*The Irish Guards
in the Great War*

THE IRISH GUARDS
IN THE GREAT WAR

THE FIRST BATTALION

by

Rudyard Kipling

SPELLMOUNT

British Library Cataloguing in Publication Data:
A catalogue record for this book is available
from the British Library

Copyright © Rudyard Kipling 1970, 1985, 1997, 2008
Maps copyright © Rudyard Kipling 1970, 1985, 2008

ISBN 978-1-86227-404-4

This edition published in 2007 by
Spellmount Limited
Cirencester Road, Chalford
Stroud, Gloucestershire. GL6 8PE
www.spellmount.com

Spellmount Limited is an imprint of NPI Media Group

1 3 5 7 9 8 6 4 2

Typesetting and origination by NPI Media Group
Printed in Great Britain

CONTENTS

PUBLISHER'S NOTE

THE PUBLISHERS would like to thank Colonel Frank Groves and his colleagues at the RHQ Irish Guards for the invaluable assistance they have given with the production of this edition. Access has been provided to the regimental records and all the photographs used have come from the Irish Guards' archives. Permission was also granted for the inclusion of the poem *The Irish Guards* the copyright for which was passed to the Irish Guards Charitable Fund by Kipling in 1918.

The publishers would also like to thank Elizabeth Inglis, the archivist of the Kipling archives at the University of Sussex; David Fox, the administrator at Bateman's and George Webb, the Editor of *The Kipling Journal* who not only wrote the Foreword to the edition but also provided valuable information about how this history was commissioned by the Irish Guards.

As far as possible the style of typesetting and punctuation of the original 1923 edition have been maintained.

FOREWORD

By GEORGE WEBB

Editor of The Kipling Journal

FOR ALL THE MAIN BELLIGERENTS, the Great War of 1914–18 was a profoundly traumatic ordeal. For the British, though they were not invaded and eventually emerged victorious, it left a lasting scar on their folk memory. The scale of the conflict and the terrible toll of casualties, especially on the trench-locked Western Front, still fascinate the reading public, as the continual appearance of new books about the war attests.

The Irish Guards in the Great War, far from being a new book, first appeared in 1923. But this fresh edition, splendidly illustrated with previously unpublished photographs of places and events described in the book, is very much to be welcomed. In its sombre, understated way, Kipling's narrative is a masterpiece, and one too long neglected. It was his utterly individual contribution to the art of regimental history. In 1923 it was hailed as setting new standards; and it has always commanded the respect of specialists on the writings of the First World War; but for the literary public in general, to whom its author here made few concessions, this grimly austere record had lapsed into oblivion, and its revival was overdue.

When he wrote it, Kipling, though long past his first exuberant flush of youthful fame and fortune, was still a tremendous literary figure, the most popular writer of English prose and verse of his day. After an apprenticeship as a very young but talented journalist in India from 1882 to 1889, he had returned to London where in 1890, aged twenty-four, he leapt to international prominence with *Barrack-Room Ballads*. Through the 1890s he kept in the public eye, not only with stories and poems about India but also with a copious flood of highly original writing about a wider world. Indeed, he was to remain tirelessly prolific until his death at seventy in 1936; even by 1914 he had published some twenty-one volumes of prose and five of verse – all still at that date in print.

None of his chosen subjects was more memorable and realistic than his affectionate and understanding depiction of the British soldier. Here was a theme which had never before had comparable literary treatment: Kipling made it his own. 'Tommy Atkins', whether in barracks or in action, whether engaged in the vicious little campaigns typical of the North-West Frontier or the long slog of the Boer War, found in his vivid prose and verse an unsentimental champion.

Though a great gulf separates the small colonial wars of Victoria's Empire from the terrible attrition of 1914–18, there is a connecting thread, in Kipling's thought and style, between his brisk accounts of early far-off battle-scenes in miniature and his soberly factual record of the Irish Guards' ordeal in France and Flanders. That link is highlighted by some comments of Henry James in 1891, in his Introduction to an American volume of Kipling's Indian stories entitled *Mine Own People*.

James singled out as the most brilliant stories those 'devoted wholly to the common soldier, and of this series it appears to me that too much good can hardly be said'. He particularly praised 'the robust attitude of the narrator, who never arranges or glosses or falsifies, but makes straight for the common and the characteristic'. He specified the deaths of the drummerboys Jakin and Lew, those dubious heroes of 'The Drums of the Fore and Aft', who had 'saved the reputation of their regiment and perished, the least mawkishly in the world, in a squalor of battle incomparably expressed'.

The same tribute can be paid to Kipling's *Irish Guards*, written some thirty years later. In a review, collected in 1929 in *The Missing Muse & Other Essays*, the historian Philip Guedalla commented:

> That sudden reputation, which startled our fathers into a dazed recognition of a new writer of English prose, was largely made by a *staccato* familiarity with war. In the later years of the last century Mr Kipling became a prose Laureate of the British Army. He learnt its idiom in dusty cantonments beyond Bombay; and he dispensed its adventures to the civilian public in short, sharp doses. Gradually it became uncertain whether he had described or invented its leading types . . . That is why one waited, when a real war came, for Mr Kipling to write about it.

Actually, Kipling was writing war-related articles, promptly re-published in book form, from the early stages of the Great War; indeed, with his vocal advocacy of national service and military preparedness he had been a Cassandra anticipating the war long before 1914. However, *The Irish Guards* both dwarfs in bulk his other output of the years 1917–22 in which he was working on it, and differs in kind from anything else he produced. It was not written to entertain or even to edify; it was not issued among his standard editions; its royalties went to a soldiers' widows' charity. Moreover, like his devoted membership of the Imperial War Graves Commission (the other official commitment which this firmly independent man accepted out of piety to the dead), the task imposed restrictions which he would normally reject – as he had done in 1915, declining to write for the War Office a history of the Battle of Ypres.

As the *Observer*'s reviewer remarked on 22 April 1923 when *The Irish Guards* appeared, regimental history is by definition:

subject to the same handicaps as the official painting of a great ceremonial . . . standards of precision, detail and convention which rest upon other authority than that of art. Mr Kipling has accepted an unwonted servitude . . . and . . . ennobled a type of composition which literature has scarcely hitherto made its own.

In *The Times* of 17 April the reviewer was John Buchan, the final volume of whose superb *History of the Great War*, today as disregarded as Kipling's Irish Guards, had appeared seven months before. He wrote:

The Irish Guards had been so fortunate as to find their historian in the greatest living master of narrative. No other book can ever be written exactly like this, and it seems likely to endure as the fullest document of the war-life of a British regiment, compiled by a man of genius who brings to his task not only a quick eye to observe and a sure hand to portray, but a rare spirit of reverence and understanding.

It is worth recalling just how the regiment were 'so fortunate as to find their historian'.

When war broke out in August 1914, Kipling's only son John, a schoolboy of nearly seventeen, stirred by the wave of patriotic enthusiasm that swept the country, volunteered for a commission in the Army. Being under age and handicapped by poor sight, he was initially rejected. He then proposed to enlist in the ranks, whereupon his father's friendship with the aged Field-Marshal Lord Roberts – whom he had first met in the 1880s in India – was used to gain the boy nomination to a commission in the Irish Guards, of which Roberts was Colonel-in-Chief. During the next twelve months John Kipling was at the depot at Warley in Essex, fairly frequently seeing his father, who also met many of his fellow-officers.

When a newly formed 2nd Battalion sailed for France in August 1915, John went with it. He was keen, well liked, evidently competent – and just eighteen. His battalion was at once deployed in the costly battle of Loos, where over-sanguine planning and hasty handling committed inexperienced British troops to frontal assault against positions impregnable to the resources and artillery at their disposal.

John was among the earliest casualties of the battle. For lack of conclusive evidence derivable from such confused and partial reports as became available from other soldiers who had seen him in action – first leading his men in the open, later wounded but still walking – he was listed as missing, believed killed.

Here a dramatic interpolation is necessary. The formula 'Missing', so common in the carnage of the Western Front, would apply officially to John Kipling for the next 77 years; it seemed certain that his body would never be unearthed. Then in June 1992, after a vigilant researcher of the Commonwealth War Graves Commission, sifting old data on the re-burial of unidentified British casualties at Loos, had shrewdly cross-checked a discrepant map-reference, an anonymous body was suddenly proved beyond doubt to be John Kipling's.

Thus one individual mystery – one of countless thousands on the Western Front – was surprisingly solved. However, it was sixty years too late to comfort the Kipling parents, who for the rest of their lives had had to bear, in addition to the loss of a son, the painful awareness that he had no known grave.

Precisely what had befallen John Kipling at 'Chalk-Pit Wood', the spot near Loos where he had last been seen alive, was unknown, though his father took immense trouble to question comrades who might have been able to supply evidence. At first he did not rule out the possibility that his son was a prisoner; and attempts were made through neutral channels to see if this was so. Moreover, Kipling's international standing was such that the Royal Flying Corps took the unusual step of dropping leaflets over the German lines near Loos to ask for help in ascertaining whether the 'son of the world-famous author' (*Sohne des weltberühmten Schriftstellers*) was dead or alive. But no news was ever received, and the assumption hardened that he was dead.

The loss added a bitterly personal dimension to Kipling's longstanding dislike of Germany; enhanced his intense regard for the fighting man now paying in blood for the civilian complacency that Kipling, Roberts and a few others had tried in vain to shake before the war; gave him a heightened feeling for his son's regiment; and made him responsive to the plea that he should write their war history.

On 8 January 1917 Colonel D.J. Proby, then Colonel Commanding at the Irish Guards Headquarters in Buckingham Gate, wrote to tell Kipling that in common with the other Guards Regiments the Irish Guards wanted a regimental history of the war. He said it had been suggested that Kipling might be willing to write it, not on business terms but as a 'memento' of his son's service; and he tactfully asked if this might be so. Kipling's acceptance was swift: within a week the matter was agreed, and a few days later arrangements were in hand to send him by registered post some of the 1st Battalion's War Diaries and maps. He started work without delay.

The result was this large book in two volumes, one devoted to each of the two battalions of the regiment, with detailed appendices and casualty lists, etc. It records the entire fortunes of the regiment, almost daily from the first landing of the battalions in France in 1914 and 1915, until their arrival in Cologne after the Armistice. It represents five and a half years of meticulous and laborious toil, from early 1917 when Kipling began to study official and private records until late in 1922 (a year in which he suffered recurrent illness and chronic pain) when after several revisions he finally approved his proofs for the printers.

By his usual standards of productivity, this was otherwise a thin period: he did little other literary work of substance until the book was dealt with. Authorities on Kipling are agreed on the mental and physical toll that it exacted. In Philip Mason's phrase, it was a 'sacrificial task'. Charles Carrington, Kipling's official biographer, called it 'the most sustained of his literary efforts'. Kipling himself told his secretary Dorothy Ponton that 'this will be my great work', and said it was 'done with agony and bloody sweat'. This last was an allusion to the general and personal tragedy he was writing about; and to his own chronic ill-health (Ponton said his last proofs were 'corrected by dint of sheer will-power'); and perhaps to the state of Ireland in those years. For Ireland was convulsed by insurgency, civil strife and partition; which, since Kipling was a passionate Unionist, was ironic accompaniment to his compilation of the heroic wartime record of largely Irish troops.

Indeed, the tragic post-war condition of Ireland may have been the reason why Kipling's well known poem, 'The Irish Guards', written in 1918 with a Great War theme, was not reprinted in 1923 as a verse prologue (a familiar Kipling device) to the regimental history. The poem, appropriately included in the present edition, is of some interest, because shortly before the war Kipling's political convictions, temporarily overriding his old respect for the doughty Irish soldier typified by Private Mulvaney of *Soldiers Three*, had provoked him into caustic comments about Ireland's Catholic south. However, after war had broken out, and particularly after his son's death with the Irish Guards, whose non-commissioned ranks had at first been exclusively Irish and mainly Catholic, this acrimonious standpoint was untenable for the regiment's war historian. The gallant loyalty of the men, matched by the steadiness of their chaplains, was a key theme; so the poem was Kipling's *amende honorable* to the Irish as a whole.

It first appeared in *The Times* on 11 March 1918, and then in a decorated limited edition, the proceeds from which, plus a £300 gift from Kipling, were donated to the regimental charity and placed in a Kipling Fund. Sir John Hall, by then Colonel Commanding at Headquarters, in a letter dated 27 March 1918, thanked Kipling for the gift of a framed manuscript of the poem. The last great German offensive, the formidable March Push, was just then at its height; and Hall went on to outline such scant news of the regiment as had come in from the reeling Front – a critical situation, heavy fighting, and an urgent need for new drafts.

The verses of 'The Irish Guards', set to the resounding music of Edward German, proved very suitable to the concert halls of 1918; and in their lyrical refrain made a valid comparison with the famous 'Wild Geese' of history and legend – Irish soldiers of fortune who in the eighteenth century had been conspicuous in the French armies, and whose successors were now on the joint English/French side. By 1923 however, lines such as 'For where there are Irish their hearts are unchanging, / And when they are changed, it is Ireland no more!' must have seemed too poignant to be published in the book.

In overall historical terms, *The Irish Guards in the Great War* is an integral part of the anti-German theme which Kipling had addressed ever since the Entente Cordiale of 1904. Certain ideas are central – that the alliance with France is sacred; that the war represents the defence of civilisation against barbarism; that Germans are Huns and apt to behave accordingly; and that the

British in general, and their war dead in particular, have been betrayed by the unforgivable pre-war complacency of liberal politicians. One of Kipling's well known 'Epitaphs of the War' was 'If any question why we died, / Tell them, because our fathers lied'. That sentiment slips out occasionally in the book, and would no doubt have done so more often if Kipling had not been consciously creating a memorial rather than re-opening controversy; writing the record of a regiment rather than a history of the war.

In military terms, Kipling used a technique to produce a result without precedent among regimental histories. It is worth examining that technique, for in John Buchan's words,

> the natural unit for the war historian is the division, and a divisional history enables the writer to make his story a recognisable part of the main movements of armies. It is different with the doings of a regiment.

How, then, did Kipling cope with the doings of his regiment, and what, apart from the predictable power and originality of the words, was the technique which struck the critics who read the book? The unnamed reviewer in the *Journal of the Royal United Services Institution* noted the exceptional scale of his use of private diaries and records:

> he has told their story from the regimental point of view, and illuminates his text with remarks and comments made by the men..

The reviewer for the *Army Quarterly* praised his adoption of

> the point of view of the unit only, confining himself exclusively to its doings and sensations . . . Regimental officers and men had an extremely limited knowledge of what was going on outside their own particular corner . . . He has therefore concentrated his efforts not so much on narrating but on interpreting what happened, on recalling in some degree the thoughts and feelings of officers and men . . . He has been singularly successful; . . . years hence, when men want to know what . . . their ancestors had to endure . . . it will be to Kipling's book that they will . . . turn.

The reviewer for the *Glasgow Herald* called the book

> the prose epic of the British infantry in France . . . probably the greatest of all war books: for though we have had many a sound book that has dealt with our men as soldiers, we have till now had no book that has dealt with our soldiers as men.

Guedalla said Kipling had succeeded in creating

an enormous panorama of one tiny section of the front line. He has drawn it in infinite detail, and with hardly an omission of any insignificant or sickening particular.

Buchan commended the work, as

> an intimate record of men's daily lives. There is room, no doubt, for the bland synoptic histories, but our successors . . . will value them less than books such as this. For they will be able to provide those 'broad and balanced' narratives for themselves; what they will never be able to achieve is the story, woven from material which is fast perishing, of the impact of war on the individual soldiers . . . amid the terror and bewilderment and ennui.

Kipling's technique, then, seems to rest upon his exceptional descriptive powers, his empathy with soldiers under breaking-strain, and his habitual passion for detail. Detail, indeed, almost numbing in its impact, calculatedly appalling in the flatness of its narration, is the hallmark of the book. Not that Kipling supposed he could get everything in, or get it all right: in the words of the *Observer* review, 'He never forgets . . . how such a tale can, at the best, but limp after the truth'.

This *caveat* is eloquently stressed in Kipling's Introduction. We are warned that 'witnesses to phases of fights die and are dispersed; the ground . . . is battered out of recognition in a few hours; survivors confuse dates, places and personalities . . . [and] the only wonder to the compiler of these records has been that any sure fact whatever should be retrieved out of the whirlpools of war.

In the same Introduction he points out that 'a battalion's field is bounded by its own vision.' Certainly, though part of his technique in this book was to vary that vision occasionally by grimly ironic comments grounded on wider perspective or hindsight, he confined his main narrative to the battalions' field; and much of it is routine reporting of a unit's detailed life — billets, rations, leave, health, sport, transport and the weather. This too is part of the technique: being true to life, it serves as foil to the terrible passages about wounds and gas and horror, and to the occasional magnificent pictures of the violent realities of action.

He felt that those who had fought and survived would appreciate why 'the compiler has loaded his records with detail . . . since in a life where Death ruled every hour, nothing was trivial'. As for other readers, he hoped they might 'find a little to interest . . . in these very details and flatnesses that make up the unlovely, yet superb, life endured for their sakes'.

The product of this remorselessly applied technique was a work of literature. It cannot be compared with other accounts of units at war. Those may have more glamour, but cannot match Kipling in highlighting the incongruities of war by calculated simplicity of depiction, conveying the unbelievable in sepia.

His impact comes from suppression of impact, restrained reiteration, horror heightened by monotone, and always 'economy of implication' – a recognised hallmark of his style. His frieze of doomed youth – stilted, bare, unimpassioned – struck perceptive observers. In Guedalla's words:

> the long line of young men stands out clearly; and . . . the dismal round of trenches, raids, billets, great offensives, camps and fatigues . . . in the long, slow interval between the sunny evening near Harmignies when a stray bullet hit the Belgian turf and someone said 'Now we can say we have been under fire,' and the driving rain and gleaming pavements of Cologne, with a General sitting his horse to watch them go by, and the drums pounding out 'Brian Boru'.

The unremitting flow of impressions, shapeless except for chronological sequence, imparts a hypnotic blend of realism and unreality, heightened by the strange beauty of the maps. These are an odd feature, with their exquisite elaboration, ornamental print and decorated margins redolent of an earlier and more romantic age – providing an incongruous setting for the battle zones, scenes of brutal fighting described without euphemism in the text. Whether Kipling simply liked this style of map, or felt it was an effective foil to the mud and blood of reality, is unclear.

But if he indulged in some cartographic frills, they were the only latitude he allowed himself. Regimental historians must be selective, but risk immediate challenge if they embroider ascertainable truth. Kipling knew this. After describing one disastrous raid by the Irish Guards he commented that every action is followed by 'interminable discussion from every point of view of every rank . . . and the more they explain, argue and asseverate, the deeper grows the confusion out of which the historian in due time weaves the accepted version – at which all who were concerned scoff.'

The anarchy of the evidence was often compounded by the mangled shapelessness of the terrain. Plans, always unrealistically definite, lost meaning as soon as troops went over the top. Although 'villages and salient points existed beautifully on such maps as were issued to the officers . . . the whole landscape happened to be one pitted, clodded, brown and white wilderness of aching uniformity.' So Kipling seldom suggests that deployment was tidy, formation was maintained, or troops had any clear idea of what was happening: he uses the very confusion as part of the atmosphere of war. This is not the classical approach to regimental history with its *penchant* for clarity, determinism and visible results. Rather he portrayed amorphous struggle mitigated only by the sustaining discipline of the regiment – which is nearer to our modern doubt whether war is ever anything but muddle.

However, caring greatly for the integrity of his history, he reported known facts, whether trifling or important, 'soberly' as he said, 'and with what truth is possible'. Eschewing sensationalism where no words were adequate to the actuality of war, he preferred to convey drama by implication. He was notably laconic when recording casualties, including his son's disappearance at Loos: this does not imply insensitivity. As he wrote of the regiment's subalterns, many were 'almost children . . . [who] came out from Warley with the constantly renewed drafts, lived the span of a Second Lieutenant's life and were spent . . . In most cases the compiler has let the mere fact suffice; since, to his mind, it did not seem fit to heap words on the doom.'

Kipling's restrained treatment of unpleasantness and horror is powerfully effective; but it does require of us a readiness to look through the austere prose to the indescribable reality. Otherwise the very spareness of the narrative may grate: for instance Edmund Blunden, himself a veteran of the trenches, reviewing the book in the *Nation & Athenaeum*, cited the utter insufficiency of phrases such as 'the annoying fights and checks round the concreted machine-gun posts'. But if such jauntiness mars an occasional sentence it never impairs the fine prose of the more compelling passages; and it can invariably be put down to one of three limitations under which Kipling was writing – the public-school levity and understatement of some young officer witnesses; the relative inarticulateness of non-commissioned sources who anyway doubted (as he said in his Introduction) if civilians would understand; and his own determination not to over-colour.

Certainly the mannered simplicity and starkness of this monumental book is achieved at the cost of what Guedalla called a 'deliberately abandoned perspective' – so it cannot be regarded as orthodox military history. For that, we can go elsewhere: what we find in *The Irish Guards* is a quarry of authentic *atmosphere*. Few books that seek to re-create the atmosphere of the Great War will be above controversy, though some have exploited the advantage of autobiography, others the freedom of fiction; but the sheaf of stylised etchings in this book are of undoubted veracity.

As Henry James had noted in 1891, Kipling 'makes straight for the common and the characteristic' – particularly in his vignettes of the private soldier's life. 'Fatigues' are sympathetically recalled; and the 'staggering and crawling, loaded with sharp angled petrol tins of water along imperfect duckboards, is perhaps a memory which will outlast all others.' Yet the troops retain a sense of humour, and are adaptable to hardship: thus 'a race accustomed to peat can miraculously make hot tea over a few fragments of ammunition-boxes or a fistful of stolen coke.'

Always there is admiration for the stoic obedience of the men – 'the inexplicable wonder of war, which orders that the soldier shall do what he is told, and shall stay where he may be put.' Likewise the saving grace of *esprit de corps*, for a man 'may join for the sake of "King and Country", but he goes over the top for the honour of his own platoon.'

As to the officers, a few come over clearly, such as the future Field-Marshal Alexander, as competent as he was popular; but a regimental history could not dilate on many of its 115 dead officers or the smaller number that survived. The most telling passages are ones of *general* application, as when Kipling describes the tension 'that springs up among officers in that last hour of waiting under the thunder of the preliminary bombardment before the word is given that hoists all ranks slowly and methodically into a bone-naked landscape.' And the confusion that usually ensues, because 'once over the top . . . the machine-gun and the lie of the ground dictate the situation to the platoon commander . . . who sees, perhaps, fifty yards about him.' And after the usual comparative failure, the usual anguished post-mortem, 'more undermining than any bodily stress', with its 'obsessions as to whether, if one had led one's platoon by such and such a deviation . . . one might have saved such and such a casualty . . . Memory brings back the face or the eyes of the dying, and the silence, always accusing, as the platoon goes forward.'

The heroes of the book are the fighting men: but essentially the fighting men of *our side*. Though there are occasional expressions of respect for the enemy's tenacity or courage, these are rare. The Germans are unforgivable for having started the war, and for the indications Kipling perceives by the end of this war that they are already looking to prepare the next. They are Huns, and are frequently called it in terms that set them below the standards of the civilisation that they have assaulted – 'the Hun tribes' and 'the inscrutable Hun mind', 'the Hun-warren'. Such terms grate today, but may be thought excusable in their context, given what Kipling had warned would happen, what had happened, and what he feared would happen again.

Bitterness about Britain's unpreparedness for war is also manifest, the villains being the politicians whose disregard of warning signs had deprived the Army of what it needed to wage effectively a continental campaign. This complaint irritated Guedalla, a loyal Asquithian Liberal, who saw as one of the few blemishes in the book Kipling's 'nagging dissatisfaction with civilians for neglecting to prepare for a war on a scale which no single soldier in Europe had foreseen'. It would have been fairer to concede that as a disregarded prophet Kipling had some right to complain; and that his 'dissatisfaction' was grounded on shortages of men and material in face of heavy enemy superiority. In one of several such comments, he had referred to basic lack of equipment in 1915, for Britain 'had not made any preparation for war till war began, and the price of this was the lives of men'.

For the Generals on the Western Front Kipling showed none of the anger that he had expressed in vitriolic verse about those in Mesopotamia:

> They shall not return to us, the resolute, the young,
> The eager and whole-hearted whom we gave:
> But the men who left them thriftily to die in their own dung,
> Shall they come with years and honour to the grave?

Presumably the proprieties of an official history made for reticence in this regard; but he did realise that the scale of the fighting, and the crucial dominance of defensive capacity on both sides, had placed warfare beyond the existing art of command. He concluded that 'bad staff-work or faulty generalship . . . were not lacking in the War, but the broad sense of justice in all who suffered from them, recognizing that all were equally amateurs, saved the depression of repeated failures from turning into demoralization.'

However, as part of the overall ironic picture, he did not conceal the fatal optimism of some of the offensive planning; the hope that each next push would produce a break-through; that cavalry in reserve would at last exploit the infantry-created gap; that open warfare and a rush through Belgium to Germany would follow. He emphasized this false expectation at Loos, where his son was killed and his battalion lost seven officers in forty minutes. The confidence of a General, that 'the greatest battle in the history of the world' and the defeat of the entrenched enemy were imminent, is made to appear more than usually fatuous. Kipling lifts his view above battalion level to comment that 'it does not seem to have occurred to anyone . . . that direct Infantry attacks . . . on works begotten out of a generation of thought . . . are not likely to find a fortunate issue.'

When it was needed, Kipling drew the wider strategic picture with great clarity; his vigorous prose is at its most memorable when describing prepared defences to be assaulted by British troops. One such example was Loos, where the German positions were 'trenched and tunnelled with cemented and floored works of terrifying permanency that linked together fortified redoubts, observation posts, concealed batteries, rallying-points and impregnable shelters for waiting reserves . . .' This excerpt is from a passage of concentrated force and cumulative detail which builds up a sense of foreboding – justified by the failure of the offensive that ensued.

Another example is the Somme, where the enemy's formidable lines of defence 'ran below and along the flanks and on the tops of five-hundred-foot downs'. A detailed description of these positions concludes: 'Belt upon belt of fifty-yard-deep wire protected these points, either directly or at such angles as should herd and hold up attacking infantry to the fire of veiled guns. Nothing had been neglected or unforeseen, except knowledge of the nature of the men who, in due time, should wear their red way through every yard of it.'

This setting for the Somme was particularly praised by Paul Fussell, who in *The Great War and Modern Memory*, published in 1975, explored the whole application of words to convey the indescribable in war. He found Kipling's description of the German lines 'admirably professional'; noting the 'almost poetic symmetrical, interlocking assonance and alliteration with which Kipling orchestrates his climax.'

This is a reminder that much of the book, despite its factuality, is highly literary and carefully composed. Sometimes this is obvious, in the use of an extraordinary phrase or striking image – the 'stamp and vomit' of a shell, the 'insolently uninterested' dead, the 'trumpeting and clanking' of the tanks. Sometimes it is half hidden, in the suggestive structuring of a sentence.

Sometimes it is best perceived by a fellow-historian who has handled similar material. Buchan was one: another was Sir Frederick Ponsonby, author of the parallel history of the Grenadier Guards. In a charming tribute to Kipling's 'wonderful book' he wrote: 'I admired particularly the way you used a broad brush with brilliant bits of colour when your material was thin . . . in my history these bits became threadbare.'

Just as Kipling varied his standpoint, rising occasionally above the battalion level to a loftier overview; and just as he varied the emotional tension of the tale, relieving accounts of horror by interludes of humour, or drabness by farce; so he varied the narrative pace, letting the banality of regimental routine become foil to superlative passages of action. One such is his account of the 1st Battalion's attack on the Somme on September 1916. It fills some eight pages, and was described by Buchan as 'a model of what a battle picture should be'.

Ten minutes before Zero, the soldiers, with 'bayonets fixed and the searching dawn-light on their faces', were kneeling to receive Absolution from their priest. Then they went over the top, into 'a blizzard of shell and machine-gun fire where all landmarks were undistinguishable'. An intermediate objective that they reached is vividly described – a shambles of a trench littered with the dead of both sides and the pitifully dying, and choked with 'the reeking, chemical-tainted fog of the high explosives'. Later, survivors of the Battalion were still trying to advance. 'Formation was gone – blown to bits long ago. Nearly every officer was down, and Sergeant after Sergeant . . . but the discipline held, and with it the instinct that made them crawl, dodge, run and stumble as chance offered and their Corporals ordered, towards the enemy and not away from him...'

The vicissitudes of the Irish Guards are thus catalogued, consistently but with varying pace, throughout the war. The regiment lost more than twice its original strength killed, and many more wounded; yet somehow its identity was not weakened but enhanced. How this paradox arose can be deduced from the book; how Kipling had recognised it was noted by Field-Marshal Templer in 1970 in his Foreword to a later book about the Irish Guards, *The Micks* by Peter Verney:

> Kipling put his heart and soul into that splendid record. He made no attempt to comment on strategy and tactics, but what he recorded, with such infinite love and labour, was the spirit imbuing a regiment.

The closing passage of Volume II movingly describes the return of the Guards Division in the spring of 1919 from the unreality of occupied Cologne to England, and their formal march through the streets of London, with 'their wounded accompanying them on foot, or in the crowded lorries'. For the Irish Guards' 2nd Battalion, the junior of the two, much reduced in strength, the occasion had special significance, as they were due for disbandment. Kipling described them as having been a 'happy' battalion, which had 'done as well as any' in 'a War that had made mere glory ridiculous'.

Now, only the memory of what they had been through would remain; and 'as they moved – little more than a Company strong – in the wake of their seniors, one saw, here and there among the wounded in civil kit, young men with eyes which did not match their age, shaken beyond speech or tears by the splendour and the grief of that memory.'

GEORGE WEBB, CMG, OBE, a retired diplomat, has been the Editor of *The Kipling Journal* (house magazine of the Kipling Society) since 1980. In 1988, with Sir Hugh Cortazzi, he edited *Kipling's Japan*. This Foreword is partly derived from an article on 'The Irish Guards in the Great War' that he wrote in the *Army Quarterly & Defence Journal*.

THE IRISH GUARDS
1918

We're not so old in the Army List,
　　But we're not so young at our trade,
For we had the honour at Fontenoy
　　Of meeting the Guards' Brigade.
Twas Lally, Dillon, Bulkeley, Clare,
　　And Lee that led us then,
And after a hundred and seventy years
　　We're fighting for France again!
　　　　Old Days! The wild geese are fighting,
　　　　　　Head to the storm as they faced it before!
　　　　For where there are Irish there's bound to be flighting,
　　　　　　And when there's no fighting, it's Ireland no more!
　　　　　　　　　　　　　　Ireland no more!

The fashion's all for khaki now,
　　But once through France we went
Full-dressed in scarlet Army cloth
　　The English – left at Ghent.
They're fighting on our side to-day
　　But, before they changed their clothes,
The half of Europe knew our fame,
　　As all of Ireland knows!
　　　　Old Days! The wild geese are flying,
　　　　　　Head to the storm as they faced it before!
　　　　For where there are Irish there's memory undying,
　　　　　　And when we forget, it is Ireland no more!
　　　　　　　　　　　　　　Ireland no more!

From Barry Wood to Gouzeaucourt,
  From Boyne to Pilkem Ridge,
The ancient days come back no more
  Than water under the bridge,
But the bridge it stands and the water runs
  As red as yesterday,
And the Irish move to the sound of the guns
  Like salmon to the sea.
    Old Days! The wild geese are ranging,
      Head to the storm as they faced it before!
    For where there are Irish their hearts are unchanging,
      And when they are changed, it is Ireland no more!
                                    Ireland no more!

We're not so old in the Army List,
  But we're not so new in the ring,
For we carried our packs with Marshal Saxe
  When Louis was our King.
But Douglas Haig's our Marshal now
  And we're King George's men,
And after one hundred and seventy years
  We're fighting for France again!
    Ah, France! And did we stand by you,
      When life was made splendid with gifts and rewards?
    Ah, France! And will we deny you
      In the hour of your agony, Mother of Swords?
    Old Days! The wild geese are fighting,
      Head to the storm as they faced it before!
    For where there are Irish there's loving and fighting,
      And when we stop either, it's Ireland no more!
                                    Ireland no more!

INTRODUCTION

THESE VOLUMES try to give soberly and with what truth is possible, the experiences of both Battalions of the Irish Guards from 1914 to 1918. The point of view is the Battalions', and the facts mainly follow the Regimental Diaries, supplemented by the few private letters and documents which such a war made possible, and by some tales that have gathered round men and their actions. As evidence is released, historians may be able to reconstruct what happened in or behind the battle-line; what motives and necessities swayed the actors; and who stood up or failed under his burden. But a battalion's field is bounded by its own vision. Even within these limits, there is large room for error. Witnesses to phases of fights die and are dispersed; the ground over which they fought is battered out of recognition in a few hours; survivors confuse dates, places and personalities, and in the trenches, the monotony of the waiting days and the repetition-work of repairs breed mistakes and false judgements. Men grow doubtful or oversure, and, in all good faith, give directly opposed versions. The clear sight of a comrade so mangled that he seems to have been long dead is burnt in on one brain to the exclusion of all else that happened that day. The shock of an exploded dump, shaking down a firmament upon the landscape, dislocates memory throughout half a battalion; and so on in all matters, till the end of laborious enquiry is too often the opening of fresh confusion. When to this are added the personal prejudices and misunderstandings of men under heavy strain, carrying clouded memories of orders half given or half heard, amid scenes that pass like nightmares, the only wonder to the compiler of these records has been that any sure fact whatever should be retrieved out of the whirlpools of war.

It seemed to him best, then, to abandon all idea of such broad and balanced narratives as will be put forward by experts, and to limit himself to matters which directly touched the men's lives and fortunes. Nor has he been too careful to correct the inferences of the time by the knowledge of later events. From first to last, the Irish Guards, like the rest of our Armies, knew little of what was going on round them. Probably they knew less at the close of the War than at the beginning when our forces were so small that each man felt himself somebody indeed, and so stood to be hunted through the heat from Mons to Meaux, turned again to suffer beneath the Soupir ridges, and endured the first hideous winter of The Salient where, wet, almost weaponless, but unbroken, he helped in the long miracle of holding the line.

But the men of '14 and '15, and what meagre records of their day were safe to keep, have long been lost; while the crowded years between remove their battles across dead Belgian towns and villages as far from us as the fights in Homer.

Doubtless, all will be reconstructed to the satisfaction of future years when, if there be memory beyond the grave, the ghosts may laugh at the neatly groomed histories. Meantime, we can take it for granted that the old Regular Army of England passed away in the mud of Flanders in less than a year. In training, morale, endurance, courage and devotion the Earth did not hold its like, but it possessed neither the numbers, guns, nor equipment necessary for the type of war that overtook it. The fact of its unpreparedness has been extolled as proof of the purity of its country's ideals, which must be great consolation to all concerned. But, how slowly that equipment was furnished, how inadequate were our first attempts at bombs, trench-mortars, duck-boards, wiring and the rest, may be divined through the loyal and guarded allusions in the Diaries. Nor do private communications give much hint of it, for one of the marvels of that marvellous time was the silence of those concerned on everything that might too much distress their friends at home. The censorship had imposed this as a matter of precaution, but only the spirit of the officers could have backed the law so completely; and, as better days came, their early makeshifts and contrivances passed out of remembrance with their early dead. But the sufferings of our Armies were constant. They included wet and cold in due season, dirt always, occasional vermin, exposure, extreme fatigue, and the hourly incidence of death in every shape along the front line and, later, in the farthest back-areas where the enemy aeroplanes harried their camps. And when our Regular troops had been expended, these experiences were imposed upon officers and men compelled to cover, within a few months, the long years of training that should go to the making of a soldier – men unbroken even to the disturbing impact of crowds and like experiences, which the conscript accepts from his youth. Their short home-leaves gave them sudden changes to the tense home atmosphere under cover of a whirl of "entertainment," they and their kin wearied themselves to forget and escape a little from that life, on the brink of the next world, whose guns they could hear summoning in the silences between their talk. Yet, some were glad to return – else why should youngsters of three years' experience have found themselves upon a frosty night, on an iron-bound French road, shouting aloud for joy as they heard the stammer of a machine-gun over the rise, and turned up the well-known trench that led to their own dug-out and their brethren from whom they had been separated by the vast interval of ninety-six hours? Many have confessed to the same delight in their work, as there were others to whom almost every hour was frankly detestable except for the companionship that revealed them one to another till the chances of war separated the companions. And there were, too, many, almost children, of whom no record remains. They came out from Warley with the constantly renewed drafts, lived the span of a Second Lieutenant's life and were spent. Their intimates might preserve, perhaps, memories of a promise cut short, recollections of a phrase that stuck, a chance-seen act of bravery or of kindness. The Diaries give their names and fates with the conventional expressions of regret. In most instances, the compiler has let the mere fact suffice; since, to his mind, it did not seem fit to heap words on the doom.

For the same reason, he has not dealt with each instance of valour, leaving it to stand in the official language in which it was acknowledged. The rewards represent but a very small proportion of the skill, daring and heroism actually noted; for no volume could hold the full tale of all that was done, either in the way of duty, under constraint of necessity and desire to keep alive, or through joy and pleasure in achieving great deeds.

Here the Irish rank and file by temperament excelled. They had all their race's delight in the drama of things; and, whatever the pinch – whether ambushed warfare or hand-to-hand shock, or an insolently perfect parade after long divorce from the decencies – could be depended upon to advance the regimental honour. Their discipline, of course, was that of the Guards, which, based upon tradition, proven experience and knowledge of the human heart, adjusts itself to the spirit of each of its battalions. Though the material of that body might be expended twice in a twelvemonth, the leaven that remained worked on the new supplies at once and from the first. In the dingy out-of-date barracks at Warley the Regimental Reserves gathered and grew into a full-fledged Second Battalion with reserves of its own, and to these the wounded officers and men sent home to be repatched, explained the arts and needs of a war which, apparently always at a stand, changed character every month. After the utter inadequacy of its opening there was a period of hand-made bombs and of loaded sticks for close work; of nippers for the abundant wire left uncut by our few guns; of remedies for trench-feet; of medicaments against lockjaw from the grossly manured Belgian dirt, and of fancy timberings to hold up sliding trenches. In due course, when a few set battles, which sometimes gained several hundred yards, had wasted their many thousand lives, infallible forms of attack and defence developed themselves, were tried and generally found wanting, while scientific raids, the evolution of specialists, and the mass of regulated detail that more and more surrounded the life of the trenches, occupied their leisure between actions. Our battalions played themselves into the game at the awful price that must be paid for improvisation, however cheery; enduring with a philosophy that may have saved the war, the deviations and delays made necessary by the demands of the various political and other organizations at home.

In the same spirit they accepted the inevitable break-downs in the business of war-by-experiment; for it is safe to say that there was hardly an operation in which platoons, companies, regiments, brigades, or divisions were not left with one or both flanks in the air. Among themselves, officers and men discussing

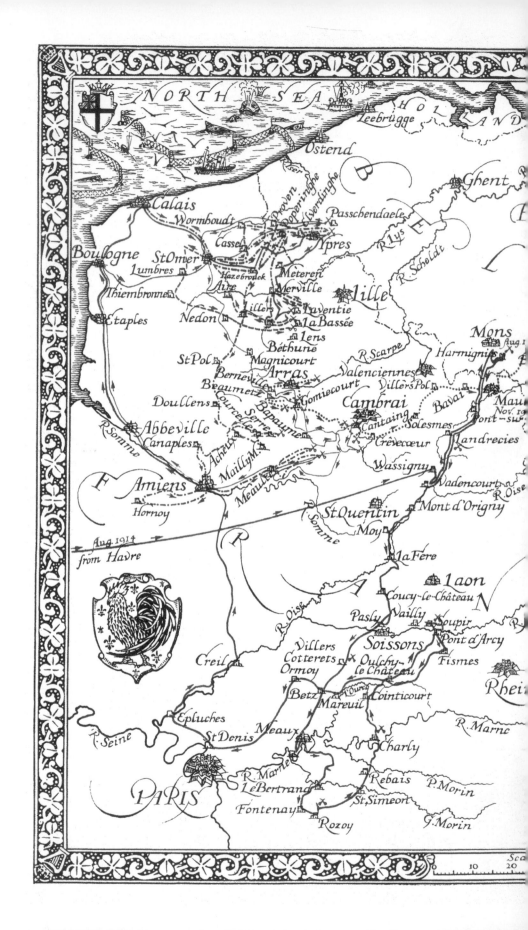

NORTH SEA

HOLLAND

Zeebrügge

Ostend

B

Ghent

Calais

Wormhoudt

Droven

Poperinghe

Verlinghe

Passchendaele

Cassel

Ypres

R. Lys

Boulogne

St Omer

Meteren

R. Scheldt

Lumbres

Hazebrouck

Merville

Lille

Thiembronne

Aire

Iller

Laventie

Etaples

Nedon

La Bassée

Mons

Aug. i.

Lens

Harmigni

St Pol

Béthune

R. Scarpe

Magnicourt

Berneville

Arras

Valenciennes

Villers Pol

Mau

Beaumetz

Gomiecourt

Cambrai

Bavai

Nov. 19

Doullens

Courcelles

Bapaume

Pont-sur

Serre

Cantaing

Solesmes

Abbeville

Acheu

Crévecœur

Landrecies

R. Somme

Canaples

Mailly M.

Wassigny

Meau

Vadencourt

R. Oise

Amiens

St Quentin

Mont d'Origny

Hornoy

Somme

Moy

Aug. 1914
from Havre

R

la Fère

Laon

Coucy-le-Château

A

N

Oise

Pasly

Vailly

Soupir

R.

Soissons

Pont d'Arcy

Creil

Villers
Cotterets

Oulchy-
le-Château

Fismes

Ormoy

Rhei

Betz

l'Ourcq

Cointicourt

Mareuil

R. Marne

Epluches

Meaux

R. Seine

St Denis

Charly

PARIS

R. Marne

Rebais

P. Morin

Le Bertrand

St Simeon

Fontenay

G. Morin

Rozoy

ITINERARY of the FIRST BATTALION IRISH GUARDS AUGUST 1914 — DECEMBER 1918.

such matters, make it quite clear how and why such and such units broke, were misled, or delayed on their way into the line. But when a civilian presumes to assist, all ranks unite against his uninformed criticisms. He is warned that, once over the top, no plans hold, for the machine-gun and the lie of the ground dictate the situation to the platoon-commander on whom all things depend and who sees, perhaps, fifty yards about him. There are limits, too, of shock and exhaustion beyond which humanity cannot be pressed without paying toll later. For which cause it may happen that a Division that has borne long agony unflinching, and sincerely believes itself capable of yet more, will, for no reason then apparent (at almost the mere rumour of noises in the night), collapse ignominiously on the same ground where, a month later, with two-thirds of its strength casualties, it cuts coolly and cleanly to its goal. And its fellows, who have borne the same yoke, allow for this.

The compiler of these records, therefore, has made little attempt to put forward any theory of what might or should have happened if things had gone according to plan; and has been scrupulous to avoid debatable issues of bad staff-work or faulty generalship. They were not lacking in the War, but the broad sense of justice in all who suffered from them, recognizing that all were equally amateurs, saved the depression of repeated failures from turning into demoralization.

Here, again, the Irish were reported by those who knew them best, to have been lenient in their judgements, though their private speech was as unrestrained as that of any other body of bewildered and overmastered men. "Wearing down" the enemy through a period of four years and three months, during most of which time that enemy dealt losses at least equal to those he received, tested human virtue upon a scale that the world had never dreamed of. The Irish Guards stood to the test without flaw.

They were in no sense any man's command. They needed minute comprehension, quick sympathy and inflexible justice, which they repaid by individual devotion and a collective good-will that showed best when things were at their utter worst. Their moods naturally varied with the weather and the burden of fatigues (actions merely kill, while fatigue breaks men's hearts), but their morale was constant because their unofficial life, on which morale hinges, made for contentment. The discipline of the Guards, demanding the utmost that can be exacted of the man, requires of the officer unresting care of his men under all conditions. This care can be a source of sorrow and friction in rigid or over-conscientious hands, till, with the best will in the world, a battalion may be reduced to the mental state of nurse-harried children. Or, conversely, an adored Company Commander bold as a lion, may, for lack of it, turn his puzzled company into a bear-garden. But there is an elasticity in Celtic psychology that does not often let things reach breaking-point either way; and their sense of humour and social duty – it is a race more careful to regard each other's feelings than each other's lives – held them as easily as they were strictly associated. A jest; the grave hearing out of absurd complaints that might turn to tragedy were the hearing not accorded; a prompt soothing down of gloomy, injured pride; a piece of flagrant buffoonery sanctioned, even shared, but never taken advantage of, went far in dark days to build up that understanding and understood inner life of the two Battalions to which, now, men look back lovingly across their civilian years. It called for a devotion from all, little this side of idolatry; and was shown equally by officers, N.C.O.'s, and men, stretcher-bearers, cooks, orderlies, and not least by the hard-bit, fantastic old soldiers, used for odd duties, who faithfully hobbled about France alongside the rush of wonderful young blood.

Were instances given, the impression might be false, for the tone and temper of the time that set the pace has gone over. But while it lasted, the men made their officers and the officers their men by methods as old as war itself and their Roman Catholic priests, fearless even in a community none too regardful of Nature's first law, formed a subtle and supple link between both. That the priest, ever in waiting upon Death or pain, should learn to magnify his office was as natural as that doctors and frontline commanders should find him somewhat under their feet when occasion called for the secular, not the spiritual, arm. That Commanding Officers, to keep peace and save important pillars of their little society, should first advise and finally order the Padre not to expose himself wantonly in forward posts or attacks, was equally of a piece with human nature; and that the priests, to the huge content of the men, should disregard the order ("What's a casualty compared to a soul?") was most natural of all. Then the question would come up for discussion in the trenches and dug-outs, where everything that anyone had on his mind was thrashed out through the long, quiet hours, or dropped and picked up again with the rise and fall of shell-fire. They speculated on all things in Heaven and earth as they worked in piled filth among the carcasses of their fellows, lay out under the stars on the eves of open battle, or vegetated through a month's feeding and idleness between one sacrifice and the next.

But none has kept minutes of those incredible symposia that made for them a life apart from the mad world which was their portion; nor can any pen re-create that world's brilliance, squalor, unreason and heaped boredom. Recollection fades from men's minds as common life closes over them, till even now they wonder what part they can ever have had in the shrewd, man-hunting savages who answered to their names so few years ago.

It is for the sake of these initiated that the compiler has loaded his records with detail and seeming triviality, since in a life where Death ruled every hour, nothing was trivial, and bald references to villages, billets, camps, fatigues and sports, as well as hints of tales that can never now fully be told, carry each their separate significance to each survivor, intimate and incommunicable as family jests.

As regards other readers, the compiler dares no more than hope that some of those who have no care for old history, or that larger number who at present are putting away from themselves odious memories, may find a little to interest, or even comfort in these very details and flatnesses that make up the unlovely, yet superb, life endured for their sakes.

RUDYARD KIPLING

1914
MONS TO LA BASSÉE

AT 5 p.m. on Tuesday, August 4, 1914, the 1st Battalion of the Irish Guards received orders to mobilize for war against Germany. They were then quartered at Wellington Barracks and, under the mobilization scheme, formed part of the 4th (Guards) Brigade, Second Division, First Army Corps. The Brigade consisted of:

> The 2nd Battalion Grenadier Guards.
>   "   2th   "   Coldstream Guards.
>   "   3th   "   Coldstream Guards.
>   "   1st   "   Irish Guards.

Mobilization was completed on August 8. Next day, being Sunday, the Roman Catholics of the Battalion paraded under the Commanding Officer, Lieut.-Colonel the Hon. G. H. Morris, and went to Westminster Cathedral where Cardinal Bourne preached; and on the morning of the 11th August Field-Marshal Lord Roberts and Lady Aileen Roberts made a farewell speech to them in Wellington Barracks. This was the last time that Lord Roberts saw the Battalion of which he was the first Commander-in-Chief.

On the 12th August the Battalion entrained for Southampton in two trains at Nine Elms Station, each detachment being played out of barracks to the station by the band. They were short one officer, as 2nd Lieutenant St. J. R. Pigott had fallen ill, and an officer just gazetted – 2nd Lieutenant Sir Gerald Burke, Bart. – could not accompany them as he had not yet got his uniform. They embarked at Southampton on a hot still day in the P. & O. SS. *Novara*. This was a long and tiring operation, since everyone was new to embarkation-duty, and, owing to the tide, the ship's bulwarks stood twenty-five feet above the quay. The work was not finished till 4 p.m. when most of the men had been under arms for twelve hours. Just before leaving, Captain Sir Delves Broughton, Bart., was taken ill and had to be left behind. A telegram was sent to Headquarters, asking for Captain H. Hamilton Berners to take his place, and the *Novara* cleared at 7 p.m.

As dusk fell, she passed H.M.S. *Formidable* off Ryde and exchanged signals with her. The battleship's last message to the Battalion was to hope that they would get "plenty of fighting." Many of the officers at that moment were sincerely afraid that they might be late for the war!

The following is the list of officers who went out with the Battalion that night:

Lieut.-Col. Hon. G. H. Morris	Commanding Officer.
Major H. F. Crichton	Senior Major.
Captain Lord Desmond FitzGerald	Adjutant.
Lieut. E. J. F. Gough	Transport Officer.
Lieut. E. B. Greer	M. Gun Officer.
Hon. Lieut. H. Hickie	Quartermaster.
Lieut. H. J. S. Shields (R.A.M.C.)	Medical Officer.
Lieut. Hon. Aubrey Herbert, M.P.	Interpreter

No. 1 Company

Capt. Hon. A. E. Mulholland.	Lieut. C. A. S. Walker.
Capt. Lord John Hamilton.	2nd Lieut. N. L. Woodroffe.
Lieut. Hon. H. R. Alexander.	2nd Lieut. J. Livingstone-Learmonth.

No. 2 Company

Major H. A. Herbert-Stepney.	Lieut. E. J. F. Gough.
Capt. J. N. Guthrie.	Lieut. W. E. Hope.
Lieut. J. S. N. FitzGerald.	2nd Lieut. O. Hughes-Onslow.

No. 3 Company

Capt. Sir Delves Broughton. Bart. (replaced by Capt. H. Hamilton Berners).	Lieut. Hon. Hugh Gough. Lieut. Lord Guernsey. 2nd Lieut. Viscount Castlerosse.
Capt. Hon. T. E. Vesey.	

No. 4 Company

Capt. C. A. Tisdall.	Lieut. Lord Robert Innes-Ker.
Capt. A. A. Perceval.	Lieut. W. C. N. Reynolds.
Lieut. R. Blacker-Douglass.	2nd Lieut. J. T. P. Roberts.

Details at the Base

Capt. Lord Arthur Hay.	2nd Lieut. Sir Gerald Burke, Bart.

They reached Havre at 6 a.m. on August 13, a fiercely hot day, and, tired after a sleepless night aboard ship, and a long wait, in a hot, tin-roofed shed, for some missing men, marched three miles out of the town to Rest Camp No. 2 "in a large field at Sanvic, a suburb of Havre at the top of the hill." Later, the city herself became almost a suburb to the vast restcamps round it. Here they received an enthusiastic welcome from the French, and were first largely introduced to the wines of the country, for many maidens lined the steep road and offered bowls of drinks to the wearied.

Next day (August 14) men rested a little, looking at this strange, bright France with strange eyes, and bathed in the sea; and Captain H. Berners, replacing Sir Delves Broughton, joined. At eleven o'clock they entrained at Havre Station under secret orders for the Front. The heat broke in a terrible thunderstorm that soaked the new uniforms. The crowded train travelled north all day, receiving great welcomes everywhere, but no one knowing what its destination might be. After more than seventeen hours' slow progress by roads that were not revealed then or later, they halted at Wassigny, at a quarter to eleven on the night of August 15, and, unloading in hot darkness bivouacked at a farm near the station.

On the morning of August 16 they marched to Vadencourt, where, for the first time, they went into billets. The village, a collection of typical whitewashed tiled houses with a lovely old church in the centre, lay out pleasantly by the side of a poplar-planted stream. The 2nd Coldstream Guards were also billeted here; the Headquarters of the 4th (Guards) Brigade, the 2nd Grenadier Guards, and 3rd Coldstream being at Grougis. All supplies, be it noted, came from a village of the ominous name of Boue, which – as they were to learn through the four winters to follow – means "mud."

At Vadencourt they lay three days while the men were being inoculated against enteric. A few had been so treated before leaving Wellington Barracks, but, in view of the hurried departure, 90 per cent remained to be dealt with. The Diary remarks that for two days "the Battalion was not up to much." Major H. Crichton fell sick here.

On the 20th August the march towards Belgium of the Brigade began, via Etreux and Fesmy (where Lieutenant and Quartermaster Hickie went sick and had to be sent back to railhead) to Maroilles, where the Battalion billeted, August 21, and thence, via Pont-sur-Sambre and Hargnies, to La Longueville, August 22. Here, being then five miles east of Malplaquet the Battalion heard the first sound of the guns of the war, far off; not knowing that, at the end of all, they would hear them cease almost on that very spot.

At three o'clock in the morning of August 23 the Brigade marched via Riez de l'Erelle into Belgian territory and through Blaregnies towards Mons where it was dimly understood that some sort of battle was in the making. But it was not understood that eighty thousand British troops with three hundred guns, disposed between Condé, through Mons towards Binche, were meeting twice that number of Germans on their front, plus sixty thousand Germans with two hundred and thirty guns trying to turn their left flank, while a quarter of a million Germans, with close on a thousand guns, were driving in the French armies on the British right from Charleroi to Namur, across the Meuse and the Sambre. This, in substance, was the situation at Mons. It supplied a sufficient answer to the immortal question, put by one of the pillars of the Battalion, a Drill-Sergeant, who happened to arrive from home just as that situation had explained itself, and found his Battalion steadily marching south. "Fwhat's all this talk about a retreat?" said he, and strictly rebuked the shouts of laughter that followed.[1]

THE RETREAT FROM MONS

The Brigade was first ordered to take up a position at Bois la Haut, close to the dirtier suburbs of Mons, which is a fair city on a hill, but the order was cancelled when it was discovered that the Fifth Division was already there. Eventually, the Irish Guards were told to move from the village of Quevy le Petit, where they had expected to go into billets, to Harveng. Here they were ordered, with the 2nd Grenadier Guards, to support the Fifth Division on a chalk ridge from Harmignies to the Mons road, while the other two Battalions of the Brigade (the 2nd and 3rd Coldstream Guards) took up position north-east of Harveng. Their knowledge of what might be in front of them or who was in support was, naturally, small. It was a hot, still evening, no Germans were visible, but shrapnel fell ahead of the Battalion as it moved in artillery formation across the rolling, cropped lands. One single far-ranging rifle-bullet landed with a *phtt* in the chalk between two officers, one of whom turning to the other laughed and said, "Ah! Now we can say we have been underfire." A few more shells arrived as the advance to the ridge went forward, and the Brigade reached the seventh kilometre-stone on the Harmignies–Mons road, below the ridge, about 6 p.m. on the 23rd August. The Irish Rifles, commanded by Colonel Bird, D.S.O., were fighting here, and Nos. 1 and 2 Companies of the Irish Guards went up to reinforce them. This was the first time that the Battalion had been personally shelled and five men were wounded. The guns ceased about dusk, and there was very little fire from the German trenches, which were rather in the nature of scratch-holes, ahead of them. That night, too, was the first on which the troops saw a searchlight used. They enjoyed also their first experience of digging themselves in, the which they did so casually that veterans of after years would hold up that "trench" as a sample of "the valour of ignorance." At midnight the Irish Rifles were ordered to retire while the Irish Guards covered their retirement, but so far they had been in direct contact with nothing.

The Battalion heard confusedly of the fall of Namur and, it may be presumed, of the retirement of the French armies on the right of the British. There was little other news of any sort, and what there was, not cheering. On front and flank of the British armies the enemy stood in more than overwhelming strength, and it came to a question of retiring, as speedily as might be, before the flood swallowed what remained. So the long retreat of our little army began.

---

[1] About this time, on a distant flank of the War, there was a very young French Lieutenant of Artillery who, in his first action, when evening came, telephoned to his superior officer as to dispositions for the night, in the sincere belief that, following the custom of all wars up to date, the guns would stop as the darkness closed. His answer was: "This will be a war in which no one ever goes to bed."

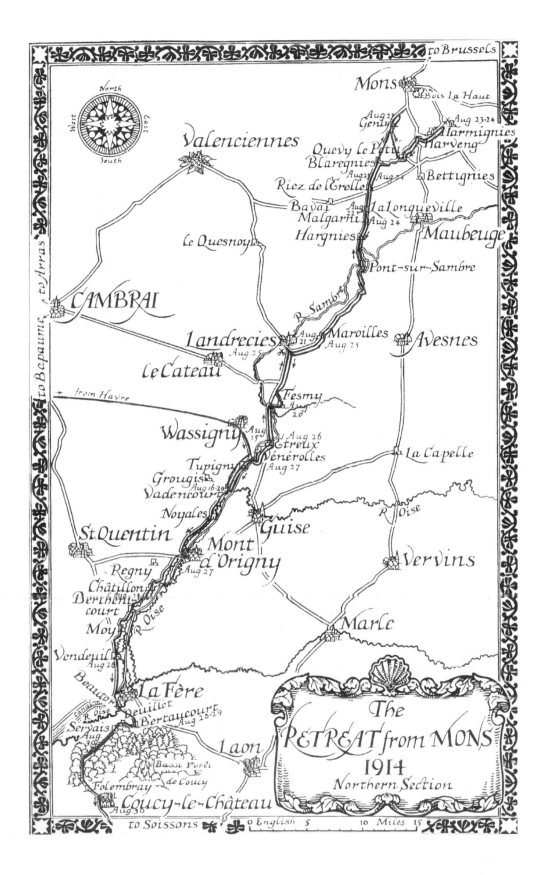

The PETREAT from MONS 1914 Northern Section

The large outlines of it are as follows: The entire British Force, First and Second Army Corps, fell back to Bavai – the First without serious difficulty, the Second fighting rear-guard actions through the day. At Bavai the two Corps diverged, not to unite again till they should reach Betz on the 1st September. The Second Army Corps, reinforced by the Fourth Division, took the roads through Le Quesnoy, Solesmes, Le Cateau, St. Quentin, Ham, Nesle, Noyon, and Crépy-en-Valois; the First paralleling them, roughly, through Landrecies, Vadencourt, La Fère, Pasly by Soissons, and Villers-Cotterêts.

At 2 o'clock in the morning of August 24 the Battalion "having covered the retirement of all the other troops," retired through the position which the 2nd and 3rd Coldstream Guards had taken up, to Quevy le Petit, where it was ordered, with the 2nd Grenadiers, to entrench another position north of Quevy le Petit (from the third kilometre-stone on the Genly – Quevy le Petit road to the tenth kilometre-stone on the Mons – Bettignies road). This it did while the whole of the Second Division retired through the position at 4 p.m., the Battalion acting as rear-guard. Their notion of "digging-in" was to cut fire-steps in the side of the handy bank of any road. At nine o'clock that night the Battalion "came out of Belgium by the same road that it had marched into Belgium" through Blaregnies, past Bavai where the First and Second Army Corps diverged, and through La Longueville to Malgarni, where they bivouacked in an orchard, "having been forty-four hours under arms." Here the first mail from England arrived, and was distributed by torch-light under the apple trees in the warm night.

On the afternoon of August 25 the Battalion reached Landrecies, an unlovely, long-streeted town in closely cultivated country. The German pressure was heavy behind them, and that evening the 3rd Coldstream Guards on outpost duty to the north-west of Landrecies on the Mormal road, were attacked, and, as history shows, beat off that attack in a night-fight of some splendour. The Battalion turned out and blocked the *pavé* entrance to the town with improvised barricades, which they lined, of stones, tables, chairs, carts, and pianos; relieved the Coldstream at 1.30 a.m., August 26; and once again covered the retirement of the Brigade out of the town towards Etreux. The men were very tired, so weary indeed that many of them slept by the roadside while waiting to relieve the Coldstream at Landrecies fight. That night was the first they heard wounded men scream. A couple of Irish Guards officers, sleeping so deeply that only the demolition by shell-fire of the house next door waked them, were left behind here, but after twenty-four hours of fantastic and, at that time, almost incredible, adventures, rejoined safely next day. It was recorded also that one of the regimental Drums was seen and heard going down Landrecies main street in the darkness, strung on the fore-leg of a gun-horse who had stepped into it as a battery went south. A battalion cooker, the sparks flying from it, passed like a fire-engine hastening to a fire, and men found time to laugh and point at the strange thing.

At Etreux, where with the rest of the Brigade the Battalion entrenched itself after the shallow pattern of the time, it had its first sight of a German aeroplane which flew over its trenches and dropped a bomb that "missed a trench by twenty yards." The Battalion fired at it, and it "flew away like a wounded bird and eventually came down and was captured by another Division." Both sides were equally inexperienced in those days in the details of air war. All that day they heard the sound of what they judged was "a battle in the direction of Le Cateau." This was the Second Army Corps and a single Division of the Third Corps under Smith-Dorrien interrupting our retirement to make a stand against four or more German Army Corps and six hundred guns. The result of that action caused the discerning General von Kluck to telegraph that he held the Expeditionary Force "surrounded by a ring of steel," and Berlin behung itself with flags. This also the Battalion did not know. They were more interested in the fact that they had lost touch with the Second Division; and that their Commanding Officer had told the officers that, so far as he could make out, they were surrounded and had better dig in deeper and wait on. As no one knew particularly where they might be in all France, and as the night of the 26th was very wet, the tired men slept undisturbedly over the proposition, to resume their retreat next day (August 27) down the valley of the Sambre, through Vénérolles, Tupigny, Vadencourt, Noyales, to the open glaring country round Mont d'Origny where the broad road to St. Quentin crosses the river. It was in Reserve that day, and the next (August 28) was advance-guard to the Brigade as the retirement continued through Châtillon, Berthenicourt, and Moy to Vendeuil and the cross-roads west of the Vendeuil – La Fère road while the Brigade marched on to Bertaucourt. After the Brigade had passed, the Battalion acted as rear-guard into Bertaucourt. Here No. 2 Company, under Major Stepney, was sent to Beautor to assist a section of the Royal Engineers in demolishing a bridge across the river there – an operation performed without incident – and in due course joined up with the Battalion again. By this time, the retreat, as one who took part in it says, had become "curiously normal" – the effect, doubtless, of that continued over-exertion which reduces men to the state of sleep-walkers. There was a ten minutes' halt every hour, on which the whole Battalion dropped where it stood and slept. At night, some of them began to see lights, like those of comfortable billets by the roadside which, for some curious reason or other, could never be reached. Others found themselves asleep, on their feet, and even when they lay down to snatch sleep, the march moved on, and wearied them in their dreams. Owing to the heat and the dust, many suffered from sore feet and exhaustion, and, since ambulance accommodation was limited, they had to be left behind to follow on if, and as best, they could. But those who fell out were few, and the Diary remarks approvingly that "on the whole the Battalion marched very well and march-discipline was good." Neither Brigade nor Battalion commanders knew anything of what was ahead or behind, but it seemed that since they could not get into Paris before the Germans and take first-class tickets to London, they would all be cut off and destroyed; which did not depress them unduly. At all events, the Battalion one evening forgot its weariness long enough to take part in the chase and capture of a stray horse of Belgian extraction, which, after its ample lack of manners and mouth had been proved, they turned over for instruction and reformation to the Transport.

From Bertaucourt, then, where the Battalion spent another night in an orchard, it marched very early on the 30th August to Terny via Deuillet, Servais, Basse Forêt de Coucy, Folembray, Coucy-le-Château, then magnificent untouched – all closer modelled country and, if possible, hotter than the bare lands they had left. Thence from Terny to Pasly, N.W. of Soissons. Here they lay down by moonlight in a field, and here an officer dreamed that the alarm had been given and that they must move on. In this nightmare he rose and woke up all platoon-officers and the C.O.; next, laboriously and methodically, his own Company; and last of all himself, whom he found shaking and swearing at a man equally drunk with fatigue.

On the 31st August the Battalion took position as right flank-guard from 9 a.m. to 3 p.m. on the high ground near Le Murger Farm and bivouacked at Soucy. So far, there had been little fighting for them since Landrecies, though they moved with the comforting knowledge that an unknown number of the enemy, thoroughly provided with means of transportation, were in fixed pursuit, just on the edge of a sky-line full of unseen guns urging the British always to move back.

VILLERS-COTTERÊTS

On the 1st September, the anniversary of Sedan, the Battalion was afoot at 2 a.m. and with the 2nd Coldstream Guards acted as rear-guard under the Commanding Officer, Colonel the Hon. G. Morris. There had been heavy dew in the night, followed at dawn by thin, miserable rain, when they breakfasted, among wet lucerne and fields of stacked corn, on the edge of the deep Villers-Cotterêts beech-forests. They fell back into them on a rumour of advancing Cavalry, who turned out to be troops of German infantry running from stack to stack and filtering into the forest on their either flank. Their first position was the Vivières – Puiseux line, a little south-west of Soucy village: the Battalion to the right of the Soucy – Villers-Cotterêts road, and the Coldstream to the left on a front of not more than a mile. Their second position, as far as can be made out, was the Rond de la Reine, a mile farther south, where the deep soft forest-roads from Soucy and Vivierès join on their way to Villers-Cotterêts. The enemy ran in upon them from all sides, and the action resolved itself into blind fighting in the gloom of the woods, with occasional glimpses of men crossing the rides, or firing from behind tree-boles. The Germans were very cautious at first, because our fire-discipline, as we fell back, gave them the impression that the forest was filled with machine-guns instead of mere trained men firing together sustainedly. The morning wet cleared, and the day grew close and stifling. There was no possibility of keeping touch or conveying orders. Since the German advance-guard was, by comparison, an army, all that could be done was to hold back as long as possible the attacks on front and flank, and to retain some sense of direction in the bullet-torn woods, where, when a man dropped in the bracken and bramble, he disappeared. But throughout the fight, till the instant of his death, Lieut.-Colonel the Hon. G. Morris, commanding the Battalion, rode from one point to another of an action that was all front, controlling, cheering and chaffing his men. And so that heathen battle, in half darkness, continued, with all units of the 4th Brigade confusedly engaged, till in the afternoon the Battalion, covered by the 2nd Coldstream, re-formed, still in the woods, a mile north of the village of Pisseleux. Here the roll was called, and it was found that the following officers were missing: Lieut.-Colonel the Hon. G. Morris, Major H. F. Crichton, Captain C. A. Tisdall, Lieutenant Lord Robert Innes-Ker, 2nd Lieutenant Viscount Castlerosse, Lieutenant the Hon. Aubrey Herbert, and Lieutenant Shields, R.A.M.C.

Captain Lord Desmond FitzGerald and Lieutenant Blacker-Douglass were wounded and left with the field-ambulance. Lieut.-Colonel Morris, Major Crichton, and Captain Tisdall had been killed. The others had been wounded and captured by the Germans, who treated them with reasonable humanity at Villers-Cotterêts till they were released on September 12 by the French advance following the first Battle of the Marne. Colonel Morris' body was afterwards identified and buried with that of Captain Tisdall; and one long rustic-fenced grave, perhaps the most beautiful of all resting-places in France, on a slope of the forest off the dim road, near the Rond de la Reine, holds our dead in that action. It was made and has been religiously tended since by Dr. Moufflers, the Mayor of the town, and his wife.

The death of Colonel Morris, an officer beloved and a man noticeably brave among brave men, was a heavy loss to the Battalion he commanded, and whose temper he knew so well. In the thick of the fight during a lull in the firing, when some blind shell-fire opened, he called to the men: "D'you hear that? They're doing that to frighten you." To which some one replied with simple truth: "If that's what they're after, they might as well stop. They succeeded with *me* hours ago."

As a matter of fact, the men behaved serenely, as may be proved by this tale. They were working their way, well under rifle-fire, across an opening in the forest, when some of them stopped to pick blackberries that attracted their attention. To these their sergeant, very deliberately, said: "I shouldn't mind them berries, lads. There's may be worrums in 'em." It was a speech worthy of a hero of Dumas, whose town Villers-Cotterêts is, by right of birth. Yet once, during their further retirement towards Pisseleux, they were badly disconcerted. A curious private prodded a hornets' nest on a branch with his bayonet, and the inhabitants came out in force. Then there was real confusion: not restored by the sight of baldheaded reservists frantically slapping with their caps at one hornet while others stung them on their defenceless scalps. So they passed out of the darkness and the greenery of the forest, which, four years later, was to hide a great French Army, and launch it forth to turn the tide of 1918.

Their march continued until 11 p.m. that night, when the Battalion arrived at Betz, where the First and Second Army Corps rejoined each other once more. No supplies were received that night nor the following day (September 2), when the Battalion reached Esbly, where they bathed – with soap, be it noted – in the broad and quiet Marne, and an ox was requisitioned, potatoes were dug up from a field, and some sort of meal served out.

The Diary here notes "Thus ended the retreat from Mons." This is not strictly correct. In twelve days the British Army had been driven back 140 miles as the crow flies from Mons, and farther, of course by road. There was yet to be a further retirement of some fifteen miles of Esbly ere the general advance began; but September 3 marks, as nearly as may be, slack-water ere the ebb that followed of the triumphant German tidal wave through Belgium almost up to the outer forts of Paris. That advance had, at the last moment, swerved aside from Paris towards the south-east, and in doing so had partially exposed its right flank to the Sixth French Army. General Joffre took instant advantage of the false step to wheel his Sixth Army to the east, so that its line ran due north and east from Ermenonville to Lagny; at the same time throwing forward the left of his line. The British Force lay between Lagny and Cortecan, filling the gap between the Sixth and Fifth French Armies, and was still an effective weapon which the enemy supposed they had broken for good. But our harried men realized no more than that, for the moment, there seemed to be a pause in the steady going back. The confusion, the dust, the heat, continued while the Armies manoeuvred for position; and scouts and aerial reconnaissance reported more and more German columns of all arms pressing down from the east and north-east.

On September 3 the 4th Brigade moved from Esbly, in the great loops of the Marne, through Meaux to the neighbourhood of Pierre Levée, where the Battalion fed once more on requisitioned beef, potatoes and apples.

THE ADVANCE TO THE AISNE

Next day (September 4), while the British Army was getting into position in the process of changing front to the right, the 4th Brigade had to cover a retirement of the 5th Brigade between Pierre Levee and Le Bertrand, and the Battalion dug itself in near a farm (Grand Loge) on the Pierre Levée – Giremoutiers road in preparation for a rear-guard attack that did not arrive. They remained in position with what the Diary pathetically refers to as "the machine-gun," till they were relieved in the evening by the Worcesters, and reached bivouac at Le Bertrand at one o'clock on the morning of the 5th September. That day they bivouacked near Fontenay, and picked up some much-needed mess-tins, boots, putties and like with which to make good more immediate waste.

On the 6th they marched through Rozoy (where they saw an old priest standing at the door of his church, and to him the men bared their heads mechanically, till he, openly surprised, gave them his blessing) to Mont Plaisir to gain touch between the First and Second Divisions of the English Army. Major Stepney, the C.O., reported to Headquarters 1st Brigade at 9 a.m. half a mile north-east of Rozoy. At the same moment cavalry scouts brought news of two enemy columns, estimated at a thousand each, approaching from the direction of Vaudoy. Nos. 3 and 4 Companies were ordered forward to prolong the line of the First Division, while Nos. 1 and 2 Companies "with the machine-gun" entrenched themselves on the Mont Plaisir road.

In the afternoon Lieutenant the Hon. H. R. Alexander, reconnoitring with a platoon in the direction of the village of Villeneuve, which was to be occupied, reported a hostile battery at Le Plessis had fired on the Battalion and killed 4 men and wounded 11. One of these, Sergeant O'Loughlin, died later. This was the Battalion's first fighting since Villers-Cotterêts, and they went into action while the bells of the quiet countryside rang for church. The battery was put out of action by our guns in half an hour, Villeneuve occupied without further opposition, and the Battalion bivouacked at Touquin on the night of the 6th September. The enemy had realized the threat to their flank in General Joffre's new dispositions, and under cover of rear-guard and delaying actions were withdrawing north all along their line.

On the 7th September the Battalion made a forced march from Touquin to Rebais, where there was a German column, but the advance-guard of the Brigade was held up at St. Simeon till dark and the Battalion had to bivouac a couple of miles outside Rebais. The German force withdrew from Rebais on the afternoon of the 7th, and on the 8th the Brigade's advance continued through Rebais northward in the direction of Boitron, which lay just across the Petit Morin river. Heavy machine-gun fire from some thick woods along the rolling ground, across the river, checked the advance-guard (the 3rd Coldstream) and the two companies of the Irish Guards who supported them. The woods, the river valley, and the village of Boitron were searched by our guns, and on the renewal of the attack the river was crossed and Boitron occupied, the enemy being heavily shelled as he retired. Here the Battalion re-formed and pressed forward in a heavy rain-storm, through a flank attack of machine-guns from woods on the left. These they charged, while a battery of our field-guns fired point-blank into the thickets, and captured a German machine-gun company of six guns (which seemed to them, at the time, a vast number), 3 officers, and 90 rank and file. Here, too, in the confusion of the fighting they came under fire of our own artillery, an experience that was to become familiar to them, and the C.O. ordered the Companies to assemble at Ferme le Cas Rouge, a village near by where they bivouacked for the night. They proudly shut up in the farm-yard the first prisoners they had ever taken; told off two servants to wait upon a wounded major; took the parole of the two other officers and invited them to a dinner of chicken and red wine. The Battalion, it will be observed, knew nothing then except the observances of ordinary civilized warfare. Second Lieutenant A Fitzgerald and a draft arrived that day.

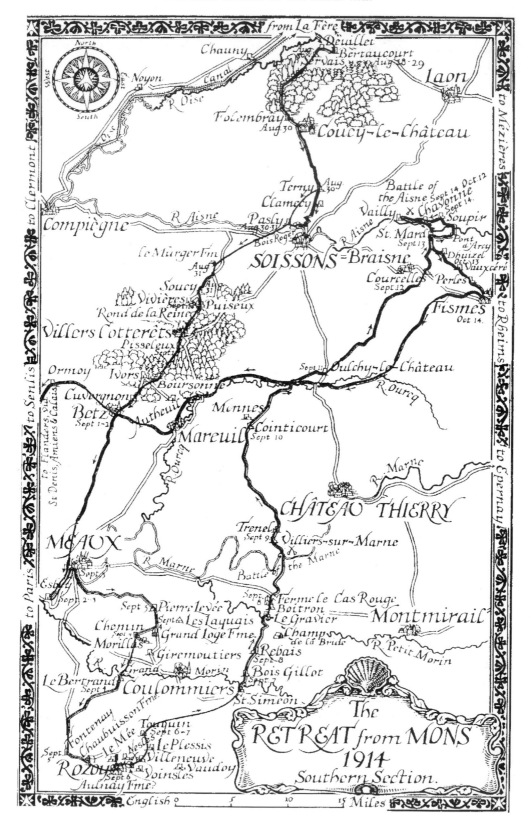

The RETREAT from MONS
1914
Southern Section.

This small affair of Boitron Wood was the Irish Guards' share of the immense mixed Battle of the Marne, now raging along all the front. Its result and the capture of the machine-guns cheered them a little.

The next five days – September 9 to 13 – had nothing but tedious marching and more tedious halts and checks, due to the congestion of traffic and the chaos in the villages that had been entered, sacked, defiled and abandoned by the enemy. The Marne was crossed on the 9th at Charly, where – the inhabitants said that the Germans detailed for the job had been too drunk to effect it – a bridge had been left ready for demolition, but intact, and by this means the First and Second Divisions crossed the river. The weather turned wet, with heavy showers; greatcoats had been lost or thrown aside all along the line of retreat; billets and bivouacs made filthy by the retreating Germans; and there was general discomfort, enlivened with continuous cannonading from the front and the appearance of German prisoners gathered in by our Cavalry ahead. And thus, from the Marne the Battalion came by way of Trenel, Villiers-sur-Marne, Cointicourt, Oulchy-le-Château, Courcelles and St. Mard to the high banks of the Aisne, which they crossed by the pontoon bridge at Pont d'Arcy on the morning of September 14 and advanced to Soupir in the hollows under the steep wooded hills.

That day, the 2nd Grenadiers formed the advance-guard of the Brigade, followed by the 3rd Coldstream, the Irish Guards and the 2nd Coldstream. After they had cleared Soupir village, the force was shelled and an attack was made by the 3rd Coldstream, the Irish Guards in support, on a steep ridge near La Cour de Soupir farm, which stood on the crest of the bluff above the river. The heavily wooded country was alive with musketry and machine-gun fire, and the distances were obscured by mist and heavy rain. The 3rd Coldstream, attacking the farm, found themselves outflanked from a ridge on their right, which was then attempted by three companies of the Irish Guards. They reached to within a couple of hundred yards of a wood cut up by rides, down which, as well as from the trenches, heavy rifle-fire was directed. Here Captain J. N. Guthrie (No. 2 Company) was wounded and Captain H. Hamilton Berners killed, while Lieutenant Watson, R.A.M.C., was shot and wounded at close quarters attending a wounded man. Here, too, the Battalion had its first experience of the German use of the white flag; for Lieutenant J. S. FitzGerald with No. 8 Platoon and a party of Coldstream under Lieutenant Cotterel-Dormer found some hundred and fifty Germans sitting round haystacks and waving white flags. They went forward to take their surrender and were met by a heavy fire at thirty yards range, which forced them to fall back. Lieutenant E. B. Greer, machine-gun officer, now brought up his two machine-guns, but was heavily fired at from cover, had all of one gun-team killed or wounded and, for the while, lost one gun. He reorganized the other gun-team, and called for volunteers from the Company nearest him to recover it. After dark Corporal Sheridan and Private Carney of No. 3 Company and Private Harrington, a machine-gunner of No. 1 Company, went out with him and the gun was brought in. A farther advance was made in the afternoon to the edge of the wood in order to clear out the snipers who held it and commanded the cultivated fields outside. Towards dusk, Captain Lord Guernsey, who was Acting Quartermaster, reported himself to the C.O., who posted him to No. 2 Company, then engaged in clearing out the snipers, in place of Captain Guthrie, who had been wounded. He went forward to assist Captain Lord Arthur Hay in command, and both were immediately shot dead.

The Battalion bivouacked in battle-outpost formation that night on the edge of the wood, and got into touch with the 60th Rifles on their right and the 2nd Grenadiers on their left. Here, though they did not know it, the advance from the Marne was at an end. Our forces had reached the valley of the Aisne, with its bluffs on either side and deep roads half hidden by the woods that climbed them. The plateaux of the north of the river shaped themselves for the trench-warfare of the years to come; and the natural strength of the positions on the high ground was increased by numberless quarries and caves that ran along it.

THE HALT AT SOUPIR

On the 15th September patrols reported that the enemy had fallen back a little from his position, and at daylight two companies entrenched themselves on the edge of the wood. Judged by present standards, those trenches were little more than shallow furrows, for we did not know that the day of open battle was ended, and it is curious to see how slowly our people broke themselves to the monotonous business of trench construction and maintenance. Even after they had dug the casual ditch which they called a trench, it cost some time and a few lives till they understood that the works could not be approached in the open as had been war's custom. Their first communication-trench was but three hundred yards long, and it struck them as a gigantic and almost impossible "fatigue."

The enemy had not fallen back more than a thousand yards from the Cour de Soupir farm which they were resolute to retake if possible. They fired on our burying-parties and shelled the trenches all through the 16th September. Patrols were sent out at dawn and dusk – since anyone visible leaving the trenches was fired upon by snipers – found hostile infantry in full strength in front of them, and the Battalion had to organize its first system of trench-relief; for the Diary of the 18th September remarks that "Nos. 1 and 4 Companies relieved 2 and 3 Companies in the trenches and were again shelled during the day"

Sniping on Hun lines was a novel experience to the Battalion. They judged it strange to find a man apparently dead, with a cloth over his face, lying in a hollow under a ridge commanding their line, who turned out to be quite alive and unwounded. His rifle was within short reach, and he was waiting till our patrols had passed to get to his work. But they killed him, angrily and with astonishment.

Lieutenant E.B. Greer, machine-gun officer, now brought up his two machine-guns, but was heavily fired at from cover, had all of one gun-team killed or wounded and, for the while, lost one gun . . .

Lieutenant Greer with his Maxim gun team, August 1914.

On the morning of the 18th September Lieut.-Colonel Lord Ardee, Grenadier Guards, arrived and took over command from Major Stepney. The following officers – the first of the long line – also arrived as reinforcements: Major G. Madden; Captain Norman Orr-Ewing, Scots Guards, attached; Captain Lord Francis Scott, Grenadier Guards, attached; Captain the Hon. J. F. Trefusis, Lieutenants George Brooke, L. S. Coke, R. H. Ferguson, G. M. Maitland, C. R. Harding, and P. Antrobus.

The Battalion reorganized as follows after less than four weeks' campaign:

Lieut.-Colonel Lord Ardee	C.O.
Major Herbert Stepney	Senior Major.
Capt. the Hon. J. Trefusis	Adjutant.
Lieut. E. J. Gough	Transport Officer.
Lieut. C. A. S. Walker	Quartermaster (acting)
Capt. Hon. A. E. Mulholland	O.C. No. 1 Company.
Capt. N. Orr-Ewing	O.C. No. 2 Company.
Capt. Lord Francis Scott	O.C. No. 3 Company.
Major G. Madden	O.C. No. 4 Company.

The trench-war was solidifying itself; for the Diary of that same day notes that the enemy "shelled the trenches and the two howitzer-guns which were in position below." Ours was an army, then, which could count and place every gun that it owned. As many as three howitzer batteries per Division had accompanied the Expeditionary Force, and more were being sent from home.

The night of the 19th was very wet. They were relieved by the 3rd Coldstream, and went into billets at Soupir, "having been in the trenches for five days." There was an alarm in the afternoon, and the machine-guns and 100 men of No. 1 Company were sent to help the Coldstream in the trenches, whilst the rest of the Battalion marched at 6 p.m. to be ready to assist the 2nd Grenadiers on the left of Cour de Soupir farm. Only "the machine-guns," however, came into action, and the Battalion returned to its billets at 10 p.m.

Much the same sort of thing occurred on the 20th – a furious fusillade from the trenches, the despatch of reinforcements up a "muddy lane," not yet turned into a communication-trench, to help the 3rd Coldstream, while Nos. 2 and 4 Companies went out to reinforce the Oxfordshire Light Infantry and to hold the road at the back of it "in case of a retirement," and the rest of the Battalion with the machine-guns stayed as a reserve in Soupir market-square. But beyond shrapnel bursting over the village and the wounding of two men by stray machine-gun bullets, there were no special incidents. Major G. Madden this day had to return to England, ill.

On the 21st the Battalion relieved the 2nd Grenadiers on the left at Soupir farm at 3.30 a.m. – the safest hour, as experience was to prove, for reliefs. Nos. 2 and 3 Companies were in trenches and Nos. 1 and 4 about 300 yards in the rear, with the Headquarters in one of the caves which are a feature of the country.

The word "dug-out" had not yet been invented. The nearest approach to it is a reference in a private letter to "a shelter-recess in the side of the trench to protect one from shrapnel." The Diary marks that the "usual alarms occurred at 6.30 when the patrol went out and the enemy fired a good deal of shrapnel without effect." Soupir, like many French villages, was full of carefully planted spies of singular audacity. One was found in an officer's room. He had appeared from a cellar, alleging that he was an invalid, but as the Gunners' telephone-wires near the cellar had been cut and our movements had been reported to the enemy with great regularity, his explanation was not accepted; nor were his days long in that land.

Patrols, too, were elastic affairs. One of them, under Lieutenant R. H. Ferguson, went out on the night of the 21st, came on the enemy's trenches half a mile out, lay down to listen to the conversation there, were all but cut off by a wandering section of snipers, and returned to their lines unmolested, after the lieutenant had shot the leading pursuer with his revolver.

On the 22nd September the Battalion – both entrenched and in reserve in the caves behind – experienced four hours' high-explosive howitzer fire, which "except for the effect on the nerves did very little damage." (They had yet to learn what continuous noise could do to break men's nerve.) This was followed by a heavy fusillade, varied by star-shells, rockets and searchlights, which lasted intermittently throughout the night. The rocket-display was new to the men. Searchlights, we know, they had seen before.

On the 23rd a telephone-line between Battalion Headquarters and the advanced trenches was installed (for the first time). Nos. 2 and 3 Companies relieved Nos. 1 and 4 in the trenches, and a man bringing back a message from No. 4 Company was killed by a sniper. The Battalion was relieved by the 3rd Coldstream in the evening and returned to its billets in the barns and lofts of Soupir village, where next day (September 24) the Diary observes they spent "a quiet morning. The men got washed and shaved, and Company officers were able to get at their companies. There are so many new officers who do not know their men that any rest day should be made use of in this manner." They relieved the 3rd Coldstream again that evening, and "digging operations to improve existing trenches and make communication-trenches were at once begun." (Here is the first direct reference in the Diary to communication-trenches, as such.)

Snipers were active all through the 25th September. The trenches were heavily shelled in the afternoon, and "one man was hit in the leg while going to fetch water." They returned to Soupir in the evening and spent the 26th standing to, in anticipation of enemy attacks which did not develop into anything more than an artillery duel, and in digging trenches for the defence of Soupir village. This work, however, had to be stopped owing to heavy shell-fire brought to bear on the working-parties – presumably through information from the many spies – and after a wearing day they relieved the 3rd Coldstream in the trenches at night. The Diary gives no hint of the tremendous strain of those twenty-four hours' "reliefs" from being shelled in a trench to being shelled in a village, nor of the inadequacy of our Artillery as it strove to cope with the German guns, nor of the rasping irritation caused by the knowledge that every disposition made was reported almost at once to the enemy.

On September 27 – a Sunday – the enemy's bands were heard playing up and down the trenches. Some attempt was made by a British battalion on the right to move out a patrol covered by the fire of No. 2 Company, but the enemy shells and machine-guns smothered every movement.

On the 28th September (their day in billets) stakes were cut out of the woods behind Soupir, while the Pioneers collected what wire they could lay hands on, as "the Battalion was ordered to construct wire entanglements in front of their trenches to-night." The entanglements were made of two or three strands, at the most, of agricultural wire picked up where they could find it. They heard heavy fighting throughout the night on their right – "probably the First Division." Both sides by now were feeling the strain of trench-work, for which neither had made preparations, and the result was an increasing tension manifesting itself in wild outbursts of musketry and artillery and camp rumour of massed attacks and breaks-through.

On the 30th September, F.-M. Lord Roberts' birthday, a congratulatory telegram was sent to him; and "a great quantity of material was collected out of which huts for the men could be built." These were frail affairs of straw and twig, half dug in, half built out, of the nearest banks, or placed under the lee of any available shelter. The very fabric of them has long since been overlaid with strata of fresh wreckage and the twig roofs and sides are rotted black under the grass or ploughed in.

The month closes with the note that, as it was a very bright moonlight night, the Battalion's usual relief of the Coldstream was "carried out up the communication-trenches." Some men still recall that first clumsy trench-relief.

October 1 was spent in perfecting communication-trenches and shelters, and "the Brigadier came up in the morning and was taken round the trenches." Two officers were sent to Chavonne to meet the 5th Brigade – one to bring the Worcesters to the Battalion's trenches, the other to show the Connaught Rangers their billets in Soupir. The 3rd Coldstream marched out of Soupir and took up the line to the left of the 2nd Grenadiers near Vailly, and next day, 2nd October, No. 1 Company of the Irish Guards dug a connecting-trench between those two. Otherwise, for the moment, life was smooth.

It may be noted, for the instruction of generations to come, that some of the Reservists grumbled at orders not to talk or smoke in the trenches, as that drew fire; and that a newly appointed platoon-officer, when he had admonished them officially, fell them out and informed them unofficially that, were there any more trouble, he would, after the C.O. had dealt with the offenders, take them on for three rounds "boxing in public." Peace and goodwill returned at once.

On the 3rd October a platoon was despatched to help the Royal Engineers in the construction of a road across a new bridge they had put up between Soupir and Chavonne. The Battalion relieved the 3rd Coldstream in its new position three-quarters of a mile east of Vailly, and next day "quietly improved trenches and head-cover," which latter is mentioned for the first time. It was all casual timber picked up off the country-side.

On the 5th October a patrol explored through the wood, in front of the right trenches, but found only dead Germans to the number of thirty and many half buried, as well as five British soldiers killed in some lost affair of a fortnight before. Private O'Shaughnessy, No. 1 Company, was shot dead by a sniper when on observation-post at the end of this wood. He had only arrived that morning with a draft of one hundred men, under Lieutenant Gore-Langton, and had asked to be allowed to go out on this duty. In the afternoon three shells burst on the road near Battalion Headquarters, and fatally wounded Lieutenant G. Brooke, who was on his way to Soupir to take over the transport from Lieutenant E. J. Gough. He was sent in to Braisne, where he died on the 7th October. The Diary notes "he would not have been found so soon had not the shells broken the telephone-wire to Headquarters. A message was coming through at the time and when communication was stopped the Signalling Sergeant sent two men to repair the wire and they found him." He was brought in to the A.D.S. at Vailly-sur-Aisne by his own men, who made the R.A.M.C. stretcher-bearers walk behind, for they would allow none but themselves to carry him. They bade him farewell before they returned to their trenches, and went out openly weeping. When he was sent to Braisne that evening, after being dressed, his own men again got an ambulance across the pontoon-bridge, which had been hitherto reckoned impassable, for his convenience. His last words to them were that they were to "play the game" and not to revenge his death on the Hun.

On the afternoon of the 6th October, which was cold and misty, the Germans pushed a patrol through the wood and our standing-patrol went out and discovered one German under-officer of the 64th (Imperial Jäger Guards) dead, and the rifle of another man.

The enemy sent out no more patrols. Men had grown to be cunning among the timber, and noticed every tree they moved under. When the Coldstream relieved the Battalion that night, one of our patrols found a felled tree had been carefully placed across their homeward path by some unknown hand – it might have been the late Jäger under-officer – who had expected to attack the patrol while it was climbing over the obstacle.

On the 7th the Battalion rested in Soupir all day, and on the 8th Lieutenant G. Brooke's body was brought in from Braisne and buried in Soupir cemetery.

The 9th was a quiet day except for an hour's shelling, and a good deal of cheering from the German trenches in the evening, evidently in honour of the fall of Antwerp. It annoyed our men for the reason that they could not retaliate. Our guns had not a round to throw away.

THE MOVE TOWARD THE SEA

The opposing lines had been locked now for close upon a month and, as defences elaborated themselves, all hope of breaking-through vanished. Both sides then opened that mutually outflanking movement towards the west which did not end till it reached the sea. Held up along their main front, the Germans struck at the Flanders plain, the Allies striving to meet the movement and envelop their right flank as it extended. A British force had been sent to Antwerp; the Seventh Division and the Third Cavalry Division had been landed at Zeebrugge on the 7th October with the idea of helping either the Antwerp force or co-operating with the Allied Armies as circumstances dictated. Meantime, the main British force was being held in the trenches of the Aisne a hundred and twenty miles away; and it seemed good to all concerned that these two bodies of British troops should be consolidated, alike for purposes of offence, command and, by no means least, supply, on the Flanders flank covering the Channel. There were obvious dangers in moving so many men from high ground across a broad river under the enemy's eye. It could only be effected at night with all precautions, but as the western pressure developed and was accentuated by the fall of Antwerp, the advantage of the transfer outweighed all risk. Our Cavalry moved on the 3rd October by road for Flanders, and a few days later the infantry began to entrain for St. Omer. The Second Corps was the first to leave, the Third Corps followed, and the First was the last.

Orders came to the Battalion on Sunday, October 11, to be prepared to move at short notice, and new clothes were issued to the men, but they did not hand over their trenches to the French till the 13th October, when they marched to Perles in the evening and entrained on the 14th at Fismes a little after noon, reaching Hazebrouck via (the route is worth recording) Mareuil-sur-Ourcq, Ormoy, St. Denis, outside Paris, Epluches, Creil, Amiens (10.15 p.m.), Abbeville (3.15 a.m.), Etaples, Boulogne, Calais and St. Omer, every stone of which last six was to be as familiar to them as their own hearths for years to come.

At 5 p.m. on the 15th the Battalion went into billets at Hazebrouck. It was a sharp change from the soft wooded bluffs and clean chalky hills above the Aisne, to the slow ditch-like streams and crowded farming landscape of Flanders. At Hazebrouck they lay till the morning of the 17th, when they marched to Boeschepe, attended church parade on Sunday the 18th, and marched to untouched Ypres via St. Kokebeele, Reninghelst and Vlamertinghe on the 20th with the Brigade, some divisional troops and the 41st Battery R.F.A. The Brigade halted at Ypres a few hours, seeing and being impressed by the beauty of the Cloth Hall and the crowded marketplace. The 2nd Coldstream and the 2nd Battalion Grenadiers being eventually sent forward, the remainder of the Brigade billeted in St. Jean, then described impersonally as "a small village about one and a half kilometres east of Ypres." They halted at the edge of the city for dinner, and the men got out their melodeons and danced jigs on the flawless *pavé*. Much firing was heard all day, and "the 2nd Coldstream came into action about 4 p.m. and remained in the trenches all night."

That was the sum of information available at the moment to the Battalion – that, and orders to "drive the enemy back wherever met." So they first were introduced to the stage of the bloody and debatable land which will be known for all time as "The Salient."

The original intention of our Army on the Flanders flank had been offensive, but the long check on the Aisne gave the enemy time to bring forward troops from their immense and perfectly prepared reserves, while the fall of Antwerp – small wonder the Germans had cheered in their trenches when the news came! – released more. Consequentiy, the movement that began on the Allies' side as an attempt to roll up the German right flank before it could reach the sea, ended in a desperate defence to hold back an overwhelmingly strong enemy from sweeping forward through Belgium to Calais and the French seaboard. Out of this defence developed that immense and overlapping series of operations centring on Ypres, extending from the Yser Canal in the north to La Bassée in the south, and lasting from mid-October to the 20th November 1914, which may be ranked as the First Battle of Ypres.

It will be remembered that the Second and Third British Army Corps were the first to leave the Aisne trenches for the west. On the 11th October the Second Army Corps was in position between the Aire and Béthune and in touch with the left flank of the Tenth French Army at La Bassée.

On the 12th of October the Third Army Corps reached St. Omer and moved forward to Hazebrouck to get in touch with the Second Army Corps on its right, the idea being that the two Corps together should wheel on their own left and striking eastward turn the position of the German forces that were facing the Tenth French Army. They failed owing to the strength of the German forces on the spot, and by October 19, after indescribably fierce fighting, the Second and Third Army Corps had been brought to a standstill on a line, from La Bassée through Armentières not noticeably differing from the position which our forces were destined to occupy for many months to come. The attempted flank attacks had become frontal all along the line, and in due course frontal attacks solidified into trench-warfare again.

North of Armentières the situation had settled itself in much the same fashion, flank attacks being outflanked by the extension of the enemy's line, with strenuous frontal attacks of his daily increasing forces.

The Seventh Division – the first half of the Fourth Army Corps – reached Ypres from Dixmude on the 14th October after its unsuccessful attempt to relieve Antwerp. As the First Army Corps had not yet come up from the Aisne, this Division was used to cover the British position at Ypres from the north; the infantry lying from Zandvoorde, on the south-east, through Zonnebeke to Langemarck on the north-west. Here again, through lack of numbers and artillery equipment, the British position was as serious as in the south. Enemy forces, more numerous than the British and Belgian armies combined, were bearing down on the British line from the eastward through Courtrai, Iseghem and Roulers, and over the Lys bridge at Menin. Later on, it was discovered that these represented not less than five new Army Corps. The Seventh Division was ordered to move upon Menin, to seize the bridge over the river and thus check the advance of further reinforcements. There were, of course, not enough troops for the work, but on the 18th October the Division, the right centre of which rested on the Ypres – Menin road, not yet lined throughout with dead, wheeled its left (the 22nd Brigade) forward. As the advance began, the Cavalry on the left became aware of a large new German force on the left flank of the advance, and fighting became general all along the line of the Division.

On the 19th October the airmen reported the presence of two fresh Army Corps on the left. No farther advance being possible, the Division was ordered to fall back to its original line, an operation attended with heavy loss under constant attacks.

On the 20th October the pressure increased as the German Army Corps made themselves felt against the thin line held by the Seventh Division, which was not amply provided with heavy batteries. Their losses were largely due to artillery fire, directed by air-observation, that obliterated trenches, men and machine-guns.

On the 21st October the enemy attacked the Division throughout the day, artillery preparations being varied by mass assaults, but still the Division endured in the face of an enemy at least four times as strong and constantly reinforced. It is, as one writer says, hardly conceivable that our men could have checked the enemy's advance for even a day longer, had it not been for the arrival at this juncture of the First Army Corps. Reinforcements were urgently needed at every point of the British line, but for the moment, the imminent danger lay to the north of Ypres, where fresh German forces, underestimated as usual, might sweep the Belgian army aside and enter the Channel ports in our rear. With this in mind, the British Commander-in-Chief decided to use the First Army Corps to prolong the British line, already, as it seemed, nearly worn through, toward the sea, rather than to strengthen any occupied sector. He posted it, therefore – until French reinforcements should arrive – to the north, or left of the Seventh Division, from Zonnebeke to Bixschoote.

Our front at that date ran from Hollebeke to Bixschoote, a distance, allowing for bends, of some sixteen miles. To protect this we had but three depleted Infantry Divisions and two Cavalry Brigades against opposed forces of not less than a hundred thousand. Moreover, the ground was hampered by the flight, from Roulers and villages in German possession, of refugees, of whom a percentage were certainly spies, but over whom it was impossible to exercise any control. They carried their goods in little carts drawn by dogs, and they wept and wailed as they straggled past our men.

THE SALIENT AND THE FIRST BATTLE OF YPRES

The orders for the Guards Brigade on October 21 to "drive back the enemy wherever met" were not without significance. All their news in billets had been of fresh formations coming down from the north and the east, and it was understood that the Germans counted with confidence upon entering Calais, via Ypres, in a few days.

The Brigade, less the 2nd Coldstream, "assembled in a field about four kilometres along the Ypres – Zonnebeke Road, and after a wait of three hours No. 4 Company of the 1st Irish Guards advanced to the support of the 2nd Grenadiers, who had been ordered to prolong the line to the right of the 2nd Coldstream. This Company and both the advanced Battalions suffered somewhat severely from shell-fire and occasional sniping." Thus coldly does the Diary enter upon what was in fact the first day of the first Battle of Ypres, in which Companies had to do the work of Battalions, and Battalions of Brigades, and whose only relief was a change of torn and blood-soaked ground from one threatened sector of the line to the next.

It was not worth while to record how the people of Ypres brought hot coffee to the Battalion as it passed through, the day before (October 20); and how, when they halted there a few hours, the men amused their hosts by again dancing Irish jigs on the pavements while the refugees clattered past; or how it was necessary to warn the Companies that the enemy might attack behind a screen of Belgian women and children – in which case the Battalion would have to fire through them.

On the evening of the 21st October the Battalion was ordered up to the support of what was left of the 22nd Brigade which had fallen back to Zonnebeke. "It came under a heavy burst of artillery fire and was forced to lie down (in a ploughed field) for fifteen minutes" – at that time a novel experience. On its way a hare started up which was captured by a man of No. 2 Company to the scandal of discipline and the delight of all, and later sold for five shillings. At Zonnebeke it found No. 4 Company already lining the main road on the left of the town and took up a position in extended order on its right, "thus establishing the line into Zonnebeke." The casualties, in spite of the artillery fire, are noted as only "one killed and seven wounded," which must have been far under the mark. The night was lit by the flames of burning houses, by which light they hunted for snipers in haystacks round the village, buried stray dead of a battalion of the Seventh Division which had left them and, by order, did a deal of futile digging-in.

The next day the 22nd Brigade retired out of Zonnebeke about a kilometre down the main road to Ypres, the Battalion and half the 2nd Coldstream conforming to the movement. This enabled the Germans to enter the north of Zonnebeke and post machine-guns in some of the houses. None the less, our patrols remained in the south end of the town and did "excellent work"; an officer's patrol, under Lieutenant Ferguson, capturing three mounted orderlies. One man was killed and 8 wounded in the Battalion that day.

On the 23rd October "the enemy brought up more machine-guns and used them against us energetically all the day." A platoon of No. 1 Company, under Lieutenant the Hon. H. Alexander, attempted an out-flanking movement through Zonnebeke, towards the church, supported by a platoon of No. 4 Company, under Lieutenant W. C. N. Reynolds, in the course of which the latter officer was wounded. The trenches were shelled with shrapnel all the afternoon, and a German advance was sprayed down with our rifle-fire. In the evening the French made an attack through Zonnebeke helped by their 75's and established themselves in the town. They also, at 9 p.m., relieved the Battalion which moved at once southwest to Zillebeke and arrived there at 2 a.m. on the morning of the 24th, when it billeted "chiefly in a brick-yard" ready to be used afresh.

The relieving troops were a Division of the Ninth French Army Corps. They took over the line of our Second Division, while our Second Division in turn took over part of the front of the Seventh Division. At the same time French Territorials relieved our First Division between Bixschoote and Langemarck, thus freeing us of all responsibility for any ground north of the Ypres – Zonnebeke road. Our Army on the 24th October, then, stood as follows: From the Zonnebeke road to a point near the race-course in the historic Polygon Wood west of Reutel was the Second Division; on its right, up to the Menin road, lay the First Division; and from the Menin road to Zandvoorde the Seventh Division with the 3rd Cavalry Brigade in the Zandvoorde trenches. Our line had thus been shortened and strengthened; but the enemy were continuously receiving reinforcements from Roulers and Menin, and the pressure never ceased.

In the early morning of the 24th October, and before the transfer of all the troops had been effected the British Ypres front was attacked throughout in force and once more the shock of the attack fell on the remains of the Seventh Division. Reserves there were none; each Battalion stood where it was in the flood and fought on front, flank and rear indifferently. The Irish Guards had a few hours' rest in the brick-fields at Zillebeke, where, by some miracle, it found its mail of home letters and parcels waiting for it. Even before it could open them it was ordered out from Zillebeke[1] along the Ypres – Menin road to Hooge to help the 20th Brigade (Seventh Division), which had been attacked on the morning of the 25th October, and parties of the enemy were reported to have broken through into Polygon Wood.

That attack, however, was repulsed during the day, and in the evening the Battalion was despatched to act in support of the 5th Brigade near Race-course (Polygon) Wood, due north of Veldhoek, where the Battalion bivouacked for the night in a ploughed field. This was the first time it had marched up the Menin road or seen the Château of Hooge, of which now no trace remains, sitting stately among its lawns.

On the 25th October, after a heavy bombardment as bombardments were then reckoned, the whole Division was ordered at dawn to advance against Reutel; the 2nd Grenadier Guards and the Irish Guards being given the work of clearing out Polygon Wood, of which the enemy held the upper half. They were advancing through the woods, and the trenches of the Worcester Battalion there, when a big shell burst in Lieutenant Ferguson's platoon, No. 3 Company, killing 4 and wounding 9 men, as far as was known. Ferguson himself, knocked down but unwounded, went back to advise No. 2 Company coming up behind him to deviate a little, "for the ground was a slaughter-house." The Battalion fought its way to a couple of hundred yards north of Reutel and was then brought under heavy rifle-

---

[1] "… and the next time I saw Zillebeke it was a deserted ruin, and the small house whose inmates had been so kind to my subalterns and me was a heap of debris." – Extract from a Company Commander's Diary.

fire from concealed trenches on a ridge. The 2nd Grenadiers on the right had, earlier, been held up by a German trench on their left, and, as dark came on, touch between the battalions there was lost, and the patrol sent out to regain it only stumbled on the German trench. The left of the Battalion lost touch by nearly a quarter of a mile with the 5th Brigade, and as the wet night closed in they found themselves isolated in darkness and dripping autumn undergrowth, with the old orders "to hold ground gained at all costs." Meantime they hung with both flanks in the air and enemy patrols on either side. The nearest supports of any kind were the trenches of the Worcesters, six hundred yards behind, through the woods; so the Battalion linked up with them by means of a double front of men, back to back, strung out tail-wise from their bivouac to the Worcesters. The manoeuvre succeeded. There was sniping all night from every side, but thanks to the faithful "tail" the enemy could not get round the Battalion to make sure whether it was wholly in the air. The casualties this day were reported as 4 killed and 23 wounded.

At 4 a.m. on the 26th October, just after the night's rain had ceased, word came from Brigade Headquarters that the 3rd Coldstream were to be expected on the Battalion's right. They arrived an hour and a half later and the Battalion attacked, again to be held up in a salient heavily enfiladed from every angle by machine-guns, and though No. 2 Company carried a couple of farm-houses outside the woods, they were forced to retire from one of them and lost heavily. An attack by the 6th Brigade in the afternoon relieved the pressure a little, and helped the Battalion to get in touch with, at least, its Brigade. Lieutenant Shields (R.A.M.C. attached) was killed here while attending our wounded. He had been remonstrated with only a few minutes before for exposing himself too much, and paid as much heed to the rebuke as did the others who succeeded him in his office. The casualties for the day were 1 officer and 9 men killed and 42 wounded. The night was memorable inasmuch as the Battalion, which had had no food for forty-eight hours, was allowed to eat its emergency rations.

There was a German attack on the night of the 27th October, lasting for less than an hour, but the advance of the 6th Brigade on the Battalion's left, together with the advance of the French still farther to the left, threatening Passchendaele, kept the enemy moderately quiet till the Battalion was relieved in the evening of the 27th by the 3rd Coldstream, settling down here and at intervals throughout the night. Major Herbert-Stepney was slightly wounded in the back by a bullet when at supper in a farm-house; 2 men were killed and 3 wounded. Captain A. H. L. McCarthy, R.A.M.C., joined for duty, replacing Lieutenant Shields.

Next morning (October 28) the 5th Brigade was attacking and the Battalion was ordered to support. It was heavily shelled again in the wood and dug itself in north-west on the race-course, where it stayed all day ready to support the Coldstream, and had a quiet time. The C.O. (Lord Ardee) went to hospital with a bad throat; Lieutenant Greer was wounded while serving his machine-gun, which had been lent to the 3rd Coldstream, and a couple of men were wounded. Drill-Sergeant A. Winspear joined the Connaught Rangers as 2nd Lieutenant – one of the earliest of the Army officers promoted from the ranks.

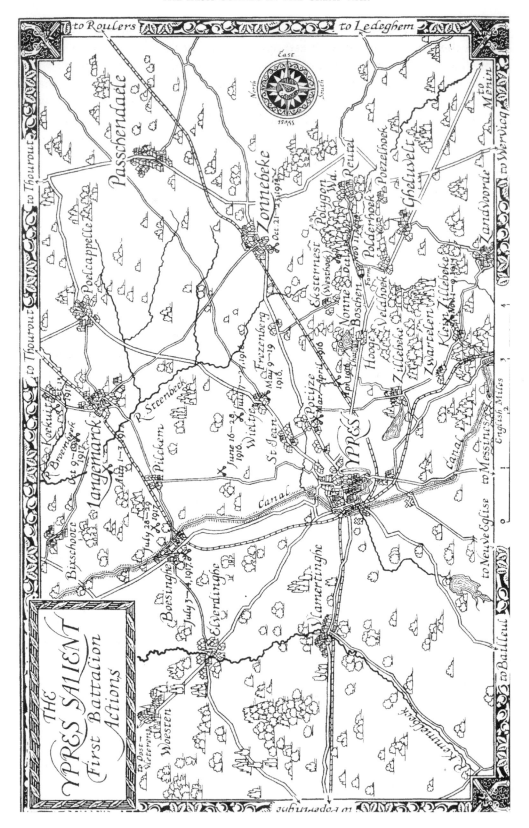

The enemy at that date were so sure of success that they made no attempt to conceal their intentions, and all our spent forces on the Ypres front were well aware that a serious attack would be opened on them on the 29th. Rumour said it would be superintended by the Kaiser himself. But, so far as the Battalion was concerned, that day was relatively quiet. The 2nd Brigade had been ordered to retake the trenches lost by the 1st Brigade east of Gheluvelt, and the Battalion's duty, with the 2nd Grenadiers, was to fill up whatever gaps might be found in a line which was mainly gaps between the left of the 2nd and the right of the 1st Brigade near Polderhoek. It reached the light railway from Gheluvelt to Polderhoek, discovered that the gap there could be filled up by a platoon, communicated with the C.O.'s of the two Brigades concerned, sent back three Companies to the 4th Brigade Headquarters, left one at the disposal of the 1st Brigade, and at night withdrew. For the moment, the line could be held with the troops on the spot, and it was no policy to use a man more than was necessary. The casualties to the men for that day were but 4 killed and 6 wounded, though a shell burst on the Brigade Reserve Ammunition Column, west of Race-course Wood, and did considerable damage.

The 30th October opened on the heaviest crisis of the long Battle of Ypres. The Battalion, to an accompaniment of "Jack Johnsons," dug trenches a quarter of a mile west of Race-course Wood in case the troops at the farther end of it should be driven back; for in those years woods were visible and gave good cover. German aeroplanes, well aware that they had no anti-aircraft guns to fear, swooped low over them in the morning, and men could only reply with some pitiful rifle-fire.

In the afternoon orders came for them and the 2nd Grenadiers to stop digging and move up to Klein Zillebeke to support the hard-pressed Seventh Division on whose front the enemy had broken through again. When they reached what was more or less the line, Nos. 1 and 2 Companies were sent forward to support the Cavalry in their trenches, while Nos. 3 and 4 Companies dug themselves in behind Klein Zillebeke.[1] A gap of about a quarter of a mile was found running from the Klein Zillebeke – Zandvoorde road north to the trenches of the 2nd Gordon Highlanders, and patrols reported the enemy in force in a strip of wood immediately to the east of it. Whether the gap had been blasted out by concentrated enemy-fire, or whether what the guns had left of our Cavalry had retired, was never clear. The Battalion was told off to hold the place and to find out who was on either side of them, while the 2nd Grenadiers continued the line southward from the main road to the canal. Beginning at 11 p.m., they dug themselves in till morning light. A burning farm-house blazed steadily all night in a hollow by Zandvoorde and our patrols on the road could see the Germans

---

[1] "At the cross-roads near Klein Zillebeke we halted, lying down on each side of the road as shells were coming over. In the centre of the road lay a dead trooper of some British Cavalry Regiment, his horse also half dead across him. A woman passed by. . . . She had all her house-hold treasures strapped on her back and held the hands of two very small children. She took no notice of any one, but I saw the two little children shy away from the dead man." – Diary of a Company Officer.

"in their spiked helmets" silhouetted against the glare as they stormed out of the woods and massed behind the fold of the ground ready for the morning's attack. Two years later, our guns would have waited on their telephones till the enemy formation was completed and would then have removed those battalions from the face of the earth. But we had not those guns. During the night the Oxfordshire Light Infantry came up and occupied a farm between the Battalion and the Gordon Highlanders and strengthened the situation a little. Company Commanders had already been officially warned that the position was serious and that they must "hang on at all costs." Also that the Kaiser himself was in front of them.

On the 31st, after an attack by the French towards Hollebeke which did not develop, the full storm broke. The Battalion, backed by two R.F.A. guns, was shelled from seven in the morning till eleven o'clock at night in such trenches as it had been able to construct during the night; while machine-gun and infantry fire grew steadily through the hours. The Companies were disposed as follows: No. 4 Company immediately to the north of the main wood; then No. 3 with No. 1 in touch with the Oxfordshire Light Infantry at a farm-house, next to the Gordons; No. 2 was in reserve at a farm with Headquarters.

On the afternoon of the 31st October, Lord Ardee arrived from hospital, though he was in no state to be out of it, and was greeted by the information that the Gordons on the left, heavily shelled, had been driven out of their trenches. The Oxford L.I. and also No. 1 Company of the Battalion which was in touch with them had to conform to the movement. The section of R.F.A. had to retire also with the Gordons and, after apologies, duly delivered among bursting German shell, for "having to look after their guns," they "limbered up and went off as though it were the Military Tournament." There was a counter-attack, and eventually the enemy were driven back and the line was re-established before night, which passed, says the Diary, "fairly quietly." The moonlight made movement almost impossible; nor could the men get any hot tea, their great stand-by, but rations were distributed. The casualties among officers that day were Lieutenant L. S. Coke killed, and buried in the garden of the farm; Captain Lord Francis Scott, Lieutenant the Earl of Kingston and Lieutenant R. Ferguson wounded. There were many casualties in the front trenches, specially among No. 3 Company, men being blown to pieces and no trace left. The depressing thing, above all, was that we seemed to have no guns to reply with.

Bombardment was renewed on the 1st November. The front trenches were drenched by field-guns, at close range, with spurts of heavy stuff at intervals; the rear by heavy artillery, while machine-gun fire filled the intervals. One of the trenches of a platoon in No. 3 Company, under Lieutenant Maitland, was completely blown in, and only a few men escaped. The Lieutenant remained with the survivors while Sergeant C. Harradine, under heavy fire, took the news to the C.O. It was hopeless to send reinforcements; the machine-gun fire would have wiped them out moving and our artillery was not strong enough to silence any one sector of the enemy's fire.

In the afternoon the enemy attacked – with rifle-fire and a close-range small piece that broke up our two machine-guns – across some dead ground and occupied the wrecked trench, driving back the few remains of No. 3 Company. The Companies on the right and left, Nos. 4 and 1, after heavy fighting, fell back on No. 2 Company, which was occupying roughly prepared trenches in the rear. One platoon, however, of No. 1 Company, under Lieutenant N. Woodroffe (he had only left Eton a year), did not get the order to retire, and so held on in its trench till dark and "was certainly instrumental in checking the advance of the enemy." The line was near breaking-point by then but Company after Company delivered what blow it could, and fell back, shelled and machine-gunned at every step, to the fringe of Zillebeke Wood. Here the officers, every cook, orderly and man who could stand, took rifle and fought; for they were all that stood there between the enemy and the Channel Ports. (Years later, a man remembering that fight said: "Twas like a football scrum. Every one was somebody, ye'll understand. If he dropped there was no one to take his place. Great days! An' we not so frightened as when it came to the fightin' by machinery on the Somme afterwards.")[1] The C.O. sent the Adjutant to Brigade Headquarters to ask for help, but the whole Staff had gone over to the 2nd Brigade Headquarters, whose Brigadier had taken over command of the 4th Brigade as its own Brigadier had been wounded. About this time, too, the C.O. of the Battalion (Lord Ardee) was wounded. Eventually the 2nd Battalion Grenadiers was sent up with some Cavalry of the much-enduring 7th Brigade, and the line of support-trenches was held. The Battalion had had nothing to eat for thirty-six hours; so the Cavalry kept the line for a little till our men got food.

A French Regiment (Territorials) on the right also took over part of the trenches of our depleted line. Forty-four men were known to have been killed, 205 wounded and 88 – chiefly from the blown-up No. 3 Platoon – were missing. Of officers, Lieutenant K. R. Mathieson had been killed (he had been last seen shooting a Hun who was bayoneting our wounded); Captain Mulholland died of his wounds as soon as he arrived in hospital at Ypres; Lieut.-Colonel Lord Ardee, Captain Vesey, Lieutenant Gore-Langton and Lieutenant Alexander were wounded, and Lieutenant G. M. Maitland, who had stayed with his handful in No. 3 Company's trench, was missing. Yet the time was to come when three hundred and fifty casualties would be regarded as no extraordinary price to pay for ground won or held. One small draft of 40 men arrived from home that night.

On November 2 the Battalion was reduced to three Companies, since in No. 3 Company all officers were casualties and only 26 men of it answered their names at roll-call. They were heavily shelled all that day. They tried to put up a little wire

---

[1] Their Brigadier, Lord Cavan, wrote on the 20th November to Captain N. Orr-Ewing, commanding the Battalion: "I want you to convey to every man in your Battalion that I consider that the safety of the right flank of the British section depended entirely upon their staunchness after the disastrous day, Nov. 1. Those of them that were left made history, and I can never thank them enough for the way in which they recovered themselves and showed the enemy that the Irish Guards must be reckoned with, however hard hit"

on their front during the night; they collected what dead they could; they received several wounded men of the day's fight as they crawled into our lines; they heard one such man calling in the dark, and they heard the enemy turn a machine-gun on him and silence him. The regular work of sending forward and relieving the Companies in the front line went on, varied by an attack from the enemy, chiefly rifle-fire, on the night of the 3rd November. On that date they received "a new machine-gun," and another draft of 60 men (under Captain E. C. S. King-Harman) several of whom were killed or wounded that same afternoon. The night was filled with false alarms, as some of the new drafts began to imagine crowds of Germans advancing out of the dark. This was a popular obsession, but it led to waste of ammunition and waking up utterly tired men elsewhere in the line.

On the 4th November there was an outburst of machine-gunning from a farm-house, not 300 yards away. One field-gun was brought up to deal with them, and some of the 2nd Life Guards stood by to help in event of an attack, but the enemy contented themselves with mere punishing fire.

On the evening of November 5 they located our one field-gun which was still trying to cope with the enemy's machine-guns, shelled it for an hour vigorously, blew up the farm-house that sheltered it, but – clean missed the gun though it had been firing at least one round every ten minutes. One of our wounded of the 1st November managed to crawl into our lines. He had been three days without food or water – the Germans, who thought he would die, refusing him both. There was heavy shelling, and about thirty casualties in the line "as far as known."

On the 6th after an hour's preparation with heavy, light, and machine-gun fire, the enemy attacked the French troops on the Battalion's right, who fell back and left the flank of the Battalion (No. 2 Company) open. The Company "in good order and fighting" fell back by platoons to its support trenches, but this left No. 1 Company practically in the air, and at the end of the day the greater part of them were missing. As the Germans occupied the French trenches in succession, they opened an enfilade fire on the Irish which did sore execution. Once again the Adjutant went to the Brigadier to explain the situation. The Household Cavalry were sent up at the gallop to Zillebeke where they dismounted and advanced on foot. The 1st Life Guards on the left were detailed to retake the Irish Guards' trenches, while the 2nd Life Guards attacked the position whence the French had been ousted. A hundred Irish Guardsmen, collected on the spot, also took part in the attack, which in an hour recovered most of the lost positions. Here Lieutenant W. E. Hope was killed, and a little later, Lieutenant N. Woodroffe fell, shot dead in the advance of the Household Cavalry. Two Companies, had these been available, could have held the support trenches after the Household Cavalry had cleared the front, but there were no reinforcements and the unceasing pressure on the French drove the Battalion back on a fresh line a couple of hundred yards behind the support trenches which the Cavalry held till the remains of the Battalion had re-formed and got some hot tea from the ever-forward cookers. In addition to Lieutenants Hope and Woodroffe killed, Captain Lord John Hamilton and Captain E. C. S. King-Harman, who had come out with the draft on the 1st November, were missing that day.

On November 7 the Battalion relieved the Cavalry at one in the morning, and dug and deepened their trenches on the edge of the wood till word came to them to keep up a heavy fire on any enemy driven out of the wood, as the 22nd Brigade were attacking on their right. That "Brigade," now reduced to two composite battalions – the Royal Welsh Fusiliers with the 2nd Queen's and the Warwicks with South Staffords – both commanded by captains, did all that was humanly possible against the pressure, but in the end, as the Diary says, "having failed to get the line required, withdrew under heavy shell-fire." Their attack was no more than one of many desperate interludes in the desperate first Battle of Ypres – a winning fight against hopeless odds of men and material – but it diverted attention for the moment from the Battalion's particular section of the line and "the enemy did not shell our trenches much." Early in the day Major Stepney, commanding, went out from the support trenches and was not seen again alive. His body was found late in the evening between the lines. The command of the Battalion now fell to Captain N. Orr-Ewing.

Since October 31, 6 officers had been killed, 7 wounded, and 3 were missing. Of N.C.O.'s and men 64 were dead, 339 wounded, and 194 missing. The total casualties, all ranks, for one week, were 613.

The remnants were made into two shrunken Companies next day (the 8th) which was a quiet one with intermittent bursts of shelling from French 75's on the right, and German heavies; the enemy eighty yards distant. Captain A. Perceval, who had been blown up twice in the past week, and Lieutenant J. S. N. FitzGerald were sent to hospital.

On the night of the 9th November the Battalion of four platoons, three in the firing line and one in reserve, was relieved by the South Wales Borderers; drew supplies and men at Brigade Headquarters, moved back through Zillebeke and marched into bivouacs near a farm south of the Ypres – Zollebeke road, where they settled down with some Oxford L.I. in deep trenches and dug-outs which had been dug by the French.

They spent the 10th in luxury; their cookers were up and the men ate their first hot meal for many days. Blankets also were issued, and a draft of about two hundred men arrived under Lieutenant Hon. W. C. Hanbury-Tracy, which brought up the strength of the reorganized two-company Battalion to 360 men. Major Webber, "S.R." (this is the first time that the Diary makes mention of the Special Reserve), arrived the day before and as Senior Officer took over from Captain Orr-Ewing. The other officers who came with him were Captain Everard and Lieutenant L. R. Hargreaves, both Special Reserve, with Lieutenant St. J. R. Pigott, and, next day, 2nd Lieutenant Straker, Machine-gun Officer, with "two new guns." All these reinforcements allowed the Battalion to be organized as two companies instead of four platoons.

On the morning of the 11th November they were moved out by way of the Bellewaarde Lake and under cover of the woods there, in support of the Oxfordshire L.I. who cleared the wood north of Château Hooge and captured some thirty prisoners of the Prussian Guards. This was the first time, to their

. . . the tone and temper of the time that set the pace has gone over. But while it lasted, the men made their officers and the officers their men by methods as old as war itself; . . .
From left to right:
CAPT. E.B. GREER (later Acting Lieut-Colonel), awarded M.C. June 1915; killed in command
   of the Second Battalion, July 1917
CAPT J.S.N. FITZGERALD, awarded the M.C. (?1916)
CAPT HON H.R. ALEXANDER (later Field-Marshal Lord Alexander of Tunis), awarded
   D.S.O. January 1916, M.C. January 1916.

knowledge, that they had handled that Corps. Though heavily shelled the Battalion lost no men and spent the rest of the day behind the O.L.I. and the Grenadiers, waiting in the rain near the Headquarters of the First Brigade (Brigadier-General FitzClarence, V.C.) to which it was for the moment attached.

It was here that one of our officers found some enemy prisoners faithfully shepherded under the lee of a protecting haystack while their guard (Oxford L.I.) stood out in the open under casual shrapnel. A change was made at once.

At 9 p.m. the Battalion was told it might go back and get tea and supplies at some cross-roads or other in the darkness behind it. The cookers never came up and the supplies were not available till past midnight on the 12th. As their orders were to return to 1st Brigade Headquarters at 2 a.m. to take part in an attack on a German trench, the men had not much sleep. The trench had been captured by the enemy the day before, but they had abandoned it and dug another, commanding, in the rear, whence they could deal with any attempt at recapture on our part. The composite force of the 2nd Grenadiers, Munster Fusiliers, Irish Guards, and Oxfordshire L.I. discovered this much, wading through mud in the darkness before dawn, at a cost to the Battalion of Webber and Lieutenant Harding and some twelve men wounded. They were caught front and flank and scattered among the shell-holes. G FitzClarence was killed by enemy fire out of the dark, and eventually the troops returned to 1st Brigade Headquarters where a Company of the Grenadiers were told off to dig trenches in a gap which had been found in the line, while the remainder, the Irish Guards and the Munsters, were sent back to the woods near Château Hooge, which were full of fragments of broken battalions, from Scots Guards to Zouaves.

The Battalion reached its destination at 6 a.m. on the 12th. Three-quarters of an hour later it was ordered up to the woods on the Gheluvelt road. They occupied "dug-outs" – the first time the Diary mentions these as part of the scheme of things – on the north side of the road near the end of the wood west of Veldhoek; sent a platoon to reinforce the Scots Fusiliers who were hard-pressed, near by; and were heavily shelled at intervals all day, besides being sniped and machine-gunned by the enemy who commanded the main road towards Hooge. None the less, they were fed that night without accident. Captains Everard and Hanbury-Tracy and 2nd Lieutenant Pigott were sent to hospital; 2nd Lieutenant Antrobus rejoined from hospital. This left to the Battalion – Captain Orr-Ewing, Captain the Hon. J. Trefusis, Adjutant R. M. C. Sandhurst, who had joined a day or so before, Lieutenant L. R. Hargreaves, and 2nd Lieutenant Antrobus, who was next day wounded in the arm by a shell. Lieutenant Walker, Acting Quartermaster, was sick, and Captain Gough was acting as Brigade Transport Officer. At that moment the strength of the Battalion is reported at "about" 160 officers and men. A draft of 50 N.C.O.'s and men arrived on the 13th November.

On November 14 they were ordered to return to 4th Brigade Headquarters and take over trenches near Klein Zillebeke from the South Wales Borderers who had relieved them there on the 9th. "The day passed much as usual," it was observed, but "the shelling was fairly heavy and the enemy gained some ground." Lieutenant and Quartermaster Hickie returned from a sick leave of two months. The Sussex Battalion relieved the Battalion in their dug-outs on the edge of the Veldhoek woods at 11 p.m.; the Battalion then moved off and by half-past three on the morning of the 15th had relieved the South Wales Borderers in their old trenches. Here they received word of the death of their Colonel, Field-Marshal Lord Roberts, from pneumonia while on a visit to the Indian troops at the front. C.S.M. Rogers and Private Murphy were selected as representatives of the Battalion to attend the funeral service at St. Omer. The Battalion spent the day, under constant shell-fire, in improving trenches, "but there was some difficulty as snipers were busy, as they had been all day." One officer wrote: "Our men are very tired and the rifles are in an awful state. It rains continuously, and it is very hard to get any sort of rifle-oil."

The 16th November, a day of snow and heavy firing, ending in an attack which was suppressed by rapid fire, was grimly enlivened by the appearance of one German deserter with two fingers shot off who announced that he "had had enough of fighting."

On the 17th November Brigade Headquarters were blown in by shell-fire, both of the Irish Guards orderlies on duty were injured, and both of the Battalion's "two new machine-guns" were knocked to pieces. There was five hours' heavy shelling from 7 a.m. till noon when the enemy came out of their trenches to attack in force, and were dealt with for an hour by the Battalion, the Grenadiers on its left and the Cavalry on its right. It was estimated that – thanks to efficient fire-control and good discipline – twelve hundred killed and wounded were accounted for in front of our trenches. Our only man killed in this attack was C.S.M. Munns who had been just recommended for his commission. He was a born leader of men, always cheerful, and with what seemed like a genuine love for fighting. A second attack, not pressed home, followed at three o'clock; another out-break of small-arm fire at half-past nine and yet another towards midnight, and a heavy shelling of the French on our right. "Then all was quiet," says the easily-satisfied record.

They endured one day longer, with nothing worse than a "certain amount of heavy shelling but not so much as usual," and on the 18th their battered remnants came out. They were relieved by a Company of the 3rd Coldstream (Captain H. Dawson) and marched off to billets at Potijze on the Ypres – Zonnebeke Road, where the men got plenty of food. Hard frost had followed the soaking wet and downpour of the previous days; snow succeeded, but there were hot meals and the hope of rest and refit at Meteren behind Bailleul, fifteen miles from Potijze.

They reached that haven on the 21st November – eight officers and 390 men in all – "desperately tired" in a cold that froze the water in the men's bottles. Not a man fell out. Captain Lord Desmond FitzGerald, recovered from his wound, arrived on the same day and took over the Adjutancy.

The Battalion had been practically wiped out and reconstructed in a month. They had been cramped in wet mud till they had almost forgotten the use of their legs: their rifles, clothing, equipment, everything except their morale and the undefeated humour with which they had borne their burden, needed renewal or repair. They rested and began to clean themselves of their dirt and vermin while the C.O. and Company Officers went round billets and companies – to see that the men had all they needed – as is the custom of our Army. It was a comprehensive refit, including everything from trousers to ground-sheets, as well as mufflers and mittens sent by H.I.H. the Grand Duke Michael of Russia. Steady platoon and company drill, which is restorative to men after long standing in dirt, or fighting in the dark, marked the unbelievably still days.

On the 23rd November the Reverend Father Gwynne, the beloved R.C. Chaplain, arrived to take up his duties; and on the 24th they were inspected by the Commander-in-Chief, Sir John French.

On the 28th a draft of 288 N.C.O.'s and men reached them, under command of Captain P. L. Reid with the following officers: Lieutenant G. Gough; 2nd Lieutenants H. S. Keating, H. Marion-Crawford, Hon. H. A. V. Harmsworth, A. C. Innes, and L. C. Lee. With this draft the strength of the Battalion stood at 700 men and 15 officers. Of the latter the Diary notes that nine are in the Special Reserve, "seven of them having done no sort of soldiering before the War." Mercifully, men lived but one day at a time, or the Diarist might have drawn conclusions which would have fallen far short of what the future was to bring, from the fact that as many as twelve machine-gunners were kept at the base by the order of the authorities. There was need to train machine-gunners, and an even greater need for the guns themselves. But the Battalion was not occupied with the larger questions of the War. They had borne their part against all odds of numbers and equipment in barring the German road to the sea in the first month-long Battle of Ypres. They knew very little of what they had done. Not one of their number could have given any consecutive account of what had happened, nor, in that general-post of daily and nightly confusion, whither they had gone. All they were sure of was that such as lived were not dead ("The Lord only knows why") and that the enemy had not broken through. They had no knowledge what labours still lay before them.

On the 3rd December, after an issue of new equipment and a visit from Sir Douglas Haig, commanding the First Army Corps, they lined the road from Meteren towards Bailleul for the visit of the King who walked down the lines of the 4th (Guards) Brigade and, after shaking hands with the four Commanding Officers of the Brigade, said: "I am very proud of my Guards and am full of admiration for their bravery, endurance, and fine spirit. I wish I could have addressed them all, but that is impossible, so you must tell them what I say to you. You are fighting a brave and determined enemy, but if you go on as you have been doing and show the same fine spirit, there can be only one end, please God, and that is victory. I wish you all good luck."

D.S.O.'s had been awarded to Captain Orr-Ewing and Captain Lord Francis Scott; and the Distinguished Conduct Medal to Company Sergeant-Major Munns, who, it will be remembered, was killed in action just after he was recommended for a commission; to Sergeant M'Goldrick, Brigade Orderly, who was one of the orderlies injured when the Brigade Headquarters were blown up on the 17th November; Corporal Riordan (wounded), Private Russell (Brigade Orderly), and Private Glynn (since wounded and missing). The King decorated

Sergeant M'Goldrick with the D.C.M. that afternoon. The others named were, from various causes, absent. It was the first of many such occasions where those honoured could not be present to receive their valour's reward.

The Diary notes the issue of cardigan waistcoats and goat-skin coats for each man, as well as of a new American pattern boot, with a hard toe which, it conservatively fears, "may not stand the wear of the old ammunition-boot." Route-marches increased in length, and the men marched as well as they ate. Indeed, they volunteered to the Brigadier, who came round once to see the dinners, that they had never been so well fed. It kept them healthy, though there were the usual criticisms from officers, N.C.O.'s, and surviving veterans of the Regular Army, on the quality of the new drafts, some of whom, it seems, suffered from bad teeth and had to be sent away for renewals and refits. As a much-tried sergeant remarked: "A man with a sore tooth is a nuisance an' a danger to the whole British Army."

On the 9th December Sir Douglas Haig came over to present the Médaille Militaire, on behalf of the French Government, to certain officers, N.C.O.'s, and men of the Guards Brigade. Drill-Sergeant Rodgers of the Battalion was among the recipients. Captain Orr-Ewing was ordered to rejoin the 1st Battalion of the Scots Guards (his own battalion), to the regret of the Battalion whose lot he had shared since September – the most capable of officers as the most popular of comrades.

A party from the Brigade was sent to Headquarters of the 11th Engineering Company "to be taught how to throw bombs made out of jam pots, which apparently are used against the enemy at close quarters in the present trench-warfare." There were at least half-a-dozen more or less dangerous varieties of these hand-made bombs in use, before standard patterns were evolved and bombing took its place as a regular aid to warfare. The "jam-pot" bomb died early but not before it had caused a sufficiency of trouble to its users. The others will be mentioned in due course.

"Aeroplane duty" was another invention of those early days. A Company was told off daily to look out for aeroplanes and, if possible, to bring them down – presumably by rifle-fire. The War was still very young.

F.-M. Earl Kitchener's appointment to Colonel of the Battalion in succession to F.-M. Earl Roberts was marked on the 12th in the following telegram from Earl Kitchener:

> His Majesty the King having been graciously pleased to appoint me to be Colonel of the Irish Guards, I desire to take the first opportunity of expressing to you and through you to all ranks how proud I am to be associated with so gallant a regiment. My warmest greetings and best wishes to you all!

The C.O. replied:

> All ranks, 1st Battalion Irish Guards, greatly appreciate the honour conferred on them by His Majesty the King, and are proud to have such a distinguished soldier as Colonel of the Regiment.

On the 13th December a further draft of 100 men and three officers arrived under Captain Mylne; the other officers being Lieutenant Antrobus who was wounded exactly a month before, and Lieutenant Hubbard. This brought the Battalion's strength to 800 with the following officers: Major the Hon. J. Trefusis, C.O.; Captain Lord Desmond FitzGerald, Adjutant; Lieutenant C. A. S. Walker, Transport Officer; 2nd Lieutenant L. Straker, Machine-gun Officer; Captain A. H. L. McCarthy, Medical Officer; Captain Rev. Father Gwynne, Chaplain; Lieutenant H. Hickie, Quartermaster. No. 1 Company, Captain E. J. Gough, Lieutenant L. Hargreaves, 2nd Lieutenant A. C. Times. No. 2 Company, Captain E. Mylne, 2nd Lieutenant H. S. Keating, 2nd Lieutenant F. H. Witts. No. 3 Company, Captain P. L. Reid, 2nd Lieutenant P. H. Antrobus, 2nd Lieutenant Hon. H. V. Harmsworth, 2nd Lieutenant H. Marion-Crawford. No. 4 Company, Lieutenant G. Gough, Lieutenant G. Hubbard, 2nd Lieutenant Lee.

Lieutenant C. A. Walker had to go to hospital with bronchitis and Lieutenant Antrobus took over from him.

Major Arbuthnot (Scots Guards) arrived on the 14th December with Queen Alexandra's presents to the Battalion which were duly issued to selected officers, N.C.O.'s, and men, but at the time, the Battalion was under two hours' notice to move either to support an attack then being delivered by the Third Division upon the wood at Wytschaete, or "for any other purpose." The attack was not a success except in so far as it pinned the enemy forces to one place, but the Battalion was not called upon to help. It lived under "short notice" for a week which naturally interfered with extended route-marches or training. Companies were sent out one by one to dig in the water-logged soil and to extemporize means of keeping their feet out of the water by "blocks of wood made in the form of a platform at the bottom of the trenches." Thus laboriously is described the genesis of what was later to grow into thousands of miles of duckboard, plain or wired.

Meantime, between the 20th and 22nd of December the fierce and unsatisfactory battle of Cuinchy, the burden of which fell heavily on our devoted Indian troops, had been fought out on a front of half a dozen miles from south of the Béthune Canal to Festubert. Nothing had been gained except the all-important issue – that the enemy did not break through. There was a long casualty-list as casualties were then counted, and the Indian Brigades were withdrawn from their wrecked and sodden trenches for a little rest. The Guards Brigade was ordered to relieve them, and on the 22nd marched out from Meteren. The Herts Territorial Battalion (to be honourably and affectionately known later as "The Herts Guards") led that first march, followed by the 2nd Coldstream, 1st Battalion Irish Guards, the 3rd Coldstream, and the 2nd Grenadiers. They billeted at Béthune where, on the 23rd December, the 2nd Coldstream in support, they took over their share of the Indian trenches near Le Touret between Essars and Richebourg l'Avoué, and on Christmas Eve after tea and the distribution of the Christmas puddings from England, the Battalion, with the Hertfordshires, relieved the 4th Dogras, 6th Jats and 9th Gurkhas. It is recorded that, the Gurkha being a somewhat shorter man than the average

Guardsman, the long Irish had to dig their trenches about two feet deeper, and they wondered loudly what sort of persons these "little dark fellas" could be.

The Christmas truce of 1914 reached the Battalion in severely modified form. They lay among a network of trenches, already many times fought over, with communications that led directly into the enemy's lines a couple of hundred yards away. So they spent Christmas Day, under occasional bombardment of heavy artillery, in exploring and establishing themselves as well as they might among these wet and dreary works. In this duty Lieutenant G. P. Gough and Lieutenant F. H. Witts and six men were wounded.

Earl Kitchener, their Colonel, sent them Christmas wishes and the King's and Queen's Christmas cards were distributed. Their comfort was that Christmas night was frosty so that the men kept dry at least.

Boxing Day was quiet, too, and only four men were wounded as they dug in the hard ground to improve their communications with the 2nd Coldstream on their left. Then the frost broke in rain, the clay stuck to the spade, the trenches began to fill, and a deserter brought news of an impending attack which turned out to be nothing more serious than a bombing affair which was duly "attended to." Some of our own shells bursting short killed one man and wounded six. Princess Mary's gifts of pipes, tobacco and Christmas cards were distributed to the men and duly appreciated.

The impossibility of keeping anything free from mud forced them to reduce their firing-line to the least possible numbers, while those in support, or billets, made shift to clean rifles and accoutrements. The days went forward in rain and wet, with digging where water allowed, and a regular daily toll of a few men killed and wounded.

On the 30th December Captain Eric Gough was killed by a stray bullet while commanding his Company (No.1) and was buried next day in a cemetery a few miles along the Béthune – Richebourg road. He had been Transport Officer since the Battalion left London in August, but had commanded a Company since the 21st November, and was an immense loss to the Battalion to which he was devoted. Lieutenant Sir G. Burke and 2nd Lieutenant J. M. Stewart came from England on the same day and were posted to No. 1 Company, now commanded by Lieutenant: Hargreaves.

The Diary ends the year with a recapitulation more impressive in its restraint than any multitude of words:

> The country round this part is very low-lying, intersected with ditches with pollarded willows growing on their banks. No sooner is a trench dug than it fills with water. . . . The soil is clay, and so keeps the water from draining away even if that were possible. In order to keep the men at all dry, they have to stand on planks rested on logs in the trenches, and in the less wet places bundles of straw and short fascines are put down. Pumping has been tried, but not with much success. The weather continues wet, and there does not seem to be any likelihood of a change. Consequently, we may expect some fresh discomforts daily.

1915
LA BASSÉE TO LAVENTIE

THEY WERE NOT DISAPPOINTED. New Year's Day was marked by the flooding out of a section of forward trenches, and by experiments with a trench-mortar, from which 2nd Lieutenant Keating and some Garrison gunners threw three bombs at an enemy digging-party a couple of hundred yards away. This is the first reference to our use of trench-mortars in the young campaign. The enemy retaliated next day by bombing, from their real trench-mortars, at a distance of seven hundred yards, the small farm-house where Battalion Headquarters lay. The bombs could be seen "coming at a very steep angle, but the house was only once hit." Daylight showed the work of the Irish trench-mortar to have been so good – it had blown a gap in the German trench – that they continued it and inflicted and observed much damage.

They were relieved on the 3rd January by the King's Royal Rifles and got to billets near Vieille Chapelle late that night. A London Gazette announced that the Distinguished Conduct Medal had been awarded No. 2535 Sergeant C. Harradine; No. 1664 Corporal C. Moran; No. 4015 Private W. Moore (since killed in action); No. 2853 Lance-Corporal W. Delaney. Also "the new decoration called the Military Cross" had been awarded to Lieutenant the Hon. H. W. Gough.

The Battalion, as a whole, had its reward for the past ten days when the Brigadier expressed his approval of the work of the Guards Brigade "and especially that of the Irish Guards."

Cleaning and refit, classes in bomb-throwing (both by hand and from rifles) under the Engineers and an elementary machine-gun class under 2nd Lieutenant Straker, filled in the week; but the most appreciated boon at Vieille Chapelle was some huge tubs in which the men could be boiled clean. Father Gwynne held service in the roofless shell-wrecked church, long since wiped out.

They took over trenches from the Worcesters on the 8th with a cold knowledge of what awaited them; for the Diary notes, the day before: "Another wet day, which will probably completely fill trenches on the left of the new line with water." But it did not fill them more than two feet deep, though the whole line was afloat, and in the communication-trenches seven men got stuck in the mud; one of them was not extricated for six hours. The relief took six and a half hours in pouring rain, with one man killed and two wounded. The front line of the Guards Brigade was held by the 3rd Coldstream on the right, the 2nd Coldstream in support; one Company of the 2nd Grenadiers in the centre, and the rest of the Battalion in support; the Irish Guards on the left, the Herts Territorials in support. The Grenadiers relieved their front Company every twenty-four hours, the others every forty-eight. This meant that Battalion C.O.'s had to spend most of their time in the front line studying what was, in effect, the navigation of canals.

On the 9th January, for example, the water averaged three feet in the trenches and, as that average rose, it was decided to leave a few strong posts in comparatively dry positions and withdraw the others along the Rue du Bois into the destroyed village of Richebourg l'Avoué. Luckily, the enemy, not two hundred yards away, had his own troubles to attend to and, despite his lavish flares and musketry-fire, our men were extricated, bodily in some instances, with but 3 killed and 2 wounded.

On the 10th January the Herts Regiment relieved them, and the whole Battalion billeted at Richebourg St. Vaast. Casualties from small-arm fire had been increasing owing to the sodden state of the parapets; but the Battalion retaliated a little from one "telescopic-sighted rifle" sent up by Lieutenant the Earl of Kingston, with which Drill-Sergeant Bracken "certainly" accounted for 3 killed and 4 wounded of the enemy. The Diary, mercifully blind to the dreadful years to come, thinks, "There should be many of these rifles used as long as the army is sitting in trenches." Many of them were so used: this, the father of them all, now hangs in the Regimental Mess.

Then trench-feet and rheumatism developed, and in forty-eight hours fifty men had to be sent to hospital for one form or other of these complaints.

A draft of a hundred fresh men arrived between the 11th and 12th of January with six officers: Captain P. S. Long-Innes, 2nd Lieutenants F. F. Graham, J. R. Ralli, R. B. H. Kemp, D. W. Gunston (Derek) and J. T. Robyns. Economy in officers and men was not yet possible; for when an officer was not in the front line he had more than all he could do to look after what comforts were obtainable for the men. Yet concessions were made to human weakness; for when the Battalion returned to its trenches on the 12th an order was received and, to some extent, obeyed that "men were not to stand in the water for *more than twelve hours at a time*." This called for continuous reliefs of the platoons, as it took a man most of his rest in billets to scrape himself moderately clean. To save the labour of portage through the mud, each man was given two days' supplies when he went into the trenches, plus some dry tea and a couple of tins of Maconochie to heat up over the braziers. The idea worked satisfactorily; for the days of the merciless air-patrols had yet to come; and the braziers flared naked to heaven while the Irish "drummed up," which is to say, stewed their tea or rations on them.

The hopeless work of improving positions in soil no stiffer than porridge was resumed, and the "telescopic-sighted rifle," in the hands of Sergeant-Major Kirk and Drill-Sergeant Bracken, who were later congratulated by the G.O.C. Second Division, continued its discreet and guarded labours among the enemy. Only 1 man was killed and 1 wounded on the 13th January, and the night of that easy day passed off quietly, "the enemy occupying himself chiefly with singing songs or playing on mouth-organs." Here and elsewhere he was given to spasms of music for no ascertainable reason, which the Irish, who do not naturally burst into song, rather resented. Between morceaux he sent up many coloured flares, while our working-parties silently completed and christened by the name of "Gibraltar" a post to command a flooded gap in the oozy line.

They were relieved on the 15th January by the Highland Light Infantry of the 3rd Brigade (Lahore Division) which was taking over the line held by the 4th (Guards) Brigade. The Battalion went back to Brigade Reserve billets at Locon.[1]

Their last week in the trenches had cost them 82 casualties including sick, but it is worth noting that, at this time, Captain McCarthy, the Medical Officer, by issuing mustard mixed with lard for the men to rub on their feet, had in three days got the better of the epidemic of "trench" or, as they were then called, "swollen" feet.

It was while in Reserve that 2nd Lieut. Keating, Bombing Instructor and in charge of the trench-mortars, lost his life and 13 men were wounded owing to the premature explosion of an old-type fused bomb with which he was instructing a class. Second Lieutenant Keating was buried next day in the cemetery near Le Touret, where many Guardsmen were already laid, and his epitaph may worthily stand as it was written – "A very capable officer, always ready to undertake any task however difficult or dangerous."

After a few days the Battalion went into Corps Reserve and spent a week in being "smartened up" behind the line with steady drill, rifle exercises, route-marching and kit inspection, on rainy days, lest life in the caked filth of the trenches should lead any one to forget the standard of the Brigade of Guards which under no circumstance allows any excuse.

Their work was interrupted by another "Kaiser-battle," obediently planned to celebrate the All Highest's birthday. It began on the 25th January with a demonstration along the whole flat front from Festubert to Vermelles. Béthune was also shelled from an armoured train run out of La Bassée, and a heavy attack was launched by Prussian Infantry on a salient of our line, held by the 1st Infantry Brigade, where it joined the French line among the tangle of railway tracks and brick-fields near Cuinchy. Owing to the mud, the salient was lightly manned by half a Battalion of the Scots Guards and half a Battalion of the Coldstream. Their trenches were wiped out by the artillery attack and their line fell back, perhaps half a mile, to a partially prepared position among the brick-fields and railway lines between the Aire – La Bassée Canal and the La Bassée – Béthune road. Here fighting continued with reinforcements and counter-attacks knee-deep in mud till the enemy were checked and a none too stable defence made good between a mess of German communication trenches

---

[1] Brigade Reserve means in readiness to move at short notice in any direction to support; all wagons standing packed day and night, except that the blankets may be used by the men. Corps Reserve takes a battalion definitely out of the line for the time being and out of reach of all except air-bombing.

and a keep or redoubt held by the British among the huge brick-stacks by the railway. So far as the Battalion was concerned, this phase of the affair seems to have led to no more than two or three days' standing-to in readiness to support with the rest of the Brigade, and taking what odd shells fell to their share.

No institutions are more self-centred than a Battalion in the face of war. "Steady drill," and Company kit inspections were carried on in the lulls of the waiting, and their main preoccupation was how much water might be expected in the new trenches when their turn came to occupy them. The Germans were devoting some of their heavy artillery to shelling the lock of the Aire – La Bassée Canal at Pont Fixe, between Givenchy and Cuinchy, in the hope of bursting it and flooding the country. They spent more than a hundred eight-inch howitzer shells on that endeavour in one day, and later – long after the lock had been thoroughly protected with sand-bags – used to give it stated doses of shell at regular intervals. Similarly, they would bombard one special spot on the line near Béthune because in '14, an armoured train of ours had fired thence at them

The Battalion had just been reinforced by a draft of 107 men and 4 officers – Captain Eric Greer, Lieutenant Blacker-Douglass, 2nd Lieutenant R. G. C. Yerburgh and 2nd Lieutenant S. G. Tallents. They were under orders to move up towards the fighting among the brick-fields which had opened on the 25th, and had not ceased since. Unofficial reports described the trenches they were to take over as "not very wet but otherwise damnable," and on the 30th January the Battalion definitely moved from Locon, with the 2nd Coldstream, via Béthune to Cuinchy. Here the Coldstream took over from the 2nd Brigade the whole line of a thousand yards of trench occupied by them; the Irish furnishing supports. The rest of the Brigade, that is to say, the Herts Territorials, the Grenadiers, and the 3rd Coldstream, were at Annequin, Beuvry and Béthune.

The Companies were disposed between the La Bassée – Béthune road and the railway, beside the Aire – La Bassée Canal. The centre of their line consisted of a collection of huge dull plum-coloured brick-stacks, mottled with black, which might have been originally thirty feet high. Five of these were held by our people and the others by the enemy – the whole connected and interlocked by saps and communication-trenches new and old, without key or finality. Neither side could live in comfort at such close quarters until they had strengthened their lines either by local attacks, bombing raids or systematised artillery work. "The whole position," an officer remarks professionally, "is most interesting and requires careful handling and a considerable amount of ingenuity."

Except for railway embankments and culverts, the country about was so flat that a bullet once started had no reason to stop. The men were billeted in solid-built Flemish houses with bullet-proof partitions, and therefore, unless noticeably shelled, were inclined to walk about in front of the houses in the daylight, till they were sternly set to work to clean their billets of months of accumulations of refuse and to bury neglected carcasses. War and all connected with it was infinitely stale already, but houses and the ruins of them had not yet been wholly wiped out in that sector.

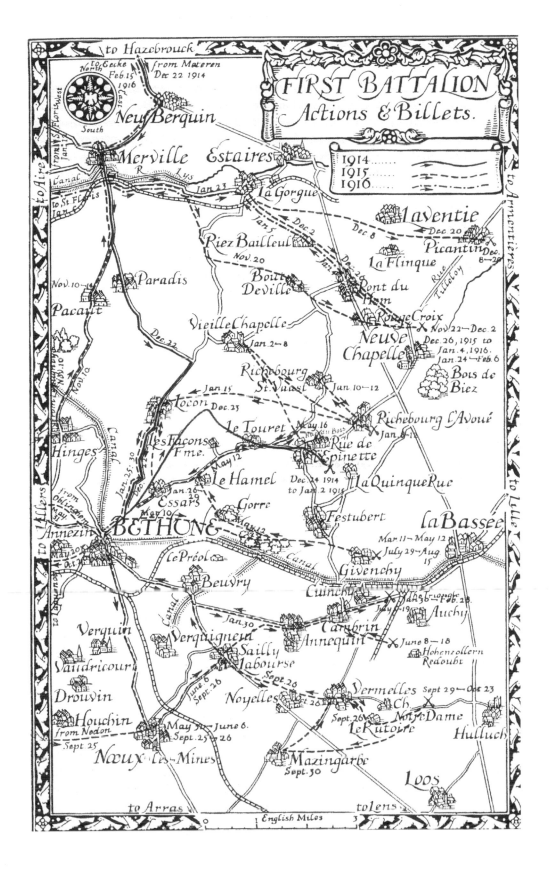

They were installed by the last day of the month with no greater inconvenience than drifts of stray bullets over the support trenches, an unsystematic shelling of Battalion Headquarters two or three hundred yards in the rear, and some desultory bombing in the complicated front line.

Early in the morning of the 1st February a post held by the Coldstream in a hollow near the Embankment, just west of the Railway Triangle – a spot unholy beyond most, even in this sector – was bombed and rushed by the enemy through an old communication-trench. No. 4 Company Irish Guards was ordered to help the Coldstream's attack. The men were led by Lieutenant Blacker-Douglass who had but rejoined on the 25th January. He was knocked over by a bomb within a few yards of the German barricade to the trench, picked himself up and went on, only to be shot through the head a moment later. Lieutenant Lee of the same Company was shot through the heart; the Company Commander, Captain Long-Innes, and 2nd Lieutenant Blom were wounded, and the command devolved on C.Q.M.S. Carton, who, in spite of a verbal order to retire "which he did not believe," held on till the morning in the trench under such cover of shell-holes and hasty barricades as could be found or put up. The Germans were too well posted to be moved by bomb or rifle, so, when daylight showed the situation, our big guns were called upon to shell for ten minutes, with shrapnel, the hollow where they lay. The spectacle was sickening, but the results were satisfactory. Then a second attack of some fifty Coldstream and thirty Irish Guards of No. 1 Company under Lieutenants Graham and Innes went forward, hung for a moment on the fringe of their own shrapnel – for barrages were new things – and swept up the trench. It was here that Lance-Corporal O'Leary, Lieutenant Innes' orderly, won his V.C. He rushed up along the railway embankment above the trenches, shot down 5 Germans behind their first barricade in the trench, then 3 more trying to work a machine-gun at the next barricade fifty yards farther along the trench, and took a couple of prisoners. Eye-witnesses report that he did his work quite leisurely and wandered out into the open, visible for any distance around, intent upon killing another German to whom he had taken a dislike. Meantime, Graham, badly wounded in the head, and Innes, together with some Coldstream, had worked their way into the post and found it deserted. Our guns and our attack had accounted for about 30 dead, but had left 32 wounded and unwounded prisoners, all of whom, with one exception, wept aloud. The hollow was full of mixed dead – Coldstream, Irish and German.

The men who remained of No. 4 Company did not settle down to the work of consolidating their position till they had found Blacker-Douglass's body. At least a couple of his company had been wounded in the first attack while trying to bring it away. Lee's body was recovered not far off.

A quarter of an hour after the post had fallen, the Engineers were up with unlimited sand-bags and helped the men who worked as they ate among the piled horrors around them, while everything was made ready for the expected German counter-attack. It did not come. Not only had the post been abandoned, but also a couple of trenches running out of it to the southward. These were duly barricaded in case the enemy were minded to work back along them at dusk. But for the rest of the day they preferred to shell; killing 2 and wounding 5 men of the two companies which were relieved by a Company of the 3rd Coldstream and one of the 3rd Grenadiers. Our men returned to billets "very tired and hungry, but very pleased with themselves." That day's work had cost us 2 officers and 8 men killed; 3 officers and 24 men wounded and 2 men missing. In return, two machine-guns, 8 whole and 24 wounded prisoners had been taken, the post recovered and, perhaps, sixty yards of additional trench with it. Such was the price paid in those years for maintaining even a foothold against the massed pressure of the enemy. It is distinctly noted in the Diary that two complete machine-guns were added to the defence of the post after it had been recaptured. Machine-guns were then valuable articles of barter, for when the French who were their neighbors wished to borrow one such article "for moral and material support," a Brigadier-General's permission had to be obtained.

This experience had shown it was better for each battalion in the line to provide its own supports, and they reorganized on the 2nd February on this basis; the 2nd and 3rd Coldstream Guards taking over the left half of the line up to within fifty yards of the Keep, while for their right, to the main La Bassée road, the 2nd Grenadiers and the Irish Guards were responsible – each with two companies in the fire trench and two in support, and all on forty-eight hours' relief.

The enemy continued to shell the captured position, killing 2 and wounding 9 men that day, but no counter-attack developed and a few days later it was decided to straighten out the front then held by the 4th (Guards) Brigade. The fighting on the 25th had left it running irregularly through the big brick-yard, before mentioned. Of the dozen or more solid stacks of brick, four or five connected by a parapet of loose bricks and known as the Keep, were in our hands. The other eight, irregularly spaced, made a most awkward wedge into our line. They were backed by a labyrinth of German trench-work, and, being shell-proof, supports could be massed behind them in perfect safety. The nearest were within bombing distance of the Keep, and, in those days, the Germans had more and better bombs than we. On every account, then, the wedge had to be cleared, the stacks and their connecting trenches overrun and the line advanced a hundred and fifty yards or so to get a better field of fire. As a preliminary, a small but necessary piece of German trench on the flanks of the Keep was captured by the Irish on the 5th February with a loss of but 2 killed and none wounded.

At 2 p.m. on the 6th of February the stacks were heavily bombarded for a quarter of an hour – a large allowance. Even "Mother," a neighboring 9·2, probably of naval extraction, took part in it, and some French artillery ringed the approaches on the German side with screens of black melenite fumes, while No. 2 Company from the front trenches swept the German parapet facing them with five minutes of that old "rapid fire" which the Germans in the salient and elsewhere had so often mistaken fort machine-gun work. Then two assaulting parties of thirty men each from Nos. 3 and 1 Companies, under Lieutenants T. Musgrave and J. Ralli, opened the attack on five of the eight stacks. The other three were fairly dealt with on the same lines

. . . the combined attack swept on through the brick-stacks . . . till – fighting, digging, cursing and sand-bagging – our men had hacked their way some seventy yards beyond their objective and dug in under a shelf of raw ground about three feet high, probably the lip of an old clay-pit.

The brickstacks at Cuinchy, February 1915.

by the 3rd Coldstream. As there was no wire left on the trench before our stacks, our party got there almost at once; but Musgrave, ahead of his men, was shot by a group of five Germans who showed fight behind a few fatal unbroken strands in the rear. They were all killed a moment later when the men came up. Then the supporting parties under Lieutenant Innes were slipped, together with the Engineers under Major Fowkes, R.E., and the combined attack swept on through the brick-stacks, in and out of the trenches and around and behind them, where the Germans were shot and bayoneted as found, till – fighting, digging, cursing and sand-bagging – our men had hacked their way some seventy yards beyond their objective and dug in under a shelf of raw ground about three feet high, probably the lip of an old clay-pit. Our guns had lifted and were choking off all attempts at possible counter-attacks, but the German supports seemed to have evaporated in the direction of La Bassée. There was a ridge in front of the captured position whence a few bullets were still dropping, but the back of the defence had been broken and, as firing diminished, first one and then two out of every three men were set digging in and filling sand-bags. The fortunes of the little campaign had gone smoothly, and when it was necessary, in the rough and tumble of the trench-work, to bring up reinforcements or more shovels and ammunition for the digging-parties, the indefatigable and brotherly Herts Territorials were drawn upon. The Coldstream had carried their share of the front and lay in line on our left, and at dusk, while the Engineers were putting up more wire, under rifle-fire at 150 yards range, the position was secure.

Our casualties, thanks to the bombardment and the swiftness of the attack, were only 1 officer and 6 men killed and 25 wounded. Father Gwynne, the Chaplain, was severely wounded by a piece of shrapnel while watching the attack "from an observation-post," which, as the Father understood it, meant as far forward as possible, in order that he might be ready to give comfort to the dying. The Coldstream gathered in twenty-eight prisoners, the Irish none, but among their spoils is entered "one Iron Cross" won rather picturesquely. At the opening of the rush the Germans made a close-range bombing-raid on one of the corners of the Keep and at last pitched a bomb on to the top of a sand-bag redoubt. This so annoyed one of our bomb-throwers, a giant of the name of Hennigan, of No. 1 Company, that he picked up a trench-mortar bomb (no trinket) which lay convenient, cut down the fuse for short range and threw it at a spot where he had caught a glimpse of a German officer. The bomb burst almost before it reached the ground, and must have made a direct hit; for nothing upon the officer was recognisable later save the Iron Cross, which in due time went to the Regimental Orderly Room. Hennigan was awarded the D.C.M.; for his bomb also blew in and blocked up the communication-trench through which the bombers came – a matter which he regarded as a side-issue compared to his "splendid bowlin'."

The Companies were relieved in the evening by a company of Grenadiers, and as they wandered back through the new-taken trenches in the winter dusk, lost their way among all manner of horrors. One officer wrote: "I fell over and became involved in a kind of wrestling-match with a shapeless Thing that turned out to be a dead man without a head . . . and so back to Beuvry, very tired and sad for the death of Tommy" (Musgrave).

There were other casualties that moved laughter under the ribs of death. A man reported after the action that his teeth were "all broke on him." His Company Officer naturally expressed sympathy but some surprise at not seeing a bullet-hole through both cheeks. "I took them out and put them in my pocket for the charge, Sorr, and they all broke on me," was the reply. "Well, go to the doctor and see if he can get you a new set." "I've been to him, Sorr, and it's little sympathy I got. He just gave me a pill and chased me away, Sorr."

A weird attempt was made at daybreak on the 7th February by a forlorn hope of some fifty Germans to charge the newly installed line at a point where the Coldstream and 2nd Grenadiers joined. They dashed out across the ground from behind a stack, the officer waving his sword, and were all killed or wounded on or close up to our wire. Men said there seemed no meaning or reason in the affair, unless it was a suicide-party of Germans who had run from the attack of the day before and had been ordered thus to die. One of their wounded lay out all day, and when the Irish were taking over the relief on the 8th some Germans shouted loudly from their trenches and one stood up and pointed to the wounded man. Said the Grenadiers who were being relieved: "Come and get him!" A couple of German stretcher-bearers came out and bore their comrade away, not thirty yards from our trench, while our men held their fire.

In the same relief it fell to the Irish to examine the body of a single German who had crept up and of a sudden peered into our front-line trench, where a Grenadier promptly shot him. He dropped on the edge of the parapet and lay "like a man praying." Since he had no rifle, it was assumed he was a bomber; but after dark they found he was wholly unarmed. At almost the same hour of the previous night another German came to precisely the same end in the same posture on the right flank of the line. Whether these two were deserters or scouts who would pretend to be deserters if captured, was never settled. The trenches were full of such mysteries. Strange trades, too, were driven there. A man, now gone to Valhalla, for he was utterly brave, did not approve of letting dead Germans lie unvisited before the lines. He would mark the body down in the course of his day's work, thrust a stick in the parados to give him his direction, and at night, or preferably when the morning fog lay heavy on the landscape, would slip across to his quarry and return with his pockets filled with loot. Many officers had seen C – 's stick at the back of the trench. Some living may like to learn now why it was there.[1]

---

[1] "I saw him slip back over the parapet in the mornin' mist, the way he always did, just behind the officer going the rounds. An' his pockets was bulgin'. I had been layin' for him a long while because I knew he had something I wanted. So I went up behind him and I said quite quiet,' C–, I'll take your night's pickin's if it's the same to you.' He knew it had to be an' to do him justice he bore it well. 'Well, anyway, Sergeant,' says he ' 'tis worth five francs to you, is it not?' 'Yes,' says I, and I gave him the five francs then an' there, an' he emptied his pockets into my hands. 'Twas worth all of five francs to me, C–'s work that night. An' he never bore me malice thereafter." – *A Sergeant's Tale.*

A draft of one hundred men, making good the week's losses, came in on the 8th February under Captain G. E. Young, Lieutenants T. Allen and C. Pease, and 2nd Lieutenant V. W. D. Fox. Among them were many wounded who had returned. They fell to at once on the strengthening and cleaning up of the new line which lay less than a hundred yards from the enemy. It supported the French line where that joined on to ours, and the officers would visit together through a tunnel under the roadway. Of this forlorn part of the world there is a tale that stands best as it was written by one of the officers of the Battalion: "And while we were barricading with sand-bags where the old trench joined the road, a dead Coldstream lying against a tree watched us with dull unobservant eyes . . . While we were trudging along the *pavé*, mortally weary (after relief), said the Sergeant to me: 'Did you hear what happened last night? You saw that dead man by the tree, Sir? Well, the covering-party they lay all round him. One of them tapped him on the shoulder an' asked him if he were asleep. And presently, the C.S.M. that came down with the relief, he whispered to the Corporal, "How many men have ye got out, Corporal?" "Five, Sir," says the Corporal. "I can see six meself," says the C.S.M. "Five belong to me," says the Corporal. "Count 'em, lad," says the C.S.M. "Five came out with me," says the Corporal, "and the sixth, faith, 'tis cold he is with watching us every night this six weeks."

For a while the days and nights were peaceful, as peace was counted round the Brick-stacks. The unspeakably foul German trenches were supplemented with new ones, communication-trenches multiplied and marked with proper signboards, and such historic main arteries as the "Old Kent Road" trench paved with bricks from the stacks. By night the front line sat and shivered round braziers in the freezing dark while bits of new-made trench fell around them, and listening-posts at the head of old saps and barricaded alleys reported imaginary night-attacks. When they worked on a captured trench they were like as not to find it bottomed, or worse still, revetted, with an enemy corpse, which the sliding mud would deliver hideously into the arms of the party. On such occasions the sensitive would be sick, while the more hardened warmed and ate their food unperturbed amid all the offal. But there were compensations.

On the 11th February, for example, it is noted that the men had baked meat and suet pudding "for the first time since the War began"; on the 13th not one man was even wounded through the whole day and night; while on the 15th more than half the Battalion had hot baths "for the first time since January." The diaries record these facts as of equal importance with a small advance by the French on their right, who captured a trench but fell into a nest of angry machine-guns and had to retire. The Battalion's share in the work was but to assist in keeping the enemy's heads down; in return for which the Germans shelled them an hour, killing 1 and wounding 5. Our men persisted in under-cutting the sides of the trench to make dug-outs, in the belief that unsupported caves of earth were safe against high explosives. Timbers and framing, indeed material of any kind, were still scarce, and doors and boards from wrecked houses were used in erecting parapets. Sand-bags were made out of old petticoats and pyjamas, and the farmers' fences supplied an indifferent sort of wire. Sand-bags, wires and stakes did not arrive at the front in appreciable quantities till the spring of 1915, and telephones about the same date. There was no abundance of any of these things till late in 1915; for the country had not made any preparation for war till war began, and the price of this was the lives of men.

The simplicity of our battery-work is shown by the joyous statement that "we now have a Gunner officer to live with us in our headquarters in the trenches and a telephone to the battery so that fire can be brought to bear quickly on any part of our front as necessity arises." At times there would be an error in the signals, whereby the Battalion coming up from billets to the trenches through the dark would be urged to make haste because their section was being attacked, and after a breathless arrival would find the artillery busied on some small affair away on a flank.

Characteristically enough, the Germans when bombarded, as they were with effect by the French, would retaliate by shelling our lines. The shells worried the Irish less than the fact that three of their officers – Major the Earl of Rosse, Lieutenant Rankin and 2nd Lieutenant D. Parsons, who arrived at 2 a.m. with a draft from home, were found to be temporarily attached to the Scots Guards. At that time the Battalion was 25 officers and 900 men strong, and the wastage from snipers and shells, both in the trench and while relieving, was not more than six daily.

There were reports that the enemy was now mining under the Brick-stacks, so a mining company was formed, and an officer experimented successfully in firing rifle-grenades point-blank from the rifle, instead of parabolically which allowed the enemy time to see them descending. This was for the benefit of a few persistent snipers seventy yards away, who were effectively removed and their dug-out set ablaze by the new form of attack.

Towards the end of the month our men had finished their trench-cleanings and brickings-up, had buried all dead that could be got at, and word went round that, if the situation on the 25th February could be considered "healthy" the Prince of Wales would visit them. The Germans, perhaps on information received (for the back-areas were thronged with spies), chose that day to be very active with a small gun, and as a fresh trench linking up with the French on the La Bassée road had been made and was visible against some new-fallen snow, they shelled that too. For this reason the Prince was not taken quite up to the front line, at which "he was rather annoyed." The precaution was reasonable enough. A few minutes after he had left a sector judged "comparatively safe" 2nd Lieutenant T. Allen was killed by a shell pitching on the parapet there. Three privates were also killed and 4 wounded by shell or bomb on that "healthy" day. The same gun which had been giving trouble during the Prince's visit was thought to be located by flash somewhere on the north side of the La Bassée road and siege-howitzers kept it subdued till the evening of the 25th, when, with the usual German scrupulosity, it began to shell the main road, by which reliefs came, at ten-minute intervals for three hours, but with no casualties as far as the Irish were concerned. One shell, duly noted, arrived near Brigade Headquarters and a battery of ours was asked to abate the nuisance. It is curious that only a few hours later the Germans were shelling a French battery not far from Béthune with ten-inch stuff which, if expended on the main road, would have disorganized our reliefs very completely. This was on the eve of going into Corps Reserve at Béthune, where the Battalion took over the College des Jeunes Filles from the Worcesters, the best billets since the war began, but, alas! furnished "with a large square where drill can take place." The month's losses had been 4 officers and 34 men killed 5 officers and 85 men wounded or 128 men in all.

At Béthune they enjoyed nine days' rest, with "steady drill and route-marches," concerts in the local theatre, inter-regimental boxing with the 2nd Grenadiers, and a Divisional football competition for a cup presented by the Bishop of Khartum. Here they defeated the 6th Field Ambulance and lost by two goals to nil to the Oxford and Bucks. L.I. Major Trefusis, C.O., Captain Mylne and 2nd Lieutenant H. Marion-Crawford went home for a week's leave – for that wonderful experience of "first leave" was now available – while Major the Earl of Rosse, who had been recovered from the Scots Guards, took over command.

NEUVE CHAPELLE

By the 9th March every one had returned and with them a draft of a hundred men under Lieutenant C. Wynter, 2nd Lieutenant T. E. Nugent and 2nd Lieutenant Hon. W. S. P. Alexander, just in time to take their share in the operations before Neuve Chapelle.

This village, which lay four miles under the Aubers Ridge, at the entrance to the open country round Lille and Tourcoing, had been in German hands since Smith-Dorrien's Corps were turned out of it on October 26th and 27th of the year before. Assuming that our troops could break through at that point, that no reinforcements could be brought up by the Germans over all their well-considered lines of communication, that the Aubers Ridge could be surrounded and held, that cavalry could follow up infantry armed with machine-guns across trenches and through country studded with fortified posts, it was considered, in some quarters, that an attack might be driven through even to Lille itself.

Our armies, penned for months in the trenches, had suffered heavy wastage, though they were being built up from behind with men, material and guns on a scale which, by all past standards, was enormous. The enemy, with infinitely larger resources, had meantime strengthened and restrengthened himself behind belt upon belt of barbed wire with uncounted machine-gun posts and an artillery of high explosives to which the world then held no equal. His hand was heavy, too, in offence, and the French Armies to the eastward felt it as soon as the spring opened. To ease that pressure, to release our troops from the burden of mere wasteful waiting, and to break, as far as might be, the edge of the enemy at the outset of the '15 campaign, were, presumably, objects of the battle only second to the somewhat ambitious project of entering Lille.

Neuve Chapelle proved . . . that unless artillery utterly root out barbed-wire trenches, machine-gun posts and fortified houses, no valour of attacking infantry can pierce a modern defensive line.

The Irish Guards resting at Neuve Chapelle, 10th March 1915.

Neuve Chapelle proved in large what the men in the trenches had learned in little throughout the winter – that unless artillery utterly root out barbed-wire trenches, machine-gun posts and fortified houses, no valour of attacking infantry can pierce a modern defensive line. More than three hundred guns – say 5 per cent of the number that our armies had in the last years of the War – opened upon Neuve Chapelle and its defences at 7.30 on the morning of March 10 for half an hour "in a bombardment without parallel!" Where the fire fell it wiped out everything above the sodden, muddy ground, so utterly breaking the defence that for a while the attack of Rawlinson's Fourth Army Corps went forward with hardly a check across shapeless overturned wreckage of men and things. Then, at one point after another, along the whole bare front, Battalions found themselves hung up before, or trapped between, breadths of uncut wire that covered nests of machine-guns, and were withered up before any artillery could be warned to their help. This was the fate of the 6th Brigade, whose part in the work on that sector was to capture two lines of trenches in front of Givenchy. Three Battalions of the 4th (Guards) Brigade – the 2nd Grenadiers, 1st Irish and 2nd Coldstream – were attached to it as Divisional Reserve, and the remaining two Battalions of the Brigade – the 3rd Coldstream Guards and the Herts Regiment under Colonel Matheson – as Corps Reserve.

The Battalion left billets near Béthune in the early dawn of the 10th March and moved to a wood just north of the Aire – La Bassée Canal, where it remained till midnight, when it went forward to take over some trenches held by the King's Liverpool and South Staffords (6th Brigade) whose attack had failed. Our guns had only succeeded in blowing an inadequate hole or two in the enemy's wire which at many places was reported as ten yards deep, and the assaulting battalions had, as usual, been halted there and cut down. The only consolation for the heavy losses in men and officers was the news that the attack farther north had gone well and that a thousand Germans had been captured.

A fresh attack was ordered on the morning of the 11th, but the bombardment was delayed by fog and did so little damage to the wire that by afternoon the idea was abandoned, and in the evening the 4th (Guards) Brigade took over the line that had been held by the 6th Brigade. They were filthy trenches, their parapets were not bullet-proof, and the houses behind them blown to pieces. Headquarters Mess lived in one cellar, the C.O. of the Battalion slept in another, and the communication-trenches were far too shallow. Part of our front had to be evacuated while our bombardment was going on as it was too close to the enemy for safe shelling. The failure of the 6th Brigade's attack in this quarter reduced the next day's operation to a holding affair of rifle and heavy-gun fire, delayed and hampered by the morning fog, and on the 13th March the Battalion went into billets at Le Préol. The battle round Neuve Chapelle itself, they were told, had yielded more prisoners; but heavy German reinforcements were being moved up.

Late that night a draft of eighty N.C.O.'s and men arrived under Lieutenant J. S. N. FitzGerald, among them the first detachment of specially enlisted (late) R.I. Constabulary – large drilled men – who were to play so solid a part in the history and the glory of the Battalion. The strength of the Battalion at that moment was 1080 with some 26 officers – much greater than it had been at any time during the War. They were all turned in to the endless work of cleaning out and draining foul trenches, and the dog's life of holding them under regular and irregular bombardments.

It was safer to relieve by daylight rather than by night, as darkness brought bursts of sudden rifle and machine-gun fire, despatched at a venture from behind the five-deep line of German *chevaux de frise* not seventy yards away. Tempting openings, too, were left in the wire to invite attack, but the bait was not taken. Neuve Chapelle had been a failure except in so far as it had shown the enemy that winter had not dulled any of our arms, and it was recognized we must continue to sit still till men and material should accumulate behind us. The documents and diaries of those weeks admit this with the unshaken cheerfulness of the race. Yet, even so, the actual and potential strength of the enemy was not realized.

Very slowly, and always with the thought at the back of the mind that the deadlock might break at any moment, the Army set itself, battalion by battalion, to learn the War that it was waging.

On the 15th of March 2nd Lieutenant H. Marion-Crawford was appointed Brigade Bombing Officer to the Guards Brigade with sixty men under him attached to the Irish Guards. The "jam-pot" grenade of 1914 was practically obsolete by now; the "stick" hand-grenade of the hair-brush type and the grenade fired from the rifle had succeeded it and were appearing on the front in appreciable quantities. The Mills bomb, which superseded all others both for hand and rifle, was not born till the autumn of 1915 and was not lavishly supplied till the opening of the next year.

On the 16th March, or five days after their share of the Battle of Neuve Chapelle had ended, and they lay in the trenches, a moaning was heard in the darkness of No Man's Land and a corporal sent out to report. He came back saying that he had got into a trench some thirty yards from the front line where he had seen a lighted candle and heard what he believed to be Germans talking. Another patrol was despatched and at last came back with a wounded man of the King's Liverpools who had been lying out since the 10th. He said he had been wounded in the assault, captured as he was trying to crawl back, stripped of boots, equipment and rations, but left with a blanket, and the enemy apparently visited him every night as they patrolled the trench. An attempt was made to capture that patrol, but in the darkness the trench was missed altogether.

The enemy celebrated the day before St. Patrick's Day and the day itself, March 17th, by several hours of brisk shelling of Givenchy, timed to catch the evening reliefs, but luckily without casualties. Queen Alexandra sent the Battalion their shamrock; telegrams wishing them good luck were duly received from Lord Kitchener, Colonel of the Battalion, Brigadier-General Nugent, and a letter from Sir Charles Monro, commanding the First Army Corps. Father Gwynne held an open-air service in the early morning, and every man was given a hot bath at Béthune. More important still, every man who wanted it had free beer with his dinner, and in those days beer was beer indeed!

They built some sort of decent life out of the monotonous hours; they came to know the very best and the very worst in themselves and in their comrades upon whom their lives and well-being depended . . .

In the trenches, October 1915.

The end of the month was filled with constructive work and the linking-up and strengthening of trenches, and the burial, where possible, of "the very old dead" – twenty-nine of them in one day – and always unrelaxing watch and ward against the enemy. At times he puzzled them, as when one evening he threw bombs just over his own parapet till it seemed that he must be busy blowing holes in his own deep wire. But it turned out at last to be some new pattern of bomb with which he was methodically experimenting. Later came a few aeroplanes, the first seen in some weeks. It may have been no more than a coincidence that the first 'planes came over on the day that the Prince of Wales was paying the Battalion another visit. But it was the continuous rifle-fire at night that accounted for most of the casualties in the trenches and during reliefs. Second Lieutenant T. Nugent was wounded in the back of the neck on the 24th by an unaimed bullet, and almost each day had its count of casualties.

The Battalion took life with philosophic calm. Food and rest are the paramount considerations of men in war. The former was certain and abundant; the latter scanty and broken. So the Commanding Officer made no comment when, one night going round the line, he found a man deeply asleep with his feet projecting into the fairway and, written on a paper on his chest, the legend:

Sleep is sweet; undisturbed it is divine,
So lift up your feet and do not tread on mine.

A certain amount of change and interest was given by the appearance on the scene of the Post Office Territorials (8th City of London), commanded by Colonel J. Harvey, an ex-Irish Guardsman, and a platoon of that Regiment was attached to the Battalion for instructional purposes. Later, three, and at last seven platoons, were placed at the disposal of the Irish Guards, whose C.O. "found them work to do." They "made themselves quite useful" but "wanted more practice in digging" – an experience never begrudged them by the generous Irish.

TRENCH-WORK AFTER NEUVE CHAPELLE

Thanks to Neuve Chapelle, a breathing-space had been won during which Territorial troops were taking their place in the front line and such supplies as times afforded were coming up. The Diary records many visits of Colonels, Brigadiers, and Inspectors of the Territorial Forces to this section, which, when it had been brought up to the Guards' standard, was considered a model for instruction. The month closed with bright moon- light and the mounting of two motor machine-guns, one south of Duck's Bill and the other in Oxford Street, for protection against aeroplanes.

April opened with the death of 2nd Lieutenant J. M. Stewart, killed before dawn while looking over the parapet of the trench at Duck's Bill, and buried at noon in the cemetery near "Windy Corner." He was one of the best of the younger officers of these days and had proved himself on many occasions. The lull after Neuve Chapelle continued, the Battalion relieving the Grenadiers every other day at 6 p.m. with almost the regularity of a civilian department. When it was fine, aeroplanes, taking no notice of the anti-aircraft artillery, ranged over them in search of certain heavy naval guns that had been reaching into enemy back-areas.

There was very little bomb-dropping on infantry, and the monotony of rifle-fire and occasional hand-bombing was only broken when our artillery, with a few shells to spare, fired into the enemy's second line near Couteleux, where the Germans, behind heavy wire, were singing and "making much noise." The effort drew a return fire of high explosives and a shell wounded 8 and killed 1 man of No. 3 Company. Our gunners said that they had killed many more than nine Germans, but sporadic outbursts of this kind were not well seen in the front line, which has to abide the result. As one officer wrote: "I am all for determined bombardment but do not appreciate minor ones, though I quite see it makes the enemy use his ammunition." The 2nd London Territorial Artillery registered their guns also, for the first time, on April 12, and a platoon of the 15th County of London with its machine-gun was attached to the Battalion for instruction.

It is no sort of discredit to the Territorials that at first they did not know what to expect in this war, and reading between the lines one sees how thoroughly and patiently the Regulars performed their extra duties of schoolmasters, guides, philosophers and friends to Battalions whose most extended training had never dreamed of an ordered existence, half underground, where all things but death were invisible, and even the transport and tendency of the wounded was a mystery of pain and confusion worked out among labyrinths of open drains.

Among the distinguished visitors to be shown the trenches was Lieut. Colonel R. S. de Haviland of the Eton O.T.C. – a man of many friends in that company. The come-and-go of visitors cheered and interested the men in the front trenches, since their presence even for a little proved that, somewhere in the world, life continued on not inconceivable lines. They jested naturally enough at those who looked on for a day or two at their hardships and went away, but the hardships were lightened a little by the very jest. Even while the Commandant of the Eton O.T.C. was with them the Battalion was energetically devising means to drain out an unspeakable accumulation of stagnant water downhill from a mine near the Shrine under the White House barricade (the White House was scarcely more than a name even then) into some German trenches at the foot of the slope. This work necessitated clearing a ditch by the roadside in which were found four German corpses, "besides pieces of other human beings," which were buried, and in due course the whole flood of abomination was decanted on to the enemy. "As it was very horrible, I don't suppose they will like it," writes one of the officers chiefly concerned.

On the same day, April 16, while 2nd Lieutenant H. Marion-Crawford, who it will be remembered was Brigade Bombing Instructor, was schooling some men of the 3rd Coldstream with live grenades, one exploded and killed him instantaneously. He had shown the greatest ability in organizing the bombing work, and his loss at that time, where bombers were being more and more leaned upon, was very seriously felt. He was buried four hours after his death in the cemetery near Givenchy.

On the 17th the Battalion went back to the College des Jeunes Filles at Béthune for a four days' rest, while its place in the trenches was taken by a couple of Territorial Battalions – the Post Office Rifles and the 15th County of London. While it was route-marched, and instructed, and washed and steadily drilled, the battle for Hill 60 was being fought with mines and hand-grenades, hand-mortars, and the first gas-shells, a score of miles to the north, where it was made known to the Germans how, man for man, their fresh and fully trained troops could not overcome ours. The demonstration cost some three thousand casualties on our side, and, it may be presumed, strengthened the enemy's intention to use gas on a larger scale in the future. But no echo of the little affair interfered with the work at Givenchy. The question was how the new Territorial Battalions would hold their trenches, and one sees in all the documents a justified pride in their teachings when the Battalion went up to the front again on the 22nd and found the Territorials were keen and had kept their trenches clean. For the Guards teach, not unsuccessfully, that unless a man is clean he cannot be the best sort of soldier.

On the night of the 22nd April the sector was held by the 15th County of London, the Irish Guards and the Post Office Rifles, the remainder of the Guards Brigade being in rest. To the normal strain of a watching front line in foul weather was added a fresh burden. A few days before, the enemy had blown a mine in an orchard about fifty yards short of our trenches. It did no damage at the time, but the R.E. Mining Officer, Lieutenant Barclay, in counter-mining towards the crater it had made, saw, through the wall of his mine, Germans engaged in turning the crater into an advanced-post. Trench-mortars were fired at once to discourage them. Then came reports of underground workings heard in other directions, and, notably, close to the parapet of a trench near the White House. This was on the evening of the 24th. Hardly had orders been given to clear the White House trench, when the ground at the junction of Lieutenant Barclay's counter-mine and the German crater went up and the Lieutenant was killed. At the same time an explosion occurred near the White House. Two privates of the Irish Guards (2845 J. Mansfield and 3975 M. Brine) volunteered to enter our mine and see what had happened. They recovered Lieutenant Barclay's body at great risk from the asphyxiating gases, and both men were recommended for the D. C .M. The explosion near the White House was, after inspection, put down as the work of a heavy shell, not a mine; but listening parties reported more underground noises and another section of trench was evacuated accordingly. To prevent the Germans consolidating themselves further in the crater which connected with Lieutenant Barclay's mine, our 4·5 howitzers bombarded it on the 25th, and it was decided to blow our end of the mine as soon as possible to prevent the enemy working up it. This was difficult, for the galleries were full of foul gas – whether leaking from some adjacent coal-pit or laid on by the enemy was uncertain. The R.E. officer who went down to lay the charges was asphyxiated and several of his men were injured.

Not till the 29th of April were the difficulties overcome; by which time the enemy had driven a fresh shaft into it. After the explosion, a field battery (17th R.F.A.) and the 47th Howitzer Battery fired a salvo at the German trenches. "There was a little rifle-fire, but soon all was quiet." Mining, like aerial and bombing work, was still in its infancy, and the information supplied by the Intelligence was said to be belated and inadequate.

An interesting point is the unshaken serenity with which the men took the new developments. They were far too annoyed at being shifted about and losing their rest to consider too curiously the underlying causes of evil. They left the 3rd Coldstream to deal with the situation and went into billets in Le Préol, and the next day (April 26) into Béthune for their hot baths. A draft of 3 officers (Captain T. M. D. Bailie and 2nd Lieutenants A. W. L. Paget and R. S. G. Paget) with 136 N.C.O.'s and men reached them on the 27th, when there was just time to give them a hot meal and send them at once to the trenches in the bright moonlight under "a certain amount of rifle-fire and intermittent shelling from small guns which did not do much damage." An enemy field-gun, long known as an unlocated pest, spent the morning busily enfilading the trenches, in spite of the assurances of our Artillery that they had found and knocked it out several times. Appeal was made to an R.A. Brigadier who, after examining the ground, left the Battalion under the impression that "it was likely a gun would be brought up early to-morrow." Nothing more is heard of the hope: but guns were scarce at that time.

There were other preoccupations for those in command. The second Battle of Ypres, that month's miracle of naked endurance against the long-planned and coldly-thought-out horror of gas, had begun near Langemarck with the choking-out of the French and Canadian troops, and had continued day after day with the sacrifice of Battalions and Brigades, Regulars and Territorials swallowed up in the low grey-yellow gas banks that threatened Ypres from Langemarck to Hill 60, or beaten to pulp by heavy explosives and the remnant riddled anew by machine-guns. Once again England was making good with her best flesh and blood for the material and the training she had deliberately refused to provide while yet peace held. The men who came out of that furnace alive say that no after-experience of all the War approached it for sheer concentrated, as well as prolonged, terror, confusion and a growing sense of hopelessness among growing agonies. If a world, at that time unbroken to German methods, stood aghast at the limited revelations allowed by the Press Censorship reports, those who had seen a man, or worse, a child, dying from gas may conceive with what emotions men exposed to the new torment regarded it, what kind of reports leaked out from clearing-stations and hospitals, and what work therefore was laid upon officers to maintain an even and unaffected temper in the Battalions in waiting. The records, of course, do not mention these details, nor, indeed, do they record when gas-protectors (for masks, helmets, and boxes were not evolved till much later) were first issued to the troops on the Givenchy sector. But private letters of the 25th April, at the time the German mine in the Orchard occupied their attention, remark "we have all been issued out with an antidote to the latest German villain . . . i.e. of asphyxiating gases . . . What they will end by doing one can hardly imagine. The only thing is to be prepared for anything."

The first "masks" were a little more than mufflers or strips of cloth dipped in lime water. A weathercock was rigged up near Headquarters dug-outs, and when the wind blew from the Germans these were got ready. False alarms of gas, due to strange stenches given off by various explosives, or the appearance of a mist over the German line, were not uncommon, and on each occasion it appeared that the C.O. had to turn out, sniff and personally pass judgement on the case. The men had their instructions what to do in case of emergency, concluding with the simple order, perhaps the result of experience at Ypres, "in event of the first line being overcome, the second immediately charge through the gas and occupy the front-line trenches."

But to return to the routine:

The casualties for the month of April were 2 officers and 8 men killed and 1 officer and 42 men wounded. The strength of the Battalion stood at 28 officers and 1133 men, higher than it had ever been before.

The following is the distribution of officers and N.C.O.'s at that time, a little less than three weeks before the Battle of Festubert.

Headquarters

Major the Hon. J. F. Trefusis	Commanding Officer.
Major the Earl of Rosse	Second in Command.
Capt. Lord Desmond FitzGerald	Adjutant.
Lieut. P. H. Antrobus	Transport Officer.
Lieut. L. S. Straker	Machine-gun Officer.
Capt. A. H. L. McCarthy	Medical Officer.
Lieut. H. Hickie	Quartermaster.
The Rev. John Gwynne (S.J.)	Chaplain.

No. 1 Company

Capt. J. N. Guthrie	2nd Lieut. V. W. D. Fox.
Lieut. R. G. C. Yerburgh	No. 2535 C.S.M. Harradine.
2nd Lieut. Hon. W. S. P. Alexander	No. 3726 C.Q.M.S. P. M'Goldrick.

No. 2 Company

Capt. E. G. Mylne	2nd Lieut. S. G. Tallents.
Lieut. Sir G. Burke, Bart	No. 3949 C.S.M. D. Moyles.
2nd Lieut. R. B. H. Kemp	No. 2703 C.Q.M.S. J. G. Lowry.

No. 3 Company

Major P. L. Reid	2nd Lieut. C. de Persse
2nd Lieut. E. W. Campbell	(attached 7th Dragoon Gds)
2nd Lieut. C. Pease	No. 2112 C.S.M. H. M'Veigh.
2nd Lieut. J. R. Ralli	No. 3972 C.Q.M.S. R. Grady.

No. 4 Company

Capt. G. E. S. Young	2nd Lieut. D C. Parsons.
Lieut. J. S. N. FitzGerald	No. 2384 C.S.M. T. Curry.
Lieut. C. D. Wynter	No. 3132 C.Q.M.S. H. Carton.

The first ten days of May passed quietly. Mines, for the moment, gave no further anxiety, bombing and bombardments were light, reliefs were happily effected, and but 1 man was killed and 1 wounded. Two officers, Lieutenant H. A. Boyse and 2nd Lieutenant R.H.W. Heard, joined on the 2nd.

THE BATTLE OF FESTUBERT

It was judged expedient while the second Battle of Ypres was in full heat that the Germans should, if possible, be kept from sending any help to their front near Arras, in Artois, which at the time was under strong pressure from the French thrusting towards Lens. To this end, our First Army was ordered to attack the German Seventh Corps over the flat ground between Laventie and Richebourg on a front of some ten miles. The affair opened very early on the morning of the 9th May with a bombardment, imposing in itself by the standards of the day, but, as before, insufficient to break the wire or crush enough of the machine-gun nests. The Germans seem to have had full information of its coming, and dealt with it severely. The whole attack from north to south – Indian, Scottish, Territorials and the rest – was caught and broken as it rolled against the well-wired German trenches.

The Battalion, whose part, then, was to maintain the right of our Army where it joined the French, heard the French guns open on the night of the 8th May, and by dawn the English gun-fire was in full swing to the north – one continuous roar broken by the deep grunt of our howitzer-shells bursting, for these were so few that we could pick them up by ear. The Guards had no concern with these matters till the trouble should thicken. Their business was to stand ready for any counter-attack and keep up bursts of rapid fire at intervals while they waited for what little news came to hand. It was uniformly bad, except that the French in the south seemed to be making some headway, and so far as aeroplanes and artillery observers could make out, there was no concentration of troops immediately in front of them. The Germans were too busy with the immediate English front to extend their commitments to the southward, and the next two days were, for the Battalion in their trenches, the quietest that they had known for some time. Then came orders to hand over to the 1st Scots Guards and rejoin the Second Division near Le Touret in readiness to carry on the attack which had broken down on the 9th. They bivouacked in the open, and the weather turned cold and wet, but the men, relieved from the trenches and assured of a change of work, sat it out "singing songs and playing games in the wet!" They had been forbidden to light fires, lest they should accidentally use the local farmers' tobacco-drying poles or hedge-stuff. And while they waited under their mackintosh sheets the Armies waited on the weather. A fresh attack was to be launched from Richebourg by the Rue du Bois, and southward as far as Festubert, but, this time, by night not by day, and after longer artillery preparation. The 5th and 6th Brigades were to open it, with the 4th (Guards) Brigade in support. It began at 11.30 on the 15th, when, at huge cost, something like half a mile in breadth and a quarter of a mile in depth of trenches was screwed out of the Germans by the morning of Sunday the 16th. The Battalion was moved from bivouac in the dawn of that day to support the 5th Brigade which had not gone so far forward as the 6th, and spent the day in trenches at Rue du Bois under incessant mixed artillery fire, which killed 1 man and wounded an officer and 28 men – the whole without being able to inflict any damage on the enemy. Indeed, the survivors of the battle here agreed that they saw no German dead other than some corpses left over from previous attacks. They returned to bivouac in wet and mist, and on the afternoon of the 17th were, with the 2nd Grenadiers, ordered to occupy the line then held by the 21st Brigade and to push forward and dig in near a farm (Cour l'Avoine) bristling with machine-guns across a stretch of dead flat, muddy ground, pitted with water-logged shell-holes. The left was to keep touch with the 6th Brigade and the right with the Grenadiers, the whole line facing north-east from Quinque Rue.

They extended in the dusk. The left flanking Company, No. 4, found no sign of the 6th Brigade, but received a message from the 5th King's Battalion that their Brigade orders were that the right of that Battalion should get into touch with the Irish but would not be up till late; so one machine-gun was sent to strengthen that company's flank. No. 2 Company, on the right flank, had reached its objective and dug itself in under bursts of raking machine-gun and rifle-fire directed against the dykes and bridges, which unfortunately wounded both Captain Mylne and Lieutenant Kemp, and the Company command devolved on 2nd Lieutenant S. G. Tallents. The left flank, meantime, was in the air without tools or sand-bags, but luckily the night was wet and it was allowed to dig itself in unmolested. The casualties for the day were only 2 officers wounded, 3 men killed and 5 wounded.

The 18th dawned in wreaths of driving rain and mist that wrapped the flats. The preliminary bombardment of Farm Cour l'Avoine was postponed for lack of good light, and in that lull a Brigadier whose men had already attacked the farm unsuccessfully came across the trenches to the Battalion and gave his experiences and recommendations. The weather made one low cluster of devastated buildings seen across the levels look remarkably like any other; and it seems pure luck that the attack, as originally intended, was not launched against the wrong objective. From noon on, the enemy began to shell the Battalion severely in its shallow trenches, and there were forty casualties while they lay waiting orders. The attack began at 4.30 p.m. Cour l'Avoine was then so bombarded by heavy shell-fire that, as usual, it seemed that nothing in or around it could live. But as soon as the attacking companies rose and showed over the ground-line, the hail of machine-gun fire re-opened, and for the next three hours the Irish suffered in the open and among the shell-holes, beaten down, as the other battalions had been before them, round the piled wreckage of Cour l'Avoine farm. In one trench, abandoned by the enemy, they fell into a neat German trap. Its parapet facing towards the British was bullet-proof enough, but the parados, though proof against the casual splinters of our shrapnel, which had no back-blast, had been pared thin enough to pass all bullets. Consequently, when the trench was occupied, accurately ranged machine-guns opened on the parados, and riddled the men to such an extent that one Company had to get out and take refuge behind what had been the parapet. The greatest distance gained in all was about three hundred yards, and this with their left flank still in the air and protected by the one machine-gun which Lieutenant Straker, the unflinching enthusiast of the weapon, had brought into a communication-trench. At last they dug in where they were; the next Brigade on the left linked up to the one-machine-gun communication-trench, and with their old friends the Herts Battalion and the East Anglian Field Company, with whom they had tested mines together, they began to consolidate. The C.O. writes: "I tried to find out what officers I had left. Out of twenty-eight there were twelve, but four of these had been left behind with the transport a day or two before." Of the eight who had come through the affair on their feet, only two were absolutely untouched. Here is the list: Captain J. N. Guthrie and 2nd Lieutenant V. W. D. Fox, killed by shellfire, while leading their Company – No. 1 – to reinforce the line; 11 officers were wounded, Major the Earl of Rosse very severely in the head by a piece of shell; Major Reid, concussion from the explosion of a shell; Captain G. E. S. Young, hand; Lieutenant H. T. A. H. Boyse, head; 2nd Lieutenant S. G. Tallents, thigh; 2nd Lieutenant J. R. Ralli, stomach; 2nd Lieutenant E. W. Campbell, head; Lieutenant Hon. W. S. P. Alexander, neck; 2nd Lieutenant R. S. G. Paget, arm; 2nd Lieutenant J. K. Greer, leg and hand; 2nd Lieutenant C. de Persse, head. Twenty-two men were killed, 284 wounded and 86 missing. The Battalion came through it all, defeated, held down at long range, but equable in temper and morale:

Small wonder that in the cheerless dawn of the 19th their Brigadier came and "made some complimentary remarks to the men who were standing about.

The four officers who had been left behind were then ordered up to fill the gaps, and in that dawn the Company commands stood: No. 1, Lieut. R. G. C. Yerburgh; 2nd Lieut. R. H. W. Heard. No. 2, Lieut. Sir Gerald Burke; 2nd Lieut. A. W. L. Paget. No. 3, Capt. T. M. D. Bailie. No. 4, Lieut. J. S. N. FitzGerald; Lieut. C. D. Wynter.

Almost at once shelling opened again, and Lieutenants Burke and Paget were wounded and 10 men killed or wounded by three high explosives bursting right over the line. It was sheer luck that, though shelled at intervals for the rest of the day, there were very few further casualties, and the Battalion returned "in small parties" to their bivouacs near Le Touret, where a hot meal, great-coats and a rum-ration awaited them. They were wet, tired, chilled and caked with dirt, and cheerful; but next day, when they paraded before going into rest while they waited for reinforcements, there was hardly a speck of mud to be seen on them. Rest-billets at Lapugnoy, some seven or eight miles back, were out of range but not out of hearing of the guns, in a valley between delightful beech-woods carpeted with bluebells. Here they lay off and rejoiced in the novel sight of unscathed trees and actual hills.

FROM FESTUBERT TO LOOS

On the 24th May General Home came to inspect and complimented them. His compliments are nowhere recorded, but it was remarked with satisfaction at his parade that the men "stood very steady and moved their arms well considering that they have not had much practice in steady drill lately." They had merely practiced unbroken discipline among the dead and the dying in a hopeless fight.

A draft of 126 men, under Lieutenant A. F. Gordon, arrived, and Lieutenant R. Rankin, who had been attached to the 1st Scots Guards since February, joined them at Lapugnoy, and the Rev. S. Knapp, R.C. Chaplain from the 25th Brigade, took temporary charge of spiritual affairs while their own Father Gwynne, who never spared himself, was trying electric treatment in Paris for lumbago, induced, as every one knew, by unsparing exposure.

On the 25th May they moved from Lapugnoy via Chocques to Oblinghem, some five miles to the north-east, a village of many and varied smells, close to an aerodrome where they lay at a moment's notice, which meant that no one could take off his boots. A new type of gas-mask was issued here, and the men drilled in the use of it. Captain A. H. L. McCarthy, the Medical Officer who had been with them since October 25, accidentally broke his arm, and his duties were taken over by Lieutenant L. W. Bain, R.A.M.C.

On the 28th May a draft of 214 N.C.O.'s and men under Lieutenant L. R. Hargreaves, 2nd Lieutenants N. F. Durant and L. C. Whitefoord, arrived, and the next day (29th) twelve more officers came in from England: Major G. H. C. Madden; Captain V. C. J. Blake; Captain M. V. Gore-Langton; 2nd Lieutenant J. T. Robyns; 2nd Lieutenant K. E. Dormer; 2nd Lieutenant Hon. H. B. O'Brien; 2nd Lieutenant R. J. P. Rodakowski; 2nd Lieutenant K. W. Hogg; 2nd Lieutenant J. Grayling-Major; 2nd Lieutenant F. H. Witts; 2nd Lieutenant W. B. Stevens; 2nd Lieutenant P. H. J. Close – bringing the Battalion up to 28 officers and 958 other ranks.

Headquarters and Companies then stood as follows:

Headquarters

Major the Hon. J. F. Trefusis	Commanding Officer.
Major G. H. Madden	Second in Command.
Capt. Lord Desmond FitzGerald	Adjutant.
Lieut. P. H. Antrobus	Transport Officer.
2nd Lieut. L. S. Straker	Machine-gun Officer.
The Rev. S. Knapp	Chaplain.
Lieut. L. W. Bain	Medical Officer.
Lieut. H. Hickie	Quartermaster.

No. 1 Company

Capt. M. V. Gore-Langton	2nd Lieut. J. Grayling-Major.
Lieut. R. C. G. Yerburgh	2nd Lieut. F. H. Witts.
2nd Lieut. R. H. W. Heard	

No. 2 Company

Capt. T. W. D. Bailie	2nd Lieut. Hon. H. B. O'Brien.
Lieut. R. Rankin	2nd Lieut. W. B. Stevens.
2nd Lieut. K. E. Dormer	2nd Lieut. L. C. Whitefoord.

No. 3 Company

Capt. V. C. J. Blake	2nd Lieut. K. W. Hogg.
Lieut. C. D. Wynter	2nd Lieut. J. T. Robyns.
2nd Lieut. N. F. Durant	

No. 4 Company

Lieut. J. S. N. FitzGerald	2nd Lieut. A. F. L. Gordon.
Lieut. L. R. Hargreaves	2nd Lieut. R. J. P. Rodakowski.
2nd Lieut. P. H. J. Close	

There is no hint of the desperate hard work of the 2nd, Reserve, Battalion at Warley, which made possible the supply at such short notice of so many officers of such quality. These inner workings of a Regiment are known only to those who have borne the burden.

On the 31st May the 4th (Guards) Brigade was shifted from Oblinghem to billets near the most unpleasing village of Noeux-les-Mines, farther south than they had ever been before, as Divisional Reserve to a couple of Brigades of the Second Division in trenches recently taken over from the French. The Brigade moved off in two columns, through Béthune down the main road to Arras, where they were seen by the Germans and shelled both en route and as they were billeting, but, as chance chose, without accident. The billets were good, though, like most in the early days, they needed cleansing, and a rumour went about that the trenches to which the Battalion was assigned were peculiarly foul, in very bad shape and would probably need re-making throughout.

Bombing classes with a new and an "absolutely safe" bomb (Mills), the routine of Company drills and exercise, sports and an Eton dinner on the 4th June, filled the warm, peaceful days till it left Noeux-les-Mines for Sailly-Labourse. This was not the sector they had expected, but one farther to the north and nearer Cuinchy. Their trenches were an unsatisfactory line with insufficient traverses, not too many dug-outs, and inadequate parapets facing fields of fast-growing corn, which marked the German front two hundred yards away. They were reached from Cambrin through a mile and a half of communication-trenches, up which every drop of water had to be carried in tins. A recent draft of fifty had increased the Battalion to over a thousand men, and, apparently by way of breaking in the new hands, it was suggested that the Battalion should dig a complete new line of trenches. They compromised, however, by improving the existing one, which they shared with the 2nd Grenadiers, changing over on the 12th June to a stretch of fifteen hundred yards, held by the 2nd Coldstream. This necessitated three companies instead of two in the front line and the fourth in support.

The enemy here confined themselves to shelling timed to catch reliefs, but rarely heavy enough to interfere with working-parties digging or wiring in the tough chalk. On one occasion a selection of coloured lights, red, green and white, had been sent up for the Battalion to test. They chose a night when the enemy was experimenting on a collection of lights of his own, but soon discovered that rocket-lights were inadvisable, as their fiery tails gave away positions and drew fire. This disadvantage might have been found out in England by the makers instead of at 1 a.m. by a wearied Commanding Officer, whose duty was to link up and strengthen his trenches, keep an eye on the baffling breadths of corn in front of him, send reconnoitering parties out on all possible occasions, procure wire and Engineers to set it up, and at the same time keep all men and material in readiness for any possible attack that might develop on the heels of the bombardments that came and went like the summer thunder storms along the tense line.

Sometimes they watched our own shells bursting in the German trenches opposite Givenchy, where the Battalion had stayed so long; sometimes they heard unexplained French fire to the southward. Next day would bring its rumours of gains won and lost, or warnings to stand-to for expected counter-attacks that turned out to be no more than the rumble of German transport, heard at night, moving no one knew whither. When our stinted artillery felt along the enemy's trenches in front of them – for the high corn made No Man's Land blind and patrol-work difficult – the German replies were generally liberal and not long delayed.

On the 17th June one such outburst of ours loosed an hour's heavy shelling, during which Staff-Captain the Hon. E. W. Brabazon (Coldstream), on his rounds to look at a machine-gun position under the Battalion Machine-gun Officer, Lieutenant Straker, was killed by a shell that fell on the top of the dug-out. Lieutenant Straker, who was sitting in the doorway, had his foot so pinned in the fallen timber that it took an hour to extricate him. Captain Brabazon, in the dug-out itself, was crushed by a beam. He was buried at Cambrin next morning at nine o'clock, while the Battalion was repairing the damage done to the blown-in trenches and the French were fighting again in the south.

The brotherly Herts Battalion had been doing all the work of digging in their rear for some time past, and on the 20th the Battalion took over their fatigue-work and their billets at Annequin and Cambrin, while the Herts went to the front line. It was hot work in that weather to extend and deepen unending communication-trenches that cut off all the air. The Prince of Wales looked in on them at Annequin and watched the German guns searching for a heavy battery which had gone elsewhere. The movements of the Heir to the Crown, even as guardedly recorded in this Diary, not to mention others, and the unofficial stories of his appearance, alone, on a bicycle or afoot in places of the most "unhealthy" character, must have been a cause of considerable anxiety to those in charge of him. He spent his birthday (June 23) visiting along the line, which happened to be quiet after a bombardment of Annequin the day before. The place drew much fire at that time, as one of our batteries lay in front of it, and a high coal dump, used as an observation-post, just behind it. The Battalion was still on fatigues and, in spite of many rumours and alerts, had suffered very little. Indeed, the total casualties of June were but 2 men killed and an officer and 22 men wounded. Meantime, the new drafts were learning their work.

The really serious blow they took was the departure at the month's end of Lord Cavan, their Brigadier, to command the Fiftieth Division. They had known and loved him as a man who understood their difficulties, who bore his share, and more, of their hardships, and whose sympathy, unsparing devotion and, above all, abounding cheery common sense, had carried them at every turn so far through the campaign.

He bid them farewell at Béthune on the 28th, where they were in billets, in these words:

I have come to say good-bye to you, as I have to go away and take command of the Fiftieth Division. I wish to thank the Irish Guards for all they have done since they have been under my command. Before the war they had had no opportunity of proving themselves worthy to take their place in the Brigade of Guards. But during the course of this war they have always conducted themselves worthy of taking their place with the other illustrious Regiments of the Brigade of Guards – and more so. It is part of all of you young officers, who have taken the place of those who have fallen, to keep up the reputation of the Battalion, and you have a difficult task, as its reputation is very high. I need hardly say how much I feel leaving the 4th (Guards) Brigade, and I would rather remain its Brigadier than be a Field-Marshal elsewhere.

General Feilding, whom you all know, is coming to take my place, and I could not leave you in better hands. I wish you all luck.

His special farewell order ran:

28th June 1915

On leaving the Brigade to take Command of a Division it would not be seemly to recall the various actions since 18th September in which it has been my privilege and my delight to command you, but I may say this – whether in action, in trenches, or in billets, no unit of the 4th (Guards) Brigade has ever disappointed me, nor has any Battalion ever fallen short of that great standard set us by our predecessors.

We welcomed the 1st Herts Territorials at Ypres, and most worthily have they borne their part with the rest of us.

To you all I convey the gratitude of a very full heart, and I wish you Good-bye and God Speed.

(Sg.) CAVAN,
Brigadier-General,
Commanding 4th (Guards) Brigade.

And for recognition of their work in the trenches for the past three weeks, the following was sent from the G.O.C. Second Division to the Officer commanding the Irish Guards:

The Brigadier-General has received the following letter from the G.O.C. Second Division, and he would like C.O.'s to arrange that all the men hear it, so that they may realise how fully their splendid efforts are appreciated both by General Horne and himself:

"Since the 4th (Guards) Brigade went into 'Z' Section on June 6th, it has really done splendid work. In addition to opening up and deepening the communication-trenches and the construction of several different minor works in rear, you have dug and wired a new line across a front of at least 2000 yards. The 4th (Guards) Brigade and the 11th Company R.E. have done great work on many previous occasions, but I think that this last achievement surpasses them all."

26th June 1915
The C.O. directs that the above is read to all platoons, and not more than one platoon at a time.

(Sd.) DESMOND FITZGERALD,
Captain Adjutant,
1st Battalion Irish Guards.

26th June 1915

It was the Brigadier's reference to their having proved themselves worthy to take place with the other regiments of the Brigade of Guards, "and more so," that delighted them most; for the Battalion felt that it had won its spurs in every field. Yet, for all that, the Diary which, under the well-worn official phrases, represents the soul of the Regiment and knows how that soul is made and tempered, emphasizes the fact that at Béthune there are some "quite good parade-grounds, where a good deal of steady drill will be carried out" and plenty of country for route-marching, where the men could learn how to bear themselves without "budging" beneath the casual shells that dropped miles behind the line.

So they "rested" at Béthune and gave a concert in the theatre, to which they invited many inhabitants of the town who, being new to the manners and customs of the Irish, "could not understand much," but a French officer sang the "Marseillaise" with great effect, and at dinner afterwards, when the Prince of Wales was among the guests, there were not only red and white roses on the table, but, according to one account, "silver spoons and forks," provided by the owner of the house. If Béthune did not yet comprehend the songs of these wild outlanders, it had full confidence in them.

CUINCHY

The first week of July saw them returned to their own old trenches at Cuinchy – the fifty-times-fought-over line that ran from the La Bassée Canal to within a hundred yards of the La Bassée – Béthune road. A couple of companies of the Herts, one on each side of the La Bassée road, lay on their right, and right of those again, the 2nd Coldstream. They boasted as many as six machine-guns in position belonging to the Battalion, and three to the 2nd Grenadiers, their relief. The trenches had not improved by use since February. There were mine-craters directly in front of them, their opposing edges occupied by our men and the enemy; the breastworks were old bursten sand-bags; fire-steps had broken down, dug-outs were inadequate against the large-size trench-mortar bombs that the Germans were using, and generally the condition and repair of things was heart-breaking to the new-comers and their Brigadier, who spent most of his time, night and day, in the front line.

Annequin, where two of the companies were billeted, had become more than ever a shell-trap full of English batteries for which the Germans were constantly searching; and, since experts told them that we now had got the upper hand of the enemy at mining, the cynical expected that, at any moment, some really big mine would go up beneath them. As an interlude, the companies in billets were employed in making dug-outs without any material; which trifling task they somehow accomplished. The big shells and the bombing from the trench-mortars forced them to deepen all dug-outs to ten or twelve feet. These were shored with bricks and topped with rails as material became more plentiful.

On the 17th July Captain A. H. L. McCarthy, R.A.M.C., who had broken his arm at Lapugnoy six weeks before, returned to duty and was made welcome. His sick-leave, which he seems to have filled with beseeching letters to the C.O., had been darkened by a prospect of being detached from the Battalion and sent to the Dardanelles. Father Gwynne, also, came back from his two months' rheumatism cure, relieving Father Knapp. He was not quite restored and so was forbidden by the C.O. to show himself in the front line for at least ten days. It is to be hoped that he obeyed, but in a battalion where the call for the priest goes out with, or before, the call for stretcher-bearers, neither shepherds nor flock are long separated under any circumstances. They tell the tale of one of their priests who, utterly wearied, dropped for an hour's sleep in a trench that was being deepened under fire. He was roused by a respectful whisper from the working-party: "We've dug to your head an' your feet, Father, an' now, if you'll get up, we'll dig out under the length of ye."

The Brigade's system of forty-eight hours' reliefs enabled them to do more in a given time than battalions who went in for four days at a stretch, as a man could carry two days' rations on him without drawing on the fatigue-parties, and the knowledge he would be relieved at the end of the time kept his edge. A Brigadier of experience could tell any section of the line held by the Brigade as far as he could see it, simply from the demeanor of the working-parties. This state of things was only maintained by unbroken discipline and the gospel that if one man can keep himself comparatively clean in all that dirt and confusion every one else can. It behoved the Battalion, also, to make and leave a good name among the French upon whom they were quartered, as well as with the enemy over against them. They were at that time, as for long afterwards, almost unmixed Irish, and for that reason, the relations between officers and men were unlike anything that existed elsewhere, even in nominally pure Irish Battalions. If there be any mystery in the training of war that specially distinguishes the Brigade of Guards from their fellows it is that the officers lie under discipline more exacting than that of the rank and file; and that even more than in any other branch of the Service they are responsible for the comfort of their men. Forced together as they were in the stark intimacy of the trenches, that at any moment may test any soul to the uttermost; revealed to each other, every other day at least, in the long and wearisome march to billets, where the companies and platoons move slowly and sideways through the communication-trenches, gambling against death – if the German heavies are busy – at each step of the road, officers and men came to a mutual comprehension and affection – which in no way prevented the most direct and drastic criticism or penalties – as impossible to describe as it would be to omit, since it was the background against which their lives ran from day to day. The Celt's national poise and manner, his gift of courtesy and sympathy, and above all the curious and incommunicable humour of his outlook in those days made it possible for him and his officers to consort together upon terms perhaps debarred to other races. When the men practiced "crime" they were thorough and inventive in the act and unequalled in the defence, as the records of some courts-martial testify. But the same spirit that prompted the large and imaginative sin and its unexpected excuse or justification (as, for example, that three sinners detected in removing a large cask of beer were but exercising their muscles in "rowling it a piece along the *pavé*") bred a crop of forceful regimental characters. Many, very many of these, have perished and left no record save the echo of amazing or quaint sayings passed from mouth to mouth through the long years; or a blurred record of some desperately heroic deed, light-heartedly conceived and cunningly carried through to its triumphant end and dismissed with a jest. The unpredictable incidence of death or wounds was a mystery that gave the Irish full rein for sombre speculation. Half an hour's furious bombardment, with trenches blowing in by lengths at a time, would end in no more than extra fatigues for the disgusted working-parties that had to repair damage. On another day of still peace, one sudden light shell might mangle every man in a bay, and smear the duckboards with blood and horrors. A night-patrol, pinned down by a German flare, where they sprawled in the corn, and machine-gunned till their listening comrades gave up all hope, would tumble back at last into their own trenches unscathed, while far back in some sheltered corner the skied bullet, falling from a mile and a half away, would send a man to his account so silently that, till the body slid off the estaminet bench, his neighbours never guessed. The ironies and extravagances of Fate were so many, so absurd, and so terrible, that after a while human nature ceased to take conscious account of them or clutched at the smallest trifles that could change a mind's current. The surest anodyne and one that a prudent commanding Officer took care to provide was that all hands should have plenty to do. To repair a breach or to cut a fire-step was not enough. There was a standard in these matters to be lived up to, which was insisted upon through all the days of trench-warfare. None knew how long the deadlock would last or when the enemy, wearied of mining, bombs and heavy artillery, might attempt a break-through. When the first line was cleaned and consolidated and finished with what was deemed then ample dug-out accommodation, supporting parties behind it had to be brought up to a like level; and so on.

The enemy at that time, on that line, interfered very little. They rigged a searchlight on one of the brick-stacks in their possession one evening, but took it down after our guns had protested. Occasionally they shelled Béthune, while trying to hit an observation balloon near the town; and sometimes they bombed with trench-mortars. There were, however, days on end when nothing could stir them up, or when a few authoritative warnings from our guns would cut short a demonstration almost as it began. They were bombed for some hours to keep them out of the craters and to cover our men at work. In this work No. 4906 Private Henry won the D.C.M. in continuing to throw bombs though twice wounded (the Irish are gifted at hurling things), till he was at last ordered off the field. The enemy replied with everything except rifle-fire and in the darkness of a rainy night "his machine-guns caused some annoyance," till, after our artillery had failed to find them, the Battalion trench-mortars silenced them and allowed us to finish digging the new trenches and sap. The whole affair lasted four hours and was carried out by No. 1 Company, under Captain M. V. Gore-Langton, at the cost of 1 man killed, 1 officer, Lieutenant the Hon. H. A. V. Harmsworth, slightly wounded, and 7 men wounded.

On the 3rd August Lieutenant H. F. Law was sent out with a patrol to examine yet another mine-crater close to the two which the Battalion had occupied on its first night. He threw bombs into it, found it empty, and the Companies began at once to dig up to it from two points and make it all their own. The enemy "interfered" with the working-parties for a while but was bombed off. At daybreak he retaliated with a methodical bombardment along the line of seven-inch minenwerfers – one every three minutes – for an hour and a half. These could be seen dropping perpendicularly ere they exploded but they did no great damage, and the rest of the day was peaceful till a sudden thunder storm made everything and everybody abominably dirty. (Additional fatigues are always more resented than additional risks of death.)

When they came up again on the 6th August they found that an enemy mine in the orchard had exploded, wounded several of the Grenadiers whom they were relieving, and done damage to some of our own work. While they were making good, the Mining Company overheard Germans at work in a gallery a few feet from one of ours. The men were withdrawn at once from the forward line till dawn, when our mine was sprung "to anticipate enemy action." It might have injured some of the enemy's work, but it certainly disorganized several of our own sap-heads which had to be re-dug.

Into the variegated activities of that morning dropped a staff officer of the First Army Corps anxious to get the C.O.'s notes and instructions on mining for new troops who might later have to hold that line "in accordance with the manner taught by experience." Captain J. H. T. Priestman of the Lincoinshires, a Sandhurst instructor, arrived with him and was attached to the sector for a few days "to see how things were carried on." As he was being taken round the trenches by the C.O. and the Adjutant, next morning, a private, on sentry with a bomber, tried to throw a bomb on his own account, but, says the Diary, "not knowing how to, he blew himself up and wounded the bomber." By breakfast time the enemy were shelling the line in enfilade from the direction of Auchy and two men were blown to pieces. A couple of hours later the bombardment was repeated with, from first to last, 6 killed and 9 wounded. The instructor was but one of many whose unregarded duty was to study at first hand every device of the enemy in action and to lecture upon it at the training-centres in England a few days later.

The Battalion relieved the Grenadiers once more on the 10th August, after another German mine had been exploded on the salient, and had carried away so much German wire that it seemed possible to effect an entry into their trenches across the new-made crater. A patrol under Lieutenant A. F. L. Gordon was therefore sent out at night but reported the slopes too steep to climb and, since another mine had gone up and destroyed four of our own sap-heads with it, the night was spent in repairing these under intermittent bomb-fire on both sides.

On the 11th August fresh attempts were made to work some sort of foothold across the crater-pitted ground into the enemy's trenches, specially at the spot where a crater had been partially filled up by the explosion of a fresh mine.

The day was quiet. Captain M. V. Gore-Langton spent the evening of it in reconnoitring the enemy's wire, went out across the partly-filled crater, found yet another crater which ran into the enemy's line, and there met one German lying out within a few yards of him, whom Private Dempsey, his orderly, killed, thereby rousing the enemy in that particular point. They opened with bombs on a party of ours at work on a sap in one of the innumerable craters, and were discomfited the moment. An hour later, Captain Gore-Langton, with one man, went out for the second time across the same crater to put up some more wire. He fell into the arms of a German bombing party, was knocked down thrice by explosions of bombs around him and only got back to the trenches with great difficulty. The C.O., Colonel Trefusis, then "remonstrated" with him on the grounds that "it is not the Company Commander's business to go out wiring." On the heels of this enterprise, a really vicious fight with machine-guns as well as bombs developed in the dark. It was silenced by four rounds of our howitzers, when the roar of the bombs stopped as though by order. A third affair broke out just on dawn when our men found enemy working-parties in craters below them and bombed with them exceedingly, for the Germans were not good long-range throwers.

On the morning of the 12th August came General Home to look at the position, which he examined leisurely from every part of the line instead of merely through the covered loopholes which had been built for his convenience. "I was glad when I got him safely out of it," wrote the C.O., for one never knows when bombs may come over." Just before they were relieved, the C.O., Colonel Trefusis, was telephoned word that he was to command the 20th Brigade and was pathetically grieved at his promotion. He hated leaving the Battalion which, after eleven months of better or worse, he had come to look upon as his own. No man could possibly wish to command a better. He was going to a Brigade where he knew no one, and his hope was that he might be allowed to remain one day more with the Battalion "when it goes to the trenches" before going into Reserve. He had his wish when they went into the line on the 14th August, and he faced the ordeal, worse than war, of saying good-bye to each company in the morning, and at evening "went round to make sure that the night Companies had plenty of bombers in the proper places." Bombs were the one tool at that time which could deal with nests of occupied craters and since the work was dangerous the Irish were qualifying for it with zeal and interest, even though they occasionally dropped or released bombs by accident.

They were relieved (August 15) by a Battalion from the 5th Brigade, who "had heard all sorts of dreadful stories about the position." "But I told them," said Colonel Trefusis, "it was not so bad, provided their bombers kept on bombing at night. Mines, of course, one cannot help, and the only way to minimize their effect is to keep as few men in the front line as possible."

And so, Colonel the Hon. J. Trefusis passes out of the Battalion's story, to his new headquarters and his new staff and bombing officers, and his brand new troops, who "simply out of curiosity to see what was going on put their heads over the parapet while under instruction and so lost two men shot through the head, which I hope will be a lesson to them."

He had commanded the Battalion since November 1914, and no sudden occasion had found him wanting. The Diary says, "It is impossible to say all that he has done for the Battalion," and indeed, high courage unbroken humour, a cool head, skill, and infinite unselfishness are difficult things to set down in words. He was succeeded in the command by Major G. H. C. Madden, who arrived from England on the 16th August, when the Battalion was in rest at Béthune and the hands of their company and platoon officers were closing upon them to make sure once more that such untidy business as mining, counter-mining and crater-fighting had not diminished smartness on parade. This was doubly needful since the 4th (Guards) Brigade ceased, on the 19th August, to be part of the First Army and became the 1st Guards Brigade in the newly formed Guards Division of four Battalions Grenadiers, four Coldstream, two Scots, two Irish, and the Welsh Guards.

The 2nd Battalion of the Irish Guards, raised at Warley, left England for France on the 17th August.

Preparations on what was then considered an overwhelming scale were under way to break the German line near Loos while the French attacked seriously in the Champagne country; the idea being to arrive at the long-dreamed-of battle of manoeuvre in the plain of the Scheldt. Guns, gas-smoke apparatus and material had been collected during the summer lull; existing communications had been more or less improved, though the necessity for feeder-railways was not at all realized, tanks were not yet created, and the proportion of machine-guns to infantry was rather below actual requirements. As compared with later years our Armies were going into action with hammers and their bare hands across a breadth of densely occupied tunnelled and elaborately fortified mining country where, as one writer observed, "there is twice as much below ground as there is above." Consequently, for the third or fourth time within a twelvemonth, England was to learn at the cost of scores of thousands of casualties that modern warfare, unlike private theatricals, does not "come right at the performance" unless there have been rehearsals.

The training of the men in the forms of attack anticipated went forward energetically behind the front lines, together with arrangements for the massing and distribution of the seventy thousand troops of the First Army (First and Fourth Corps) assigned to the attack. For the next six weeks or so the Irish Guards were under instruction to that end, and the trenches knew them no more.

There was a formal leave-taking as they left Béthune for St. Hilaire, when the ex-4th (Guards) Brigade was played out of Béthune by the band of the 1st King's Liverpools and marched past General Home, commanding the Second Division, between lines of cheering men. A company of the trusty Herts Territorials, who had been with the Brigade since 1914, took part in the ceremony. It was repeated next day before Sir Douglas Haig at Campagne and again in the Central Square of St. Omer, when Sir John. French thanked all ranks for "the splendid services they had rendered" and was "much impressed with their soldier-like bearing."

Major-General Home's special farewell order ran as follows:

18th August 1915

The 4th (Guards) Brigade leaves the Second Division to-morrow. The G.O.C. speaks not only for himself, but for every officer, non-commissioned officer, and man of the Division when he expresses sorrow that certain changes in organization have rendered necessary the severance of ties of comradeship commenced in peace and cemented by war.

For the past year, by gallantry, devotion to duty, and sacrifice in battles and in the trenches the Brigade has maintained the high traditions of His Majesty's Guards and equally by thorough performance of duties, strict discipline, and the exhibition of many soldier-like qualities, has set an example of smartness which has tended to raise the standard and elevate the morale of all with whom it has been associated.

Major-General Home parts from Brigadier-General Feuding, the officers, non-commissioned officers, and men of the 4th (Guards) Brigade with lively regret – he thanks them for their loyal support, and he wishes them good fortune in the future.

(Sd.) .J.W. ROBINSON,

Lieut.-Colonel,

A.A. & Q.M.G. Second Division.

General Haig on the 20th August handed the following Special Order of the Day to the Brigade Commander:

HEADQUARTERS 1ST ARMY,

20th August 1915

The 4th (Guards) Brigade leaves my command to-day after over a year of active service in the field. During that time the Brigade has taken part in military operations of the most diverse kind and under very varied conditions of country and weather, and throughout all ranks have displayed the greatest fortitude, tenacity, and resolution.

I desire to place on record my high appreciation of the services rendered by the Brigade and my grateful thanks for the devoted assistance which one and all have given me during a year of strenuous work.

(Sd-) D. HAIG,

General Commanding 1st Army.

And the reward of their confused and unclean work among the craters and the tunnels of the past weeks came in the Commander-in-Chiefs announcement:

GUARDS DIVISION,

The Commander-in-Chief has intimated that he has read with great interest and satisfaction the reports of the mining operations and crater fighting which have taken place in the Second Division Area during the last two months.

He desires that his high appreciation of the good work performed be conveyed to the troops, especially to the 170th and 176th Tunnelling Cos. R.E., the 1st Battalion Irish Guards, the 1st Battalion K.R.R.C., and the 2nd Battalion South Staffordshire Regiment.

The G.O.C. Second Division has great pleasure in forwarding this announcement.

(Sd-)H. P. HORNE,
Major-General,
Commanding Second Division.

Second Division,
21.8.15.

They lay at Eperlecques for a day or two on their way to Thiembronne, a hot nineteen-mile march during which only five men fell out. It was at St. Pierre between Thiembronne and Acquin that they met and dined with the 2nd Battalion of the Regiment which had landed in France on the 18th August. There are few records of this historic meeting; for the youth and the strength that gathered by the cookers in that open sunlit field by St. Pierre has been several times wiped out and replaced. The two battalions conferred together, by rank and by age, on the methods and devices of the enemy, the veterans of the First enlightening the new hands of the Second with tales that could lose nothing in the telling, mixed with practical advice of the most grim. The First promptly christened the Second "The Irish Landsturm," and a young officer, who later rose to eminent heights and command of the 2nd Battalion, sat upon a table under some trees, and delighted the world with joyous songs upon a concertina and a mouth-organ. Then they parted.

LOOS

The next three weeks were spent by the 1st Battalion at or near Thiembronne in training for the great battle to come. They were instructed in march-discipline, infantry attack, extended-order drill and field-training, attacks on villages (Drionville was one of them selected and the French villagers attended the field-day in great numbers) as well as in bussing and debussing against time into motor-buses which were then beginning to be moderately plentiful. Regimental sports were not forgotten – they were a great success and an amusement more or less comprehensible to the people of Thiembronne – and, since the whole world was aware that a combined attack would be made shortly by the English and French armies, the officers of the Guards Brigade were duly informed by Lieutenant-General Haking commanding the Eleventh Army Corps, to which the Guards Division belonged, that such, indeed, was the case.

The domestic concerns of the Battalion during this pause include the facts that 2nd Lieutenant Dames-Longworth from the 2nd Middlesex was attached on the 9th September "prior to transfer" to the Irish Guards; Captain C. D. Wynter, Lieutenant F. H. Witts and 2nd Lieutenant W. B. Stevens were transferred (September 10) from the 1st to the 2nd Battalion, and 2nd Lieutenants T. K. Walker and T. H. Langrishe transferred on the same day from the 2nd to the 1st, while Orderly-Room Quarter-master-Sergeant J. Halligan, of whom later, was gazetted a 2nd Lieutenant to the Leinster Regiment. Captain L. R. Hargreaves was on the 13th "permitted to wear the badge of Captain pending his temporary promotion to that rank being announced in the *London Gazette*," and the C.O., Major G. H. C. Madden, was on the 6th September gazetted a temporary Lieutenant-Colonel. These were the first grants of temporary rank in the Battalion.

On the 18th September the C.O.'s of all the Battalions in the Guards Division motored to the Béthune district, where a reconnaissance was made "from convenient observation-posts" of the country between Cuinchy and Loos that they might judge the weight of the task before them.

It was a jagged, scarred and mutilated sweep of mining-villages, factories, quarries, slag-dumps, pitheads, chalk-pits and railway embankments – all the plant of an elaborate mechanical civilization connected above ground and below by every means that ingenuity and labour could devise to the uses of war. The ground was trenched and tunnelled with cemented and floored works of terrifying permanency that linked together fortified redoubts, observation-posts, concealed batteries, rallying-points and impregnable shelters for waiting reserves. So it ran along our front from Grenay north of the plateau of Notre Dame de Lorette, where two huge slag-heaps known as the Double Crassier bristled with machine-guns, across the bare interlude of crop land between Loos and Hulluch, where a high German redoubt crowned the slopes, to the village of Haisnes with the low and dangerous Hohenzollern Redoubt south of it. Triple lines of barbed wire protected a system of triple trenches, concrete-faced, holding dug-outs twenty feet deep, with lifts for machine-guns which could appear and disappear in emplacements of concrete over iron rails; and the observation-posts were capped with steel cupolas. In the background ample railways and a multitude of roads lay ready to launch fresh troops to any point that might by any chance be forced in the face of these obstacles.

Our Armies were brought up for the most part on their own feet, and lay in trenches not in the least concreted; nor were our roads to the front wholly equal to the demands on them. The assaulting troops were the First and Fourth Army Corps (less some troops detached to make a feint at Festubert and Cuinchy) disposed in the trenches south from the line of the Béthune – La Bassée Canal to the Vermelles – Hulluch road. Their work, as laid down, was to storm Auchy – La Bassée, Haisnes, capture the Hohenzollern Redoubt to the south-west of it and the immensely fortified Mine-head Pit 8 (with which it was connected), the Hulluch quarries, equally fortified, and the long strip of wood beside them, and the village of Cité St. Elie between Hulluch and Haisnes. South of the Vermelles – Hulluch road, the Fourth Army Corps was to occupy the high ground between Loos and Lens, including the redoubt on Hill 69; all the town of Loos, which was a museum of veiled deaths, the Double Crassier, the Chalk-Pit, the Redoubt on Hill 70 on the Loos – Haisnes road, and the village of Cité St. Auguste. After which, doubtless, the way would be open to victory. The Eleventh Army Corps formed the main infantry reserve and included the newly formed Guards Division, the Twenty-first and Twenty-fourth Divisions of the New Army and the Twenty-eighth. The Twenty-first and Twenty- fourth were brought up between Beuvry and Noeux-les-Mines; the Twenty-eighth to Bailleul, while the Guards Division lay in reserve near Lillers, ten miles north-west or so from Souchez; the Third Cavalry Division near Sains-en-Gohelle, and the British Cavalry Corps at Bailleul-les-Pernes ten miles west of Noeux-les-Mines, in attendance on the expected break-through.

On the 21st September the Battalion was inspected by Lord Kitchener at Avroult, on the St. Omer Road – the first time it was ever paraded before its Colonel-in-chief – who in a few brief words recalled what it had already done in the War and hinted at what lay before it. Lord Cavan commanding the Guards Division, in wishing the men God-speed on the eve of "the greatest battle in the world's history," reminded them that the fate of future generations hung on the issue and that great things were expected of the Guards Division. They knew it well enough.

By a piece of ill-luck, that might have been taken as an omen, the day before they moved from Thiembronne to the front, a bombing accident at practice caused the death of Lance-Sergeant R. Matthews and three men, which few casualties, on the eve of tens of thousands to come, were due subjects of a court of inquiry and a full report to Headquarters. Then they marched by Capelle-sur-Lys to Nedon in mist and gathering rain as the autumn weather broke on the 24th, and heard the roar of what seemed continuous bombardment from Vimy to La Bassée. But it was at dawn on the 25th September that the serious work of the heavy guns began, while the Division crawled in pouring rain along congested roads from Nedon to Noeux-les-Mines. All they could see of the battle-front was veiled in clouds of gas and the screens of covering smoke through which our attacks had been launched after two hours of preliminary bombardment. Our troops there found, as chance and accident decreed, either broken wire or half-obliterated trenches easy to overpass for a few hundred yards till they came to the uncut stuff before which the men perished as their likes had done on like fields. So it happened that day to the 6th Brigade of the First Division north of La Bassée, and the 19th Brigade south of it; to the 28th Brigade of the Ninth Division by the Hohenzollern Redoubt and Pit 8. These all met wire uncut before trenches untouched, and were slaughtered. The 26th Brigade of the Ninth Division broke through at a heavy cost as far as Pit 8, and, for the moment, as far as the edge of the village of Haisnes. The Seventh Division, working between the Ninth Division and the road from Vermelles to Hulluch, had better fortune. They penetrated as far as the edge of Hulluch village, but were driven back, ere the day's end, to the quarries a thousand yards in the rear. One Brigade, the 1st of the First Division of the Fourth Army on their right, had also penetrated as far as the outskirts of Hulluch. Its 2nd Brigade was hung up in barbed wire near Lone Tree to the southward, which check again exposed the left flank of the next (Fifteenth Highland) Division as that (44th, 45th, and 46th Brigades) made its way into Loos, carried Hill 70, the Chalk-Pit and Pit 14. The Forty-seventh Division on the extreme right of the British Line at its junction with the French Tenth Army had to be used mainly as a defensive flank to the operation, since the French attack, which should have timed with ours, did not develop till six hours after our troops had got away, and was then limited to Souchez and the Vimy Ridge.

At noon on the 25th September the position stood thus: the First Army Corps held up between the Béthune – La Bassée Canal and the Hohenzollern Redoubt; the Seventh Division hard pressed among the quarries and houses by Hulluch; the Ninth in little better case as regarded Pit 8 and the Redoubt itself the Highland Division pushed forward in the right centre holding on precariously in the shambles round Loos and being already forced back for lack of supports.

All along the line the attack had spent itself among uncut wire and unsubdued machine-gun positions. There were no more troops to follow at once on the heels of the first, nor was there time to dig in before the counter-attacks were delivered by the Germans, to whom every minute of delay meant the certainty of more available reserves fresh from the rail. A little after noon their pressure began to take effect, and ground won during the first rush of the advance was blasted out of our possession by gun-fire, bombing and floods of enemy troops arriving throughout the night.

Both sides were now bringing up reserves: but ours seem to have arrived somewhat more slowly than the Germans.

The Guards Division had come up on foot as quickly as the traffic on the roads allowed, and by the morning of the 26th the 1st Brigade (2nd Grenadiers, 2nd and 3rd Coldstream, and 1st Irish) were marched to Sailly-Labourse. The weather had improved, though the ground was heavy enough. Loos still remained to us, Hulluch was untaken. The enemy were well established on Hill 70 and had driven us out of Pit 14 and the Chalk-Pit Quarry on the Lens – La Bassée road which had been won on the previous day. It was this sector of the line to which the 2nd and 3rd Brigades of the Guards Division were directed. The local reserves (21st and 24th Divisions) had been used up, and as the Brigade took over the ground were retiring directly through them. The 1st Guards Brigade was employed in the work of holding the ground to the left, or north, of the other two Brigades. Their own left lay next what remained of the Seventh Division after the furious wastage of the past two days.

On the afternoon of the 26th September the 2nd and 3rd Coldstream, with the 2nd Grenadiers in support, occupied some trenches in a waste of cut-up ground east of a line of captured German trenches opposite Hulluch. The 1st Irish Guards lay in trenches close to the wrecked water-tower of the village of Vermelles, while the confused and irregular attacks and counter-attacks broke out along the line, slackened and were renewed again beneath the vault of the overhead clamour built by the passage of countless shells.

The field of battle presented an extraordinary effect of dispersion and detachment. Gas, smoke and the continuous splash and sparkle of bombs marked where the lines were in actual touch, but behind and outside this inferno stretched a desolation of emptiness, peopled with single figures "walking about all over the place," as one observer wrote, with dead and wounded on the ground, and casualties being slowly conveyed to dressing-stations – every one apparently unconcerned beneath shell-fire which in old-time battles would have been reckoned heavy, but which here, by comparison, was peace.

A premature burst of one of our own shells wounded four men of the Battalion's machine-gun group as it was moving along the Hulluch road, but there were no other casualties reported, and on Sunday 27th, while the village of Vermelles was being heavily shelled, No. 2 and half of No. 3 Company were sent forward to fetch off what wounded lay immediately in front of them on the battle-field. There was need. Throughout that long Sunday of "clearing up" at a slow pace under scattered fire, the casualties were but eleven in all – 2nd Lieutenant Grayling-Major, slightly wounded, one man killed and nine wounded. Three thousand yards to the left their 2nd Battalion, which, with the 2nd and 3rd Guards Brigades, had been set to recapture Pit 14 and Chalk-Pit Wood, lost that evening eight officers and over three hundred men killed and wounded. Officer-losses had been very heavy, and orders were issued, none too soon, to keep a reserve of them, specially in the junior ranks. Lieutenants Yerburgh and Rankin, with 2nd Lieutenants Law, Langrishe and Walker, were thus back to the first-line Transport to be saved for contingencies. Second Lieutenant Christy and twenty men from the base joined on the same day. The Battalion lay at that time behind the remnants of the 20th Brigade of the Seventh Division, whose Brigadier, Colonel the Hon. J. Trefusis, had been their old C.O. His Brigade, which had suffered between two and three thousand casualties, was in no shape for further fighting, but was hanging on in expectation of relief, if possible, from the mixed duties of trying to establish a line and sending out parties to assist in repelling the nearest counter-attack. Fighting continued everywhere, especially on the left of the line, and heavy rain added to the general misery.

By the 28th September we might have gained on an average three thousand yards on a front of between six and seven thousand, but there was no certainty that we could hold it, and the front was alive with reports – some true, others false – that the enemy had captured a line of trench here, broken through there, or was massing in force elsewhere. As a matter of fact, the worst of the German attacks had spent themselves, and both sides were, through their own difficulties, beginning to break off their main engagements for the bitter localized fightings that go to the making of a new front.

In rain, chalky slime and deep discomfort, after utter exhaustion, the broken battalions were comparing notes of news and imperturbably renewing their social life. Brigadier-General Trefusis slips, or wades, through rain and mud to lunch with his old Battalion a few hundred yards away, and one learns indirectly what cheer and comfort his presence brings. Then he goes on with the remnants of his shattered Brigade, to take over fresh work on a quieter part of the line and en route "to get his hair cut."

The Battalion, after (Sept. 29) another day's soaking in Vermelles trenches, relieved the 3rd Brigade, First Division, in front-line trenches just west of Hulluch.

The ground by Le Rutoire farm and Bois Carré between the battered German trenches was a sea of shell-craters and wreckage, scorched with fires of every sort which had swept away all landmarks. Lone Tree, a general rendezvous and clearing-station for that sector of the line and a registered mark for enemy guns, was the spot where their guides met them in the rainy, windy darkness. The relief took four hours and cost Drill-Sergeant Corry, another N.C.O., and a private wounded. All four Company Commanders went ahead some hours before to acquaint themselves with the impassable trenches, the Battalions being brought on, in artillery formation, by the Adjutant.

On the 30th September, the English losses having brought our efforts to a standstill, the troops of the Ninth French Army Corps began to take over the trenches defending Loos and running out of the ruins of that town to Hill 70. Foch and D'Untal in their fighting since the 27th had driven, at a price, the Germans out of Souchez, and some deceptive progress had been made by the Tenth French Army Corps up the Vimy heights to the right of the English line. In all, our Armies had manufactured a salient, some five miles wide across the bow of it, running from Cuinchy Post, the Hohenzollern Redoubt, the Hulluch Quarries, the edge of Hill 70, the south of Loos, and thence doubling back to Grenay. On the other hand, the enemy had under-driven a section south of this at the junction of the Allied forces running through Lens, Liévin, Angres, by Givenchy-en-Gohelle over the Vimy heights to the Scarpe below Arras. There may, even on the 30th, have remained some hope on our part of "breaking through" into the plain of the Scheldt, with its chance of open warfare to follow. The enemy, however, had no intention of allowing us any freedom of movement which localized attacks on his part could limit and hold till such time as his reserves might get in a counter-attack strong enough to regain all the few poor hundreds of yards which we had shelled, bombed and bayoneted out of his front. The fighting was specially severe that day among the rabbit-warrens of trenches by the Hohenzollern Redoubt. Sections of trenches were lost and won back or wiped out by gun-fire all along a front where, for one instance of recorded heroism among the confusion of bombs and barricades, there were hundreds unrecorded as the spouting earth closed over and hid all after-knowledge of the very site of the agony.

A section of trench held by the Scots Fusiliers on the immediate left of the Irish Guards was attacked and a hundred yards or so of it was captured, but the Battalion was not called upon to lend a hand. It lay under heavy shell and sniping fire in the wet, till it was time to exchange the comparative security of a wet open drain for the unsheltered horrors of a relief which, beginning in the dusk at six, was not completed till close on two in the morning. The last company reached their miserable billets at Mazingarbe, some three miles away across a well-searched back-area at 6 a.m. One N.C.O. was killed and ten N.C.O.'s and men were wounded.

They spent the next three days in the battered suburbs of Mazingarbe while the Twelfth Division took over the Guards' line and the Ninth French Army Corps relieved the British troops who were holding the south face of the Cuinchy – Hulluch – Grenay salient. The 1st Battalion itself was now drawn upon to meet the demands of the 2nd Battalion for officers to make good losses in their action of the 27th. Five officers, at least, were badly needed, but no more than four could be spared – Captain J. S. N. FitzGerald, as Adjutant, Lieutenant R. Rankin, Lieutenant H. Montgomery, who had only arrived with a draft on the 1st October, and 2nd Lieutenant Langrishe. Officers were a scarce commodity; for, though there was a momentary lull, there had been heavy bomb and trench work by the Twenty-eighth Division all round the disputed Hohenzollern Redoubt which was falling piece by piece into the hands of the enemy; and attacks were expected all along the uncertain line.

THE HOHENZOLLERN TRENCHES

On October 3 the Guards Division relieved the Twenty-eighth round the Hohenzollern and the Hulluch quarries. The 3rd Brigade of the Division was assigned as much of the works round the Hohenzollern as yet remained to us; the 1st Brigade lay on their right linking on to the First Division which had relieved the Twelfth on the right of the Guards Division. The 2nd Guards Brigade was in reserve at Vermelles. The 1st Battalion acted as reserve to its own, the 1st Brigade, and moving from Mazingarbe on the afternoon of the 3rd bivouacked in misery to the west of the railway line just outside Vermelles. The 2nd Grenadiers, in trenches which had formed part of the old British front line north-east of the Chapel of Notre Dame de Consolation, supported the 2nd and 3rd Coldstream who held the firing-line in a mass of unsurveyed and unknown German trenches running from St. Elie Avenue, a notorious and most dismal communication-trench, northwards towards the Hohenzollern Redoubt, one face of which generously enfiladed our line at all times. The whole was a wilderness of muck and death, reached through three thousand yards of foul gutters, impeded by loops and knots of old telephone cables, whose sides bulged in the wet, and where, with the best care in the world, reliefs could go piteously astray and isolated parties find themselves plodding, blind and helpless, into the enemy's arms.

Opinions naturally differ as to which was the least attractive period of the War for the Battalion, but there was a general feeling that, setting aside the cruel wet of The Salient and the complicated barren miseries of the Somme, the times after Loos round the Hohenzollern Redoubt and in the Laventie sector were the worst. Men and officers had counted on getting forward to open country at last, and the return to redoubled trench-work and its fatigues was no comfort to them. But the work had to be done, and the notice in the Diary that they were "responsible for improving and cleaning up the trenches as far as the support Battalions" – which meant as far as they could get forward – implied unbroken labour in the chalky ground, varied by carrying up supplies, bombs and small-arm ammunition to the front line. There were five bombing-posts in their sector of the front with as many sapheads, all to be guarded. Most of the trenches needed deepening, and any work in the open was at the risk of a continuous stream of bullets from the Hohenzollern's machine-guns. High explosives and a few gas-shells by day, aerial torpedoes by night, and sniping all round the clock, made the accompaniment to their life for the nine days that they held the line.

Here is the bare record. On the 6th October, two men killed and three wounded, while strengthening parapets. On the 7th, Lieutenant Heard and three men with him wounded, while superintending work in the open within range of the spiteful Hohenzollern. On the 8th, six hours unbroken bombardment, culminating, so far as the Battalion knew, in an attack on the 2nd Coldstream whom they were supporting and the 3rd Grenadiers on their left. The Grenadiers, most of their bombers killed, borrowed No. 1 Company's bombers, who "did good work," while No. 1 Company itself formed a flank to defend the left of the Brigade in case the Germans broke through, as for a time seemed possible. Both Grenadiers and Coldstream ran out of bombs and ammunition, which the Battalion sent up throughout the evening until it was reported that "all was normal again" and that the Germans had everywhere been repulsed with heavy loss. The Battalion then carried up rations to the Coldstream and spent the rest of the night repairing blown-in ammunition trenches. They had had no time to speculate or ask questions, and not till long afterwards did they realize that the blast of a great battle had passed over them; that the Germans had counter-attacked with picked battalions all along the line of the Cuinchy – Hulluch – Grenay Salient and that their dead lay in thousands on the cut-up ground from Souchez to Hohenzollern. In modern trench warfare any attack extending beyond the range of a combatant's vision, which runs from fifty yards to a quarter of a mile, according to the ground and his own personal distractions, may, for aught he can tell, be either an engagement of the first class or some local brawl for the details of which he can search next week's home papers in vain.

The Battalion got through the day with only six men killed, eleven wounded and one gassed, and on the 9th, when they were busiest in the work of repairing wrecked trenches, they were informed that certain recesses which they had been cutting out in the trenches for the reception of gas-cylinders would not be required and that they were to fill them in again. As a veteran of four years' experience put it, apropos of this and some other matters: "Men take more notice, ye'll understand, of one extra fatigue, than any three fights."

A few aerial torpedoes which, whether they kill or not, make unlimited mess, fell during the night, and on the morning of the 10th October Captain M. V. Gore-Langton – one of the Battalion's best and most efficient officers – was shot through the head and killed by a German sniper while looking for a position for a loophole in the parapet. He was buried six hours later in the British Cemetery at Vermelles, and the command of his company devolved on Lieutenant Yerburgh. Our own artillery spent the day in breaking German wire in front of the Hulluch quarries at long range and a little more than a hundred yards ahead of our trenches. Several of our shells dropped short, to the discomfort of the Irish, but the wire was satisfactorily cut, and two companies kept up bursts of rapid fire during the night to stay the enemy from repairing it. Only five men were killed and five wounded from all causes this day.

On the 11th our guns resumed wire-cutting and, besides making it most unpleasant for our men in the front trenches, put one of our own machine-guns out of action, but luckily with no loss of life.

The tragedy of the day came later when, just after lunch, a shell landed in the doorway of Headquarters dug-out, breaking both of Colonel Madden's legs, and mortally wounding the Rev. Father John Gwynne, the Battalion's R.C. chaplain (Colonel Madden died in England a few weeks later). The Adjutant, Lord Desmond FitzGerald, was slightly wounded also. The other two occupants of the dug-out, Captain Bailie, who had gone through almost precisely the same experience in the same spot not three days before, and the Medical Officer, were untouched. It was difficult to get two wounded men down the trenches to the Headquarters of the supporting Battalion, where they had to be left till dark. And then they were carried back in the open – or "over-land" as the phrase was. Father Gwynne died next day in hospital at Béthune, and the Battalion lost in him "not merely the chaplain, but a man unusually beloved." He had been with them since November of the previous year. He feared nothing, despised no one, betrayed no confidence nor used it to his own advantage; upheld authority, softened asperities, and cheered and comforted every man within his reach. If there were any blemish in a character so utterly selfless, it was no more than a tendency, shared by the servants of his calling, to attach more importance to the administration of the last rites of his Church to a wounded man than to the immediate appearance of the medical officer, and to forget that there are times when Supreme Unction can be a depressant. *Per contra*, Absolution at the moment of going over the top, if given with vigour and good cheer, as he gave it, is a powerful tonic. At all times the priest's influence in checking "crime" in a regiment is very large indeed, and with such priests as the Irish Guards had the good fortune to possess, almost unbounded.

Colonel Madden was succeeded by Captain Lord De FitzGerald as Commanding Officer, and the rest of the day was spent in suffering a bombardment of aerial torpedoes, very difficult to locate and not put down by our heavy guns till after dark. Besides the three wounded officers that day three men were wounded and three killed.

On the morning of the 13th, after heavy shelling, a bomb attack on the 2nd Grenadiers developed in the trenches to the right, when the Battalion brought up and detonated several boxes for their comrades. Their work further included putting up 120 scaling-ladders for an attack by the 35th Brigade.

. . . the Battalion lost in Father Gwynne "not merely the chaplain, but a man unusually beloved" . . . He feared nothing, despised no one, betrayed no confidence . . . and comforted every man within his reach.

Father Gwynne at Le Préol, March 1915.

Next day they were relieved by the 7th Norfolks, 35th Brigade of the North Midland Division of Territorials, and went to rest at Verquin, five or six miles behind the line. It took them nearly seven hours to clear the trenches; Colonel Madden, on account of his wounds, being carried out on a sitting litter; Lord Desmond FitzGerald, who, as Adjutant, had been wounded when Father Gwynne had been killed, overdue for hospital with a piece of shrapnel in his foot, and all ranks utterly done after their nine days' turn of duty. They laid them down as tired animals lie, while behind them the whole north front of the Cuinchy – Hulluch Salient broke into set battle once again.

A series of holding attacks were made all along the line almost from Ypres to La Bassée to keep the enemy from reinforcing against the real one on the Hohenzollern Redoubt, Fosse 8, the Hulluch Quarries and the heart of the Loos position generally. It was preceded by bombardments that in some cases cut wire and in some did not, accompanied by gas and smoke, which affected both sides equally. It was carried through by men in smoke-helmets, half-blinding them among blinding accompaniments of fumes and flying earth, through trenches to which there was no clue, over the wrecks of streets of miners' cottages, cellars and underground machine-gun nests, and round the concreted flanks of unsuspected artillery emplacements. Among these obstacles, too, it died out with the dead Battalions of Regulars and Territorials caught, as the chances of war smote them, either in bulk across open ground or in detail among bombs and machine-gun posts.

There was here, as many times before, and very many times after, heroism beyond belief, and every form of bravery that the spirit of man can make good. The net result of all, between the 27th of September and the 15th of October, when the last ground-swell of the long fight smoothed itself out over the unburied dead, was a loss to us of 50,000 men and 2000 officers, and a gain of a salient seven thousand yards long and three thousand two hundred yards deep. For practical purposes, a good deal of this depth ranked as "No Man's Land" from that date till the final break-up of the German hosts in 1918. The public were informed that the valour of the new Territorial Divisions had justified their training, which seemed expensive; and that our Armies, whatever else they lacked at that time and it was not a little – had gained in confidence: which seemed superfluous.

AFTER LOOS

But the Battalion lay at Verquin, cleaning up after its ten days' filth, and there was Mass on the morning of the 14th, when Father S. Knapp came over from the 2nd Battalion and "spoke to the men on the subject of Father Gwynne's death," for now that the two Battalions were next-door neighbours, Father Knapp served both. No written record remains of the priest's speech, but those who survive that heard it say it moved all men's hearts. Mass always preceded the day's work in billets, but even on the first morning on their return from trenches the men would make shift somehow to clean their hands and faces, and if possible to shave, before attending it, no matter what the hour.

Then on the 14th October they moved from Verquin to unpleasing Sailly-Labourse, four miles or so behind the line, for another day's "rest" in billets, and so (Oct. 17) to what was left of Vermelles, a couple of miles from the front, where the men had to make the wrecked houses habitable till (Oct. 19) they took over from the Welsh Guards some reserve-trenches on the old ground in front of Clerk's Keep, a quarter of a mile west of the Vermelles railway line.

The 20th October was the day when the 2nd Battalion were engaged in a bombing attack on the Hohenzollern, from which they won no small honour, as will be told in their story. The 1st Battalion lay at Vermelles, unshelled for the moment, and had leisure to make "light overhead cover for the men against the rain." The Division was in line again, and the Battalion's first work was to improve a new line of trenches which, besides the defect of being much too close to the Hohenzollern, lacked dug-outs. In Lord Desmond FitzGerald's absence, Major the Hon. H. R. Alexander from the 2nd Battalion took command of the Battalion, and they relieved the 2nd Coldstream on the 21st and resumed the stale routine – digging saps under fire, which necessitated shovelling the earth into sand bags and emptying it out by night; dodging snipers and trench-mortars, and hoping that our own shells, which were battering round the Hohenzollern, would not fall too short; fixing wire and fuses till the moon grew and they had to wait for the dawn-mists to cloak their work; discovering and reconnoitring old German communication-trenches that ran to ever-new German sniping-posts and had to be blocked with wire tangles; and losing in three days, by minenwerfers, sniping, the fall of dug-outs and premature bursts of our own shells, 7 men killed and 18 wounded. The two (1 and 2) went back to Vermelles, while 3 and 4 took over the support-trenches from the 3rd Coldstream, reversing the process on the 24th October.

When letters hint at "drill" in any connection, it is a sure sign that a Battalion is on the eve of relief. For example, on the 24th, 2nd Lieutenant Levy arrived with a draft of fifty-eight men, a sergeant and two corporals, who were divided among the companies. The Diary observes that they were a fair lot of men but "did not look too well drilled." Accordingly, after a couple of days' mild shelling round and near Vermelles Church and Shrine, we find the Battalion relieved by the Norfolks (Oct. 26). All four companies worked their way cautiously out of the fire-zone – it is at the moment of relief that casualties are most felt – picked up their Headquarters and transport, and marched for half of a whole day in the open to billets at pleasant, wooded Lapugnoy, where they found clean straw to lie down on and were promised blankets. After the usual clean up and payment of the men, they were ordered off to Chocques to take part in the King's Review of the Guards Division at Haute Rièze on the afternoon of the 28th, but, owing to the accident to His Majesty caused by his horse falling with him, the parade was cancelled.

"Steady drill" filled the next ten days. Lieutenant the Hon. B. O'Brien started to train fresh bombing-squads with the Mills bomb, which was then being issued in such quantities that as many as twenty boxes of them could be spared for instruction. Up till then, bombs had been varied in type and various in action. As has been pointed out, the Irish took kindly to this game and produced many notable experts. But the perfect bomber is not always docile out of the line. Among the giants of 15 was a private against whom order had gone forth that on no account was he to be paid on pay-days, for the reason that once in funds he would retire into France at large "for a day and a night and a morrow," and return a happy, hiccuping but indispensable "criminal." At last, after a long stretch of enforced virtue, he managed, by chicane or his own amazing personality, to seduce five francs from his platoon Sergeant and forthwith disappeared. On his return, richly disguised, he sought out his benefactor with a gift under his arm. The rest is in his Sergeant's own words: "'No,' I says, 'go away and sleep it off,' I says, pushin' it away, for 'twas a rum jar he was temptin' me with. ' 'Tis for you, Sergeant,' he says. ' You're the only man that has thrusted me with a centime since summer.' Thrust him ! There was no sergeant of ours had not been remindin' me of those same five francs *all* the time he'd been away – let alone what I'd got at Company Orders. So I loosed myself upon him, an' I described him to himself the way he'd have shame at it; but shame was not in him. 'Yes, Sergeant,' he says to me, ' full I am, and *this* is full too,' he says, pattin' the rum jar (and it was!), 'an' I know where there's plenty more,' he says, ' and it's all for you an' your great trustfulness to me about them five francs.' What could I do? He'd made me a laughing-stock to the Battalion. An awful man! He'd done it all on those five unlucky francs! Yes, he'd lead a bombin' party or a drinkin' party – his own or any other Battalion's; and he was worth a platoon an' a half when there was anything doing, and I thrust in God he's alive yet – him and his five francs! But an awful man!"

Drunkenness was confined, for the most part, to a known few characters, regular and almost privileged in their irregularities. The influence of the Priest and the work of the Company Officers went hand in hand here. Here is a tribute paid by a brother officer to Captain Gore-Langton, killed on the 10th October, which explains the secret. "The men liked him for his pluck and the plain way in which he dealt with them, always doing his best for the worst, most idle, and stupidest men in our company. . . . One can't really believe he's gone. I always expect to see him swinging round a traverse." The Battalion did not forget him, and while at Lapugnoy, sent a party to Vermelles to attend to his grave there.

On the 31st October Lieut.-Colonel R. C. McCalmont arrived from commanding a Battalion of the New Ulster Army Division and took over the command from Major Alexander, who reverted to the 2nd Battalion, from which he had been borrowed.

LAVENTIE

On the 10th of the month the Guards Division were for duty again on the Laventie sector, which at every time of the year had a bad reputation for wet. The outcome of Loos had ended hope of a break-through, and a few thousand yards won there against a few thousand lost out Ypres way represented the balance of the account since November 1914. Therefore, once again, the line had to be held till more men, munitions and materials could be trained, manufactured and accumulated, while the price of making war on the spur of the moment was paid, day in and day out, with the bodies of young men subject to every form of death among the slits in the dirt along which they moved. It bored them extremely, but otherwise did not much affect their morale. They built some sort of decent life out of the monotonous hours; they came to know the very best and the very worst in themselves and in their comrades upon whom their lives and well-being depended; and they formed friendships that lasted, as fate willed, for months or even years. They lied persistently and with intent in their home letters concerning their discomforts and exposure, and lent themselves to the impression, cultivated by some sedulous newspapers, that the trenches were electrically-lighted abodes of comfort and jollity, varied with concerts and sports. It was all part of the trial which the national genius calls "the game."

The Battalion (Lieut.-Colonel R. McCalmont commanding was at Pacaut, due north of Béthune, on the 11th, at Merville on the 14th, training young soldiers how to use smoke helmets – for gas was a thing to be expected anywhere now – and enjoying every variety of weather, from sodden wet to sharp frost. The effects of the gas-helmet on the young soldiers were quaintly described as "very useful on them. 'Twas like throwin' a cloth over a parrot-cage. It stopped *all* their chat."

On the 20th November they took over reserve-billets from the 1st Scots Guards near Bout Deville, and the next day, after inspection of both Battalions by General Feilding, commanding the Division, and the late Mr. John Redmond, M.P., went into trenches with the happy fore-knowledge that they were likely to stay there till the 2nd of January and would be lucky if they got a few days out at Christmas. It was a stretch of unmitigated beastliness in the low ditch-riddled ground behind Neuve Chapelle and the Aubers Ridge, on the interminable La Bassée – Estaires road, with no available communication-trenches, in many places impassable from wet, all needing sand-bags, and all "in a very neglected state, except for the work done by the 2nd Guards Brigade the week before the Battalion moved in." (It is nowhere on record that the Guards Division, or for that matter, any other, was ever contented with trenches that it took over.) The enemy, however, were quiet, being at least as uncomfortable as our people. Even when our field-guns blew large gaps in their parapets a hundred yards away there was very little retaliation, and our casualties on relief – the men lay in scattered billets at Riez Bailleul three miles or so up the road – were relatively few.

In one whole week not more than four or five men were killed and fifteen or sixteen wounded, two of them by our own shrapnel bursting short while our guns experimented on block-houses and steel cupolas, as these revealed themselves. Even when the Prince of Wales visited the line at the Major-General's inspection of it, and left by the only possible road, "Sign Post Lane," in broad daylight in the open, within a furlong of the enemy, casualties did not occur! There is no mention, either, of any of the aeroplane-visitations which sometimes followed his appearances. As a personal friend of one of the officers, he found reason to visit along that sector more often than is officially recorded.

At the beginning of the month the 1st Guards Brigade was relieved by the 3rd of its Division, and the Battalion handed its line over to the 4th Grenadiers, not without some housewifely pride at improvements it had effected. But, since pride ever precedes a fall, the sharp frost of the past week dissolved in heavy rain, and the neat new-made breastworks with their aligned sand-bags collapsed. If the 4th Grenadiers keep veracious diaries, it is probable that that night of thaw and delayed reliefs is strongly recorded in them.

La Gorgue, under Estaires, upon the sluggish Lys in sodden wet weather (December 3-8) gave them a breathing space for a general wash-up and those "steady drills" necessary to mankind. The new stretch that they took over from their own 2nd Battalion was about two miles north of their previous one and south-east of Laventie, running parallel to the Rue Tilleloy, that endless road, flanked, like all others hereabouts, with farmhouses, which joins Armentières to Neuve Chapelle. The ground was, of course, sop, the parapets were perforable breastworks, but reliefs could arrive unobserved within five hundred yards of the front, and the enemy's line lay in most places nearly a quarter of a mile from ours. More important still, there was reasonable accommodation for Battalion Headquarters in a farm-house (one of the many "Red Houses" of the war) which, by some accident, had been untouched so far, though it stood less than a mile from the front line. Where Headquarters are comfortable, Headquarters are happy, and by so much the more placable. Only very young soldiers grudge them protection and warmth.

For a few days it was a peaceful stretch of the great line that buttressed on Switzerland and the sea. Christmas was coming, and, even had the weather allowed it, neither side was looking too earnestly for trouble.

A Company of Welsh Fusiliers with their C.O. and Adjutant came up for eight days' instruction, and were distributed through the Battalion. The system in the front line at that moment was one of gangs of three, a digger, an armed man, and a bomber, relieving each other by shifts; and to each of these trios one Welshman was allotted.

The Welsh were small, keen and inquisitive. The large Irish praised their Saints aloud for sending them new boys to talk to through the long watches. It is related of one Welshman that, among a thousand questions, he demanded if his tutor had ever gone over the top. The Irishman admitted that he had. "And how often does one go over?" the Welshman continued. "I'll show you. Come with me," replied the other Celt, and, moving to a gap in the parapet, lifted the Welshman in his arms that he might the better see what remained, hung up in German wire, of a private of some ancient fight – withered wreckage, perhaps, of Neuve Chapelle. "*He* went over wanst," said the Irishman. The working-party resumed their labours, and men say that that new boy put no more questions "for the full of the half of an hour – an' that's as long as a week to a Welshman."

All four companies were held in the first line except for three posts – Picantin, Dead End and Hougoumont – a few hundred yards behind that were manned with a platoon apiece, but on the 12th December rumours of a mine made it wise to evacuate a part of the right flank till one of our 9·2's should have searched for the suspected mine-shaft. Its investigations roused the enemy to mild retaliation, which ended next day in one of our men being wounded by our own 9·2, and three by the enemy's shrapnel – the first casualties in four days.

The wet kept the peace along the line, but it did not altogether damp the energies of our patrols. For a reason, not explained officially, Lieutenant S. E. F. Christy was moved to go out with a patrol and to hurl into the German lines a printed message (was it the earliest workings of propaganda?) demanding that the Germans "should surrender." There is no indication whether the summons was to the German army at large or merely to as many of them as lay before the Battalion; but, the invitation being disregarded, Lieutenants Christy and Law made themselves offensive in patrol-work to the best of their means. On one excursion, the latter officer discovered (December 15) a water-logged concrete-built loophole dug-out occupied by Germans. Being a hardened souvenir-hunter, he is reported to have removed the official German name-board of the establishment ere he went back for reinforcements with a view to capturing it complete. On his return he found it abandoned. The water had driven the enemy to a drier post, and the cutting-out expedition had to be postponed. Too long in the line without incident wears on every one's temper, but luck was against them and an attempt on the 20th December by a "selected party" under some R.E.'s and Lieutenants Law and Christy was ruined by the moonlight and the fact that the enemy had returned to their concrete hutch and were more than on the alert. By the light of later knowledge the Battalion was inclined to believe that the dug-out had been left as bait and that there were too many spies in our lines before Laventie.

On the 21st December the Battalion came out for Christmas and billeted at Laventie, as their next turn would be in the old sector that they had handed over to the 4th Grenadiers three weeks ago. The same Battalion relieved them on this day, and, as before, were an hour late in turning up – a thing inexcusable except on one's own part.

Their Adjutant's preoccupations with officers sick and wounded; N.C.O.'s promoted to commissions in line battalions, and the catching and training of their substitutes; and with all the housekeeping work of a Battalion in the field, had not prevented him from making strict and accurate inquiries at

Headquarters as to "what exactly is being sent out for Christmas Day. Is it plum-pudding only or sausages alone? Last year we had both, but I should like to know for certain."

All things considered (and there was no shelling), Christmas dinner at La Gorgue 1915 was a success, and "the C.O. and other officers went round the dinners as at home" in merciful ignorance that those of them who survived would attend three more such festivals.

Major-General Lord Cavan, Commanding the Guards Division, who had been appointed to command the newly formed Fourteenth Corps,[1] addressed the officers after dinner and half-promised them the Christmas present they most desired. He spoke well of the Battalion, as one who had seen and shared their work had right to do, saying that "there might be as good, but there were none better," and added that "there was just a hope that the Guards Division might eventually go to his Corps." They cheered.

The quiet that fell about Christmastide held till the birth of the New Year, which the inscrutable Hun mind celebrated punctually on the hour (German time) with twenty minutes' heavy machine-gun and rifle fire in the darkness. One killed and one wounded were all their casualties.

Here is the roll of the Officers and Staff of the Battalion as the year ended in mud, among rotten parapets and water-logged trenches, with nothing to show for all that had gone before save time gained and ground held to allow of preparation for the real struggle, on the edge of which these thousand soldiers and all their world stood ignorant but unshaken.

Lieut.-Colonel R. C. A. McCalmont	Commanding Officer.
Major Lord Desmond FitzGerald	Adjutant.
Lieut. T. E. G. Nugent	a./Adjutant.
Hon. Lieut. H. Hickie	Quartermaster.
Capt. P. H. Antrobus	Transport.
Lieut. C. Pease	Brigade Company.
Lieut. L. C. Whitefoord	Brigade Company.
Lieut. J. Grayling-Major	Depot.
Capt. Rev. A. H. A. Knapp, O.P	Chaplain.
Capt. P. R. Woodhouse, R.A.M.C.	Medical Officer.
No. 108 Sgt.-Major J. Kirk	Sgt.-Major.
No. 176 Q.M.S. J. M. Payne	Q.M.S.
No. 918 Drill-Sgt. T. Cahill	Senior Drill-Sgt.
No. 2666 Drill-Sgt. G. Weeks	Junior Drill-Sgt.
No. 1134 O.R.Cr.-Sgt. P. Matthews	Orderly-Room Sgt. at Base.
No. 3933 Sgt-Dr. W. Cherry	Sgt.-Drummer.

---

[1] He was succeeded by Major-General Feuding in command of the Guards Division; Brigadier-General Pereira commanding the 1st Guards Brigade

No. 1119 Sgt. R. Nugent — a./Pioneer-Sgt.
No. 837 Armr.-Q.M.S.S. Bradley — Armr.-Q.M.S.
No. 3874 Sgt. M. Greaney — Transport-Sgt.
No. 4166 Sgt. J. Fawcett — Signalling-Sgt.
No. 2900 Sgt. P. J. Curtis — Orderly-Room Clerk.

No. 1 Company

Capt. R. G. C. Yerburgh — (3726 C.Q.M.S. P. M'Goldrick.)
Lieut. D. J. B. FitzGerald — 3303 a./C.Q.M.S. J. Glynn.
2562 C.S.M. P. A. Carroll

No. 2 Company

Capt. V. C. J. Blake — 3949 C.S.M. D. Voyles.
Lieut. C. E. R. Hanbury — 999 C.Q.M.S. H. Payne.

No. 3 Company

Capt. T. M. D. Bailie — (2112 C.S.M. H. M'Veigh.)
Capt. A. F. L. Gordon — 3972 C.Q.M.S. R. Grady.
Lieut. S. E. F. Christy — 2922 a./C.S.M. J. Donolly.
Lieut. K. E. Dormer.

No. 4 Company.

Capt. P. S. Long-Innes — 2nd Lieut. M. B. Levy.
Lieut. Hon. H. B. O'Brien — 3632 C.S.M. M. Moran.
  (Bombing Officer) — (2122 C.Q.M.S. T. Murphy.)
Lieut. R. J. P. Rodakowski — 798 a./C.Q.M.S. J. Scanlon.

1916

THE SALIENT
TO THE SOMME

BRIGADIER-GENERAL G. FEILDING, D.S.O., as we know, succeeded Lord Cavan in the command of the Guards Division, and the enemy woke up to a little more regular shelling and sniping for a few days till (January 4) the 1st Guards Brigade was unexpectedly relieved by a fresh Brigade (the 114th), and the Battalion moved to billets in St. Floris which, as usual, were "in a very filthy condition." There they stayed, under strong training at bombing and Lewis-gunnery, till the 12th. Thence to Merville till the 23rd, when Lieutenant Hon. H. B. O'Brien, a specialist in these matters, as may have been noticed before, was appointed Brigade Bombing Officer. The bomb was to be the dominant factor of the day's work for the next year or so, and the number of students made the country round billets unwholesome and varied. There is a true tale of a bombing school on a foggy morning who, hurling with zeal over a bank into the mist, found themselves presently being cursed from a safe distance by a repairing party who had been sent out to discover why one whole system of big-gun telephone-wires was dumb. They complained that the school had "cut it into vermicelli."

The instruction bore fruit; for, so soon as they were back in the trenches at Ebenezer Farm, which they had quitted on the 4th, bombing seems to have been forced wherever practicable. A weak, or it might be more accurate to say, a sore point had developed on the front in a crater thrown up by one of our own mines, which it was necessary to sap out to and protect by intermittent bombing. This brought retaliation and a few casualties nightly. A trench-mortar battery was imported to deal with the nuisance and, as might be expected, drew the enemy's artillery.

On the 28th January a single stray bullet in the dark found and killed Captain V. C. J. Blake, No. 2 Company, while he was laying out some work in wire for his company; and a bombing attack round the mine-crater ended in three other ranks killed and one wounded.

On February 1 our mine-shaft in the same locality flooded without warning and drowned a couple of men in a listening-post. Our pumps could make no impression on the water; it was difficult to put up any head-cover for the men in the forward sap, and the enemy's wire was being strengthened nightly and needed clearing away. This was routine-work undertaken by our artillery who blew gaps in it in three places, which the Battalion covered with machine-gun fire. It kept the enemy reasonably quiet, and H.R.H. Prince Albert, who was out on a tour from England, breakfasted with Battalion Headquarters the same morning (February 5). Once again the enemy's information must have been inaccurate or delayed since there is no mention of any shelling or aeroplane work on Headquarters.

They came out of the line on the 7th and billeted near Merville. Reckoned by their standards it had been an uneventful stretch of duty, and those officers who could be spared had gone on short leave; for there was a rumour that leave would be stopped after the 20th of the month. The French and their English allies knew well that the great German attack on Verdun was ripening (it opened in the third week of February), and the world had no doubt of the issues that depended upon that gate to the heart of France holding fast. The whole long line stiffened to take the weight of any sudden side-issue or main catastrophe that the chance of war might bring about. But a Battalion among hundreds of Battalions knows as little what its own movements mean as a single truck in a goods yard knows of the import and export trade of Great Britain. The young officers snatched their few hours' leave at home, loyally told their people that all was going well, returned – "to a most interesting lecture on the Battle of Neuve Chapelle," delivered at La Gorgue by a Divisional Staff Officer, and to an inspection of the 1st Guards Brigade by Lord Kitchener on a vile wet day when they were all soaked to the skin (February 10), and "to the usual routine in very poor weather."

Lord Desmond FitzGerald, being now Second in Command by seniority, resigned his adjutancy and was succeeded by Lieutenant T. E. G. Nugent; No. 2, Captain Blake's, Company was commanded by Major the Hon. A. C. S. Chichester, fresh from home, and Father S. Knapp, their priest, who had been transferred to the 1st London Irish, was followed by Father J. Lane-Fox from the same Battalion. Of the six Fathers who served the two Battalions, two – Fathers Gwynne and S. Knapp, D.S.O., M.C. – were killed, one – Father F. M. Browne, M.C. – wounded twice, and one – Father F. S. Browne, M.C. – wounded once.

On the face of it nothing could have been quieter and more domestic than their daily life round Merville, and after a week of it they were moved (February 16) north towards Steenvoorde, in a hurricane of wind and rain, to the neighbourhood of Poperinghe, on the Ypres – Poperinghe – Dunkirk road, and a camp of tents, mostly blown down, and huts, connected, for which small ease they were grateful, by duck-boards. This brought them into the Second Army area and into the Fourteenth Corps under Lord Cavan, precisely as that officer had hoped. He explained to them there was "a small German offensive" on the left of the line here, and that "if it came to anything" the Brigade might be wanted.

The "small offensive" had opened on the 13th with a furious bombardment of the extreme southern end of the Ypres Salient between the Ypres – Comines Canal and Ypres – Comines railway, a little to the south of Hill 60, followed by the springing of five mines under the British front line and an infantry attack, which ended in the capture by the enemy of four or five hundred yards of trench and the low ridge called "The Bluff," over which they ran. The affair bulked big in the newspaper-press of the day; for a battalion, the 10th Lancashire Fusiliers, was literally buried by one of the mine explosions. The German gain was well held, but prevented from extending by a concentration of our artillery, and later on (March 2) the whole position was recaptured after desperate fighting and the line there came to rest.

For the first time the Battalion seems impressed by the hostile aircraft with which The Salient was filled. Poperinghe and Hazebrouck were bombed almost as soon as they came in, and their camp was visited by four aeroplanes at high noon, after a snowfall, which showed up everything below. They had been attending a demonstration to prove the harmlessness of a flammenwerfer if only one lay flat on the ground and let the roaring blast hiss over. Ribald men have explained, since, that these demonstrations were more demoralizing than the actual machine in action, especially when, as occasionally happened, the nozzle of the flame-shooter carried away and, in the attempts to recontrol the thing, the class, bombed from above and chased by fire below, broke and fled.

But the whole Salient was a death-trap throughout. The great shells crossed each other's path at every angle, back and forth, single or in flights. For no certain cause that our line could guess, fire would concentrate itself on some half-obliterated feature of the landscape – a bank, the poor stumpage of a wood, a remnant of a village or the angle of a road, that went out in smoke, dust and flying clods, as though devils were flinging it up with invisible spades. The concentrated clamours would die down and cease; the single shells would resume their aimless falling over a line of fields, with the monotony of drips from a tap, till, again, it seemed as though one of them had found something worthy of attention and shouted back the news to its fellows who, crowding altogether in one spot, roared, overturned, and set alight for five or ten wild minutes or through a methodical half-hour. If the storm fell on bare ground, that was churned and torn afresh into smoking clods; if upon men in trenches, on relief, or with the transport, no eye could judge what harm had been done; for often where it had seemed as though nothing could live, dispersed units picked themselves up and reformed, almost untouched, after inconceivable escapes. Elsewhere, a few spurts of stinking smoke in a corner might cover all that remained of a platoon, or have ripped the heart out of a silent, waiting company. By night, fantastic traceries of crossing fire-lines ran along the shoulder of a ridge; shrapnel, bursting high, jetted a trail of swift sparks, as it might be steel striking flint; dropping flares outlined some tortured farm-house among its willow-stumps, or the intolerable glare of a big shell framed itself behind a naked doorway; and coloured lights dyed the bellies of the low clouds till all sense of distance and direction was lost, and the bewildered troops stumbled and crawled from *pavé* to pot-hole, treading upon their old dead.

Dawn brought dirty white desolation across yellow mud pitted with slate-coloured water-holes, and confused by senseless grey and black lines and curled tangles of wire. There was nothing to see, except – almost pearl-coloured under their mud-dyed helmets – the tense, preoccupied faces of men moving with wide spaces between their platoons, to water-floored cellars and shelters chillier even than the grave-like trenches they had left, always with the consciousness that they were watched by invisible eyes which presently would choose certain of them to be killed. Those who came through it, say that the sense of this brooding Death more affected every phase of life in The Salient than in any other portion of the great war-field.

The German offensive on the Bluff and the necessary measures of retaliation did not concern the Battalion for the moment. After a few days' aimless waiting they were sent, in bitter cold and snow, to rest-camp at Calais for a week. They were seven hours slipping and sliding along the snow-covered roads ere they could entrain at Bavichore Street, and untold hours detraining at the other end; all of which annoyed them more than any bombing, even though the C.O. himself complimented them on their march "under very trying circumstances." The Irish, particularly in their own Battalions, have not the relief of swearing as other races do. Their temperament runs to extravagant comparisons and appeals to the Saint, and ordinary foul language, even on night-reliefs in muddy trenches choked with loose wires and corpses, is checked by the priests. But, as one said "What we felt on that cruel Calais road, skatin' into each other, an' – an' apologizin', would have melted all the snows of Europe that winter."

Bombing instruction and inter-platoon bombing matches on Calais beach kept them employed.

On March 3, during practice with live bombs, one exploded prematurely, as several others of that type had done in other battalions, and Major Lord Desmond FitzGerald was so severely wounded that he died within an hour at the Millicent Sutherland (No. 9 Red Cross) Hospital. Lieutenant T. E. G. Nugent was dangerously wounded at the same time through the liver, though he did not realize this at the time, and stayed coolly in charge of a party till help came. Lieutenant Hanbury, who was conducting the practice, was wounded in the hand and leg, and Father Lane-Fox lost an eye and some fingers.

Lord Desmond FitzGerald was buried in the public cemetery at Calais on the 5th. As he himself had expressly desired, there was no formal parade, but the whole Battalion, of which he was next for the command, lined the road to his grave. His passion and his loyalty had been given to the Battalion without thought of self, and among many sad things few are sadder than to see the record of his unceasing activities and care since he had been Second in Command cut across by the curt announcement of his death. It was a little thing that his name had been at the time submitted for a well-deserved D.S.O. In a hard-pressed body of men, death and sickness carry a special sting, because the victim knows

– and in the very article of death feels it – what confusion and extra work, rearrangement and adjustments of responsibilities his enforced defection must lay upon his comrades. The winter had brought a certain amount of sickness and minor accidents among the officers, small in themselves, but cumulatively a burden. Irreplaceable N.C.O.'s had gone, or were going, to take commissions in the Line; others of unproven capacities had to be fetched forward in their place. Warley, of course, was not anxious to send its best N.C.O.'s away from a depot choked with recruits. The detail of life was hard and cumbersome. It was a lengthy business even to draw a typewriting machine for use in the trenches. Companies two-thirds full of fresh drafts had to be entrusted to officers who might or might not have the divine gift of leadership, and, when all was set, tomorrow's chance-spun shell might break and bury the most carefully thought-out combinations. "Things change so quickly nowadays," Desmond FitzGerald wrote not long before his death; "it is impossible to see ahead." And Death took him on Calais beach in the full stride of his power.

He had quietly presented the Battalion the year before with service Drums. "No mention need be made of who paid." They were the only battalion of the Brigade which lacked them at that time, and they had been the only battalion to bring them out of the beginning of the war, when, during the retreat from Mons, "the Artillery drove over the big Drum at Landrecies."

Temporary Captain A. F. L. Gordon followed Lieutenant Nugent as Adjutant, and the Rev. F. M. Browne from G.H.Q. replaced Father Lane-Fox. They moved into the Salient again on the 6th March billeting at Wormhoudt, and were told several unpleasant things about the state of the line and the very limited amount of "retaliation" that they might expect from their own artillery.

The snow stopped all training except a little bombing. Opinion as to the value of bombs differed even in those early days, but they were the order of the day, and gave officers the chance to put in practice their pet theories of bowling. A Commanding Officer of great experience wrote, a year later, after the Battle of Arras, thanking Heaven that that affair had "led to the rediscovery of the rifle as a suitable weapon for Infantry," adding, "I swear a bomb is of all weapons the most futile in which to specialize."

The French were as keen on the bomb as the rest of the world, and parties of officers visited our bombing competitions at Wormhoudt, where the Battalion lay till the 16th March, moving to billets (Brandhoek) near Vlamertinghe for St. Patrick's Day and the sports sacred to the occasion. They were played into camp by a Naval party to the tune of "A Life on the Ocean Wave," not a little to their astonishment. A little later they were to be even more astonished.

Then the 1st Guards Brigade took over their sector of the Fourteenth Division's new front from the Sixth Division and, as usual, complained that the trenches which ran from the east of the town were in bad condition. The Brigade Reserve camp near Vlamertinghe was not much better. It is significant that, at this date, a train, specially oiled and treated to run noiselessly through the night, used to take the reliefs right up into Ypres – a journey that did not lack excitement.

On the 23rd March, as the Battalion was going into the trenches on the Ypres Canal bank, the meaning of that "Naval party" at Vlamertinghe became plainer. Three Naval officers and twenty-five petty officers on special leave appeared among them for the purpose of spending a happy four days with them at their labours. They wore the uniforms of private soldiers without pack or equipment, and were first seen joyously walking and talking on a well-observed road, which combination of miracles led the amazed beholders to assume that they were either lunatics or escaped criminals of the deepest dye; and it was a toss-up that the whole cheery picnic-party was not arrested – or shot to save their lives. One officer, at least, had the liveliest memories of chaperoning for several hours a Naval officer with a passion for professional souvenirs in the shape of large-calibre shell fragments. "I've never been at the wrong end of this size gun before," the mariner would say as the German heavies fell. "It's tremendously interesting! I *must* just make sure about that fuse, if you don't mind." The host, to whom 5·9's, and much larger, were no novelty (for the Canal bank dug-outs did not keep them out), had to feign an interest he did not feel, till it dawned on the sailor that if he pursued his investigations too far he would be cut off by German patrols. The visitors all agreed that ships, under normal circumstances, were the Hotel Ritz compared to the daily trench-routine of the Army. We vaingloriously fired several rounds from a 9·2 to please the Senior Service who, naturally, had seen such things before. The enemy replied with two days' full "retaliation" after the Navy had left.

Yet, as things went in The Salient, it was, like their reserve camp, "not too uncomfortable." Though there was only one workable communication-trench (The Haymarket) to their line, and that a bad one, the main St. Jean road could be used after dark at reasonable risks. No work was possible by daylight, but, except for general and indiscriminate shelling, they lived quietly, even when, as happened on the first night (March 23), No. 1 Company and Headquarters were solemnly misguided down the Menin road in the dark *over* Hell Fire Corner to within a few hundred yards of Hooge and returned "without even being fired at." The Regimental Transport, too, managed to come up as far as Potijze with supplies, on three of the four nights of the Battalion's first tour, and had no casualties, "though the woods were regularly shelled." This was an extraordinary stroke of luck for the Battalion since other transport had suffered severely.

The outstanding wonder that any one in The Salient should be alive at all, is not referred to in the Diary. Men who watched the shape of that cape of death, raken by incessant aeroplanes and cross-cut by gun-fire that fell equally from the flanks and, as it seemed, the very rear, sometimes speculated, as did the French in the livelier hells of Verdun, how long solid earth itself could hold out against the upheavals of the attack. Flesh and blood could endure – that was their business – but the ground on which they stood did not abide. As one man said: "It 'ud flee away in lumps under the sole of your foot, till there was no rest anywhere."

Their first four days' tour saw three men killed in the line by a single whizz-bang in a dug-out; one wounded, and an officer, Lieutenant R. J. P. Rodakowski, slightly hit by a piece of shrapnel. They buried their dead by night at Potijze. Reliefs were the real difficulty; for the line and the roads were continuously shelled, and at any moment in the dusk they might find their only sound communication-trench impassable. They watched it go up from end to end, one dreadful night on the 29th of March, when they were in support and the Grenadiers in the line, and the King's Company was wiped out almost to a man. It was a prelude to an attack that never arrived – a suddenly launched, suddenly arrested, wantonness of destruction. Coming, going, standing or sitting still gave no minute of guaranteed safety. A party returning from home-leave were caught by a single shell in the streets of Ypres on April 2. Sergeant-Major Kirk and a private were killed, and a N.C.O. and three men were wounded. Men dropped, too, almost in the hour when they took their leave. They worked up the line of nights, half the shift at a time repairing damage, and the remainder standing by for attacks.

On the 3rd April, after an untouched turn of duty, eight men were wounded by blind fire during the relief.

At Poperinghe, on April 4, they were billeted in the Convent which supplied them with Variety Entertainments, Cinemas, Band Concerts and performing troupes, all liable at any moment to be dispersed by the enemy's artillery or 'planes and therefore doubly precious. The Battalion had its share of professional honour, too, in a matter of ceremonial. As regards the outside world the Brigade of Guards is one; as regards the various battalions of it, there are allowable internal differences of opinion. Consequently when a Russian General, late Chief of the Staff to the Grand Duke Nicholas of Russia, visited Poperinghe, and the 1st Battalion of the Irish Guards – out of five Guards Battalions within reach – was chosen as the one for him to inspect, life smiled upon them, and they rose to the occasion. Hear the words of an observer, experienced, if not altogether disinterested: "The day (April 5) was lovely, and our fellows, in spite of their months of trench-work, did magnificently. The wonderful precision of their drill excited the admiration even of officers belonging to some of the other regiments. The Huns missed a grand opportunity"

The Huns had their revenge a few days later when the Battalion's billets and Headquarters at Poperinghe were suddenly, on April 11, shelled just as the Battalion was going into line at Ypres. The thing began almost with a jest. The Regimental Chaplain was taking confessions, as is usual before going up, in Poperinghe Church, when the building rocked to bursts of big stuff obviously drawing nearer. He turned to open the confessional-slide, and smelt gas – chlorine beyond doubt. While he groped wildly for his gas-helmet in the dusk, the penitent reassured him: "It's all right, Father. I've been to Divisional Gas School to-day. That smell's off my clothes." Relieved, the Padre went on with his duties to an accompaniment of glass falling from the windows, and when he came out, found the porch filled with a small crowd who reported: "Lots of men hit in an ambulance down the road." Thither ran the Padre, to meet a man crazy with terror whom a shell-burst had flung across the street, half-stripped and blackened from head to foot. He was given Absolution, became all of a sudden vehemently sick, and dropped into stupor. Next, on a stretcher, an Irish Guardsman crushed by a fallen wall, reported for the moment as "not serious." As the priest turned to go, for more wounded men were being borne up through the dusk, the lad was retaken by a violent haemorrhage. Supreme Unction at once was his need. Captain Woodhouse, R.A.M.C., the regimental doctor, appeared out of the darkness, wounded in the arm and shoulder, his uniform nearly ripped off him and very busy. He had been attending a wounded man in a house near headquarters when a shell burst at the door, mortally wounded the patient, killed one stretcher-bearer outright and seriously wounded two others. The Padre, dodging shells en route, dived into the cellars of the house where he was billeted, for the Sacred Elements, went back to the wayside dressing-station, found a man of the Buffs, unconscious, but evidently a Catholic (for he carried a scapular sewed in his tunic), anointed him, and – the visitation having passed like a thunderstorm – trudged into Ypres unworried by anything worse than casual machine-gun fire, and set himself to find some sufficiently large sound cellar for Battalion Mass next morning. The Battalion followed a little later and went underground in Ypres – Headquarters and a Company in the Carmelite Convent, two Companies in the solid brick and earth ramparts that endure to this day, and one in the cellars of the Rue de Malines.

It was the mildest of upheavals – a standard-pattern affair hardly noted by any one, but it serves to show what a priest's and a doctor's duties are when the immediate heavy silence after a shell-burst, that seems so astoundingly long, is cut by the outcries of wounded men, and the two hurry off together, stumbling and feeling through the dark, till the electric torch picks up some dim, veiled outline, or hideously displays the wounds on the body they seek. There is a tale of half a platoon among whom a heavy gas-shell dropped as they lay in the flank of a cutting beside a road. Their platoon-commander hurried to them, followed by the Sergeant, calling out to know the extent of the damage. No one replied. The question was repeated. Then: "Speak up when the Officer's askin'," cried the scandalized Sergeant. But even that appeal failed. They were all dead where they lay, and, human nature being what it is, the Sergeant's words became a joke against him for many days after. But men cannot live in extreme fear for more than a very limited time. Normal little interests save them; so while they lay in cellars by candle-light at Ypres and worked stealthily at night, the Battalion found time to make a most beautiful Irish Star, four feet across, of glass and pounded brick from the rubbish of the Convent garden. It was a work of supererogation, accomplished while cleaning up the billets, which drew favourable notice from high authorities.

On the 16th April they were shifted to relieve the 2nd Grenadiers at Railway Wood north-west of Hooge. This was almost the most easterly point of The Salient on the north of the Menin road by the Roulers railway, and ranked as quite the least desirable stretch of an acutely undesirable line. In addition to every other drawback, the wood welled water at every pore, for the Bellewaarde Beck brought to it all the drainage from the Bellewaarde ridge, and even the trenches on high ground were water-logged. They were bombed from overhead as soon as they moved in; Hell Fire Corner was shelled on the 17th April and six men were wounded.

The 18th April was quiet, only two men wounded, and "except for violent bombardments north and south, and an attack on Wieltje and other places," so was the 19th. Wieltje was two thousand yards, and the "other places" even farther away. The "disturbance" was nothing more than principal German attacks on four different fronts of The Salient, among mud and mud-filled shell-holes and craters of old mines where men sank and choked where they fought waist-deep in the dirt, where the clogged rifles were useless, and the bomb and the bayonet were the only hope. From any reasonable point of view The Salient was a particularly weak position, always worth an attack in the intervals of its regular use as a Gunnery school for German artillery. The enemy knew that we were on the way to take the pressure off the French at Verdun, which had been a factory of death since February, and argued that it would be well to make trouble anywhere they could. They chose the First and Second Canadian Divisions round Ypres, and fought them for two days, with very little profit beyond filling more shell-holes with more dead.

At that date men had learned by experience the comparative values of their flanking Divisions and the battalions immediately beside them. When a local attack fell on some of these, those unaffected would rest as unconcernedly as the watch below takes its ease when the watch on deck is struggling with the squall. The syren-like hoot of the gas-horns, one or two miles off, might break their rest on relief, but the Division involved being known to be adequate, the Battalion was not roused and "spent a quiet day." Other Divisions, new to the line, caused anxiety and interfered with regular routine, till they had shaken into place; and yet others might be always trusted to hoot and signal for help on the least provocation. These peculiarities would be discussed in the cantonments and coffee-bars of the rest-areas, or, later, out on the roadside with an occasional far-ranging German shell to interrupt a really pleasant inter-Battalion or Divisional argument where, if report is true, even the Military Police sometimes forgot to be impartial. And there were unambitious, unimproving units quite content to accept anything that their predecessors had left them in the way of open-work parapets, gapped sand-bags and smash traverses. Against these, experienced corps builded, not without ostentation, strong flanks so that if their neighbours went of a sudden, they themselves might still have a chance for their lives. The Irish had a saying of their own — a sort of lilting call that ran down the trenches at odd times – to the effect that God being in his Heaven and "the Micks in the line, all was well. Pom-pom!" Every Battalion, too, had its own version of the ancient war-song which claims that they themselves were in the front line with their best friends of the moment immediately behind them, but that when they went to look for such-and-such a Battalion with whom they were unfriends for the moment, they were blessed (or otherwise) if they could find them.

Theirs was the misfortune to be the only Battalion of the Division available for fatigues during their sixteen days' tour; so they supplied parties without intermission, both to the trenches round Railway Wood, and in battered Ypres in the cellars where they rested by candle-light to the accompaniment of crashing masonry and flying pavement blocks. A fatigue-party, under Lieutenant T. K. Walker, carrying Engineers' stuff to near Railway Wood, was caught and shelled on the 24th, on the last two hundred yards or so of utterly exposed duckboards, every piece of which the enemy guns had taped to a yard. The water-logged soil made any sort of trenches here out of the question. Men slid and staggered across the open under their loads till the shells chose to find them, or they reached Railway Wood and found some cover in the mine which was always being made there and always pumped out. Lieutenant Walker and four men were killed at once, and seven men were wounded, of whom two afterwards died. It was as swift as the shelling of Headquarters at Poperinghe on the 11th; and Captain Woodhouse, the M.O., had to get forward to the wreckage under a heavy fire of shells and aerial torpedoes. With, or not far from him, went, crawled, ran or floundered the priest; for if by any means the body could be relieved, repaired or eased, so could the soul. It is true that both these men more or less respected direct orders not to expose themselves too much; but they suffered from curious lapses of memory.

Then Spring came to The Salient in one swift rush, so warm and so windless that, at the end of April, when they were in rest under leafing trees at Poperinghe, it was possible to dine in shirt sleeves in the open by candle and starlight. The gentle weather even softened the edge of war for a day or two, till Ypres and the neighbourhood were vigorously shelled on the 5th May. The Battalion was then in Ypres prison and the cellars beneath it, where some unloved enthusiast had discovered that there was plenty of room for drill purposes in the main gaol-corridor, and drilled they were accordingly to the music of the bombardments. On such occasions men were sometimes seen to "budge," i.e. roll their eyes in the direction of plaster and stones falling from the ceiling, for which heinous "crime" their names were justly taken.

On the 9th May they relieved the 2nd Grenadiers on the left sector of their Brigade's front at Wieltje, where what were once trenches had been bombed and shelled into a sketchy string of bombing-posts – or as a man said, "grouse-butts." It was perhaps one degree worse than their stretch at Hooge and necessitated companies and posts being scattered, as the ground served, between what was left of Wieltje, St. Jean and La Brique. The enemy opened by shelling the Reserve Company (No. 4) at St. Jean and wounding eight men, while their machine-gun fire held up all work in the front line where No. 1 Company was trying to dig a communication-trench through old dirt and dead to No. 2 Company in support.

The demonstration might have meant anything or nothing, but to be on the safe side and to comply with Brigade orders, regular observation and snipers' posts were posted henceforward, and Lieutenant Rodakowski was struck off all trench duties as "Intelligence (and Sniping) Officer." The arrangements and supervision of a dozen or so snipers, imaginative, stolid or frankly bored, as the case might be, and the collation of their various reports based (for very little could be actually seen) on the Celtic imagination operating at large; the whole to be revised and corrected from hour to hour by one's own faculties of observation and deduction; make Intelligence work a little strenuous.

On the 12th May St. Jean, which included Battalion Headquarters, half-way between St. Jean and Wieltje, was heavily shelled for eight hours of the night with heavy stuff – but no casualties beyond a couple of men wounded.

On the 18th May, when they were in the line once more, the enemy who had recently been remarkably quiet made an attempt to rush a bombing-post, but, says the Diary, "Lieutenant Tisdall and 4182 Private A. Younge came upon them unexpectedly, and owing to the former's coolness and the latter's vigorous offensive action with rifle and bombs, the hostile party, about twenty, fled." The Diary is never emotional in such little matters as these, and the officers concerned say less than nothing. It is the old-timers among the men who cherish memories of the "vigorous offensive" action. No pen dare put on paper the speech of the orderly who, with rifle and bomb, erupts along the trench or over the edge of the shell-crater either in deadly silence or with threatenings and slaughter in his own dialect, and, when the quick, grisly business is over, convulses his associates with his private version of it. The orderly got the D.C.M. and the officer the Military Cross.

The enemy retaliated next night by shelling the support line and wounded seven men just as the Battalion was going into rest and was relieved late, which they noticed with deep displeasure, by a Battalion of the Twentieth Division.

The 20th May saw them in the clean back-area at the pleasant well-treed village of Longuenesse, three miles south-west of St. Omer, all together in good billets and plenty of clean straw at one farm; Headquarters at a neighbouring château, the 2nd Coldstream, their particular friends, with them, and the other battalions of their Brigade at villages near by. The weather was good; for a week at least work was reasonable, and they all went to pay a visit disguised as a "Battalion Drill" to the parade ground of the cadet-school at Blendecques, of which Lieutenant J. Halligan, late Orderly-Room Quartermaster-Sergeant of the Battalion, was Adjutant. It is reasonable to infer that the Russian General at the Poperinghe camp got no better in the way of a ceremonial parade than did their old comrade.

The shadow of preparations for the Somme fell over them afterwards. They dug quadruple lines of trenches and assaulted them in full kit with gas helmets; and found time, between whiles, to hold a Boxing competition, at which the 12th Lancers arrived with "their Private Young," who was defeated by the Battalion's Company-Sergeant-Major Voyles. These things are as sacred as the Eton dinner at St. Omer on the 3rd June, which seven officers from the Battalion attended.

On the 7th June they moved on a twelve-mile march to Hondeghem, under Cassel, en route for a Poperinghe camp once more, and developed several cases of sore feet. This was put down to a "bad issue of socks," but it supports the theory of the Sergeants' Mess, that nothing but careful inspection, coupled with steady route-marching, can "put a foot" on men who have been paddling in trench-mud with twisted, water-logged boots.

At Poperinghe they were coolies again till they went into line on the 15th June. A permanent fatigue-party of 150, under 2nd Lieutenants Hegarty and Earle, was sent to the Engineers near Ypres. Another, a hundred strong, helped to bury field-cables by night at Brielen on the Ypres – Elverdinghe road, a place much sought after by the enemy's artillery. But digging is reckoned better than drill, and their next tour of duty was to be a wearisome one. Lieutenant J. N. Marshall from the Entrenching Battalion joined on the 15th, and Lieutenant J. K. Greer took command of No. 1 Company, Lieutenant Law being on a course.

They relieved the 11th Essex and the 8th Bedfordshires (Sixth Division) on the night of the 16th, in the surprisingly short time of one hour, which was nearly a record and showed that all hands were abreast of their work. Their new sector lay north-west of Wieltje and due north of Ypres, covering the Ypres – Pilckem road, with supports at Lancashire Farm, and the Battalion Headquarters amid loose bricks and mud on the Canal bank. The trenches were bad; only one communication-trench (Skipton Road) was moderately dry, and the parapets were thin, low and badly gapped, which gave enemy snipers their chance. Two men were killed outright the first day; one died of wounds and four were wounded.

No Man's Land at this point was several hundred yards deep, and covered with long grass and weeds. The periscopes soon learned to know that poppies and thistles grew brightest and tallest round the edges of shell- holes, and since shell-holes meant cover, all patrols directed their belly-flat course to them.

On the 18th June officer patrols went out to look at the enemy's wire. Second Lieutenant F. H. N. Lee was wounded in the leg while close to it, and was carried back by 3836 Corporal Redmond; dying later of gangrene. Another officer, Lieutenant Hon. P. Ogilvy, ran by mistake into wire on his return journey, and had to fight his way back with his orderly. One man was killed and one wounded, besides the wounded officer.

On the 19th Lieutenant J. N. Marshall, while out with a working-party, was sniped in the arm, but finished his work before reporting it. A man was killed and two were wounded. "The day was normal – probably the quietest of the tour," says the Diary, but one may be certain that certain inconspicuous German snipers were congratulating themselves on their bag. The bulk of the trouble came from five old dug-outs known as the "Canadian dug-outs," some two or three hundred yards away, which had once been in our hands. These had been wired round collectively and individually, and their grass-grown irregular moundage made perfect snipers' nests.

The Battalion lay, from the 21st to the 23rd June, in shelters round and cellars beneath Elverdinghe Château, the trees of which were still standing, so that it was possible to put in an inspection and a little drill beneath them, but careful watch had to be kept for hostile aeroplanes. Drill under these circumstances is discipline of the highest. "'Tis not the dhrill, ye'll understand, but the not budgin' in the ranks that's so hard to come by. For, ye'll understand, that you can't help liftin' an eye when you hear *them* buzzin' above. And, of course, if a man budges on parade, he'll be restless when he's shelled."

Our Artillery had been cutting German wire on the front of the Division with the idea of raids to follow. Consequently, there was night-firing on both sides when the Battalion went back on the 24th. The trenches had been a little improved, and one man only was killed and one wounded by the snipers.

On the 26th June four men were sniped. On the 27th June wire-cutting by our guns drew heavy retaliation from the enemy. Lieutenant F. L. Pusch, D.S.O., as brave a man as the War made, who had only come up from the Entrenching Battalion a few days before, was sniped and killed at once. He had gone with his orderly to pick up a wounded man in a trench, and both were hit by the same bullet. The sniper did his best to kill Private Carroll, who dragged the wounded man and the officer's body under cover. Private Carroll was awarded the Military Medal for this. Four dead and seven wounded were that night's total.

The 28th June was the worst of that tour. The enemy opened on the trenches and supports through night and day with everything available, down to aerial torpedoes, killing five men and wounding eight.

The casualties for a "quiet" twelve days' tour, including three days only in the front line, were three officers and forty-seven other ranks killed and wounded. Some of the credit of this must go to the German snipers, who, working without noise or display, gave the Battalion the idea there was nothing much doing. The brutal outcry of artillery, its visible effect on the ground – above all, the deadly accuracy of the single aimed shells on the well-registered trench from which none must move – upset men sometimes more than repeated single casualties in the front line, which can be hurried off round the traverses without rousing more than a few companions.

They lay for a week beneath the trees near Poperinghe and started inter-platoon bombing competitions to "accustom the men to throw over-arm without jerking." These little events forbade monotony, and were sometimes rather like real warfare, for not every one can be trusted to deliver a ball accurately when he is throwing in against time.

THE SOMME

Meanwhile, Verdun had been in the fire since February, there was no sign of the attacks on it weakening, and France and the world looked uneasily at that dread point of contact where men and stuff consumed as the carbon of arc-lights consumes in the current. It was time that England should take the strain, even though her troops were not fully trained or her guns yet free to spend shell as the needs of the War demanded. What had gone before was merely the initial deposit on the price of national unpreparedness; what was to come, no more than a first installment. It was vital to save Verdun; to so hold the enemy on the Western front that he could not send too much help to his eastern line or his Austrian allies, who lay heavy on the Italian Army: most vital, to kill as many Germans as possible.

The main strength, the actual spine of the position, so far as the British front was concerned, was some twenty-five miles of high ground forming the water-shed between the Somme and the rivers of southern Belgium, which ran, roughly, from Maricourt in the south, where our line joined the French, to Gomiecourt in the north. Here the enemy had sat for two years, looking down upon France and daily strengthening himself. His trebled and quadrupled lines of defence, worked for him by his prisoners, ran below and along the flanks and on the tops of ranges of five-hundred-foot downs. Some of these were studded with close woods, deadlier even than the fortified villages between them; some cut with narrowing valleys that drew machine-gun fire as chimneys draw draughts; some opening into broad, seemingly smooth slopes, whose every haunch and hollow covered sunk forts, carefully placed mine-fields, machine-gun pits, gigantic quarries, enlarged in the chalk, connecting with systems of catacomb-like dug-outs and subterranean works at all depths, in which brigades could lie till the fitting moment. Belt upon belt of fifty-yard-deep wire protected these points, either directly or at such angles as should herd and hold up attacking infantry to the fire of veiled guns. Nothing in the entire system had been neglected or unforeseen, except knowledge of the nature of the men who, in due time, should wear their red way through every yard of it.

Neither side attempted to conceal their plans. The work of our airmen would have been enough to have warned the enemy what was intended, even had his own men overlooked the immense assembly of troops and guns in a breadth of country that had been remodeled for their needs, above ground and below. Our battalions in The Salient, where the unmolested German aeroplanes bombed them, knew well enough that, in the phrase of the moment, "everything had gone south," and our listening-posts in the front line round Ypres could tell very fairly when a German "demonstration" was prompted by natural vice or orders to cover a noisy withdrawal of their guns in the same direction. It did not need placards in English, "Come on, we are ready for you!" which were hoisted in some of the German trenches on that Somme front to make men wiser than they had been for weeks past.

Side by side with this elaborate and particular knowledge, plus a multitude of camp-rumours, even more circumstantial, was the immense incuriousness that always exists in veteran armies. Fresh drafts would pour out from England filled with vain questions and the hope of that immediate "open warfare," so widely advertised, to be told they would know all about it when their turn came, and that, meantime, deep trenches were not bad things after all. When they had looked for a little on the full face of war, they were content to copy their elders and ask no questions. They understood it was to be a wearing-out battle. Very many men had already been worn out and cast aside in the mere detail of preparation, in building the light and broad-gauge railways of supply and the roads beside them; in fetching up and installing timber, hutments, hangars, telephones, hospitals, pipe-lines for water, and the thousand other necessaries of mechanical war. As it happened to individuals, so, they knew, would it be with the battalions, brigades and divisions of all the Armies which General Rawlinson on the 1st of July moved up against that fortress of a whole countryside, called in history "The Somme."

And while that storm gathered and broke, the Battalion went with its horrible necessary work in The Salient till the hour should come for it and its Division to be cast into the furnace and used up with the rest.

On the 7th July they moved as a support to the broken and filthy banks of the Canal north of Ypres and sat in dug-outs connected by a tunnel and begirt with water and mud. Except for a mere nightly fatigue of a couple of hundred men, the Diary noted that "there was no training possible but there was little shelling." The 2nd Grenadiers were in the line which the Battalion relieved (11th July) on a broken and marshy front, between Buffs Road and Forward Cottage with Battalion Headquarters near St. Jean and the 3rd Coldstream on their left. They were shelled during relief, when Lieutenant Christy, who, but a little while before, had just escaped a sniper's bullet through a loophole, was killed.

That same morning four Germans wormed their way through the rank grass and broken ground and for a while almost captured an isolated post of six men of No. 1 Company. They tried, indeed, to march them off as prisoners, but the Irish edged away under cover of the next platoon's fire, and all got back safely. The day closed with heavy bombardments from 5·9's. An officer and three other ranks killed and seventeen wounded were counted as a light casualty-list "considering the bad cover." No man could stand upright for an instant, and all repairs, parapets and drainage work were done at night, stooping and crawling between spurts of machine-gun hose-work.

The 13th July was another "light" day with but seven men wounded. Second Lieutenant G. V. Williams joined from the base and Major C. F. Fleming went sick on the 14th. The sector being rather too active and noisy of nights just then, a patrol under Lieutenant J. N. Marshall went out to see what the enemy might intend in the way of digging a sap across "No Man's Land." The Lieutenant was wounded in the side as he left the trench, but insisted on doing his work and was out two hours; for which he paid by having to go into hospital a month later. Their casualties on the 15th, when they were relieved by the 2nd Grenadiers and went back to their dug-outs by the Canal, were five wounded, one of whom died. Out of this tense life were suddenly chosen an officer and twenty men to form part of the contingent representing our armies at the French Review in Paris on the 14th July. They were chiefly veterans of 1914, and under Captain J. S. N. FitzGerald, then of the 2nd Battalion, repaired to a bright clean city where a man could hold up his head, walking in unchoked streets between roofed and glazed houses: and the day after the glittering affair was over they returned to their brick-heaps and burrows in the Flanders mire.

to Béthune to Le...

Vimy

Chelers
from Ypres
Nov. 1917
Béthonsart
Villers~Brulin
Tinques
Bethencourt
Ecoivres
Farbu
Tinquette
to St Pol
Bray
Ecurie
Averdoingt
Penin
Maizières
Agnez~les~Duisans
Anzin
St Nicola
Ambrines
Givenchy~le~Noble
Avesnes~le~Comte
Wanquetin
Warlus
ARR
Beaufort
Hauteville
Dec. 6. 1917
to Jan. 21.
1918
Berneville
Liencourt
Simencourt
Gd Rullecourt
Barly Beaumetz~les~Loges
Bretencourt
Sombrin
Bavincourt
June 7
to July 5
Rivière Blaireville
Ap. 13. Nov. 16.
Saulty
Ap. 15~24
Bailleulmont
Ransart
Boisleux~
au~Mon
Bo
La Cauchie
Berles~
au~Bois
Hendecourt
Adinfer
Aug. 2
Pommier
au~Bois
Moyenneville
Ap. 2
Har
Warlincourt
Bienvillers~
au~Bois
Douchy
Ayette
Mondicourt
Ablainzevelle
Courcelles~
le~Comte
Gomiecourt
Thièvres
Couin
Bucquoy
Achiet~le~Grand
Sarton
Bois de Warnimont
Courcelles~au~Bois
Serre
Bapaum
Authie
Bus~les~Artois
Colincamps
Aug. 16—20
Aug. 23
Vauchelles
Bertrancourt
Auchonvillers
Beau
Louvencourt
Aug. 1
Mailly~Maillet
Hamel
Gueudecou
Englebermer
Flers

North
West East
South

R. Ancre

Delville
Wood
Guillemont
Montauban
Bern
Harde
court
Albert
Fricourt
Maricourt
Mar
Méaulte
Citadel
Br...
Dernancourt
Bronfay Fm.
Treux
Ville
Happy
Valley
C
Heilly
Morlan
court
Somme
Méricourt
l'Abbé
Dec.
1916
May
21, 1917
Bray

to Cassel
May 30.
Aug.
Oct.
to Hornoy. Oct. 10.
0 1 2 3 Eng
4

to Doullens

to Amiens

THE SOMME
First Battalion
1916..... 1917..... 1918.....

On the Battalion's next turn (July 18–22), suspecting that the enemy might be newly relieved, our patrols worked hard night after night to catch prisoners for identification purposes. 2346 Lance-Corporal Hennigan, a regimental "character" and a man of strong powers of leadership, with 5743 Private O'Brien, of whom, too, many tales are told, were marked as "very prominent in the work." But the Germans took great care not to leave men or corpses about, and they got nothing for their toil.

On the 23rd July orders came that the expected term of rest was to be cancelled as the Division would go "elsewhere," which all knew meant towards the Somme. There were five days yet ere the Battalion drew clear of The Salient, each day with its almost unnoticed casualty that in the long run makes the bulk of the bills of war, and brings home the fact that the life-blood of the Battalion is dripping away. The support platoons were reckoned lucky to have only one man killed on the 23rd after bombardment by a six-inch high-explosive gun. Captain Pollok, who took over command of No. 1 Company on the same day, was wounded two days later just after relief by a machine-gun bullet; and their last "normal" day in the trenches gave one Sergeant killed and three other ranks wounded.

They were relieved on the 27th July, after dark as usual, by the 1st Royal Warwicks, "recently come from the south, having been in the fighting there." The Warwicks knew "The Somme." They looked on the clean, creosoted, deep-bayed, high-parapeted trenches they were to hold and announced that they would feel "cushy" in such a line. "Cushy!" said the Brigade. "Wait till you've had to live in 'em!" "But," said the Warwicks, "you see, we've been fighting." The large Guardsmen looked at the little worn Linesmen and swallowed it in silence. The Fourth Division, to which the Warwicks belonged, had been part of that terrible northern attack along the line from Serre to Fricourt, which had spent itself in vain against the German defence a month before, and had been ground and milled day by day since. But all that the Diary notices is that that last relief was "carried out smoothly and quietly" in what to the Warwicks, after their experience, must have been grateful peace.

After their three weeks in dug-outs, the Battalion rested and washed south of merry Poperinghe which had been heavily shelled and for some days completely evacuated.

Between March 18 and July 18, excluding four weeks in rest, they had lost four officers and thirty other ranks killed; five officers and a hundred and fifty-three other ranks wounded – a total of one hundred and ninety-two, in the mere routine of the slow days.

There was a saying of the War, "no one notices weather in the front line"; and it is curious that, so soon as the Battalion was above ground, walking under naked skies with light and air all round it men dwelt on weather as almost a new discovery. They found it hot when the Division entrained at Proven for St. Pol. Forty-two trains took the Division and forty-seven lorries bore the Battalion itself from St. Pol to Bouque-Maison on the Doullens road. There, Headquarters were in an orchard beneath unbarked trees with leaves on the branches and a background of gun-voices from the Somme, to remind the men who laughed and talked in that shadow and sun what waited for them after this short return to real life.

They moved on the 4th August to Vauchelles-les-Authies, the match-board huts of which, on the trampled ground, have been likened to a "demobbed poultry show." It lay just off the well-worn Doullens – Albert road, now flooded with a steady current of troops and material. They waited there for ten days. During that time 2nd Lieutenant Cook (4th Connaught Rangers), Lieutenant T. Butler-Stoney from the Entrenching Battalion and Lieutenant N. Butler from Hospital joined them.

The Regimental Band arrived from England for a three months' tour. The officer who accompanied it wore a wound-stripe – the very first which the Battalion collectively had ever seen and men wondered whether wound stripes would become common, and how many one might accumulate. It was removed from the officer by laughing friends, as a matter something too suggestive in present company and the Band played in the still warm evenings, while the dust of feet going Sommeward rose and stretched unbroken along the Doullens Albert *pavé*. Here the very tree boles, before they began to be stripped and splintered by shell-fire, were worn and rubbed beneath the touch of men's shoulders and gnawed by the halted horses.

The King came on the 9th August to visit the Division. Special arrangements were impossible, so bombing-assault practice went on, while the officers of the Battalion were presented to him "in the orchard where the messes were pitched." He made no orations, uttered no threats against his enemies, nor guaranteed the personal assistance of any tribal God. His Regiments merely turned out and cheered the inconspicuous car as long as they could see it. But there is a story that a Frenchman, an old Royalist, in whose wood some officers had rigged a temporary hut of which he highly disapproved, withdrew every claim and complaint on the promise that the chair in which the King of England had sat should be handed over to him, duly certificated. Which was done.

On the 11th the Brigade moved over the open country via Louvencourt and Bertrancourt to the woods south of Mailly-Maillet, a six-mile march in hot and dusty weather, and the Brigade (2nd Grenadiers, 3rd Coldstream, 2nd Coldstream in reserve and 1st Irish Guards in support) took over trenches east of Englebelmer and "well within the shell area." Thiepval and the Schwaben Redoubt across the Ancre were only a thousand yards away and unsubdued; and, for a while, it looked as though that weary corner of death was to be the Guards' objective. But, next day, orders came to move out of the line again, back to high and breezy Louvencourt in warm rain, taking over billets from the 2nd Sherwood Foresters and, by immense good luck, coming across a heaven-sent Expeditionary Force Canteen, a thing not often found in front-line billets. Upon this, pay was at once arranged for, and every one shopped at large. The incident stayed in their minds long after the details of mere battles were forgotten, and "that canteen at Louvencourt" is a landmark of old memories.

By this date the Battle of the Somme was six weeks old, and our troops had eaten several – in some places as much as five or six – thousand yards deep into the area. Two main attacks had been delivered – that of the 1st July, which had lasted till the 14th, and that of the 14th, which went on till the end of the month. From Serre to Ovillers-la-Boisselle the Germans' front stood fast; from Ovillers-la-Boisselle to the junction with the French armies at Hardecourt, the first tremendous system of their defence had been taken literally a few score yards at a time, trench by trench, village by village, quarry by quarry, and copse by copse, lost, won, and held again from three to eight or nine times. A surge forward on some part of the line might succeed in making good a few hundred yards of gain without too heavy loss. An isolated attack, necessary to clear a flank or to struggle towards some point of larger command, withered under enormous far concentrations of enemy guns, even as the woods withered to snapped, charred stickage. At every step and turn, hosts of machine-guns at ground-level swept and shaved the forlorn landscapes; and when the utmost had been done for the day, the displaced Germans seemed always to occupy the crest of some yet higher down. Villages and woods vanished in the taking; were stamped into, or blown out of, the ground, leaving only their imperishable names. So, in the course of inconceivable weeks, fell Mametz and the ranked woods behind it, Contalmaison, Montauban, and Caterpillar Wood, Bernafay, Trônes Wood, Longueval, and the fringe of Delville (even then a charnel-house among shattered stumps), both Bazentins, and Pozières of the Australians. The few decencies and accommodations of the old settled trench-life were gone; men lived as best they could in the open among eternal shell-holes and mounds of heaped rubbish that were liable at any moment to be dispersed afresh; under constant menace of gas, blinded with the smoke-screens of local attacks, and beaten down from every point of the compass either by enemy fire, suddenly gathered and loosed, or that of their own heavies searching, from miles off, some newly cleared hollow or sky-line of the uplands where our troops lay indistinguishable from the skinned earth.

Battalions, Brigades and Divisions went in to the fight, were worn down in more or in less time, precisely as the chances of the ground either screened or exposed them for a while to the fire-blasts. Sometimes it was only a matter of hours before what had been a Brigade ceased to exist – had soaked horribly into the ground. The wastage was brought down and back across the shell-holes as well as might be, losses were made good, and with a half, two-thirds, or three-quarters, new drafts, the original Battalion climbed back to its task. While some development behind the next fold of land was in progress or brought to a standstill, they would be concerned only with the life-and-death geography of the few hundred yards immediately about them, or those few score yards over which profitable advances could be made. A day, even an hour, later, the use and value of their own hollow or ridge might be altogether abolished. What had been a hardly won foothold would become the very pivot of a central attack, or subside into a sheltered haven of refuge, as the next dominating ridge or lap

An isolated attack . . . withered under enormous far concentrations of enemy guns, even as the woods withered to snapped, charred stickage. At every step and turn, hosts of machine-guns at ground-level swept and shaved the forlorn landscapes; . . .

Mametz Wood, 1916.

of the large-boned French landscape was cleared. Equally suddenly, even while the men thanked God for their respite, German batteries or a suddenly-pushed-forth chain of German machine-guns would pound or spray their shelter into exposed torment once more.

As one philosopher of that unearthly epoch put it some time afterwards: "We was like fleas in a blanket, ye'll understand, seein' no more than the next nearest wrinkle. But Jerry and our Generals, ye'll understand, they kept us hoppin'."

"Our Generals," who, it may be presumed, knew all the wrinkles of the blanket, shifted the Brigade on the 16th August opposite Serre on the far left of the line, which was not destined to be pierced till the next year. It was a fleeting transfer to another Army Corps; their own, the Fourteenth, under Lord Cavan, having joined the Fourth Army. They took over from the Somerset L.I. (61st Brigade) a set of trenches which, after their experiences in The Salient, struck them as dry, deep and good, but odd and unhomely. They had been French, were from six to nine feet deep, paved in places with stone, which our men had never seen in trenches before, and riveted with strange French stick work. The dugouts, too, were not of their standard patterns. The front line was badly battered, but reliefs could be effected in broad daylight without casualties. The activities and comforting presence of our aeroplanes impressed them also as a contrast to Ypres, where, naturally, our troops for the moment held only a watching brief and every machine that could be spared had gone to the Somme. The dead of the opening battles lay thick about the place. The Irish buried two hundred of a Division that had passed that way, five weeks or so before, and salved, with amazement at its plenty, the wreckage of their equipment. "There's the world and all out there, Sorr," said a man returning from his work. "The very world an' all! Machine-guns and" – his voice dropping in sheer awe – "rum-jars!" They were unmolested, save by a few minenwerfers. Undertaker's work does not hearten any troops, and they were glad to get back to hutments in the untouched woods behind Authie, near their old "poultry-show." During these days 2nd Lieutenants J. N. Ward and T. Gibson joined from home, the latter going to the first-line transport and Captain L. R. Hargreaves took over No. 2 Company on joining from home on the 20th.

On the 23rd August they moved with the Brigade across to Beauval on the Doullens – Amiens road (where camps and hutments almost touched each other), and on the 25th embarked at Canaples in a horror called a "tactical train," which was stuffed with two thousand of their Brigade. After slow and spasmodic efforts it bore them quite fifty kilometers in seven hours to Méricourt l'Abbé, whence they marched to Méaulte in a green hollow under the downs, and found themselves once more in their own Fourteenth Corps under Lord Cavan. More immediately to the point, and a thing long remembered, their billets were damp, dirty and full of fleas; the weather that was destined to ruin the campaign broke in torrents of rain, and the continuous traffic of stuff had knocked the very bowels out of all the hard-worked roads. This was the first time they realized what the grey clinging Somme mud could do.

They trained in that wet at bombing, at assaulting from trenches, at visual signaling to aeroplanes, and at marking out trenches by night with white tapes, as scores of thousands had done before them, while the roar of the guns rose and dropped without explanation, like the tumult of unseen crowds; and rumours and contradictory orders for standing fast or leaving on the instant kept them in tension for ten days. But, most wonderful of all to the men from The Salient, where silence and guarded movement were automatic, was the loud life of this open-air world of troops around them – men and guns spread over the breadth of counties – horses in the open by thousands ranked in endless horse-lines – processions of roaring lorries and deep-rumbling heavy guns; and, only a few miles away – the War in full blast. It was possible to catch a ride in a lorry and go up and see "The War," as the saying ran. Yonder but a very little way, stretched horizons, downs and tablelands as far as imagination could range. All the firmament groaned to the artillery hidden and striving within them; and statelily, and regularly and unceasingly, the vast spaces of open were plumed with vertical columns of changeful shell-smoke. Men perceived that everything they had known, till then, had been a field-day. Here was The War!

A story that a wonderful new weapon would soon appear was very general. Some one had half-seen or been told about the tanks in their well-screened shelters; one or two over-zealous English journals had been industriously hinting at the developments of science; the enemy was uneasy, and, German-fashion, had issued portentous instructions to his men to be on their guard against something. But, however short his training, the British Infantryman is a born scoffer. "We had heard about moving forts that weighed thirty ton," said one of them. "Whatever it might be, we knew we'd have to take the thick o' the coffee."

The local battles and operations on the southern stretch of the front, now immediately in front of the Battalion, were almost as indistinguishable as waves on a beach that melt into or rise out of each other in the main flood. But there was a fresh tidal movement at the beginning of September, when our whole line attacked again, in conjunction with the French. We gained nothing of any account in the north, but in the south Guillemont fell, and, after desperate attack and counter-attack, almost all of Ginchy and the whole thousand-yard-square of Delville Wood and the south end of High Wood.

The net result up to the middle of September had been to advance and establish the centre of our line on the crest of the high ground from Delville Wood to the road above Mouquet Farm (Thiepval and its outworks still untaken), so that we had observation over the slopes ahead. From Delville Wood eastward to Leuze – historically known as "Lousy" – Wood, overlooking the little town of Combles on our right flank, our advance held the main ridge of land there, but had not gone beyond it. Still farther east, across the valley where Combles stood, the French were working north along the heights towards Sailly-Saillisel, three thousand yards away. Their line was pinched on the right by the big St. Pierre Vaast woods, fortified throughout. Their left was almost equally constricted by the valley where Combles, among its quarries and hidden shelters, squatted and dealt death, which all the heights to the north – Morval, Lesboeufs and Le Transloy – joined, with Sailly-Saillisel and St. Pierre Vaast in the east, to make more sure. It was necessary, then, to free the ground at the junction of the two armies in the direction of Morval, which commanded far too complete a fire; and also beyond Ginchy towards Lesboeufs where the out- lying spurs of high land raked "Lousy" Wood.

That clearing-up, a comparatively small detail on a vast front, fell to the lot of the Fourteenth Army Corps (Lord Cavan commanding), which lay between Ginchy village and Leuze Wood. The Corps was made up of the Fifty-sixth London Territorial Division, on the extreme right or east, next to the French; the Sixth Division, a little north of Leuze Wood, facing the Quadrilateral, a veiled defensive work as strong as ample time and the ground could make it, and destined to turn the fortunes of that day; and on the left of the Sixth, again, the Guards Division in front of what remained of Ginchy, Ginchy Farm and Orchard, all strongly held by the Germans, and some battered brick-fields hard by.

Lord Cavan did not overstate the case in his message to the Guards Division just before the attack when he wrote: "The Corps Commander knows that there are difficulties to be cleared up on the left and in front of the 1st Guards Brigade and on the right of the 2nd Guards Brigade, but the Commander-in-Chief is of opinion that the general situation is so favourable that every effort should be made to take advantage of it, etc., etc."

A Battalion looks at life from a more limited standpoint. Brigade Orders issued on the 11th September announced: "The French Army will attack the enemy defences between Combles Ravine and Martinpuich on Z day, with the object of seizing Morval, Lesboeufs, Gueudecourt and Flers, and breaking through the enemy's defences." But what interested the Irish, who prefer fighting light, even as the Frenchman can shuffle into action under all his high-piled possessions, was the amount of weight they would have to carry up there. It included two days' rations, a couple of bombs, two extra bandoliers of ammunition, a pick or a shovel and three sandbags per man, plus wire-cutters and other fittings. On the other hand, great-coats and packs were discarded and cardigan waistcoats worn beneath their jackets.

On the 10th September the Battalion, with the 1st Brigade, moved in from Méaulte to the valley behind Carnoy, and, after dark that night, Nos. 3 and 4 companies, under Major T. M. D. Bailie, were ordered up through Bernafay Wood to a line of what passed for trenches behind Ginchy, and next morning Nos. 1 and 2 (Captain Hargreaves and Captain Rankin) bivouacked in some old trenches at the north end of Bernafay, where they were used in carrying-fatigues for the 3rd Guards Brigade, then in the front line. The other two companies were heavily shelled in their Ginchy trenches, and lost seven killed and thirteen wounded. A bombing accident in bivouac the day before had also wounded six men.

On the 12th September No. 1 Company, stationed in a small copse near Trônes Wood, which was choked with wreckage and dead, had three of their Lewis-gunners killed and five wounded by a single shell.

On the 13th September the Battalion spent a quiet day (with only one killed and seven wounded), except for a deadly tiring fatigue of carrying bombs to Guillemont under shell-fire. Our artillery began on the 12th, and continued day and night without much break till the hour of advance on the 15th, when it changed to the duly ordered stationary and creeping barrages of the field-guns.

THE 15TH SEPTEMBER

On the evening of the 14th, the 1st Brigade of Guards moved out to the shell-holes and fragments of trench that formed their assembly-positions, on a front of five hundred yards between Delville Wood and the northern flank of Ginchy. There it lay in the cold with the others till "Zero," 6.20 a.m. of the 15th. The 2nd and 3rd Coldstream had the front line, for they were to lead the attack. The 2nd Grenadiers lay behind to support them and consolidate the first objective – a line of trench about twelve hundred yards north-east – and to hold it till the 1st Irish Guards came up and had passed through them. Then, if the flanks were secure, the 2nd Grenadiers were to come on and support in turn. The 1st Irish Guards were to pass through the 2nd and 3rd Coldstream after the latter Battalions had reached the third objective, another line of trench twenty-five hundred yards off, and were thence to go on and take the final objective – the northern outskirts of Lesboeufs, thirty-five hundred yards from their jumping-off place. There was a limited objective, three hundred yards beyond the first, which worked in with the advance towards Flers of the divisions on the left of the Guards from Delville Wood to Martinpuich. It was supposed to concern only the Battalion (2nd Coldstream) on the left flank of the 1st Brigade.

Incidentally, it was announced that as soon as all the objectives had been seized, "Cavalry would advance and seize the heights ahead."

The Battalion formed up north-west of Ginchy in two lines, facing north-east – Nos. 3 and 4 Companies in the first line; 1 and 2 in the second on the right, commanded as follows:

No. 1, Lieutenant J. K. Greer, M.C.
No. 2, Captain R. Rankin.
No. 3, Captain C. Pease.
No. 4, Captain P. S. Long-Innes.

Captain L. R. Hargreaves, Lieutenants the Hon. P. J. Ogilvy, and B. Rodakowski, 2nd Lieutenant T. C. Gibson, and C.S.M. Voyles and Farrell were left in reserve Lieutenant L. C. Whiteford and his section of the Brigade Machine-gun Company was attached to the Battalion.

They waited the hour and occupied themselves, many times over, with trivial details, repetitions of orders and comparisons of watches and compasses. (Their compass-bearing, by the way, was N. 37, or within a shade of North North-east.) Every one noticed that every one else fussed a little, and rather resented it. The Doctor and the Priest seemed to loom unnaturally large, and the Sergeants were busier than was necessary over short-comings, till, ten minutes or so before Zero, Father Browne, who had given Absolution, spoke to the Companies one by one as they knelt before him, their bayonets fixed and the searching dawn-light on their faces. He reminded them that that day was one set apart to Our Lady, and, ere many minutes, not few of them would be presenting their homage to Her in person. They realized that he told no more than truth.

Through some accident, Zero had been a little mistimed, and the troops left their lairs, not under the roar and swish of their own barrage, but in a silence which lasted perhaps less than a minute, but which seemed endless. They felt, one man averred, like amateur actors upon whom the curtain unexpectedly rises. The enemy, not looking for the attack, were only expending occasional shots, which emphasized the awful loneliness and exposure of it all, till, with a wrench that jerked the ground, our barrage opened, the enemy's counter-barrage replied, and through a haze of flying dirt No. 1 Company of the Irish saw a platoon of Coldstream in front of them crumped out of existence in one flash and roar. After that, the lines moved into a blizzard of shell and machine-gun fire where all landmarks were undistinguishable in the upheaval of explosives. ("We might as well have tried to guide ourselves by the waves of the sea – the way they spouted up.")

There naturally cannot be any definite or accurate record of the day's work. Even had maps been issued to the officers a week, instead of a day or so, before the attack; even had those maps marked all known danger-points – such as the Ginchy – Flers sunk road; even had the kaleidoscopic instructions about the Brown and Yellow lines been more intelligible, or had the village of Ginchy been distinguishable from a map of the pitted moon – once the affair was launched there was little chance of seeing far or living long. The two leading platoons of No. 3 Company following the Coldstream, charged, through the ripping fire that came out of Ginchy Orchard, to the German first-line trench which ran from the sunken road at that point. The others came behind them, cheering their way into the sleet of machine-gun fire. The true line of advance was north-easterly, but the 2nd Guards Brigade on the right of the 1st, caught very heavily by the German barrage on their right flank, closed in towards the 1st Brigade and edged it more northward; so that, about an hour and a half after the advance began, what the countless machine-guns had left of the Irish found itself with three out of its four Company Commanders already casualties, all officers of No. 2 Company out of action, and the Second in Command, Major T. M. D. Bailie, killed. They were held up under heavy shelling, either in front of German wire, or, approximately, on the first-line objective – a battered German trench, which our artillery had done its best to obliterate, but fortunately had failed in parts. With the Irish were representatives of every unit of the 1st and 2nd Brigades, mostly lacking officers, and some fresh troops of the Fourteenth

Division from the left of the line. Outside their area, the Sixth Division's attacks between Ginchy Telegraph and Leuze Wood had failed, thanks to a driving fire from the Quadrilateral, the great fortified work that controlled the landscape for a mile and a half so the right flank of the Guards Division was left in the air, the enemy zealously trying to turn it – bomb versus bayonet.

Judgement of time and distance had gone with the stress and roar around. The two attacking battalions (2nd and 3rd Coldstream) of the 1st Brigade had more or less gone too – were either dead or dispersed into small parties, dodging among smoking shell-holes. The others were under the impression that they had won at least two of the three objectives – an error due to the fact that they had found and fought over a trench full of enemy where no such obstacle had been indicated. Suddenly a party of snipers and machine-guns appeared behind the Irish in a communication-trench, fired at large, as much out of bewilderment as design, wounded the sole surviving Company Officer of the four companies (Lieutenant J. K. Greer), and owing to the jamming of our Lewis-guns got away to be killed elsewhere. A mass of surrendering Germans, disturbed by the advance of a Division on the left, drifted across them and further blinded the situation. Nobody knew within hundreds of yards where they were, but since it was obvious that the whole attack of the Division, pressed, after the failure of the Sixth Division, by the fire from the Quadrilateral, had sheered too far towards the left or north, the need of the moment was to shift the men of the 2nd Guards Brigade back along the trench towards their own area; to sort out the mixed mass of officerless men on the left; and to make them dig in before the vicious, spasmodic shelling of the congested line turned into the full roll of the German barrage.

They cleared out, as best they could, the mixed English and German bodies that paved the bottom of the trench, and toiled desperately at the wreckage – splinters and concrete from blown-in dug-outs, earth-slides and collapses of head-cover by yards at a time, all mingled or besmeared with horrors and filth that a shell would suddenly increase under their hands. Men could give hideous isolated experiences of their own – it seemed to each survivor that he had worked for a life-time in a world apart – but no man could recall any connected order of events, and the exact hour and surroundings wherein such and such a man – private, N.C.O., or officer – met his death are still in dispute. It was a still day, and the reeking, chemical-tainted fog of the high explosives would not clear. Orders would be given and taken by men suddenly appearing and as suddenly vanishing through smoke or across fallen earth, till both would be cut off in the middle by a rifle bullet, or beaten down by the stamp and vomit of a shell. There was, too, always a crowd of men seated or in fantastic attitudes, silent, with set absorbed faces, busily engaged in trying to tie up, stanch, or plug their own wounds – to save their own single lives with their own hands. When orders came to these they would shake their heads impatiently and go on with their urgent, horrible business. Others, beyond hope, but not consciousness, lamented themselves into death. The Diary covers these experiences of the three hours between 8 a.m. and 11 a.m. with the words:

Even had maps marked all known danger-points – such as the Ginchy – Flers sunk road . . . or had the village of Ginchy been distinguishable from a map of the moon – once the affair was launched there was little chance of seeing far or living long.

German dead on the Ginchy-Flers sunk road.

"In the meantime, despite rather heavy shelling, a certain amount of consolidation was done on the trench while the work of reorganization was continued." In the meantime, also, some of the Coldstream Battalions, mixed with a few men of the Irish Guards, the latter commanded by Lieutenant W. Mumford, had rushed on into the wilderness beyond the trench towards the Brown line, or what was supposed to be the Brown line, three hundred yards or so ahead, and for the moment had been lost. About half-past eleven the Commanding Officer, the Adjutant, and 2nd Lieutenant G. V. Williams and Lieutenant L. C. Whitefoord of the 1st Guards Brigade Machine-gun Company, who represented all that was left of the officers, went forward with all that was left of the Irish Guards and all available, not too badly wounded Coldstreamers, towards the next objective. Every one was glad to step out from the sickening trench into the wire-trapped, shell-ploughed open whence the worst of the German barrage had lifted, though enemy machine-guns were cropping it irregularly. Their road lay uphill through a field of rank, unweeded stuff, and, when they had topped a little rise, they saw what seemed, by comparison, untouched country where houses had some roofs on them and trees some branches, all laid out ahead in the hot sunshine between Flers and Lesboeufs. There were figures in the landscape too – Germans on the move with batteries and transport – an enemy in sight at last and, by the look of them, moving away. Then a German field-battery, also in the open, pulled up and methodically shelled them. They came upon a shallow trench littered with wreckage, scraped themselves in, and there found some more of the Division, while the German battery continued to find them. In the long run, that trench, which had been a German covered-way for guns, came to hold about sixty of the 1st Irish Guards, thirty of the 2nd Grenadiers under Captain A. F. S. Cunningham, and a hundred or so of both Battalions Coldstream under Colonel J. V. Campbell, the senior officer present. Somewhere on the left front of it, fifteen of the Irish were found lying out in shell-holes under C.S.M. Carton and Sergeant Riordan. They were in touch, so far as touch existed then, with the 9th Rifle Brigade on their left, but it was not advisable to show one's head above a shell-hole on account of enemy machine-guns which were vividly in touch with everything that moved. Their right was all in the air, and for the second time no one knew – no one could know – where the trench in which they lay was situated in the existing chaos. They fixed its position at last by compass-bearings. It was more or less on the line of the second objective, and had therefore to be held in spite of casualties. The men could do no more than fire when possible at anything that showed itself (which was seldom) and, in the rare intervals when shelling slackened, work themselves a little farther into the ground. At this juncture, Captain L. R. Hargreaves, left behind with the Reserve of Officers in Trônes Wood, was ordered up, and reached the line with nothing worse than one wound. He led out a mixed party of Coldstream and Irish to a chain of disconnected shell-holes a few hundred yards in advance of the trench. Here they suffered for the rest of the afternoon under the field-battery shelling them at less than half a mile, and the regular scything of the machine-guns from the Quadrilateral on their right. A machine-gun detachment, under Lieutenant L. C. Whitefoord, went with them, and Lieutenant W. C. Mumford and 2nd Lieutenant F. S. L. Smith with their little detachments of Irish and Coldstream came up later as reinforcements. That scattered forward fringe among the shell-holes gave what help it could to the trench behind it, which filled up, as the day wore on, with more Irish and Coldstream working their way forward. Formation was gone – blown to bits long ago. Nearly every officer was down, and Sergeant after Sergeant succeeding to the command, had dropped too; but the discipline held, and with it the instinct that made them crawl, dodge, run and stumble as chance offered and their Corporals ordered, towards the enemy and not away from him. They had done so at first, shouting aloud in the massed rush of the full charge that now seemed centuries away in time, and worlds in space. Later, as they were scattered and broken by fire, knowing that their Battalion was cut to pieces, they worked with a certain automatic forlorn earnestness, which, had any one had time to think, was extremely comic. For instance, when a Sergeant came across a stray private meditating longer than seemed necessary at the bottom of a too-tempting shell-hole, he asked him gravely what he thought he was doing. The man, dazed and shaken, replied with an equal gravity that he did not know. "Then," said the Sergeant, "get on forward out o' this an' maybe ye'll find out." and smote him dispassionately with the flat of a spade. The man, without a word, rose up, lifted his head once more into the bullet-torn air, and pitched forward, dead, a few paces farther on. And, at one time, in a terrible waiting pause, when it was death to show a finger, they saw one man out on a flank suddenly taken by madness. He lifted himself up slowly, and as slowly marched across the open towards the enemy, firing his rifle in the air meantime. The bullets seemed to avoid him for a long while, till he was visibly jerked off his feet by several that struck him all together. The stiff, blind death-march ended, and the watching Irish clicked their tongues for wonder and pity.

The Battalion had had no communication with Brigade Headquarters or any one else since early morning. It lacked supports, lights, signals, information, wood, wire, sand-bags, water, food and at least fifty per cent of its strength. Its last machine-gun had been knocked out, and it had no idea what troops might be next on either side. As the sun went down, word came from the advanced party in the shell-holes where the wrecked machine-gun lay, that the Germans were massing for a counter-attack on the Blue line of what had been the third objective. They could be seen in artillery formation with a mass of transport behind them, and it passed the men's comprehension why they did not come on and finish the weary game. But the enemy chose to wait, and at the edge of dusk the Irish saw the 2nd Scots Guards attacking on their right through a barrage of heavy stuff – attacking and disappearing between the shell-bursts. The attack failed: a few of the Scots Guards came back and found places beside the Irish and Coldstream in the trench. Night fell; the enemy's counter-attack held off; the survivors of the advanced party in the shell-holes were withdrawn to help strengthen the main trench; and when it was dark, men were sent out to get into touch with the flanks. They reported, at last, a battalion of the Duke of Cornwall's on their left and the 2nd Grenadiers on their right. In the protecting darkness, too, water and rations arrived from the Ginchy – Lesboeufs road, by some unconsidered miracle-work of Captain Antrobus and the other Battalion Transport Officers; and throughout the very long night, stragglers and little cut-off parties, with their wounded, found the trench, reported, fed, and flung themselves down in whatever place was least walked over – to sleep like the dead, their neighbours. Ground-flares had at last indicated the Battalion's position to our night-scouting contact aeroplanes. There was nothing more to be done except – as one survivor put it – "we was busy thryin' to keep alive against the next day."

The dawn of September 16 pinned them strictly to their cramped position, for the slope behind them ran in full view of the enemy. Moreover, enemy aeroplanes had risen early and taken good stock of the crowded shallow trench where they lay; and in due time the enemy artillery began to scourge them. But some of our Batteries had moved up in the night, and one little field-battery that the Irish thought very kindly of all that day, distracted their tormentors, so that, though they were shelled with H.E. and shrapnel as a matter of principle from dawn to dark, they could still make shift to hang on. The only orders they received from the Brigade that day were to maintain their positions and stand by to support an attack by the 3rd Brigade. That attack, however, never was launched. They lay still and watched, between bursts of shelling, a battalion on their left attacking some German trenches south of Gueudecourt. This happened once in the morning and once in the afternoon. Small stooping or crawling figures crept out for a while over the face of the landscape, drew the German guns, including those that were shelling the Irish trench, upon their advance, wavered forward into the smoke of it, spread out and disappeared – precisely as the watching Guards themselves had done the day before. The impression of unreality was as strong as in a cinema-show. Nothing seemed to happen that made any difference. Small shapes gesticulated a little, lay down and got up again, or having lain down, rose no more. Then the German guns returned to bombarding the Brown-line trench, and the men lying closer realized that the limelight of the show had shifted and was turned mercilessly upon themselves again. All they wanted was relief – relief from the noises and the stenches of the high explosives, the clinging horror of the sights nearest them, and from the tension that lay at the back of the minds of the most unimaginative. The men were dumb – tired with mere work and suffering; the few officers doubly tired out by that and the responsibility of keeping awake and thinking consecutively, even when their words of command clotted on their tongues through sheer weariness. The odds were heavily in favour of a German attack after dark; and a written warning from the rear said it would certainly come in the course of the night. A party of explorers sent to look for defences, found some sections of barb-wire on trestles in the wreck of an enemy trench behind them. It was man-handled and brought away by lengths and, in some fashion, set up before the trench so that the enemy might not actually roll over them without warning.

Fresh rumours of German counter-attacks arrived after midnight, in the way that information blows back and forth across a battle-field in reaction. The men were once more roused – in a burst of chill rain – to strengthen the outpost line. They must have made some noise about it, being more than half asleep at the time, but the enemy, so far from attacking, opened with long-range small-arm fire and sent up a myriad lights. That riot died down at last, and when the Battalion's third down in the line had well broken, a company of Lincolns from the 62nd Brigade came up to the trench, and said their orders were to relieve. The light was full enough now to reveal them very clearly, and "a rapid relief was effected with some difficulty." The enemy shelled till they reached the shelter of the ridge behind and there, at last, drew clear of the immediate aspect of war. Other scattered parties of the Battalion, with little knots of lightly wounded men, joined them on their way to the southern edge of Bernafay Wood, where they took reckoning of their losses. They had still seven officers left, including 2nd Lieutenant T. F. MacMahon, who with some forty men had been left behind in Divisional Reserve on the 16th, and the whole of the working platoon which had not been in action "rejoined the Battalion practically intact." The "working platoon," which was made up of two men from each platoon, was popularly credited with fabricating Headquarters dug-outs at enormous distances from the firing-line and was treated rather as a jest by men not lucky enough to be drawn for it. As for the rest, Major T. M. Bailie, Lieutenant C. R. Tisdall, Lieutenant L. C. Whiteford, and 2nd Lieutenant N. Butler were killed. Captain C. Pease and Lieutenant J. K. Greer died of wounds. Captain P. S. Long-Innes, Captain R. Rankin, Lieutenant A. C. W. Innes, 2nd Lieutenants H. C. Holmes, T. Butler-Stoney, and Count J. E. de Salis were wounded; and there were over 330 casualties in the other ranks. The total casualties in the Brigade were 1776.

No one seems to recall accurately the order of events between the gathering in Bernafay Wood and the arrival of the shadow of the Battalion in camp at the Citadel. The sun was shining; breakfast was ready for the officers and men near some trees. It struck their very tired apprehensions that there was an enormous amount of equipage and service for a very few men, and they noticed dully a sudden hustling off of unneeded plates and cups. They felt as though they had returned to a world which had outgrown them on a somewhat terrifying scale during all the ages that they had been away from it. Their one need, after food eaten sitting, was rest, and, when the first stupor of exhaustion was satisfied, their sleep began to be broken by dreams only less horrible than the memories to which they waked.

SEPTEMBER 25

But the cure was ready to hand. On the evening of the 18th September, in wet and cold weather, the Brigadier sent the Battalion a letter of praise and prophecy:

As your Brigadier I wish to express my feelings as to your most gallant work on the 15th September 1916 in the operations at Ginchy. The advance from the Orchard in the face of machine-gun fire is equal to anything you have yet accomplished in this campaign, and once more the 1st Battalion Irish Guards has carried out a most magnificent advance and held ground gained in spite of the most severe losses. In this, your first campaign, you are upholding the highest standard of bravery and efficiency for your successors and more praise than that I cannot give you. You may be called upon in the very near future to carry out similar work and I know you will not fail.

(Sd-) C. E. PEREIRA,
Brigadier-General,
Commanding 1st Guards Brigade.

This meant that they would be moved again as soon as they could stand up, and would go into their next action with at least 50 per cent new drafts and half their proper allowance of officers. Indeed, they were warned, next day, with the rest of their Division for further operations in the "immediate future," and the work of re-making and re-equipping the Battalion from end to end, saved them from that ghastly state of body and soul which is known as "fighting Huns in your sleep."

On the 19th, Major T. M. D. Bailie's body was brought back from the front and buried in the cemetery in the centre of the camp at Carnoy, and on the same day Lord Cavan, commanding the Corps, rode over and spoke to the officers on horseback of the progress of the campaign, of what had so far been accomplished on the Somme, what was intended for the future, and specially, as bearing on their next battle, of what their Artillery had in store for the enemy. It was a simple, unadorned speech, the substance of which he repeated to the N.C.O.'s, then wished the gentlemen of His Majesty's Foot Guards all good fortune and rode away.

The Division had expected to be used again as soon as might be, but their recent losses were so heavy that every Battalion in it was speculating beneath its breath how their new drafts would shape. It is one thing to take in men by fifties at a time and weld them slowly in The Salient to a common endurance; it is quite another to launch a Battalion, more than half untried recruits, across the open against all that organized death can deliver. This was a time that again tested the Depot and Reserve Battalion whose never-ending work all fighting Battalions take for granted, or mention only to blame. But Warley and Caterham had not failed them. Over three hundred recruits were sent up immediately after the 15th and 16th, and on the 20th September the re-made Battalion, less than six hundred strong, with ten officers, marched out of Citadel Camp to its detestable trenches on Ginchy Ridge. The two Coldstream Battalions of the 1st Brigade held the front line there; the 2nd Grenadiers in reserve, and the 1st Irish Guards in support.

The ground was not yet a sea of mud, but quite sufficiently tenacious. "The area allotted" was old trenches and newish shell-holes with water at the bottom, in "the small rectangular wood east of Trônes Wood." They were employed for three or four days in cleaning up the litter of battle all about the slopes and piling it in dumps, while the enemy shelled them more or less regularly with large black 5·9 shells – a very fair test of the new draft's nerves. The stuff would drop unheralded through the then leafy woods, and explode at large among the shelters and slits that the men had made for themselves. They took the noise and the shaking with philosophy as their N.C.O.'s testified. (" There was some wondherin' in the new drafts, but no budgin', ye'll understand.")

Reading between lines one can see that the R.C. Priest, the Reverend Father F. M. Browne, was busy in those days on spiritual affairs, for he was hit in the face on the 23rd, "while visiting a neighbouring battery," so that Mass on the 24th – the day before their second Battle of the Somme – was celebrated by the Reverend Father Casey. They were shelled, too, that Sunday in the wood, a single unlucky shell killing two men and wounding thirteen. The last available officer from the base, Lieutenant A. H. Blom, had joined the night before; all drafts were in; the ground was assumed to be walkable (which was not the case), and about 9 p.m. of a pitch-black Sunday night the Battalion left the wood and reached its assembly-trench, an extraordinarily bad and unprotected one, about midnight. They were promiscuously shelled in the darkness, and the trench, when found, was so narrow that they had to stand on the edge of it till the Battalion that they relieved – it did not keep them waiting long – got out. No. 1 Company (Captain L. R. Hargreaves), No. 2 Company (Captain the Hon. P. J. Ogilvy) were in the front line, the latter on the right, No. 3 Company (Lieutenant A. H. Blom), and No. 4 Company (Captain Rodakowski) about 150 yards behind with the Battalion Headquarters, in a diagonal communication-trench well bottomed with water. 2nd Lieutenant T. C. Gibson was wounded on the way up, and was replaced by 2nd Lieutenant T. F. MacMahon who had been left in Regimental Reserve.

The idea of the day's work for the 25th was less ambitious than on the 15th, and the objectives were visible German trenches, not imaginary lines on uniformly undistinguishable landscapes. Here is the Brigade-Major's memorandum for the 1st Brigade on the lie of the land, issued on the 22nd September: They were to attack and carry the village of Lesboeufs, up the Ginchy – Lesboeufs road, about fifteen hundred yards, on a front, again, of five hundred yards; the Irish Guards leading the attack throughout on the left of the 1st Brigade, and the 2nd Grenadiers on the right. It was in essence the clearing out of a badly shaken enemy line by the help of exceedingly heavy barrages.

1ST GUARDS BRIGADE No. 262

The forthcoming attack differs from the last in that the whole scheme is not such an ambitious one. The distance to the first objective is about 300 yards, to the second objective 800 yards, and to the last objective about 1300 yards. In each case the objective is a clearly defined one, and not merely a line drawn across the map.

Between our present front line and the first objective there is only "No Man's Land." During the next two nights this should be actively patrolled to ensure that our attack is not taken by surprise by some unknown trench, and in order that Officers and N.C.O.'s may have a knowledge of the ground.

It would also be of great assistance to the Artillery if reports as to the actual distance to the Green line were sent in.

The ground slopes down to Lesboeufs, beyond which there is a distinct hollow with a plateau the same level as Lesboeufs beyond. On reaching the final objective Officers and N.C.O.'s should understand the necessity for pushing patrols out to command this hollow and give warning or prevent counter-attacks forming up here.

Large-scale maps of Lesboeufs have been sent to all battalions. These should be carefully studied by all Officers and N.C.O.'s, and especially by those of the companies detailed for the cleaning up of Lesboeufs.

All runners and signallers should know the position of the advanced Brigade Report Centre, and that the best means of approach to it will probably be down the communication-trench T.3.c and T.8.b.

Finally, it cannot be too much impressed on assaulting troops the necessity for clinging to our own barrage. It will be an attack in which this should be comparatively easy, and on which the success of the whole operation may depend.

(Sd.) M. B. SMITH, Captain,
Brigade-Major,
1st Guards Brigade.

September 22, 1916.

The Battalion's own task was to clear the three objectives laid down, supported by the 3rd Coldstream, to clean out the northern portion of Lesboeufs village, and above all to secure their flanks when they halted or were held up. They waited in their trenches while our guns, hour after hour, sluiced the roads they were to take with an even downpour of shell along the trenches to be attacked – over Lesboeufs and its hidden defences, and far out into the untouched farming land beyond. It was a fine sunny morning that hid nothing. At 12.35 our barrage locked down two hundred yards ahead of the troops, and No. 1 and 2 Companies moved out with the rest of the line towards the first German trench three hundred yards away. The enemy put down a barrage at once on our front support and communication-trenches, which caused a good many casualties (including Captain R. J. P. Rodakowski and the Doctor) in Nos. 3 and 4 Companies who were moving up as a second wave. Eventually, these Companies found it less hampering to leave the crowded trench and come out over the open. So far, our artillery work was altogether a better business than on the 15th. The Companies moved almost leisurely behind the roaring arch-of-triumph of the barrage, till the leading line reached the first trench with its half-finished dug-outs. Here they found only dazed German survivors begging to be taken out of that inferno to the nearest prisoners' kraal. Some of these captures, officers included, sincerely expected to be slaughtered in cold blood.

The 2nd Grenadiers, on the right of the 1st Irish Guards, had been unlucky in their position, for the wire in front of their sector being veiled by high crop, our guns had missed it. That Battalion suffered heavily in officers and men, shot down as they tried to work their way through by hand; but they never lost touch, and the advance went on unbrokenly to the next point – a sunken road on the east side of Lesboeufs, five hundred yards ahead of the first objective. All four Companies of the Irish were together now – Lieutenant Blom of No. 3 had been wounded at the first trench and 2nd Lieutenant T. F. MacMahon took over. They reached the downward slope to the sunk road and, as at the first objective, found most of their work had been done for them by the barrage. Even while they congratulated themselves and sent off a pigeon, as well as runner messages, to report the capture to Battalion Headquarters, which, "somewhat broken" by the German shelling, had arrived in the first-taken trench, fire fell on them from the south. Our own guns, misranging across the fields, were supposed to be responsible for this; and a second pigeon was despatched praying them to cease, but "there were a number of casualties" before the advance to the last objective began. This was shown on the map as just east of Lesboeufs village, and east again of another sunken road. The final surge forward included a rush across uprooted orchards and through wrecked houses, shops and barns, with buildings alight or confusedly collapsing round them, and the enemy streaming out ahead to hide in shell-holes in the open. There was not much killing at this point, and, thanks to the tanks and the guns, a good deal less machine-gun fire than might have been expected. The Battalion dug in in a potato field a few hundred yards beyond the village, where the men providently laid aside the largest potatoes for supper, if so be they should live till that meal. In the meantime our guns were punching holes into the open land behind Lesboeufs, where parties of dislodged enemy had taken shelter. These preferred, at last, to bolt back through that storm and surrender to our men digging, who received them with derisive cheers – "for all the world as though they had been hares in a beat." Then came the tragedy. Our barrage, for some reason or other, wavered and stopped almost on the line where the men were digging in, and there hung for a long while – some accounts say a quarter of an hour, others two hours. At any rate, it was long enough to account for many more casualties. Captain L. R. Hargreaves, who had fought wounded through the 15th, was here so severely wounded that he died while being carried back, and Captain Drury-Lowe of the King's Company of the 1st Grenadiers, digging in on the Irish left, was killed – both casualties by one shell. The 2nd Grenadiers, all Company Officers down, were in touch on the right, but the left was still doubtful, for the attack there had been held up at Gueudecourt village, and the 3rd Guards Brigade had to make a defensive flank there, while a company of the 3rd Coldstream was moved up to help in the work.

In modern war no victory appears till the end of all, and what is gained by immense bloodshed must be held by immense physical labour of consolidation, which gives the enemy time to recover and counter-attack in his turn. The Irish dug and deepened and strengthened their line north of Lesboeufs, while the enemy shelled them till afternoon, when there was a breathing-space. A German counter-attack, on the left of the Guards Division, was launched and forthwith burned up. The shelling was resumed till night, which suddenly fell so quiet, by Somme standards, that supplies could be brought up without too much difficulty. As soon as light for ranging came on the 26th, our men were shelled to ground again; and an attempt of three patrols to get forward and establish posts of command on a near-by ridge brought them into a nest of machine-guns and snipers. The Diary remarks that the patrols located "at least one machine-gun," which is probably a large understatement; for so soon as the German machine-gunners recovered breath and eyesight, after or between shells, they were up and back and at work again. By the rude arithmetic of the ranks in those days, three machine-guns equalled a company, and, when well posted, a battalion.

The Battalion was relieved on the evening of the 26th by its sister (the 2nd) Battalion, who took over the whole of Lesboeufs ruins from the Brigade; and the 1st Irish Guards went back with the others through Bernafay Wood, where they fed, to camp once more at the Citadel.

In the two days of their second Somme battle, which they entered less than six hundred strong and ten officers, they had lost one officer, Captain Hargreaves, died of wounds, and five wounded, and more than 250 casualties in other ranks. Add these to the casualties of the 15th, and it will be seen that in ten days the Battalion had practically lost a Battalion. The Commanding Officer, Colonel McCalmont, the Adjutant, Captain Gordon, and Lieutenant Smith were the only officers who had come unwounded through both actions.

General Pereira, commanding the 1st Guards Brigade, issued the following order on the 27th September:

You have again maintained the high traditions of the 1st Guards Brigade when called upon a second time in the Battle of the Somme. For five days previous to the assault the 2nd and 3rd Battalion Coldstream Guards held the trenches under constant heavy shell-fire and dug many hundred yards of assembly and communication trenches, this work being constantly interrupted by the enemy's artillery. The 2nd Battalion Grenadier Guards and the 1st Battalion Irish Guards, though under shell-fire in their bivouacs, were kept clear of the trenches until the evening of 24th September and were given the task of carrying by assault all the objectives to be carried by this Brigade. Nothing deterred them in this attack, not even the fact that in places the enemy wire was cut in the face of rifle and machine-gun fire, and in spite of all resistance and heavy losses the entire main enemy defensive line was captured.

Every Battalion in the Brigade carried out its task to the full.

The German Reserve Division, which includes the 238th, 239th, and 240th Regiments, and which opposed you for many weeks at Ypres, left the Salient on the 18th September. You have now met them in the open, a worthy foe, but you have filled their trenches with their dead and have driven them before you in headlong flight.

I cannot say how proud I am to have had the honour of commanding the 1st Guards Brigade in this battle, a Brigade which has proved itself to be the finest in the British Army.

The Brigade is now under orders for rest and training, and it must now be our object to keep up the high standard of efficiency, and those who have come to fill our depleted ranks will strive their utmost to fill worthily the place of those gallant officers and men who have laid down their lives for a great cause.

(Sd.) C. E. PEREIRA,
Brigadier-General,
Commanding 1st Guards Brigade.

September 28, 1916.

Lord Cavan had sent the following message to General Pereira:

Hearty thanks and sincere congratulations to you all. A very fine achievement splendidly executed.

To which the Brigadier had replied:

Your old Brigade very proud to be able to present you with Lesboeufs. All ranks most gratified by your kind congratulations.

And so that little wave among many waves, which had done its work and gained its few hundred yards of ground up the beach, drew back into the ocean of men and hutments below the slopes of the Somme. The new drafts were naturally rather pleased with themselves; their N.C.O.'s were reasonably satisfied with them, and the remnant of the officers were far too busy with reorganization and re-equipment to have distinct notions on any subject except the day's work. It was a little later that heroisms or horrors, seen out of the tail of the eye in action, and unrealized at the time, became alive as rest returned to the body and men compared dreams with each other, or argued in what precise manner such and such a comrade had died. There was bravery enough and to spare on all hands, and there were a few, but not too many, decorations awarded for it in the course of the next month. The Battalion took the bravery for granted, and the credit of the aggregate went to the Battalion. They looked at it, broadly speaking, thus: "There was times when ye'll understand if a man was *not* earnin' V.C.'s for hours on end he would not keep alive – an' even *then*, unless the Saints looked after him, he'd likely be killed in the middest of it." In other words, the average of bravery required in action had risen twentyfold, even as the average of shots delivered by machine-guns exceeds that of many rifles; and by the mercy of Heaven, as the Irish themselves saw it, the spirit of man under discipline had risen to those heights. Captain L. R. Hargreaves (killed on the 25th) and Captain P. S. Long- Innes (wounded), with Lieutenant G. V. Williams (who was knocked unconscious and nearly killed by shell-fire on the 25th), were given the Military Cross for the affair of the 15th. Drill-Sergeant Moran, a pillar of the Battalion, who had died of wounds (it was he who had asked the immortal question about "this retreat" at Mons), with Private Boyd, received the D.C.M., and Sergeant Riordan (wounded and reported missing) the Bar to the same medal. Lance-Corporal J. Carroll, Privates M. Kenny, J. O'Connor, J. White and Lance-Corporal Cousins had the Military Medal – all for the 15th.

For the 15th and 25th combined, Lieutenant Walter Mumford and 2nd Lieutenant T. F. MacMahon won the Military Cross; and Sergeant P. Doolan and Private G. Taylor the Military Medal.

For the 25th, temporary Captain the Hon. P. Ogilvy received the Military Cross; acting Company Sergeant-Major McMullen, the Bar to his D.C.M.; and Privates Whearty, Troy and M. Lewis, the Military Medal. Captain Gordon, the Adjutant, was recommended for an immediate M.C., which he received with the next New Year honours at the same time as the C.O. received a D.S.O.

It was not an extravagant reward for men who have to keep their heads under hideous circumstances and apply courage and knowledge at the given instant; and after inconceivable strain, to hold, strengthen and turn desperate situations to their platoon's or company's advantage. The news went into Warley and Caterham, and soured Drill-Sergeants, dead-wearied with the repetition-work of forming recruits to fill shell-holes, found their little unnoticed reward in it. (" Yes. *We* made 'em – with the rheumatism on us, an' all; an' *we* kept on makin' 'em till I got to hate the silly faces of 'em. An' what did we get out of it? ' Tell Warley that their last draft was dam' rabbits an' the Ensigns as bad.' An' after that, it's Mil'try Crosses and D. C. M.'s for *our* dam' rabbits!")
The Battalion returned to the days of small, detailed, important things – too wearied to appreciate compliments, and too overworked with breaking in fresh material to think.

On the 27th, 2nd Lieutenant R. B. S. Reford joined from the base on the 28th, 2nd Lieutenant T. F. MacMahon with a party was sent to rest-camp for a week. On the 30th, Captains the Earl of Kingston and H. T. A. Boyse joined and took over command of Nos. 1 and 3 Companies.

REST-CAMPS AND FATIGUES

On the 1st October, a Sunday, after Mass celebrated by a French interpreter, which did not affect the devotion of the Battalion, the whole Brigade were embarked in one hundred and forty "French Army charabancs," a new and unforeseen torment, and driven via Amiens from Fricourt to rest-camp at Hornoy. Much must have happened on that pleasure-trip; for the Diary observes that the drivers of the vehicles were "apparently over military age, many of the assistants being natives." One is left in the dark as to their countries of origin, but one's pity goes out to all of them, Annamite, Senegalese, or Algerian, who helped to convey the newly released Irish for eight hours over fifty jolting miles.

The Battalion found good billets for themselves, and the Brigade Machine-gun Company in Hornoy itself, where the inhabitants showed them no small kindness. "Owing to small numbers, officers were in one Mess," says the Diary, and one can see the expansion of that small and shrunken Company as the new drafts come in and training picks up again.

On the 3rd October, 2nd Lieutenants J. J. Fitzwilliam Murphy and J. N. Nash joined; on the 4th, the Reverend P. J. Lane-Fox joined for duty; on the 5th, 2nd Lieutenant the Hon. D. O'Brien came in sick with the draft of a hundred and fifty-two and went down sick, all within forty-eight hours, his draft punctually delivered. Major the Hon. T. Vesey also joined as Second in Command during the course of this month.

They paraded on the 5th October for the Divisional Commander, Major-General Feilding, who presented the ribbons to the N.C.O.'s and men who had been awarded medals and complimented the Battalion on its past work. Second Lieutenant E. Budd (and five other ranks), 2nd Lieutenant E. M. Harvey, with a draft of ninety-five, not counting eleven more who had joined in small parties, and 2nd Lieutenants A. L. Bain, H. H. Maxwell, and J. J. Kane all came in within the next ten days. Captain R. G. C. Yerburgh, on rejoining from the Central Training School at Havre, was posted to the command of No. 4 Company; and on the 8th October, a team, chiefly officers, greatly daring, played a Rugby football match against "a neighbouring French Recruit Battalion," which campaign seems to have so inspired them that they all attended a Divisional dinner that night at 1st Brigade Headquarters at Dromesnil. There is, alas! no record of that match nor of what the French Recruit Battalion thought of it; but just before their departure from Hornoy they played a Soccer match against the 26th French Infantry, and next day the C.O. and all Company Officers rode over to that regiment to see how it practised the latest form of attack over the open. Thus did they combine instruction with amusement, and cemented the Sacred Alliance.

They dined also with their own 2nd Battalion, who were billeted five miles away – a high and important function at Hornoy where Brigadier-General Butler, formerly in command of the 2nd Battalion, was present, with all the officers of both Battalions. The band of the Welsh Guards assisted and they all drank the health, among many others, of the belle of Hornoy, who "responded with enthusiasm." Further, they played a football match against their brethren and won; entertained the village, not forgetting the 26th French Infantry, with their Drums; drove all ranks hard at Company drills and Battalion attacks; rehearsed the review for the approaching visit of H.R.H. the Duke of Connaught, and welcomed small detachments as they came in. The last was 2nd Lieutenant D. A. B. Moodie with fifty, on the 26th October, when Lieutenant H. F. S. Law rejoined the Battalion from his Intelligence duties with the Ninth Corps. Drill-Sergeant J. Orr assumed the duties of 2nd Lieutenant from November 2.

The Mess was now full again. The dead of the September Somme had almost passed out of men's memories till the war should be over and the ghosts return;

and the Battalion, immortal however much it changes, was ready ("forty over strength") for the bitter winter of '16–'17.

On the 7th November they were warned to move back into line and celebrated it by an officers' dinner (thirty-seven strong) of both Battalions at the Hotel London, Hornoy.

On the 10th they regretfully quitted that hospitable village for the too familiar camping grounds near Carnoy beyond Méaulte, which in winter becomes a marsh on the least provocation. They were accommodated "in bell-tents in a sea of mud" with weather to match.

Next day (11th November) they shifted to "a sort of camp" near Montauban, "quite inadequate" and served by bottomless roads where they were shelled a little after Mass – a proof, one presumes, that the enemy had news of their arrival.

On the 13th November, in cold but dry weather, they took over a line of trench north of Lesboeufs between that village and Gueudecourt. These were reached by interminable duckboards from Trônes Wood and up and over the battered and hacked Flers ridge. There were no communication-trenches and, in that windy waste of dead weed and wreckage, no landmarks to guide the eye. Trench equipment was utterly lacking, and stick and strand had to be man-handled up from Ginchy. In these delectable lodgings they relieved the 7th Yorkshire and the 8th South Staffordshires losing one man wounded by shell-fire, and Major the Hon. T. E. Vesey was sent down sick as the result of old wounds received at Loos and in '14. The Somme was no place for such as were not absolutely fit, and even the fittest had to pay toll.

Shelling for the next three days was "continuous but indiscriminate." Four men were killed, fourteen wounded and three disappeared – walked, it is supposed, into enemy ground. The wonder was there were not more such accidents. Wiser men than they would come up to the front line with a message, refuse the services of a guide back because, they protested, they knew every inch of the ground and – would be no more seen till exhumation parties three or four years later identified them by some rag of Guards' khaki or a button.

The Battalion was relieved by the 2nd Grenadiers at midnight (16th November), but were not clear till morning, when they crawled back to camp between Carnoy and Montauban, packed forty men apiece into the icy-chill Nissen huts, supposed to hold thirty, and were thankful for the foul warmth of them. Thence they moved into unstable tents on the outskirts of Méaulte, on the Bray road, where the wind funnels from all parts of the compass, and in alternate snow, rain and snow again, plumbed the deeps of discomfort. When frost put a crust on the ground they drilled; when it broke they cleaned themselves from mud; and, fair or foul, did their best to "improve" any camp into which fortune decanted them.

It was a test, were one needed, that proved all ranks to the uttermost. The heroism that endures for a day or a week at high tension is a small thing beside that habit of mind which can hold fast to manner, justice, honour and a show of kindliness and toleration, in despite of physical misery and the slow passage of bleak and indistinguishable days. Character and personality, whatever its "crime-sheet" may have been, was worth its weight in gold on the Somme, where a jest counted as high as a rumration. All sorts of unsuspected people came to their own as leaders of men or lighteners of care. There were stretcher-bearers, for instance, whose mere presence and personality steadied half a platoon after the shell-burst when, picking themselves up, men's first question out of the dark would be: "Where's So-and-so?" And So-and-so would answer with the dignity of Milesian Kings: "I'm here! Ca-arry on, lads!"

So, too, with the officers. In the long overseeing of endless fatigues, which are more trying than action, they came to understand the men with a thoroughness that one is inclined to believe not many corps have reached. Discipline in the Guards, as has been many times pointed out, allowed no excuse whatever for the officer or the man; but once the punishment, or the telling off, had been administered, the sinner and the judge could, and did, discuss everything under Heaven. One explanation which strikes at the root of the matter is this: "Ye'll understand that in those days we was all countin' ourselves for dead men – sooner or later. 'Twas in the air, ye'll understand – like the high stuff comin' over."

On Sunday, the 27th November, the day of the Requiem Mass for the Irish Guards in Westminster Cathedral, a requiem mass was said in Méaulte Church and they moved out to a French camp ("Forked Tree"), south of the town where the big French huts held a hundred men apiece, but cook-houses, etc., were all to build and the "usual routine improvement work began again." Their Brigade Bombing Officer, Lieutenant the Hon. H. B. O'Brien, was appointed Staff Captain to the 1st Guards Brigade, and Captain R. G. C. Yerburgh left to be attached to the 2nd Guards Brigade H.Q. Staff for instruction in staff duties.

They were visited by their Corps and Divisional Commanders, inspected by their Brigadier and route-marched till the 3rd December, when they moved to Maltz Horn Camp.

It had been decided that the British Army should, by degrees, take over a stretch of the French line from Le Transloy to a point opposite Roye; and the Battalion's share of this was about a thousand yards of trench at Sailly-Saillisel, held by the 160th Regiment of the Twentieth Corps (Corps de Fer). The front line ran a little in front of what had once been that long and prosperous village on the ridge, and, though not continuous, "it held in places." The support-line, through and among the wreck of the houses, was dry and fairly good. That there were no communication-trenches was a small matter – men preferred to take their chances in the open to being buried in trench mud – but there was no road up to it and "the going was heavy."

Once installed (December 6), after a prompt and workmanlike French relief, which impressed them, they found the 156th French Infantry on their right, a Coldstream Battalion on their left, and an enemy in front disposed to be quiet "except when frightened" or suspecting reliefs, when he would drop very unpleasant barrages on the support-line.

They were relieved on the 9th December by the 2nd Grenadiers who were late, because they were "constantly delayed by digging men out of mud." From Bois de la Haie, the long, thin slip of wood under Morval whence the relief started at a quarter past five in the evening, the distance to the Battalion's sector might be two miles. That relief was not completed till half-past one on the morning of the 10th – say eight hours to cover four or five miles in one continuous nightmare of mud, darkness, loss of touch and the sudden engulfment of heavily loaded men. A Grenadier Battalion claims to hold the record (fifteen hours) for the extrication of one man. Six or eight hours was not uncommon. They were shelled, of course, on their arrival and lost Sergeant Wylie, killed, and eleven wounded. Captain R. V. Pollok joined from home on that day and took over command of No. 1 Company. Major E. B. Greer, on loan from the 2nd Battalion, who had commanded the Battalion temporarily, handed over to Captain the Hon. H. R. Alexander, D.S.O., acting C.O. in place of Colonel R. McCalmont on leave. Captain the Earl of Kingston had to go into hospital on the 10th – "result of an old wound" – and on the 13th December Lieutenant J. J. V. F. Murphy – "exposure."

On the 12th December, after a day's rest in a muddy camp near Montauban, they marched to Combles through the blackened site of Guillemont to relieve the 2nd Battalion on a more southerly sector, to furnish working-parties for the railway-lines that were spreading stealthily north and east, to help lay down plank roads – not the least burdensome of fatigues, for the "planks" were substantial logs – and to make the front line a little less impossible. It was an easy turn, with very little shelling or sniping, "both sides being only able to reach their front line by going over the open." When to this is added full moonlight and a fall of snow, moderation is imposed on every one till they are under cover. Otherwise a local battle might have developed – and what is the use of local battles where both sides are stuck in the mud, and no help can be sent to either? This question would be put to the Staff when, from the comfortable security of their decent dug-outs, they lectured the front line, and were invited mirthfully to come up and experiment for themselves.

The Battalion had eleven wounded in three days, and returned to Bronfay to find their allotted camp already filled up by Gunners. Then there was confusion and argument, and the Quartermaster – notable even among Quartermasters – "procured" fuel and braziers and got the men more or less warmed and fed. "The muddle," says the Diary sternly, "was due to no proper arrangements being made to find out to whom Camp 108 belonged before the Battalions were moved into them." Thus, on paper at least, did the front line get back at the Staff.

They returned to the Combles area on the 18th, relieved their sister Battalion in less than three hours, and in fine frosty weather, helped by the enemy's inactivity, improved the trenches, lost five killed and one wounded, and on their return found Camp 108 also "improved" and devoid of Gunners.

The year closed well. Their Christmas turn (December 25–27, when they missed their Christmas dinners) was almost bloodless. The reliefs went smoothly, and though a thaw made the trenches cave here and there, but four men were wounded, and in their New Year turn, only one.

About Christmas the Brigade, to their deep regret, lost their Brigadier-General C. Pereira – promoted to command the Second Division, and in him, one of the best friends that they ever had. He knew the Battalion very personally, appreciated its value, and fought for its interests with devotion and a strong hand.

Nothing is said in the Diary of any attempts on the enemy's part to fraternize, and the New Year was "seen in without any incident," which means that no bursts of artillery marked the hour. And on the 3rd January the whole of the Guards Division went out of the line for refit. The Twentieth Division took its unenvied place, and the 1st Battalion Irish Guards lay at Sandpits Camp near Méaulte.

The strain was beginning to tell. They had had to transfer Lieutenant F. S. L. Smith and 2nd Lieutenant J. Kane to the 2nd Battalion "owing to shortage in that Battalion on account of sickness," and their own coolies were in need of rest and change. The strongest cannot stand up beyond a certain point to exposure, broken rest, alarums all round the clock; laborious physical exertions, knee or mid-thigh deep in mud; sweating fatigues, followed by cooling-off in icy blasts or a broth of snow and chalk-slime; and – more undermining than any bodily stress the pressure that grows of hourly responsibility. Sooner or later, the mind surrenders itself to a mill-round of harassing obsessions as to whether, if one had led one's platoon up or down by such and such a deviation – to the left or the right of a certain dead horse, for example – if one had halted longer there or whipped up more cautiously elsewhere – one might have saved such and such a casualty, entombment in the mud, or some other shrieking horror of the night. Reason insists that it was not, and could not have been, one's own fault. Memory brings back the face or the eyes of the dying, and the silence, always accusing, as the platoon goes forward. When this mood overtakes an officer he does well to go into rest for a while and pad his nerves, lest he arrive at that dreadful stage when he is convinced that his next turn of duty will see all his men destroyed by his own act. Between this last stage and the dragging weariness, the hoarse Somme cold, and the foul taste in the mouth which are mere signs of "beginning to be fed up," there is every variety of derangement, to be held in check by the individual's own character and that discipline which age and experience have devised to hold him when everything else has dropped away. It is the deadly journey, back and forth to the front line with material, the known and foreseen war in darkness and mud against the natural perversity of things, that shifts the foundations of the soul, so that a man, who scarcely regards Death hunting him at large by the hour, will fall into a child's paroxysms of rage and despair when the wire-strand rasps him across the knuckles or the duckboard for the hundredth time tilts sideways underfoot. "Ye'll understand," says the voice of experience, "the fatigues do it in the long run." All of which the Diary will dismiss with: "A few fatigues were found in this area."

The Somme was one overwhelming fatigue.

1917
THE SOMME TO GOUZEAUCOURT

THE BEGINNING of the year saw the British Armies, now more than fifty Divisions strong, holding a front of a hundred and ten miles from Ypres to within a short distance of Roye. Thus, allowing for changes imposed by the fluctuations of war and attack, they lay:

The Second Army had the Salient; the First centred on Armentières; the Third carried on to the south of Arras, where the Fifth held all along the valley of the Ancre and a portion of the old British line on the Somme. The Fourth joined the French left wing near Roye, and the French pressure worked in with ours.

From the Salient to the Somme battle-front, our line's business was to draw as much as possible of the enemy's strength. Therefore, our raids on that part of the line, during the latter half of 1916, were counted by the hundred; and in all that time, at no point on any given day there, could the Germans feel secure against our irruptions.

On the Somme our pressure was direct and, except for the weather, worked as continuously as a forest fire in fallen pine-needles. A fold of the hills might check it there; a bare ridge or a sodden valley hold it elsewhere for the while; but always it ate north and east across the stricken country, as Division after Division gathered, fought, won foothold, held it, dug in, and gave place to their unspent fellows beneath the cover of the advancing guns. Here is a mere outline of the work of a few weeks:

The affairs of the 15th and 25th of September (1916), when the Fourth Army pushed the line past Lesboeufs and Flers and beyond Gueudecourt on the right, knocked out, as we know, both Battalions of the Irish Guards for the time being. On the 27th and 28th of September the Second and First Canadian Divisions, with the Eleventh and Eighteenth of the Second Army Corps, captured Thiepval, the Stuff and Schwaben Redoubts on the left of the line; while the Fifty-fifth and New Zealand Divisions made possible an advance on Le Sars and Eaucourt l'Abbaye villages in the centre, which, after four days' continuous fighting by the Forty-seventh, Fiftieth and Twenty-third Divisions, ended in the taking of Eaucourt l'Abbaye and Le Sars.

On the 7th of October the French Army attacked in the direction of Sailly-Saillisel, the Fourth Army chiming in along its whole front from Lesboeufs to Destremont Farm, which had been taken by the Twenty-third Division on the 29th September. In this affair the Twenty-third Division captured Le Sars, and the Twentieth Division over a mile of trenches east of Gueudecourt.

Then the treacherous weather broke once more, and the battered and crumbled ground held their feet till a few days of dry cold were snatched for an attack in the direction of Courcelette by four Divisions (Fourth Canadian, Eighteenth, Fifteenth and Thirty-ninth), where a fresh line was needed.

On the 23rd October, and on the 5th November again, as side-issues while waiting on the weather for a serious attack on Beaumont-Hamel, a couple of Divisions (Fourth and Eighth) went in with a French attack against St. Pierre Vaast Wood, where a tangle of enemy trenches at the junction of the two armies was slowly smoked and burned out.

The 10th of November (after one day's fine weather) gave the Fourth Canadian Division a full day's fighting and, once more, a thousand yards of trench in the Courcelette sector.

On the 13th of November the Battle of the Ancre opened from Serre to east of the Schwaben Redoubt (Thirty-first, Third, Second, Fifty-first, Thirty-ninth and Nineteenth Divisions), with the intention of gaining command of both banks of the river, where it entered the enemy lines six or seven miles north of Albert. This was a sector of the old German front to the west, which had thrown back our opening attack of July 1, and had grown no more inviting since. Serre itself, helped by the state of the ground before it, was impossible, but Beaucourt, Beaumont-Hamel, and a portion of the high ground above it, with the village of St. Pierre-Division in the valley, were, in the course of the next few days, captured and held.

All the above takes no count of incessant minor operations, losses and recaptures of trenches, days and nights of bombing that were necessary to silence nests of subterranean works, marked on the maps of peace as "villages"; nor of the almost monotonous counter-attacks that followed on the heels of every gain. So long as movement was possible the Somme front was alive from end to end, according as one hard-gained position gave the key to the next, or unscreened some hitherto blinded works. Against every disadvantage of weather and over ground no troops in history had before dared to use at that season, the system and design of the advance revealed itself to the enemy. Their counter-attacks withered under our guns or died out in the fuming, raw-dug trenches; the slopes that had been their screens were crowned and turned against them; their infantry began to have no love for the blunt-nosed tanks which, though not yet come to the war in battalions, were dragging their smeared trails along the ridges; the fighting aeroplanes worried them, too, with machine-gun fire from over-head; photographers marked their covered ways by day and our heavy bombers searched them by night, as owls search stubble for mice. It all cost men and stuff, and the German Army Command had little good news to send back to the German Tribes.

Yet the last six months of 1916 had advanced our front no more than some eight miles – along the Albert – Bapaume road. At no point were we more than ten miles from our beginnings. All that showed on the map was that the enemy's line to the north had been pinched into a salient which, starting from just east of Arras, followed the line of the old German front built up two years before, through Monchy-au-Bois, Gomiecourt and Serre to the high white grounds above Beaumont-Hamel. Thence it turned east across the Ancre, seven or eight kilometres north of Arras, skirted Grandcourt, crossed the arrow-straight Albert road by the dreary Butte de Warlencourt, ran north-east of Gueudecourt, and on the rim of the rise above Le Transloy, till it crossed the Péronne – Bapaume road just north of Sailly-Saillisel. Here it swung south-east from Rancourt and Bouchavesnes down the long slopes to the Valley of the Somme, and its marshes west of Péronne. Thence, south-westerly by Berny-en-Santerre, Ablaincourt to the outskirts of Chaulnes, ending at Le Quesnoy en-Santerre, where the French took on. The twenty-five-mile stretch from Le Transloy to Le Quesnoy was the new section that had been handed over to the British care, piece by piece, at the end of the year.

To meet this pinch and all that they could see that it meant, the Germans had constructed, while they and the weather held us, elaborate second and third lines of defence behind their heavily fortified front. The first barrier – a double line of trenches, heavily wired, ran behind Sailly-Saillisel, past Le Transloy to the Albert – Bapaume road, Grévillers and Loupart woods, and via Achiet-le-Petit to Bucquoy.

Parallel to this, at a distance ranging from one to two miles, was a new line through Rocquigny, Bapaume and Ablainzevelle, almost equally strong and elaborate. Behind it, as every one understood, was a thing called the Hindenburg Line, known to the Germans as "Siegfried" – a forty-mile marvel of considered defences with branches and spurs and switches, one end of which lay on St. Quentin and the other outside Arras. This could be dealt with later, but, meantime, the enemy in the Arras – Le Transloy salient were uneasy. The attacks delivered on selected positions; the little inter-related operations that stole a few hundred yards of trench or half a village at a leap, or carried a gun-group to a position whence our batteries could peer out and punish; above all, the cold knowledge that sooner or later our unimaginative, unmilitary infantry would shamble after the guns, made them think well of lines in their rear to which they could retire at leisure.

Verdun had not fallen; very many of their men lay dead outside its obliterated forts, and so very many living were needed to make good the daily drain of the Somme that they had none too many to spare for Austrian or Turkish needs. Their one energetic ally was the weather, which, with almost comic regularity, gave them time after each reverse to draw breath, position more guns, reorganize reliefs, and explain to their doubting public in Germany the excellence and the method of their Army's plans for the future. The Battle of the Ancre, for instance, was followed by an absolute deadlock of six weeks, when our armies – one cannot assault and dig out Battalions at the same time – dropped everything to fight the mud, while our front line wallowed in bottomless trenches where subalterns took from three to six hours to visit their posts on a front of one quarter of a mile.

Bitter frosts set in with the first weeks of the New Year and the "small operations" began at once, on our side, round such portions of the Beaumont-Hamel heights as the enemy still clung to. Here the Third, Seventh and Eleventh Divisions fought, shift by shift, for the rest of January and won the high ground needed for our guns to uncover against Serre and Grandcourt, which were the keys of the positions at the corner of the Arras – Le Transloy salient. Thanks to our air-work, and the almost daily improvement in the power and precision of our barrages, that little army came through its campaign without too heavy losses, and still further cramped the enemy's foothold along the Ancre, while the rest of the line enjoyed as much peace as the Somme allowed them when "there was nothing doing."

MARKING TIME

The Guards Division, after their ten days' rest and clean-up at Sandpits Camp, Méaulte, supplied one Brigade to take over a new sector of trench opposite St. Pierre Vaast Wood on the extreme east of things and left their 1st Brigade in Reserve at Méaulte, Ville-sous-Corbie and Méricourt l'Abbé. The latter camp was allotted to the Irish Guards who had to send one company for permanent fatigues to the Railway Station – all the valley here was one long siding for men and supplies – and another to the back of Bernafay Wood for Decauville construction, while the remainder were drilled and instructed in their specialities. This was the time in our Armies' development when nearly every third man was a "specialist" in some branch or another except, as Company Officers remarked under their breaths, the rifle and its bayonet. The men's deferred Christmas dinners (it will be remembered they had been in the line on the day itself) were duly issued by half a Battalion at a time in the big cinema-hall in camp, and, lest the Transport Officer should by any chance enjoy himself, their transport chose this time of rest to develop "contagious stomatitis," a form of thrush in the mouth, and had to be isolated. Still, setting aside the cold, which does not much trouble well-fed men, the Battalion had some pleasant memories of its rest by the river. Leave was possible; smoking-parties made themselves in the big huts; the Sergeants gave a dinner, which is a sure sign of well-being; there were cinemas for the men, and no one troubled himself too much for the noise of the guns ten miles upstream.

It is difficult to rediscover a Battalion's psychology at any given time, but so far as evidence goes they had not too black doubts as to the upshot of the campaign, though every platoon kept its loud-voiced pessimists who foretold that they would take root in the trenches for evermore and christened the R.O.D. locomotives "Roll on Duration!"

On the 1st February (1917) in "cold, bright weather with snow on the ground," the 1st Brigade were once again in Divisional Reserve near Carnoy, ready to relieve the 3rd Coldstream near Rancourt on the recently-taken-over French sector, in trenches a little westerly of St. Pierre Vaast Wood which is under Sailly-Saillisel. In the wood itself lay a dreadful mine-crater of the old days, filled, as it seemed, with dead French Colonial troops – browned and blackened bodies, their white skulls still carrying jaunty red caps. Our wondering patrols used to look down into it sometimes of moonlight nights.

They moved out on the 2nd February via Maricourt and Maurepas, left No. 2 Company under canvas in Maurepas Ravine, distributed the rest in shelters and dug-outs and resumed their watch. The frozen ground stopped much digging or "improvements," and the enemy's front line gave no trouble, but a few small shells were sent over, one of which hit 2nd Lieutenant J. Orr temporarily in command of No. 1 Company and wounded a couple of men. The rest of their turn – February 2 to 6 – was quiet, for the new-fallen snow gave away the least movement on either side. While they crouched over their braziers and watched each other, the operations round Serre and at the nose of the Arras – Le Transloy salient began again as the earth's crust hardened. The Sixty-third Division hammered its way for a day and a night up the southern slopes of Serre, and our guns were threatening the line of enemy trenches from Grandcourt westward. This move unkeyed the arch of his local defences at this point, and next day he evacuated Grandcourt and such of his front as lay between Grandcourt and the Stuff Redoubt.

By the 7th February our troops had carried forward to midway between Beaucourt and Miraumont, and on the 10th February the Thirty-second Division took in hand the business of shifting the enemy out of what remained to him in the Beaumont Valley. Their advance brought Serre village into direct danger from our artillery, and any farther move on our part up the valley of the Ancre would make Serre untenable.

On the 17th February that move was made by three Divisions (Second, Eighteenth and Sixty-third) before dawn, through heavy mist on the edge of a thaw, and in the face of a well-contrived barrage that caught the battalions forming up. But the positions and observation-points, already gained, helped our guns to help the infantry, broke up the enemy's counter-attacks with satisfactory losses, and, in the next few days, gave us good command over the enemy's artillery dispositions in the valley of the Upper Ancre and a fair look into his defences at Pys and Miraumont. Then the game stood thus: If Miraumont, which lay at our mercy, were taken, Serre would go; if Serre went, Puisieux-au-Mont and Gomiecourt, the pillar of the old German western defences, would be opened too; and it was no part of the German idea to cling to untenable positions, whose loss would have to be explained at home where people were asking why victory delayed so long. Not only was the whole of the Arras – Le Transloy salient shaking by now; there was the prospect of indefinite wastage to no good end all along the rest of the Somme front, and though the

The frost broke in the third week in February, and the last state of the ground was worse even than it had been throughout the rainy autumn. Trenches caved in badly; . . . tanks were immobilized five feet deep and the very bellies of the field-guns gouged into the mud.

The Somme, east of Albert, 1917.

weather, till then, had blunted the following weight of each following blow, many considerations pointed to a temporary withdrawal of a few miles in order to advance the more irresistibly at a more fitting time. Slowly, methodically then, with careful screens of veiled machine-guns behind them, and a series of scientifically chosen artillery positions, equally capable of supporting a counter-attack, or checking and destroying any too inconvenient body of pursuers, the enemy moved back into ground not yet churned and channelled by shell or traffic, over untouched roads which he had kept in perfect order, to this very end; and left us to follow through bottomless valleys of desolation.

The frost broke in the third week in February, and the last state of the ground was worse even than it had been throughout the rainy autumn. Trenches caved in badly; dumps sank where they were being piled; the dirt and the buttresses of overhead shelters flaked and fell away in lumps; duckboards went under by furlongs at a time; tanks were immobilized five feet deep and the very bellies of the field-guns gouged into the mud. Only our airmen could see anything beyond or outside the present extreme discomfort, but the mists that came punctually with the thaws helped to baffle even their eyes.

On the 24th February the enemy had evacuated his positions in front of Pys, Miraumont and Serre: next day his first system of defence, from Gueudecourt to west of Serre, running through half-a-dozen fortified villages, was in our hands.

At the end of the month, Puisieux-au-Mont, with Gomiecourt and its defences, were occupied by us. The Germans had pulled themselves cleanly out of the worst of the salient.

By March they were back on their fortified Le Transloy – Loupart line, except that they still held the village of Tries above Miraumont, which was linked up to the Le Transloy – Loupart line by a peninsula of wired trenches. Tries was carried by the Second and Eighteenth Divisions on the 10th March.

As soon as our guns were able to concentrate on the Le Transloy – Loupart line itself which they did the day after, the enemy, leisurely as always, released it, and fell back on and through his next line, a mile or two behind – Rocquigny – Ablainzevelle – steadied his rearguards, and continued his progress towards the Hindenburg defences, withdrawing along the whole front from south of Arras to Roye. By the 17th of March word was given for a general advance of our troops in co-operation with the French.

To go back a month. Rumours of what was to be expected had cheered the camps for some time past; and just as the fall of single rocks precedes the collapse of an undermined quarry-face, so the German line had crumbled in certain spots long before their system readjusted itself throughout. Front trenches, far removed from actual points of pressure, observed that life with them was quieter than even the state of the weather justified, and began to make investigations.

When the Battalion went up, as usual, on the 15th February to relieve the 2nd Grenadiers in the trenches a little north of Rancourt and opposite St. Pierre

Vaast Wood, their casualties for the four days were but three killed and five wounded. "Practically no sniping and very occasional shelling." They treated it lightly enough, for it was here that the sentry told the conscientious officer who had heard a shell drop near the trench: "Ah, it fell quite convenient here" – a jerk of his thumb over his shoulder, and as an afterthought – "Twas a dud, though." The ground was still hard, and, to the men's joy, they could not dig.

Captain R. J. P. Rodakowski arrived from the base on the 18th of the month. The thaw caught them in camp at Maurepas, just as the enemy's withdrawal got under weigh, and their turn in trenches from the 23rd to 26th February was marked by barrages let down on them of evenings, presumably to discourage curiosity. So they were ordered at short notice to send out a couple of officer's patrols from their left and right companies to reconnoitre generally, and see if the enemy were failing back. The first patrol, under 2nd Lieutenant Shears, an N.C.O., three bombers, and three "bayonet-men," spent a couple of hours among the wire, were bombed but returned unhurt. The second, also of seven men, under Lieutenant Browne, were seen by the enemy, headed back to our lines, but made a fresh outfall, which carried them to the wire where, "finding a weak spot, they cut their way through it" and won within a few yards of the enemy's parapet when they were bombed. They used up their own supplies and came back with a good report, and four men and Lieutenant Browne wounded. On their information a raid was arranged for the next day to take over a couple of hundred yards of the enemy's trench, but it was cancelled pending developments elsewhere. They lost two killed and thirteen men and one officer wounded in this tour, and went back to routine and "specialist" training in a camp near Billon on the last day of February.

Their domestic items for the next fortnight, which, like the rest of March, was cold and stormy, run as follows: 2nd Lieutenant A. L. Bain went to the Fourteenth Corps School for a fortnight at Méaulte, which, in that weather, was no special treat; and Lieutenant E. H. Shears to Headquarters Lewis-gun School at Le Touquet, a much superior place. Lieut.-Colonel R. C. A. McCalmont left on the 3rd March to take over command of the 3rd Infantry Brigade just south of the Somme, and had a tremendous send-off from the Battalion. He was succeeded in the command by Major the Hon. H. R. Alexander, D.S.O., M.C., and Major G. E. S. Young came over from the 2nd Battalion as Second in Command – as it proved, for all too brief a time. The specialist training continued, and "open warfare" was practised by companies. There was an irreverent camp-jest just then that whenever the enemy abandoned one quarter of a mile of trench, the five nearest British army corps forsook every other game to practise "open warfare." The Battalion learned also attacks on triple lines of trenches, the creeping barrage being personified by their drums and those of the 2nd Coldstream. In this sort of work, men say, there is a tendency to lean a little too heavily on such a barrage, which had to be checked by taking the offender's name. ("So, ye'll understand, ye catch it both ways; for if ye purshue the live barrage ye'll likely to be killed; an' if you purshue a dhrummy barrage too close, your name's in the book. That's War!")

THE SOMME ADVANCE

By the middle of March the German line was giving all along; and when the Battalion moved up into Brigade Reserve on the 12th, they understood an advance was close at hand. Their allotted and sketchy stretch of trench, which they took over from the 4th Grenadiers (on the 13th March), was at Sailly-Saillisel, of evil associations, and on the 14th, on information received after active patrolling under Lieutenant E. Budd and Lieutenant Bagenal, the German front line ahead was reported clear and at once occupied. Then they were committed to a muddle of German works in the direction of Le Mesnil-en-Arrouaise, which were named after the Idols of the Tribes. There was nothing to see or to steer by except devastated earth, mud, wire, scraps of sand-bags, heaped rubbish and carcasses. The whole line went forward on the 15th, the 1st Battalion Irish Guards in touch by patrol with their 2nd Battalion on their right and on the left with the 2nd Coldstream. No one knew exactly what was in the enemy's mind, or how far his retirement was extending, but an hour after the Battalion had started they came under long-range machine-gun and heavy artillery fire while they were consolidating "Bayreuth" trench. Major G. E. S. Young was so badly wounded this day by a shell, which came through a Company Headquarters dug-out he was visiting, that he died in hospital a fortnight later and was buried at Grove Town cemetery, and Lieutenant Walter Mumford, M.C., was slightly wounded in the leg. The next trench, "Gotha," was also under gun-fire. They simply moved forward, it seemed, into registered areas, where they were held up, as by a hose of high explosives, till the enemy had completed his local arrangements. Then his artillery on that sector would withdraw across clean, hard country; some long-range machine-gun or sniping work might continue for a while; and then all would be silent, with the sudden curious silences of the Somme, till the next step forward was made on our side and dealt with as above. Thus the Battalion worked through the emptied German trenches and dug-outs, and on the 20th March held a line from Le Mesnil-en-Arrouaise to Manancourt on the Tortille River. The German retreat was as orderly as an ebb-tide. In the north, Bapaume had been taken on the 17th March by the First and Second Australian Divisions, and Péronne was occupied on the 18th by the Forty-eighth Division. Beyond Bapaume, our troops entered the third and last – Beugny–Ytres – line of German trench and wire-work that lay between them and the Hindenburg defences four or five miles behind it across open country. From Péronne southward to close upon Germaine, where we were in touch with the French, our advance-parties had crossed the Somme and spread themselves, as far as the state of the ground allowed, in – it could hardly be called pursuit so much as a heavy-footed following up of the enemy, and making our own roads and tracks as we moved. We found everything usable thoughtfully destroyed, and had to reconstruct it from the beginnings, ere any further pressure could be exercised.

The German front before Arras was unaffected by their withdrawal, and here preparations of every conceivable sort were being piled up against the approaching battle of the Ancre where from Croisilles to Vimy Ridge our Third and First Armies broke through on a front of fifteen miles on April 9, and after a week's desperate fighting, hampered as usual by the weather, carried that front four miles farther eastward, captured 13,000 prisoners and 200 guns; and, through the next month, fought their road up and into the northern end of the Hindenburg Line near Bullecourt whose name belongs to Australia.

On the 23rd of March the Battalion was taken out of its unmolested German trenches and marched to Combles, where it was used in road-making between Frégicourt, Bullet Cross-roads and Sailly-Saillisel, till the 5th of April. There was just one day in that stretch without rain, hail or snow, and when they were not road-making they buried dead and collected salvage and were complimented by the commanding officer of Engineers on their good work. As the men said: "It was great days for the Engineers – bad luck to'em – but it kept us warm."

Their total losses for March had been one officer, Major G. E. S. Young, killed and one, Lieutenant Walter Mumford, M.C., slightly wounded; fourteen other ranks killed and forty wounded – fifty-six in all or less than 10 per cent of the Battalion's strength at the time. Second Lieutenant H. V. Fanshawe joined on the 30th March.

On the 6th April they changed over to Railway construction on the broad-gauge track between Morval and Rocquigny. The men camped at one end of Le Transloy village and Battalion Headquarters in the only house (much damaged) that still stood up. Here they stayed and slaved for a week, in hail and snow and heavy frosts at night; and were practically reclothed as their uniforms were not in the best of condition. ("Ye could not have told us from – from anything or anybody ye were likely to meet in those parts, ye'll understand. But – one comfort – we was all alike – officers an' all.") A village that has not been too totally wrecked is a convenient dump to draw up. The men "improved" their camp and floored their tents out of material at hand, and were rewarded by finding usable German stores among the ruins. One sees how their morale held up, in spite of dirt, iron-rust and foul weather, from the fact that they went out of their way to construct even as they had done at Ypres – "a magnificent Irish Guards Star of glass and stones all surrounded by a low box-hedge." Nor was it forgotten that they were soldiers; and, in spite of the railway-work, and the demands of the Sappers, some of the "specialists" and occasionally a company could be trained at Le Transloy. Even training is preferable to "fatigues," and on the 15th of April they were taken in hand in good earnest. They marched twelve miles in pouring rain to a camp at Bronfay where "a very strict course of platoon training for all ranks was undertaken." It began with twenty minutes' walking or running (in the usual rain or snow) before breakfast at 7.30, and it continued with a half-hour's break till half-past twelve. "Even after three days there was an appreciable improvement in drill and smartness," says the Diary, and when their Brigadier inspected them on the 22nd April he was pleased to compliment. Of afternoons, every one seemed to lecture to every one else according to their seniority; the Brigadier on "Outposts"; the Commanding Officer – Major

R. Baggallay – on "Advance and Rear Guards"; the officers to the platoon-sergeants on every detail of life saving or taking, and when their own resources failed, the C.O. of the 2nd Coldstream lectured all officers and sergeants of the 1st Brigade on "the Attack in open warfare." It was a very thorough shaking-up – foot and transport – from the "specialist" to the cook's mate; and it culminated in No. 5 Platoon (Lieutenant E. Budd) being chosen to represent the Battalion at the Brigade Platoon competition in Drill, Arms Drill, Musketry, Bayonet-fighting and a tactical exercise. The 2nd Grenadiers platoon won, but No. 5 justified itself by taking a very close second place. Survivors, who remember, assert that the platoons of those days were in knowledge, strength and virtue immeasurably above all known standards of fighting men. ("And in the long run, d'ye see, they went with the rest. All gone! Maybe there'll be one or two of 'em left – policemen or tram-conductors an' such like; but in their day an' time, ye'll understand, there was nothing could equal them.")

The lighter side of life was supplied by the 3rd Coldstream's historic and unparalleled "Pantomime," which ran its ribald and immensely clever course for ten consecutive nights, when the cars of the Staff might be seen parked outside the theatre precisely as in the West End.

On the 1st May they resumed work on the Etricourt – Fins railroad and made camp among the ruins of the village for the next three weeks in fine hot weather. The officers and N.C.O.'s were exercised freely at map-reading (which on the Somme required high powers of imagination), sketching reports and compass-work, and occasionally officers and N.C.O.'s made up a platoon and worked out small tactical exercises – such as the rush-in on and downing of a suddenly raised machine-gun after barrages had lifted. The men were kept to the needs of railway and transport, but it was an easy life in warm, grassy Etricourt after months of mud and torn dirt. A swimming-bath was dug for them; there were wildflowers to be gathered, and an orchard in blossom to show that the world still lived naturally, and their work was close to their parade-grounds. Men spoke affectionately of Etricourt where shell-holes were so few that you could count them.

A home draft had brought the Battalion six pipers who on the 4th of May "played at Retreat for the first time," and thereafter followed the Battalion's fortunes. As everybody knows, Irish pipes have one drone less than the Scottish, but it is not commonly understood that the piper in his close-fitting saffron kilt plays them almost without any movement of the body – a point of difference that has puzzled very many Scots regiments. That immobility, as the Pipe-Major observed on an historic occasion, is "one of the secrets of the Regiment."

On the 20th of May they marched – not without some discomfort from an artillery Brigade which was trying to use the same road at the same time – from Etricourt to Curlu on the Somme, where they were once more billeted in houses. Here, after so many weeks of making their own camps to their own minds, they were introduced to other people's housekeeping, and found the whole village "left in a filthy condition by previous troops." So they cleaned it

On the 23rd of March the Battalion was taken out of its unmolested German trenches and marched to Combles, . . . There was just one day in that stretch without rain, hail or snow, and when they were not road-making they buried dead and collected salvage . . .

The road to Combles, 1917.

up and trained and learned from the Divisional Gas Officer of Transport how gas-helmets should be adjusted on horses – to which some of the scared beasts hotly objected; and they bathed by companies in the warm Somme, making a picnic of it, while the long-drawn Battle of the Ancre in the north died down to mere bloody day-and-night war among the villages covering the Hindenburg Line and its spurs. The talk in the camps turned on great doings – everything connected with the front line was "doings" – against Messines Ridge that looks over the flat shell-bitten Salient where there is more compulsory trench-bathing than any man wants. It had commanded too much of that country for too long. At its highest point, where Wytschaete village had once stood, it over-looked Ypres and the British positions around, and was a menace over desolate Plugstreet far towards Armentières. Rumour ran that arrangements had been made to shift it bodily off the face of the earth; that populations of miners had burrowed there through months, for miles; that all under-ground was riddled with workings where men fought in the dark, up and down tunnels that caved, round the sharp turns of boarded and bagged galleries, and on the lips of black shafts that dropped one into forty-foot graves. Yet, even were Messines Ridge wiped out, the enemy had large choices of commanding positions practically all round The Salient, and it seemed likely, by what news sifted into their area, that the Guards might be called upon before long to help in further big doings, Ypres way – perhaps a "break-through" towards Lille.

THE SALIENT AND BOESINGHE

The Salient had been the running sore in our Armies' side since the first. Now that we had men, guns and material, it looked as if it might be stanched at last. A Battalion does not think beyond its immediate interests – even officers are discouraged from trying to run the War by themselves – but it did not need to be told that it had not been fattened up the last few weeks for Headquarters' pleasure in its appearance. Men know when they are "for it," and if they forget, are reminded from the doors of crowded estaminets and canteens, or from the tail-boards of loaded lorries as their comrades fleet by in the dusk. They were not surprised when orders came for a shift.

On the evening of the 30th May they were taken by train from their camp, via Amiens, Abbeville and Boulogne and St. Omer to Cassel in thirteen or fourteen hours, and from Cassel marched back along the well-known *pavè* nearly to St. Omer again and billeted between La Crosse and the dingy, wide railway-crossing at Fort Rouge. All the country round was busy raising crops; every old man, woman and child working as long as light lasted. Their only available training-ground was the Forest of Clairmarais, with its two characteristic wooded hills that stand up behind St. Omer. Here they were taught "wood-fighting" in addition to other specialities, and the Mess found time to give a dinner of honour to a friendly Field-Ambulance (Irish in the main) to whom they had, on various occasions, owed much. Scandal asserts that the guests departed, in the dawn, on their own stretchers. Here, too, on the 6th June they entered for the Brigade Horse-show and won first prize for the best-turned-out limber-and-pair, and seconds for water-cart and cooker-and-pair – no small thing when one considers what is the standard of excellence in Brigade Transport.

On the next day (June 7), the nineteen mines of Messines went up together in the dawn. The three Army Corps (Second Anzac and Ninth and Tenth Corps) loosed behind them, broke forward over Messines and Wytschaete, and the whole German line from Armagh Wood to Plugstreet was wrenched backwards from a mile to two miles all along. Messines was a singularly complete and satisfactory affair, including some seven thousand prisoners and, better still, a multitude of dead, killed off in counter-attacks. It opened the road for the third Battle of Ypres which was to win more breathing-space round the wreck of the city. Unlike Arras, where there was almost unlimited space for assembly in subterranean caves and cellars, every preparation in The Salient had to be carried out under the enemy's eyes on known and registered ground lacking shelter above or below. Thus the attack, which was to cover a front of fifteen miles, demanded as much effort and pre-arrangement as any operation that had till then been undertaken in the whole course of the War. Those were made and carried through among, and in spite of, the daily demands of continuous local operations, with the same thoroughness and fixedness of purpose as when the Brigade competed for its little prizes and trophies at Renescure horse-show

On the 12th June the Battalion marched thirteen miles for musketry to Moringhem in the bare, high down-country behind Acquin, where two men collapsed with heat-stroke. A century ago the drill-book laid down that unaimed battalion-fire from "Brown Bess" should never be opened at over four hundred yards. They practised slow and rapid firing with fixed bayonets at two and three hundred; company sharp-shooters using figures at the same range.

On the 16th June the first drawing in towards The Salient began. They camped that night at Ouderzeele north of Cassel, after such heat as made several of the men fall out by the way, and on the 17th bivouacked in sheds and shelters in the woods south-east of Proven on the Poperinghe Road, where the cultivation, all unaffected by the War half-a-dozen miles off, was as thick as ever, and, except for "specialist" training in the woods, it was difficult to find the men work. The men bore this quite calmly.

As a sign of the times Lieutenant H. Hickie, who had been on leave, arrived and "again took over his duties as Quartermaster" on the 20th June. Lieutenant J. H. Nash left on the same date for the Army Central School, and on the 22nd Captain R. Rodakowski and Lieutenant W. Joyce were detailed for courses of instruction at Le Touquet Lewis-gun School.

On the 23rd June Major-General Sir A. J. Godley, commanding the Second Anzac Corps, came over on a visit to the Battalion and inspected the men, and day by day the pieces required for the next move on the chessboard of war were pushed into their places along The Salient. The Fifth Army – of four

Corps and some Divisions – under General Gough was to take the weight of the affair between Klein Zillebeke and Boesinghe, while the First French Army – First and Fifty-first Divisions – would relieve the Belgians from Boesinghe to Noordschoote and extend the line along the Yser Canal north of Ypres to Steenstraate. The Guards Division was to lie next them on the extreme left of our line at Boesinghe.

On the 25th June the Battalion moved from Proven into the edge of the battle-area near Woesten, a couple of miles or so behind Boesinghe itself, and came under the fire of a long-range German naval gun which merely cut up the fields round them. Both sides were now hard at work in the air, trying to put out each other's eyes; and a German aeroplane brought down one of our observation-balloons hideously alight, close to Woesten camp. All The Salient hummed with opposing aircraft, the bombing of back-areas was cruel and continuous, and men had no rest from strain. But our batteries, profiting by the help of our machines, hammered the enemy line as it had not been hammered there since war began. Oil-drums, gas and thermit shells were added to the regular allowances sent over, and, whenever chance offered, raiding-parties dove in and out of the front lines sharking prisoners for identification. The Battalion's share in this work was the usual fatigue – "unloading trucks" and the like, beneath intermittent artillery-fire which, on the 29th June, ended in three direct hits on the farm-house (Roussel Farm) near Elverdinghe, where they lay. One man was killed outright and three others wounded. Their regular routine-work of death had begun again.

On the 1st of July they went into line on the Boesinghe sector, relieving the 2nd Coldstream on the west or near sector of the Yser Canal. Their trenches were of the usual built-up, sand-bagged type. Headquarters were at Bleuet Farm, well under fire of all kinds, and though they managed their relief at night with little shelling, early next morning Lieutenant E. Shears was killed by shell. It was a bad sector in every way, for not only did the Battalion link on here to the Belgian army – later relieved by the French – on their left, and any point of junction of Allied forces is always severely dealt with, but the enemy were kept in tension by constant raids, or the fear of them, all along the line. This meant that their S.O.S. signals went up on the least provocation and their barrages followed with nervous punctuality. Added to this, fatigue-work was very heavy, not only in repairs but in supply; and the necessary exposure of the carrying-parties led to constant casualties.

On the 5th July, for instance, at two in the morning, gas shells fired from projectors (the Germans were searching the line in earnest that night) fell on a working-party of No. 4 Company. Nineteen men were at once prostrated, of whom one died then and there, and two a few days later; while Lieutenant Bagenal was slightly affected. (It is difficult, especially in the dark, to keep working-parties, who have to work against time, inside their gas-masks.) They were shelled for the rest of the day with no further casualties.

On the 6th July, Major Hon. H. R. Alexander leaving for England to attend the Officers' course at Aldershot, Captain R. R. C. Baggallay took over the command,

and on the 8th July they were relieved by the 3rd Coldstream and bivouacked at Cardoen Farm, where they spent two days nominally resting – that is to say, supplying one hundred and ten men each night for the detestable work of carrying-parties to the front line. Lieut.-Colonel Rocke, D.S.O., commanding since May 24, returned from leave on July 8, but unluckily on the 11th, when the Battalion was in line, in the wreck of Boesinghe Village (Headquarters at Boesinghe Chateau), slipped and broke his shoulder while going round the trenches, and Captain Baggallay again took over command. There was steady well- ranged shelling all that day, particularly on Boesinghe Chateau, in the rear of which the Aid-post and Headquarters of No. 1 Company lay. Battalion Headquarters were shelled for half an hour separately. No. 3 Company's Headquarters in the support-line were wrecked by direct hits, and the entire Company shelled out, while the whole of the back lines were worked over, up and down. All repairs had to be built up with sand-bags, for the ground was too marshy to give useful dirt, and the labour was unending.

On the 12th July they were shelled more heavily than the previous two days on exactly the same places, and their Transport, which till now had had reasonable luck, was caught fetching up water and rations. The four Company Quartermaster-Sergeants and the Mess-Sergeant were wounded, a horse and groom killed, and, later on, the Transport Officer was slightly gassed. ("Tis the Transport, ye'll understand, that has to take all Jerry's back-chat after dhark, an' no chance of replyin'.") By night they found carrying-parties to fill dumps – five of them – each dump seeming to those serving it more exposed and undesirable than the other four put together.

On the 14th of July there was a German raid, preceded by an hour's "box" barrage of trench mortars, 77's, and machine-guns, on two platoons of No. 4 Company then in the front line behind the Canal. A shrapnel-barrage fell also on the supports. A "box" barrage is a square horror of descending fire cutting off all help, and ranks high among demoralizing experiences. Luckily, the line was lightly held, and the men had more or less of cover in dug-outs and tunnels in the Canal bank. A Lewis-gun post in a covered emplacement, almost on the bed of the Canal itself, was first aware, through the infernal racket, of Germans crossing the Canal, and fired at them straight down the line of its bed. They broke and disappeared in the rank weed-growth, but there was another rush over the parapet of the line between two sentry groups in the firing-bays. The trenches were alive by then with scattered parties stumbling through the black dark, and mistaking each other for friends or enemies, and the ruin of the works added to the confusion. As far as can be made out, one officer, Lieutenant H. J. B. Eyre, coming along what was left of a trench, ran literally into a party of the enemy. His steel helmet and revolver, all chambers fired, were found afterwards near the wreck of a firing-bay, but there was no other trace. It was learned later that he had been mortally wounded and died that evening. In trench-raids, when life, death or capture often turn on a step to the left or the right, the marvel was that such accidents were not more frequent.

A wounded German was captured. He had no marks of identification, but said he belonged to a Schleswig Regiment, and that the strength of the raid was intended to be two hundred. It did not, as the men said, 'feel' anything like so many, though the wild lights of explosion that lit the scene showed large enemy parties waiting either in the bed of the Canal or on the opposite bank. These, too, vanished into the dark after their comrades in the trenches had been turned out. Probably, it was but an identification fray backed by a far-reaching artillery "hate" that troubled all the back areas even up to Elverdinghe.

Our front-line casualties in the affair were but one officer and one man missing and one wounded. Yet the barrage blew the men about like withered leaves, covered them with mud, plastered them with bits of sand-bags, and gapped, as it seemed, fathoms of trench at a stroke, while enemy machine-guns scissored back and forth over each gap. The Companies in the support-line who watched the affair and expected very few to come out of it alive, suffered much more severely from the shrapnel-barrage which fell to their share.

It was their last tour in the trenches for ten days, and it closed with heavy barrages on the front and back lines, while they were being relieved by the 1st Coldstream. This continued till our guns were asked to reply, and after ten minutes made them cease. The Battalion left the trenches in a steady downpour of wet and entrained from Elverdinghe for Proven, whence they moved into the training-area at Herzeele, where a representation of the ground to be attacked on the day of battle, with its trenches and farms, was marked out, and had to be studied by company commanders, N.C.O.'s and men according to their rank and responsibility. The officers' Mess at Herzeele was in the quaint old three-storied tower, built when the Spaniards held rule in the Low Countries.

From the 16th to the 23rd July their mornings were spent at every sort of drill – smoke-helmet drill, musketry, wiring, Lewis-gun, etc., and their afternoons in going over the training-ground and practising attacks. All that time the weather was perfect. As soon as they moved away to Proven and into the battle-area on July 25 heavy rain began, which, as on the Somme, where the Devil duly looked after his own, was destined to baulk and cripple the battle. For an introduction to their next month's work, the Battalion, roused at 2 a.m. on that day by gas-alarms from the front, provided over five hundred men for working-parties to get stuff into the front line; lost ten men killed by shell-fire and one officer, Lieutenant H. H. Maxwell (who had come unscathed through the raid of the 14th), and seven men wounded; and next evening moved to their own place, a distance of two-and-a-half miles, with two-hundred-yards intervals between the platoons, under casual shell-fire.

They camped (July 27) in support near Bleuet Farm, and, that evening, had word that our aeroplanes reported no Germans could be seen in the German front line system, and that the 3rd Coldstream had sent patrols forward who were already established across the Canal. As a matter of fact, the enemy was holding his front line in chains of single posts, preferring rather to fight for it than in it; and was relying on his carefully hidden ferro-concrete block-houses – later known as "pill-boxes" – which, as he had arranged them in the torn and marshy landscape, and along the line of the Ypres – Staden rail, could hold up and dissipate any average infantry attack. They were impervious to anything except direct hits of big stuff. Their weakness was the small size of the slit through which their machine-guns operated, and a certain clumsiness in the arrangement of the gun itself which made it difficult to depress. Consequently, cool heads could crawl up and under, and rush the thing at close quarters.

Whether the enemy believed there would be no serious attack at the junction of the French and British arms in the Boesinghe sector, or whether he drew his men out of the front line to give room for his barrages, may never be known. It is certain, however, that he left his front line immediately facing the Guards Division empty, and that miscalculation enabled the Guards to launch their attack without having first to fight their way across the Canal. The Coldstream had possessed themselves promptly of the evacuated trenches, and there stayed for some time before the enemy realized what had happened, sent aeroplanes to locate the raiders, and tried – without success – to shell them back again. It was a quick, well-thought-out coup that saved very many good lives.

On the 28th July the Battalion, after various contradictory orders, was sent forward in the evening to relieve the left of the 3rd Coldstream in the outpost-line. There was a report that the enemy meditated an attack on that Battalion at their junction with the Thirty-eighth Division on their right. (It must be remembered that the French, who had had some difficulty in getting their guns forward, were not in place, and their First Division lay on the left of the Guards.) Up, then, went the Battalion in the evening and took over the outpost-line from Douteuse House, to where it joined the French forces. Two platoons of No. 2 Company, under Captain R. Rodakowski, crossed the Canal in the mud on improvised bridges of slabs of wood nailed across rabbit-wire and canvas, and lay up in an old German front line. The other two platoons occupied the old British front line on the Canal bank. Battalion Headquarters and Aid-post were at the Chateau, as usual. No. 1 Company (Captain W. C. Mumford, M.C.) in support, and No. 4 Company (Captain Law, M.C.) had a couple of platoons forward and two back. They were all shelled equally through that night with gas and lachrymal shells, *plus* barrages on Headquarters and the various lines of support. The gas was responsible for six casualties, chiefly among signallers and orderlies, whose work kept them on the move. Nothing could be done to strengthen the newly occupied trenches, as there was no wire on the spot; for the R.E. parties, trying to bring it up, were pinned till daylight by back-barrages.

On the 29th July a patrol was sent out to look at a concrete blockhouse which our artillery reported they were unable to destroy with the guns that were in use at the moment. The patrol drew fire from the blockhouse, went on into the dark, and found that the enemy's line behind it was held by small posts only. Returning, it would seem that they were fired at again, an N.C.O. and a man being wounded, but they wounded and captured a prisoner, who said that the post held twenty men. Whereupon that block-house was "kept under observation" by small parties of our men, under Lieutenant Budd, M.C. Next morning they observed five or six of the enemy lying out in shell-holes round the blockhouse, which was too small for the whole of its garrison. This overflow was all sniped in due course, till the blockhouse, with fourteen unwounded prisoners, surrendered, was absorbed into our outpost-line, and held against the enemy's fire. Considering that fire at the time – which included 5·9's, 4·2's, and ·77's – it was a neatly expeditious affair. The Battalion was relieved by the 1st Grenadiers and the Welsh, and went back to camp in the Forest area to spend the 30th July preparing themselves and their souls for the morrow's work.

The Guards Division lay, as we know, between the First French Division on its left and our Thirty-eighth Division on its right; the line of the Ypres – Staden railway with its blockhouses marking the limit between the two British Divisions. This was an awkward junction, which caused trouble later. Four objectives were laid down. The first was the nearest German system of trenches, which had lain under searching artillery-fire for some time, and would not be difficult; the second, six hundred yards farther on, ran parallel to the Pilckem road; the third an imaginary line a hundred yards beyond the well-known Iron Cross Kortikaar   Cabaret road, beyond Pilckem Ridge, and the last went up to the Steenbeek River. The total depth of the run was about two miles from the Canal bank

The 2nd (Ponsonby's) and the 3rd (Seymour's) Brigades were to take the first three objectives, after which the 1st (Jeffreys' Brigade), following close behind, was to come through and take the fourth. The 2nd Brigade, which was on the right of the Division, held the front from the Ypres – Staden railway-bridge over the Canal to Boesinghe Bridge. The 3rd Brigade continued the line to the left for six hundred yards. The 1st Brigade, less the 1st Irish and the 3rd Coldstream, which were under the direct orders of General Feilding, G.O.C. Guards Division, was in reserve.

Our barrages, conceived on a most generous scale, were timed to creep at a hundred yards in four minutes. They were put down at 3.50 a.m., July 31, a dark, misty morning on the edge of rain, and the whole attack went forward with satisfying precision so far as the Guards Division was concerned. The various objectives were reached at the given times, and level with the French advance. By eleven o'clock the farthest was in our hands, and what difficulties there were arose from the Division on the Guards' right being held up among unreduced blockhouses enfilading them from the railway line.

Meantime, the 1st Battalion Irish Guards spent the day, after breakfast at a quarter-past five, in reserve round the little two-roomed, sand-bagged and concreted Chasseur Farm, where there was an apple-tree with all its leaves on, under half an hour's notice to move up if required. But no order came. They were shelled intermittently all day, with a few casualties, and Captain F. S. Law was slightly wounded. The evening, as pessimists prophesied, closed in heavy rain, and the ground began to go. They stayed where they were till the afternoon of the 1st August, when word came to take over the line held by the 3rd Grenadiers and the 1st Coldstream on the first, second and third objectives.

They moved out in rain into the usual wilderness of shell-holes filling with water, but for the moment were not shelled. No. 4 Company went by daylight to its positions on the first objective – Cariboo Wood and some half-wiped-out German trench-systems in a partly destroyed wood. The other companies waited till dusk before distributing themselves on the Green line – the third objective – which was about a thousand yards this side the Steenbeek River. While the move was in progress, a Brigade of the Thirty-eighth Division reported that they had been shelled out of their advanced positions on the river and were falling back, which, as far as could be seen, would leave the right flank of the Guards Division in the air. If this were so, and the dusk and the rain made it difficult to judge, it was imperative to put everything else aside and form a defensive flank along the railway line that separated the two Divisions. The Companies were diverted accordingly, hastily re-directed in the dark, and, when all was done, the Brigade that had made the trouble went back to its original position on the farther objective. There was small choice of sleeping-places that night. Such German blockhouses as came handiest were used for Battalion and Company Headquarters, while the Companies lay out in the wet and talked about the prospect of hot meals. They were not very severely shelled, but when August 2 broke in heavy rain and the Brigade on their right continued to send up S.O.S.'s at intervals, thereby obliging them to maintain their flank on the railway line, they felt that "conditions were becoming exceedingly trying," as the Diary says. Then came a relief, which was at least a change. The 1st Scots Guards relieved the two platoons of No. 4 Company back in Cariboo trenches, where the shelling was light; and later, as darkness fell, set the other Companies free to go forward and relieve the 2nd Grenadiers at the front of things. The change-over took five hours, and in the middle of it the Brigade on their right once more sent up S.O.S.'s, which brought down a German barrage, and necessitated every one "standing to" for developments. It proved a false alarm, and "no action was taken by the enemy" – an omission which it is conceivable the Guards Division rather regretted. Beyond question that Brigade had been badly held up among the blockhouses, and had been savagely shelled in and out of shell-holes that bewilder troops; but – till their own trouble comes – no troops go out of their way to make excuses for a nightmare of S.O.S.'s. ('There's enough fatigues, ye'll understand, when you're *out* o' the line. Extra fatigues in action, like defensive flanks, is outrageous!')

They were shelled and rained upon throughout the whole of the night of the 2nd August, and on the evening of the 3rd, still in ceaseless rain, were relieved by the 1st Scots Guards and marched through mud, water and darkness, over broken ground "beyond description" to Elverdinghe Siding, where they were packed into trucks at five in the morning and taken to Poll Hill Camp near Bandaghem for training.

Their casualties, all things reckoned, had been very light. They had gone into action on the 31st July with 26 officers and 1002 other ranks and had lost only 2 officers and 125 other ranks from all causes.

They moved out in the rain into the usual wilderness of shell-holes filling with water, but for the moment were not shelled . . .

On the banks of the Yser Canal after the attack on 31st July 1917.

The total casualties for the twelve Battalions of the Guards Division in the action had been 59 officers and 1876 men in two days; and rain falling without a break for the next four days drowned out the sad fight. The enemy's line had been pushed back from Bixschoote, through Frezenberg, Westhoek, Stirling Castle and Shrewsbury Forest down to Hollebeke. At that stage our Armies, as had happened so often on the Somme, were immobilized. The clay ground was cullendered and punched by the shells into chains of pools and ponds. All valleys and hollows turned into bogs where, if men wandered from the regular tracks across them, they drowned or were mired to death. If they stayed on the plankings the enemy's guns swept them away. When all had been done that man could do, the first phase of the third Battle of Ypres closed in a strengthened conviction that all the Powers of Evil were in strict alliance with Germany. Our Armies held off seven counter-attacks along the line, settled themselves in it and then, perforce, waited for the weather to clear.

It rained on and off till the 15th August, and, as most of the corn in the fields round Poll Hill Camp had, owing to the wet, not been cut, training ground was limited just at the very time when the new German system of holding a line with a chain of carefully camouflaged posts called for a change in attack methods. So the Battalion was practised in "surprise situations" – i.e. discovering invisible enemies with machine-guns in shell-holes that turned the advancing line into a ragged scattering 'scrum.' Their dummy barrages were slowed, too, as the Diary says, "to enable the surprise situations to be dealt with and to give time for the line to re-form behind the barrage after having dealt with these situations." This was a kind of work for which, like bombing, the Irish had considerable natural aptitudes. It was summed up, unofficially, thus: "In the ould days, a trench was a trench, ye'll understand, an' something to lay hould upon. Third Ypres was fallin into nothin' and then findin' 'twas two pill-boxes an' a fort on your flank." Therefore, the specialist in the shape of the Lewis-gunner and the "mopper-up" who dealt with the debris of attacks were important persons and were instructed accordingly when the Battalion was not indented upon for working-parties on the gun-tracks and bridges round Boesinghe.

THIRD YPRES AND THE BROEMBEEK

On August 1, Lieutenant the Hon. P. J. Ogilvy joined the Battalion and took over No. 1 Company from Acting Captain W. C. Mumford, who had been appointed Town Major of the busy and occasionally battered town of Elverdinghe; and Lieutenant E. Budd took over the 4th Company from Acting Captain H. F. d'A. S. Law, wounded.

On the 15th August, the eve of the Langmarck attack, they were put on one hour's notice, which was withdrawn the next day, when six Divisions (the Forty-eighth, Eleventh, Fifty-sixth, Eighth, Twentieth and Twenty-ninth) struck again along the line from the Menin road to our junction with the French in the north. The weather once more blinded our aeroplanes so that our artillery could not deal effectively with the counter-attacks; the pill-boxes held up our infantry, and though prisoners, guns and a little ground round Langemarck were gained, the line of The Salient from St Julien southwards stood as it had since the first. The Battalion was peacefully at bomb-practice on that day, and by some oversight a live bomb got mixed up with the dummies, and caused thirteen casualties, luckily none of them very serious, and the training went forward. As the crops were cut ground was gradually extended and every one was worked hard at practice attacks; for they understood that their lot would be cast in The Salient for some time.

On the 27th August medal ribbons were presented by the General of the 1st Brigade to those who had won honour in the Boesinghe battle, either by their cool-headedness in dealing with 'surprise situations' or sheer valour in the face of death or self-devotion to a comrade; for there was every form of bravery to choose from. Lieutenant E. Budd received the bar to his Military Cross, and Sergeant (a/C.S.M.) P. Donohoe (No. 3056), No. 1910 Sergeant (a/C.S.M.) F. M'Cusker, No. 3224 Corporal E. M'Cullagh, No. 4278 Lance-Corporal J. Vanston, No. 7520 Private S. Nulty, No. 5279 Private J. Rochford (bar to Military Medal), No. 10171 Lance-Corporal S. McHale, Military Medal; No. 10161 Lance-Corporal W. Cooper, D.C.M.

The following N.C.O.'s and men were unable to be present on parade, but were awarded honours during the past month: No. 4512 Sergeant J. Balfe, No. 3146 Lance-Corporal F. Coyne, No. 4386 Sergeant Macdonald, No. 6078 Private J. Martin, Military Medal; No. 4884 Private D. O'Brien, Croix de Guerre.

On the last days of August they marched to Proven siding and entrained for Elverdinghe and thence to Dulwich Camp, well known as being 'some what exposed and liable to long-range shell-fire.' They were used at once by the greedy R.E.'s for burying cables and making artillery-tracks preparatory to the next move in the interminable third Battle of Ypres.

From the 1st to the 4th September they, with the 1st Guards Brigade, were in support to the 3rd Guards Brigade which was in the line, and sent up about half their strength for carrying-parties every night. The line, swampy and overlooked by the high ground under Houthuist Forest to the north and north-east, consisted of posts in shell-holes – the shell-holes being improved only just sufficiently to make them "habitable." The standard of comfort in The Salient at that time was lower than on the Somme, where men were dying, at least, dry. All posts were elaborately concealed from overhead observation, for the enemy aeroplanes roved over them, bombing and machine-gunning at large. Though the Battalion was lucky in its four days' turn, it lost on the night of the 4th September 2nd Lieutenant G. P. Boyd and four men killed and twenty-three wounded. Some of the other Battalions in support suffered severely from bombing raids, and all back-areas were regularly raked over so that troops might be worried by loss of sleep.

From the 5th to the 8th they lay in Rugby Camp, in reserve to the 2nd Coldstream and 2nd Grenadiers of their own Brigade in the front line. Here they enjoyed a 'fairly quiet time,' and had only to find a hundred men or so per night for forward-area work. Rugby, Dulwich and the other camps were all duly and regularly bombed, shelled and gassed, but that was accepted as part of the daily and nightly work.

On the 9th they were up at the front among the "just sufficiently habitable shell-holes" of the Green line beyond the Iron Cross Kortikaar – Cabaret road from the Ypres – Staden railway to the junction with the French. Their guides met them at Bois Farm, fifteen hundred yards back, and since, once among the holes, all food sent up risked the life or mutilation of a man, they carried two days' rations and picked up their water from a Decauville railway that ran to the terminus (daily bombed and bombarded) on the Wijden Drift road. While the last two Companies (Nos. 2 and 4) were getting their tins at rail-head, an hour and a half's barrage was dropped on them and twenty-seven men were killed or wounded. Relief was delayed in consequence till one on the morning of the 10th, and, about an hour later, a wandering covey of eight Germans, who had lost their way in the dark, were rounded up by the forward platoons of No. 3 Company (2nd Lieutenant Corry, D.C.M.). It was a small brisk fight, and it came pleasantly after the barrage at railhead, and the shelling that befell them from three to half-past five. They were annoyed, too, by low-flying enemy aeroplanes who fired at the men in the posts but as a rule missed them. A deserter came in and patrols were sent out to see where the nearest enemy post might be. One was located near the railway line in front of the right Company. Exploration work of this sort in such a blind front as the enemy had arranged here, ends only too often in patrols losing their way as the eight Germans had done; and Company Officers do not like it.

On the 11th September, after some artillery work on our side, the enemy guns carried out a shoot on the pill-boxes occupied by the right (No. 1 Company) while their infantry were "unusually active," probably because the Thirty-eighth Division on the Guards' right was being relieved that night by the Twentieth. As a side-issue of the fight the Battalion on their left was attacked, which, so far as the Irish Guards were concerned, meant that the left Company, No. 2, swiftly manufactured a fresh post on their left to improve communication with their neighbours, and prevent the enemy working round their flank through the remnants of a wood. In this work they had to disperse with rifle-fire several parties of the enemy who might have interfered with their arrangements, and Captain T. F. MacMahon was wounded. This bald record covers a long, tense night of alarms and fatigues, and fatigue-parties dropping like partridges where the barrage found them, to creep forward as soon as it was lifted; and, somewhere on the left, the crackle and blaze of an attack on a battalion which was entirely capable of taking care of itself.

Their relief on the night of the 13th by the 1st Scots Guards was "very much delayed." Two detachments got lost, one through the guide being killed and the other "through the guide losing himself." Yet it was a very dark, and, therefore, theoretically a safe, night, with very little shelling – proof of the utter uncertainty of every detail connected with war.

They had lost in that fortnight one officer (2nd Lieutenant Boyd) and fourteen men killed; one officer, Captain T. F. MacMahon, and seventy-eight other ranks wounded. For the rest of the month they were training in camps – Cariboo and Poll Hill – of which the former was not out of reach of shell-fire, and studied new methods of attack to combat the enemy's new methods of defence in his protected and fortified shell-holes. These he now held in depth, one shell-hole post covering or flanking the next, so that men fought their way up a landscape of miniature redoubts, invisible to guns, almost invisible to aeroplanes, and much more expensive to reduce than the narrow-slotted pill-boxes.

On the 21st September their Brigadier-General Jeffreys saw the Battalion on parade, near Proven, and bade them farewell on his promotion to command the Nineteenth Division. He was succeeded in command of the 1st Brigade by General C. R. C. de Crespigny. On the 27th Lieut.-Colonel R. V. Pollok commanding the Battalion, who had been on leave, returned and took over from Captain A. F. L. Gordon acting in his absence. On the 29th Lieutenant B. Reford who had been Assistant-Adjutant took over No. 3 Company vice Captain T. F. MacMahon, wounded on the 11th, and 2nd Lieutenant T. S. V. Stoney joined for duty on the 25th.

Among the honours mentioned as awarded to the men that month for gallantry and devotion to duty was the D.C.M. to 5279 Private J. Rochford for "gallantry, devotion to duty and organizing ability" when employed as a stretcher-bearer with a working-party on September 3, the night that Lieutenant Boyd and twenty-eight men were killed or wounded by bombs. This, it may be noted, is that Rochford whose presence steadied, and whose jests diverted, whole platoons upon the Somme, and for whose health the men inquired first after the platoon or working-party had been shelled.

And while they trained, with the utter self-absorption of men concerned in the study of methods of taking man's life, The Salient heaved and flamed day after day with German counter-attacks as our guns covered the adjustment and reinforcements and protection of artillery troops and material in preparation for the battle of September 20. As usual, the weather broke on the eve of it. Ten Divisions (Nineteenth, Thirty-ninth, Forty-first, Twenty-third, First and Second Australians, Fifty-fifth, Fifty-eighth and Twentieth) attacked from near Hollebeke in the south to Langemarck in the north; pushed back the line on the whole length of their attack; gained one mile outwards along the desperate Menin road, established themselves in Polygon Wood, broke eleven counter-attacks, took over 3000 prisoners and left as many enemy dead. It was followed up on the 26th September by another attack, on a six-mile front from south of the Menin road to north east of St Julien, in which six Divisions (Thirty ninth, Thirty-third, Fifth and Fourth Australians, Fifty-eighth and Fifty-ninth) once more moved our line forward along that frontage, in some places nearly half a mile. Our movement clashed, almost to the minute, with German counter-attacks by fresh Divisions launched to recover the ground they had lost on the 20th September, and the fighting was none the lighter for that coincidence.

The 3rd October saw the weather break again just as fighting was resumed on a seven-mile front from the Menin road to the Ypres – Staden railway. Twelve Divisions went in here (the Thirty-seventh, Fifth, Twenty-first, Seventh; First, Second, and Third Australians; the New Zealand; Forty-eighth, Eleventh, Fourth and Twenty-ninth). Reutel, Nordemhoek and Broodseinde villages were taken, Abraham Heights gained, the Gravenstafel spur cleared by the New Zealanders; three fresh German Divisions were caught by our guns almost in the act of forming up for attack, and 5000 prisoners were passed back. The enemy's losses here were very satisfactory and mainly due to our gun-fire.

On the 5th October, then, so far as the Guards Division was concerned, the line of our working front ran through Poelcappelle and thence back to the Ypres – Staden railway at a point some thousand yards north of Langemarck. From that point it merged into the old line gained on the 20th of September which followed the Broembeek River at a short distance to the south of it, towards our junction with the French, and thence lost itself in the flooded areas beyond Noordschoote. No weight of attack had fallen on that sector of the front since September 20 when Langemarck had been captured, and the French line, with ours, advanced in the direction of Draibach and Houthulst Forest.

THE BROEMBEEK

It was decided to renew the attack, in combination with the French here, on the 9th October, from north-west of Langemarck across the Ypres – Staden railway down to a point in the line gained on the 4th October, east of Zonnebeke, on a front of six miles. The weather prepared itself in advance. Rain began punctually on the 7th, continued through the 8th, and made the going more than usually unspeakable. It affected the Guards Division principally, since their share of the work involved crossing the little valley of the Broembeek river which, should it continue to flood, offered every possible opportunity for holding up troops under fire, loss of direction (since men never move straight across bogs) and engulfment of material. The Broembeek was a stagnant ditch, from twenty to thirty feet wide and from two to five deep, edged with shell-holes and, in some parts, carrying vertical banks four or five feet deep. There was, mercifully, no wire in it, but night-patrols sent out the week before the battle of the 9th reported it could not be crossed without mats.

The 1st Brigade of the Division, which lay in reserve while the 3rd Brigade held the front line, had trained for several days at Poll Hill Camp over ground "marked" to represent the ground that the Battalion would have to attack over. The certainty of being drenched to the skin on a raw October night as a preliminary to tumbling from shell-hole to shell-hole till dawn between invisible machine-guns and snipers was left to the imagination of the men.

On October 6, "the details to be left out of the attack departed to join the Guards Divisional Reinforcement Battalion at Herzeele." Men say that the withdrawal of these reprieved ones on the eve of action was as curious a sight as the arrival of a draft. ("For ye'll understand, at that time o' the War, men knew 'twas only putting off what was bound to happen.")

Then, in foul weather, the Battalion entrained for Elverdinghe with the 3rd Coldstream of their Brigade. The idea was that the 1st Brigade (De Crespigny's) would attack parallel to the line of the Ypres – Staden railway on their right, about three hundred yards from it, the 2nd Brigade (Sergison-Brooke's) on their left next against the French, with the 3rd Brigade (Seymour's) in support. This last Brigade had been very heavily used in making arrangements for the Division to cross the Broembeek, piling dumps and helping to haul guns into fresh positions through the mud. The farthest objective set, for the advance, was the edge of the Houthulst Forest, three thousand yards across semi-fluid country with no landmarks other than the line of smashed rail on their right, and whatever fortified houses, farms, pill-boxes and shell-holes they might encounter during their progress. When they had overcome all obstacles, they were instructed to dig in on the edge of the Forest.

At 9.30 on the night of the 8th, in heavy rain, the Battalion marched from Abingley Camp to their assembly lines (these all duly marked by tapes and white signboards, which, to the imaginative, suggest grave yards) from Elverdinghe to Boesinghe Road, up "Clarges Street" to Abri Wood, and then to Cannes Farm till they met the guides for their assembly areas at Ruisseau Farm. From here began the interminable duckboards that halt and congest the slow-moving line; and it was not till four in the morning that the Battalion was formed up and moved off. The rain had stopped a little before midnight and a late moon came to their help.

The Companies were commanded as follows: No. 1, Captain the Hon. P. J. Ogilvy; No. 2, Lieutenant D. S. Browne; No. 3, Captain R. B. S. Reford; No. 4, Lieutenant N. B. Bagenal.

There was some shelling as they got into their assembly positions at 5.20 a.m., but casualties were few. The 2nd Grenadiers and 2nd Coldstream led off under a few minutes' blast of intense fire from field-guns and Stokes mortars, crossed the Broembeek and were away. At 6.20 the 1st Irish Guards and 3rd Coldstream followed them. The Battalion's crossing-place at the river, which, after all, proved not so unmanageable as the patrols reported, had no bridges, but there was wire enough on the banks to have made trouble had the enemy chosen that time and place to shell. They went over in three-foot water with mud at the bottom; re-formed, wet and filthy, and followed the 2nd Grenadiers who had captured the first and second objectives, moved through them at 8.20 and formed up on the right of the 3rd Coldstream under the barrage of our guns for their own advance on the final objective – the edge of the Forest.

So far, barring a tendency to bear towards the right or railway side, direction had been well kept and their losses were not heavy. The Companies deployed for attack on the new lines necessitated by the altered German system of defence — mopping-up sections in rear of the leading companies, with Lewis-gun sections, and a mopping-up platoon busy behind all.

Meantime, the troops on the Battalion's right had been delayed in coming up, and their delay was more marked from the second objective onward. This did not check the Guards' advance, but it exposed the Battalion's right to a cruel flanking fire from snipers among the shell-holes on the uncleared ground by the Ypres – Staden line. There were pill-boxes of concrete in front; there was a fortified farm buried in sand-bags, Egypt House, to be reduced; there were nests of machine-guns on the right which the troops on the right had not yet overrun, and there was an almost separate and independent fight in and round some brick-fields, which, in turn, were covered by the fire of snipers from the fringes of the forest. Enemy aircraft skimming low gave the German artillery every help in their power, and the enemy's shelling was accurate accordingly. The only thing that lacked in the fight was the bayonet. The affair resolved itself into a series of splashing rushes, from one shell-hole to the next, terrier-work round the pill-boxes, incessant demands for the Lewis-guns (rifle-grenades, but no bombs, were employed except by the regular bombing sections and moppers-up who cleared the underground shelters), and the hardest sort of personal attention from the officers and N.C.O.'s. All four Companies reached the final objective mixed up together, and since their right was well in the air, by the reason of the delay of the flanking troops, they had to make a defensive flank to connect with a battalion of the next Division that came up later. It was then that they were worst sniped from the shell-holes, and the casualties among the officers, who had to superintend the forming of the flank, were heaviest. There was not much shelling through the day. They waited, were sniped, and expected a counter-attack which did not come off, though in the evening the enemy was seen to be advancing and the troops on the Battalion's right fell back for a while, leaving their flank once more exposed. Their position at the time was in a somewhat awkward salient, and they re-adjusted themselves – always under sniping-fire – dug in again as much as wet ground allowed, and managed in the dark to establish connection with a Battalion of Hampshires that had come up on their right.

They spent the night of the 9th October where they lay, in the front line, while the enemy sniped them, shelled their supports, or put down sudden wandering barrages from front to back. Every Company Commander had been killed or wounded during the day; their Medical Officer (Captain P. R. Woodhouse, M.C.) was wounded at duty on the 10th, the men were caked with mud and ooze, worn to their last nerves and badly in need of food and hot drinks. There was no infantry action on their front, however, throughout the 10th, and in the evening they were relieved by two Companies of the 1st Grenadiers; the other two Companies of that Battalion relieving the 2nd Grenadiers in the support-line. The battle, which counted as "a successful minor operation" in the great schemes of the third Battle of Ypres, had cost them four officers killed in action on the 9th, one died of wounds on the 11th, seven officers and their doctor wounded in the two days; forty-seven other ranks killed; one hundred and fifty-eight wounded, and ten missing among the horrors of the swampy pitted ground. The list runs:

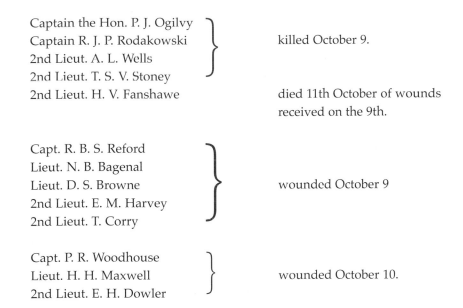

Captain the Hon. P. J. Ogilvy
Captain R. J. P. Rodakowski
2nd Lieut. A. L. Wells   killed October 9.
2nd Lieut. T. S. V. Stoney

2nd Lieut. H. V. Fanshawe   died 11th October of wounds received on the 9th.

Capt. R. B. S. Reford
Lieut. N. B. Bagenal
Lieut. D. S. Browne   wounded October 9
2nd Lieut. E. M. Harvey
2nd Lieut. T. Corry

Capt. P. R. Woodhouse
Lieut. H. H. Maxwell   wounded October 10.
2nd Lieut. E. H. Dowler

It took them eight hours along the taped tracks and the duckboards to get to Rugby Camp behind Boesinghe, where they stayed for the next two days and drew a couple of officers and a hundred men from the Divisional Reinforcement Battalion to replace some of their casualties.

On the 13th October they, with their Brigade, took over the support-line on the old battle-front from various units of the 2nd and 3rd Guards Brigade. The 2nd Grenadiers relieved the 1st Grenadiers in the front line on the right and the 2nd Coldstream the Welsh Guards on the left sector. The Battalion itself was scattered by companies and half-companies near Koekuit – Louvois Farm, Craonne Farm, and elsewhere, relieving companies and half-companies of the other Battalions, and standing by to attend smartly to the needs of the forward battalions in case of sudden calls for more bombs, small-arm ammunition and lights. They were instructed, too, to be ready to support either flank should the troops there give way. But the troops did not give way; and they had nothing worse to face than heavy shelling of the supports at night and the work of continuing the duckboard-tracks across the mud. Most of the men were "accommodated in shell-holes and small, shallow trenches," for water stopped the spade at a couple of feet below ground; but where anything usable remained of the German pill-boxes, which smelt abominably, the men were packed into them. It was in no way a pleasant tour, for the dead lay thick about, and men had not ceased speaking of their officers of the week before – intimately, lovingly, and humorously as the Irish used to do.

More than most, the advance on Houthulst Forest had been an officers' battle; for the work had been broken up, by the nature of the ground and the position of the German pill-boxes, into detached parties dealing with separate strong points, who had to be collected and formed again after each bout had ended. But this work, conceived and carried out on the spur of the moment, under the wings of Death, leaves few historians.

They were relieved on the 16th October by the 20th Lancashire Fusiliers of the 104th Brigade on their right, returned to Elverdinghe through Boesinghe, and entrained for a peaceful camp at Proven. During their three days' tour, Lieutenant R. H. S. Grayson and fourteen other ranks were wounded, mainly by shell, and two other ranks were killed.

They had begun the month of October with 28 officers and 1081 other ranks. They had lost in sixteen days 252 other ranks and 14 officers killed or wounded. Now they were free for the time to rest, refit and reorganize in readiness, men said, to be returned to the Somme. ("Ye'll understand that, in those days, we had grand choice of the fryin'-pan or the fire.")

THE RETURN TO THE SOMME AND CAMBRAI

The Salient, with its sense of being ever over-looked and constricted on every side, fairly represents the frying-pan: the broad, general conflagration of the Somme, the fire. They quitted the frying-pan with some relief, entrained at Proven with the 3rd Coldstream and the 1st Brigade Machine-gun Company, detrained at Watten between the Bois du Ham and the Forêt d'Eperlecques, beyond St. Omer, and marched to the pleasant village of Bayenghem-les-Eperlecques, where they had the satisfaction of meeting the 6th Border Regiment just marching out of the billets that they were to occupy. The place was an intensive training-camp, specializing in all the specialities, but musketry above all. The Somme was open country, where, since they had left it, multitudes of tanks had come into use for the protection of troops, and troops thus protected do not need so many bombers to clear out shell-holes as they do in The Salient, where tanks stick and are shelled to bits in the mud. The inference was obvious! They enjoyed compulsory and voluntary musketry, varied with inspections and route-marchings.

On the 21st October His Royal Highness the Duke of Connaught visited them as senior Colonel of the Brigade of Guards, was introduced to all the officers, spoke to most of the N.C.O.'s and the men who had been decorated during the war. The Battalion was formed up in "walking out" order in the streets of the village to receive him. It is alleged by survivors that the Sergeants saw to it that never since the Irish Guards had been formed was there such rigorous inspection of "walking out" men before they fell in. ("We looked like all Bird-cage Walk of a Sunday.")

On the 24th there joined for duty a draft of six officers, Major R. R. C. Baggallay, M.C., Lieutenant G. K. Thompson, M.C., and 2nd Lieutenants C. E. Hammond, F. G. de Stacpoole, T. A. Carey, and E. C. G. Lord. Lieutenant D. J. B. FitzGerald was transferred from the 1st to the 2nd Battalion on the 25th, which was the day chosen for an inspection of the whole Division by Sir Douglas Haig, in cold weather with a high wind.

On the 6th November General Antoine, commanding the First French Army Corps, which had lain on the Division's left at Boesinghe, was to present French medals gained by the Division, but, thanks to the wet, parade, after being drawn up and thereby thoroughly drenched, was dismissed and the medals presented without review. Lieut.-Colonel R. V. Pollok, commanding the Battalion, received the Croix de Guerre. It is all a piece with human nature that the miseries of a week in liquid mud among corpses should be dismissed with a jest, but a wet parade, which ruins three or four hours' careful preparation, regarded as a grievous burden for every one except the N.C.O.'s, who, by tradition, are supposed to delight in "fatigues" of this order.

Their three weeks' training came to an end on the 11th November, when they moved thirteen miles, in torrents of rain, to the village of Ecques, which was filled with Portuguese troops, and began a long march. They did not know their destination, but guessed well where they were going.

Some had all the reasons in the world to know that the Division would relieve the French on half-a-dozen different named sectors. Others were certain that it would attack independently quite elsewhere. Even Italy, where the Caporetto disaster had just taken place, was to the imaginative quite within the bounds of luck. But their line of route – twelve or thirteen miles a day in fine weather – dropped always south and east. From Ecques it crossed the Lys at Thérouanne; held over the worn road between St Pol and Béthune, till, at Magnicourt-le-Comte, came orders that all kits were to be reduced and sent in to St Pol. Elaborate reasons were given for this, such as lack of transport owing to troops being hurried to Italy, which dissipated the idea of light wines and macaroni entertained by the optimists, and deceived no one. If they turned left when they struck the St Pol – Arras road, it would not be the French whom they were relieving. If they held on south, it would be the old Somme ground. And they held on south to Beaufort, marching by daylight, till the 18th of October found them in a camp of huts outside Blaireville and well in the zone of aeroplane observation. They moved under cover of darkness that night to a camp of tents at Gomiecourt between wrecked Bapaume and battered Arras.

The bare devastated downs of the Somme had taken them back again, and they were in the Fifth Corps, Third (Julian Byng's) Army. It was revealed at Divisional Headquarters' conference on the night of the 19th that that Army was on the eve of attack. There would be no preliminary bombardments, but an outrush of tanks, with a dozen infantry Divisions on a six-mile front from Gonnelieu to the Canal du Nord near Hermies.

The affair might be a surprise for an enemy whom our pressure on The Salient had forced to withdraw a large number of troops from the Somme front. If the tanks worked well, it ought to result in the breaking through of the triple-trench-system of the Hindenburg Line, which had been immensely strengthened by the Germans since their leisurely retirement thither in April. We might expect to push on across their reserve system three or four miles behind the Hindenburg Line. We might even capture Cambrai twelve thousand yards from our jumping-off place, though that would be a side-issue; but, with luck, our attack would win us more high ground towards the north and the north-east, whence we could later strike in whichever direction seemed most profitable. Secrecy and hard hitting would be of the essence of the contract, since the enemy could bring up reinforcements in a couple of days. Meantime the Guards Division would stand by at two hours' notice, ready to be used as required. If Cambrai were taken, they would be called upon to hold it and make good. If it were not, then the battle would rank as a raid on a big scale, and the Division might be used for anything that developed. That same day Major Baggallay, M.C., carried out a road reconnaissance of the front at Doignies and Demicourt north of Havrincourt Wood. The situation there betrayed nothing. "Apparently the whole of that front sector was habitually very quiet."

Twenty-four hours later, it was alive and roaring with our tanks rooting through the massed wire of the Hindenburg Line, the clamour of half-a-dozen Divisions launched at their heels and the smashing fire of our guns in advance of them and their covering smokescreens; while far to north and south dummy attacks, gas and artillery demonstrations veiled and confused either flank. The opening day was, beyond doubt, a success. The German line went out under the tanks, as breakwaters go out under the race of a tide; and from Gonnelieu to north of Hermies three systems of their defence were overrun to a depth of four or five miles. By the 21st November our attack had punched out a square-headed salient, ten miles across the base, the southerly side of which ran along the high ground of the Bonavis Ridge, more or less parallel to the St Quentin – Escaut Canal from Gonnelieu to Masnières which latter place we held. The easterly side lay from Masnières through Noyelles-sur-l'Escaut and Cantaing to Fontaine-Notre-Dame and Bourlon Wood. This latter, as the highest point of command, was the key of the position on our north flank. Thence, the northerly flank of the salient ran roughly westward from the wood, south of Moeuvres till it joined our original front north of Boursies. About one half of the salient was commanded by German guns from the north of Bourlon Wood, and the other half from the south in the direction of the Bonavis Ridge.

Besides these natural disadvantages there were large numbers of our Cavalry hopefully disposed on the main routes in readiness for the traditional "breakthrough," the harrying of enemy communications, etc. November on the Somme is not, however, quite the best season for exploits of horse, sabre and lance.

Meantime, the Battalion spent the 20th November, and till the evening of the 21st, at two hours' notice in camp near Barastre, and on the 23rd November moved to bivouac just west of the village of Doignies behind Demicourt on the edge of the "habitually very quiet sector" before mentioned. The 1st and 3rd Brigades Guards Division had been detailed to relieve two brigades of the Fifty-first Division in the line attacking Fontaine-Notre-Dame village at the extreme north tip of the salient a dozen miles away; and on the evening of the 23rd November they received verbal orders to get away from Doignies. At the moment the Battalion was moving off, came written orders that the whole of its first-line transport should accompany it; so a verbal order was sent to the transport officer to bring it on in rear of the Brigade column. That was the beginning of some not too successful Staff work and some unnecessary wanderings in the dark, complicated by the congestion of the roads and the presence of the ever-hopeful cavalry. The Battalion, its transport all abroad, crossed the Canal du Nord from Doignies and waited by the roadside till Lieut.-Colonel Follett, commanding the Brigade, rode into Graincourt, picked up guides from the 152nd Brigade, brought on the Battalion another couple of thousand yards to the cross-roads at La Justice, found fresh guides from the Gordons and Argyll and Sutherland Highlanders and moved downhill straight into line at Cantaing mill after "a good and quiet relief," at 3.20 a.m. on the morning of the 24th. Fighting had been going on day and night since the 20th for the possession of Bourlon Wood and village, where the Fortieth Division had been worn to a skeleton in alternate attack and counter-attack, but there was no trouble that dawn or day on the Cantaing sector where the Battalion lay and listened to the roar of the battle a mile and a half to the north. Their concern was to improve their line and find out where on earth the Staff had lost their first-line transport. It appeared that varying orders had been given to the transport for the different Battalions, complicated by general instructions to follow their own units by the light of nature; and there the orders stopped. Naturally, as the roads boiled with traffic, all transport was promptly stood aside to let troops get ahead, with the result that after many adventures in the dark, including the collapse of a bridge over the Canal du Nord when half the loads had crossed, the Battalion's transport got into Ribecourt at five in the morning, still without any orders, found that no one knew where Brigade Headquarters might be, billeted themselves in a wrecked farm and managed to get into touch with their Battalion in the afternoon of the 24th. About this time, the Fortieth Division with the tanks attacked Bourlon village, captured the whole of it, only to be fought out by the enemy on the following day. The Wood had not at that time gained its dark name in history. All that the waiting Battalion at Cantaing reports on the 25th November, while wood and village fumed like the infernos that they were, is "no fighting on the Battalion front, although there was heavy fighting on the left."

It broke out again on the 26th towards evening (the fifth day of continuous battle), when the 4th Grenadiers of the 3rd Guards Brigade were sent up to support the Fortieth Division and, on the way thither, went through a heavy German barrage as though they were on parade.

But the high ground above Bourlon Wood and Fontaine-Notre-Dame gave the enemy an artillery and observation command which enabled them to sweep our front and back areas in the northern half of the salient almost as they chose. Pressure, too, was beginning to develop on the flanks. The forty-eight hours in which the enemy could bring up fresh troops had grown to nearly a week, and they had used every hour of it. In no way could the situation be called healthy, but were the Bourlon Ridges won, at least our gain of ground might be held. So it was decided that the 2nd Guards Brigade, 3rd Grenadiers, 1st Coldstream,

2nd Irish Guards and 1st Scots Guards, together with the 4th Grenadiers and the Welsh Guards borrowed, should on the 27th attack Fontaine village and Bourlon Wood. They did so attack; they were cut to pieces with machine-gun fire in the advance; they were shelled out of Bourlon Wood; they were counter-attacked by heavy reinforcements of the enemy; they had no reinforcements; they fell back on Fontaine village in the evening; they withdrew from it in the darkness and fell back on La Justice. It was a full failure with heavy casualties and the news went back, with the speed of all bad news, to the 1st Brigade, which had been relieved on the 26th, the 1st Irish Guards lying at Ribecourt in the ruined farm where their transport had taken refuge. They should have been in a trench outside the village, but a Battalion of another Division was found in possession of it, and so was not disturbed.

GOUZEAUCOURT

There was no shelter against the driving snowy rain, and the men, without great-coats or blankets, were "very cold, wet and miserable." The next day was no better, and on the 29th the Fifty-ninth Division took over their area from them while the Guards Division was rearranged thus: the 3rd Brigade at Trescault, the 2nd at Ribecourt, and the 1st at Metz-en-Couture, a wrecked red-brick village, once engaged in the sugar-beet industry, lying on and under a swell of the downs some four thousand yards west of Gouzeaucourt. The Divisional Artillery was at Flesquières, more than four miles away. The Battalion's march to Metz was badly delayed by blocks on the road and a general impression spread that trouble was not far off. Individually, the soldier is easy to deceive: collectively, a battalion has the sure instinct of an animal for changes in the wind. There were catacombs in Metz village where one Company was billeted whereby it was nearly choked to death by foul gases.[1] This seemed all of a piece with the bad luck of the tour, and the dawn of the 30th November was ushered in by single shells from a long-range gun which found them during the night. Half an hour after they had the order to move to Heudicourt and had digested a persistent rumour that the enemy were through at Gonnelieu; telegrams and orders began to pour in. The gist of them was that the line had undoubtedly cracked, and that the Brigade would move to Gouzeaucourt at once. But what the Brigade was to do, and under whose command it was to operate, were matters on which

---

[1] These were vast cellars reached by a hundred steps, and at the bottom of them resided a very old soldier, who did little more than "boil the hot water for the officers' baths" and look after a certain mascot-goat which had been given them by a French Corps. When the order to move at once came, the darting words of the Officer in Charge of the Goat to that aged man were: "Now, you look after the goat and our blankets, and don't walk about upstairs. You needn't worry about yourself. If you're taken prisoner we'll send you lots of parcels. Look after the goat and hang on to our blankets." He did.

telegrams and orders most livelily conflicted. Eventually, the Division as a whole was assigned to the Third Corps, the 3rd Brigade was ordered to come up from Trescault and help the 1st, and the various C.O.'s of the Battalions of the 1st Brigade rode forward to see for themselves what was happening. They had not far to go. Over the ridge between Gouzeaucourt and Metz poured gunners, carrying their sights with them, engineers, horses and infantry, all apparently bent on getting into the village where they would be a better target for artillery. The village choked; the Battalion fell in, clear of the confusion, where it best could, and set off at once in artillery formation, regardless of the stragglers, into the high and bare lands round Gouzeaucourt. There were no guns to back them, for their own were at Flesquières.

As was pointed out by an observer of that curious day – "'Tis little ye can do with gun-sights, an' them in the arums av men in a great haste. There was men with blankets round'em, an' men with loose putties wavin' in the wind, and they told us 'twas a general retirement. We could see that. We wanted to know for why they was returnin'. We went through 'em all, fairly breastin' our way and – we found Jerry on the next slope makin' prisoners of a Labour Corps with picks an' shovels. But some of that same Labour Corps they took their picks an' shovels and came on with us."

They halted and fixed bayonets just outside Gouzeaucourt Wood, the Irish on the left of the line, their right on the Metz – Gouzeaucourt road, the 3rd Coldstream in the centre, the 2nd Coldstream on the right, the 2nd Grenadiers in reserve in Gouzeaucourt Wood itself. What seems to have impressed men most was the extreme nakedness of the landscape, and, at first, the absence of casualties. They were shelled as they marched to the Wood but not heavily; but when they had passed beyond it they came under machine-gun fire from the village. They topped the rise beyond the Wood near Queen's Cross and were shelled from St. Quentin Ridge to the east. They overran the remnant of one of our trenches in which some sappers and infantry were still holding on. Dismounted cavalry appeared out of nowhere in particular, as troops will in a mixed fray, and attached themselves to the right of the thin line. As they swept down the last slope to Gouzeaucourt the machine-gun fire from the village grew hotter on their right, and the leading company, characteristically enough, made in towards it. This pulled the Battalion a little to the right, and off the road which was supposed to be their left boundary, but it indubitably helped to clear the place. The enemy were seen to be leaving in some haste, and only a few of them were shot or bayoneted in and out among the houses. The Battalion pushed in through the village to the slope east of it under Quentin Mill, where they dug in for the night. Their left flank was all in the air for a while, but the 3rd Brigade, which had been originally ordered to come up on the right of the 1st, was diverted to the left on the Gouzeaucourt – Villers – Plouich line, and they got into touch with the 4th Grenadiers. There was no attempt to counter-attack. Tanks were used on the right during the action, but they do not seem to have played any material part in the Battalion's area, and, as the light of the short and freezing November day closed, a cavalry regiment, or "some cavalry," came up on the left flank.

The actual stroke that recovered Gouzeaucourt had not taken more than an hour, but the day had cost them a hundred and thirty men killed, wounded and missing; Lieutenant N. F. Durant killed, Lieutenant (Acting Captain) Joyce, Lieutenant G. E. F. Van der Noot, Lieutenant G. K. Thompson, M.C., and 2nd Lieutenant P. M. Riley wounded. All the casualties were from machine-gun fire; men dropping at the corners of streets, across thresholds in cellars, and in the angles of wrecked walls that, falling on them, hid them for ever.

A profane legend sprang up almost at once that the zeal shown by the Guards in the attack was because they knew Gouzeaucourt held the supplies of the Division which had evacuated it. The enemy had been turned out before he could take advantage of his occupation. Indeed, a couple of our supply-trains were found untouched on rail at the station, and a number of our guns were recaptured in and around the place. Also, the Divisional rum-supply was largely intact. When this fact came to light, as it did – so to say – rum-jar by rum-jar, borne joyously through the dark streets that bitter night, the Brigade was refreshed and warmed, and, men assert, felt almost grateful to the Division which had laid this extra "fatigue" on them. One grim incident stays in the minds of those who survived – the sight of an enormous Irishman urging two captives, whom he had himself unearthed from a cellar, to dance before him. He demanded the jigs of his native land, and seemed to think that by giving them drink his pupils would become proficient. Men stood about and laughed till they could hardly stand; and when the fun was at its height a chance shell out of the darkness to the eastward wiped out all that tango-class before their eyes. ("Twas like a dhream, ye'll understand. One minute both Jerries was dancin' hard oblige him, an' then – nothin', nothin' – nothin' – of the three of them!")

The next day, orders came for the Guards Division to continue their work and attack on a front of two miles along the line of the ridge a thousand yards east of Gouzeaucourt, which ran south through Gonnelieu village and Gauche Wood to Villers Hill. Tanks, they were told, would help and the Divisional Artillery would put down barrages. The Fifty-ninth Division would be on their left and the Cavalry Division on their right. The 1st Guards Brigade were assigned Gauche Wood; the 3rd Brigade had the much more difficult problem of rushing Gonnelieu village in the event of another Division who were attacking it that morning (1st December) failing to make headway. The 1st Brigade's attack on Gauche Wood was undertaken by the 2nd Grenadiers on the right, the 3rd Coldstream, in reserve, in their trenches. They assembled before dawn on the 1st December, waited a while for a promised detachment of tanks and finally started off without them. Their artillery support was meagre, and the troops had to cover three-quarters of a mile over grassy land to the fringe of the wood. The enemy's first barrage fell behind them; the wood itself was crammed with much more effective machine-guns, but, once it had been entered, the issue became a man-to-man affair. Then some tanks turned up and some cavalry, the latter an hour late. The tanks were eventually withdrawn, as they found no trenches to crush in the wood and drew much shell-fire in the open; but the cavalry, which included Bengal Lancers, were of good use on the right flank of the attack. The two Guards Brigades, one attacking Gonnelieu to the north, the other Gauche Wood to the south, drew a little apart from each other as the men closed in where the machine-gun fire was hottest, and about nine o'clock the 1st Irish Guards sent up a company (No. 1) to fill the gap which developed on both sides of the Gouzeaucourt – Gonnelieu road, the boundary between the Brigades.

They do not seem to have been called upon to do more than sit, suffer and be shelled till evening, when they were relieved by a company of the 1st Coldstream and went back in the hard black frost to their bivouac in Gouzeaucourt Wood. Gauche Wood was won and held, but Gonnelieu, its houses and cellarages crammed with machine-guns, was a hopeless proposition from the first, to troops lacking tanks or adequate artillery aid. The sole excuse for attempting it was that the enemy's pressure was heavy and increasing on all three sides of the Cambrai salient (Bourlon Wood in the north was the point of most actual danger) and had to be met by whatever offered at the times and near the places. The 3rd Brigade was held up by the inevitable machine-gun in trenches in front of Gonnelieu and round the cemetery on its eastern outskirts; and there it stayed, under circumstances of extreme misery, till the 3rd December, when the 1st Brigade came back from Gouzeaucourt Wood to relieve. The 1st Irish Guards, numbering, then, four hundred and fifty battle-strength, who took over the 2nd Scots Guards' and half the 1st Grenadiers' line, were allotted what might be termed "mixed samples" of trench. No. 1 Company, for instance, held six hundred yards of superior wired line, evidently an old British reserve-line, with the enemy dug in sixty yards away. No. 3 Company on its right had a section mostly battered to bits and further weakened by an old communication-trench running up to the enemy, which had to be blocked as soon as possible. No. 2 Company was even less happily placed; for the enemy inhabited the actual continuation of their trench, so that they worked with their right flank grossly exposed. Two platoons of No. 4 Company lay close behind No. 2 to cover a gap; while the other two platoons in Flag Ravine, four or five hundred yards back, by the railway-line, were all the reserve the Battalion possessed east of Gouzeaucourt Wood. By some unexplained mercy of Providence that night, the next day and the next day's night were "quiet" in the sense that there was no actual attack. The men sat in the trenches and froze; for the frost held day and night, and the enemy shelled the line at their will, with trench-mortars from near at hand and heavier stuff from the ridges beyond. Just before dawn, on the 5th December, they put down a very heavy mixed barrage behind the front line and a trench-mortar one on the line itself, and then attacked the two weak spots – No. 2 and No. 3 Companies' position – with armoured bombers. The barricade to the communication-trench of No. 3 Company was blown in by a direct mortar-hit and a rush followed. No. 2 Company's trench was also

But in the area that we held lay a sample of the great Hindenburg line . . . Men saw it with their own eyes, explored its recesses wonderingly, followed down the terrible lanes that the tanks had cut in its hundred-yard-deep beltings of wire . . .

The Hindenburg Line.

rushed end-on from the right, and three or four bays of it were taken. At this point, the Irish left the trenches all filling with the enemy, got out into the open, where for the moment there was no mortar-fire, and dealt with the invaders from outside, bombing and shooting downwards into the heavily moving queues. The Germans wore their packs, "from which it may be inferred," says the Diary delicately, "that they meant to occupy our trenches." This, and their scientific armour, proved their undoing, and when – presumably to make doubly sure – an infantry attack swarmed out in two lines from Gonnelieu, it was broken up by our rifle and machine-gun fire, till it turned round and fled. Hereupon, says the Diary, "they were heavily bombed by their own side," presumably as an example to His Majesty's Guards of Prussian discipline. The casualties in the Battalion were one officer, 2nd Lieutenant Carey, and four other ranks killed; and about thirty wounded, mainly by bombs and mortars. But the affair was waste-work on both sides; for Gonnelieu was never taken by our arms. Our line here, in the next day or so, fell back on Gauche Wood; and of all the salient won at the Battle of Cambrai between the 20th and the 23rd of November, all that remained by the 7th of December was a stretch of country perhaps four thousand yards deep running from the Gouzeaucourt – Cambrai road to north of Demicourt. On the other hand, a cantle had been taken out of our old front line from opposite Vendhuille to Gonnelieu. But in the area that we held lay a sample of the great Hindenburg Line with its support-systems, its ten-foot-deep concreted and camouflaged trenches, covered gun-ways, machine-gun wells and shafts, and the whole detail of its immensely advertised impregnability. Men saw it with their own eyes, explored its recesses wonderingly, followed down the terrible lanes that the tanks had cut in its hundred-yard-deep beltings of wire, and settled themselves thankfully in its secure dug-outs, not foreseeing the days next spring when they would be swept out of it all like withered leaves. Cambrai was no success, but it would be unjust to hold it, as some wearied and over-wrought souls did, an unrelieved failure. The enemy had not achieved their purpose, which was to cut off all our troops in the salient, and were quite willing to break away and wait till the transfer of fresh Divisions from the collapsed Russian front should be methodically completed. We, on our part, were equally ready to cut our losses, for we had no men to spare. The Guards Division was moved out of the battle-area on the 6th December, being relieved by troops of the Ninth Division. On the evening of their own private battle the Battalion handed over their none too pleasant trenches to the 5th Cameron Highlanders, and went back to bivouac in Gouzeaucourt Wood after a "very good relief," which drew from the Diary the tribute that the Camerons were a "fine Battalion." Had they been an hour late in that cutting wind across the slopes, a cohort of angels with fiery swords would have been put down as hopeless.

They moved from the Wood next day to Etricourt down the long road through Fins, and at Etricourt entrained for Beaumetz-les-Loges on the Arras – Doullens road which they reached late at night, cold and empty, and were not billeted at Berneville, two or three kilometres to the north-east, till midnight.

They had lost, in November and December, two officers killed; Lieutenant N. F. Durant on the 30th November, who had joined on the 1st of that month, and 2nd Lieutenant T. A. Carey, killed on the 5th December, joined on the 24th October. (The average expectation of an officer's life in those days on the Somme was still about six weeks, though some were so lucky they survived for months.) Four officers had been wounded in the same period: Lieutenants G. K. Thompson, Lieutenant (Acting Captain) Joyce; G. E. F. Van der Noot, and 2nd Lieutenant P. M. Riley, all on the 30th November. The following officers joined in November and December: Lieutenants Zigomala, B. F. Crewdson, D. J. B. FitzGerald and J. N. Ward; and 2nd Lieutenants H. A. A. Collett, A. W. G. Jamrack and C. A. J. Nicholson.

At Beaumetz-les-Loges they lay till the end of the year, cleaning up, refitting, drilling, and not forgetting their football – the 2nd Scots Guards beat them in the third round of the Divisional Football Competition at Arras – or their Company Christmas dinners. These were the fourth that the Battalion had eaten within sound of the weary guns, but if any one had told them that their next would be celebrated in stately steam-heated barracks at Cologne, hospital would have been his portion. They could not have been called happy or hopeful at that time; for they knew, as all our armies did, that the year's gain had been small, and the work ahead of them, now that the German divisions, released from Russia, were pouring westward, would be heavy. But for the moment they were free of the Somme and its interminable duckboards that led men to death or hard work; its shell-holes floored with icy snow-water, the grave-like chill of its chalk trenches, and the life-sapping damps of the uplands on which they had lain out from nights till mornings.

Here is a memory of those days presented by the teller as a jest. "Ay! Gouzeaucourt and Gonnelieu! I'm not like to forget'em. I was back from leave, ye'll understand; no more anxious to die than the rest of us. An' there was some new men, too – new young lads just come over. My kit was all new too, me bein' back from leave. Our C.S.M. dhrew me attention to it one of those merry nights we was poachin' about in No Man's Land. 'Tis a pity says he, 'ye did not bring the band from Cate also,' says he. ''Twould have amused Jerry.' My new kit was shqueakin' an' clicking the way could have heard it a mile. Ay, Gouzeaucourt an' the trenches outside Gonnelieu! Jerry was usin' trench-mortars at his pleasure on us those nights. They was crackin' on our heads, ye'll understand. An' I was in a bay with two men. Wan was a new young man, an' the trench-mortars was new to him. Could? It was all of that! An' Jerry crackin' this dam' trench-mortar stuff of his on our heads will. It put the wind up me! Did I tell you other man in the bay was dead? He was. That finished me new young man. He kep' trying to make himself smaller an' smaller against the trench mortars. In the end of it, he laced his arrums round his ankles – he did – an' rocked to an' fro, whishperin' to the Saints. Shell-shock? Oh, yes,'t was all that. Presently I heard Mr. – comin' the rounds, walking outside the trench. Ye see more when ye're outside a trench, but 'tis no place I'm fond of without orders. 'Ai are ye all cosy down there, Sergeant?' says he. Yes, 'cosy' was his word! Knoin' him well 'Why wud we not be cosy, Sorr?' says I, an' at that he drops into the bay to have a look. We was cosy enough, all three of us – the dead man dead an' stiffenin' in the frost, an' this fine new young lad of ours embracin' his own ankles an' rockin' back an' forth, an' me so sorry my leave was up. Oh! we was the cosiest party in the whole dam' front line that night; and for to make it all the cosier, me new young man, as soon as he set eyes on Mr. – , he flung his arrums around his neck, an' he let out a yell, an' he hugged him like a gurrl. I had to separate 'em! I've laughed at it since, an' so did Mr. – an', begad, I remember laughin' at it at the time. Ay, 'cosy,' Mr. – said. That was the word! So I laughed. Otherwise, there *was* not much laughin', ye'll understand, at Gouzeaucourt an' them 'cosy' trenches before Gonnelieu."

1918
ARRAS TO THE ARMISTICE

THE LULL lasted till the 2nd of January when they marched via Warlus to Arras and were billeted in the prison there. Battalion Headquarters were a luxurious house in the Rue d'Amiens, with a whole roof and all windows repaired with canvas. It was hard frosty weather, binding everything tight – of the kind that must be paid for when thaw comes.

At that moment our line, on the Somme side, ran from Lens just behind Oppy, through Roeux, five miles east of Arras, south to Bullecourt, south-easterly towards Boursies, round the Flesquières – Ribecourt salient that Cambrai fight had won for us, curved back between Gonnelieu and Gouzeaucourt, and thence dropped, skirting St. Quentin and the valley of the Oise, to the junction with the French at Barisis, south of that river. This length, of close on seventy miles, was held, from Barisis to Gouzeaucourt, by Byng's Third Army, and from Gouzeaucourt to Gavrelle, by Gough's Fifth Army. North of this, the First Army took on. The working and reserve strength of the Third and Fifth Armies at the opening of 1918 was twenty-nine infantry and three cavalry Divisions. So far as our arms were concerned, everything on the French and Belgian fronts was at a standstill. The Somme had cost very heavily throughout the year, and there was, or was said to be, a scarcity of men. The situation appears to have been met by reducing the number of battalions in the brigades from four to three apiece. This released the odd battalions to make what, on paper, and in the journals, looked like additional brigades, but threw extra work, which nowhere appeared as news, on the whole of the Army administration in the field. Sir Douglas Haig's despatches refer guardedly to the reorganization, which he hints "to some extent affected" the fighting efficiency of the units concerned. The sentiments of Commanders more directly concerned were, perhaps, less publishable; for it rarely improves an old Army in the field to lace it at the last moment, before a general attack, with new brigades composed of battalions suddenly disassociated from the units with whom they have been working. But thus was created the 4th Guards Brigade, by lopping off the 4th Grenadiers, the 2nd Irish Guards, and the 3rd Coldstream from their respective Brigades, and attaching them to the Thirty-first Division. Further, it was necessary for the British Armies to take over another stretch of nearly thirty miles from the French on the right – approximately from Barisis to Vendhuille on the Oise – and this brought the British front up to one hundred and twenty-five miles total length.

Our enemy lay less under such burdens. His released divisions, aeroplanes and guns were decently entraining from the Russian front, and arriving on the Somme in good order, a fact of which our Staff, and in a very short time all our Armies, were perfectly aware. ("We could feel Jerry pilin' up and pilin' up against us in those days, ye'll understand.") So, as may have been pointed out, every one stood by to prepare for the worst. The Guards Division, now of nine battalions, instead of twelve, was assigned to the defences before Arras, the hinge on which the coming trouble might be expected to turn. Their trench and post system ran north and south across the Scarpe with its lagoon and marshes, by Roeux – all old and much used ground, but which had the advantage of being served both by canal and a light rail from Arras.

The Battalion, which had trained and bombed in the town till the 8th January, relieved the 3rd Grenadiers in the reserve trenches of the right sub-sector of this defence, on the 9th January, in heavy snow. Lancer Avenue, which commanded a fine view of our own lines and the enemy's, and posts K, L and M just off it (all south of the river), took half the strength. The remainder garrisoned Crump and Cordite Reserve trenches on the north, and supplied an isolated and unpleasant post (F) between the river and the lagoon which could only be reached with comfort after dark, when an officer, twenty men, a Lewis-gun, and a couple of signallers watched there in case an enterprising enemy should be minded to raid along the tow-path.

Next day it thawed and the old horrors of Ypres Salient were their portion. The snow vanished, leaving terrible mud. The day passed quietly. Nos. 1 and 3 Companies had to find "a carrying-party for front Companies in the evening." The story behind the entry tells itself. The enemy did not add himself to their burdens. A patrol, under 2nd Lieutenant H. A. Collett, went out the next night (January 11) five hundred yards into No Man's Land – from F post – saw and heard nothing. F post was always a ghostly sort of place, where bullets whistled by without explanation between the furred tree-trunks along the tow-path; and the marshy ground behind it was filled with shell-holes, rusty wire and the black dead of forgotten fights. The ruins of Roeux across the river, suddenly leaping to shape in the flare of Very lights, looked down on it like the skeleton of a fortress on a stage, and single unexpected shells spattered mud across the cold waters.

On the 13th January they relieved the 2nd Grenadiers at the front in a fresh assortment of decayed posts – Scabbard Alley, Scabbard Support, Welford Reserve and the like, whose names even to this day make men who served there shiver. As thaw and rain worked on them, the trenches "all fell in great lumps."

"Why troops who had held them all the summer had done nothing to revet them and prepare for the winter, I cannot think," one indignant sufferer wrote. "But that is always the fault of the British Army. It *will* not look ahead." He prophesied better than he knew. Then he went to visit his posts, where the men were already half buried in mud. The enemy assisted our repairing-parties with trench-mortars at intervals, till orders went forth that, though our mortars were nowise to stir up trouble, when once it began they would retaliate for just five minutes longer than the enemy. By the misfortune of a faulty shell, one of our Stokes guns burst on the 14th, killing or wounding eight men. However, it was noted that the enemy transferred his attentions for the next few days to a battalion of East Lancashires on our right.

On the 15th all wiring and defence-work ceased – "employed solely on trying to keep trenches passable." In spite of which the mud gained. Men's boots were pulled off their feet, and it is on joyous record that when Captain Gordon, the Adjutant, tried to get up Johnson Avenue, their only communication-trench, he stuck up to his waist in mud and water and, lest he should be engulfed, had to wriggle out of his gum-boots, which came up to his thighs, and continue in his socks. The gum-boots, empty, sank out of sight like a wreck on the Goodwins. They reconnoitred new tracks for the reliefs, across duckboards running in full view of the enemy, who, luckily, had their own conditions to fight, and let a couple of our patrols invade No Man's Land unmolested, prowl round two machine-gun posts and even enter a German front line, "being too busy talking and hammering to notice us." The sodden sand-bags of the revetments bulged outwards and met across the trenches. The men worked day and night, and blessed every battalion's remotest ancestry that had ever used, and neglected, that accursed line.

On the 17th January they were relieved by the 2nd Grenadiers, which merely meant their reverting to Crump Trench, Cordite Reserve, Ceylon Avenue, etc., where, all being equally impassable, every movement had to be effected in the open.

Our Artillery chose the 18th to be very active from their positions round Battalion Headquarters near the railway cutting behind, whereby there was some enemy retaliation that the mired front line could have spared. ("Every one is looking like the worst form of tramp – standing, walking, sleeping and eating mud.")

On the 19th they got it worse, and when No. 1 Company paraded in the dawn dark (they were in dug-outs below the rail embankment) to go to work, a shell which dropped at the entrance killed one (but he was the cook), wounded two of their number, and destroyed the whole cooking-outfit. Captain A. F. L. Gordon, M. C., was also slightly wounded on that date, but not enough to send him to hospital. He was riding into Arras with Captain Woodhouse, the M.O. – also a man of charmed lives – and just behind the railway embankment came in for a complete barrage of heavy stuff, intended for Battalion Headquarters. Neither he, nor any one else, ever understood why they were not blown to pieces. The doctor's horse wounded was the only other casualty.

On the 22nd January, the relieved 2nd Grenadiers having handed over news of the discovery of a German listening-post which seemed to be used only by night, a scheme was arranged to occupy it while it was empty, and astonish the enemy on their return. But the enemy never came, though 2nd Lieutenant Stacpoole and a party of seven, with blackened faces and smoked bayonets, lay out for them all night. It was the same with a German working-party, fifty strong, located by our patrols on the 22nd, sought on the 23rd, and found missing. The enemy were anxious not to give any chances just then, for identifications; and, though they raided generously in other directions, left the Guards' sector by the Scarpe unvisited. They delivered mortar bombardments when reliefs were due, and were attended to by our Artillery at dusk with a desultory but at the same time steady shelling, just enough to keep the five principal offenders' crews in their dug-outs. It worked admirably, and all enemy mortars, as registered on the maps, were quiet for a whole evening. After one such treatment (the night of the 25th January) they drenched the Decauville railway, just when the Battalion had railed back to Arras on relief by the 1st Grenadiers, with an hour's intense barrage of gas-shells, and a sprinkling of 5·9's and 4·2's. Battalion Headquarters were waiting to follow, and all the men had been sent down the line because rail-head was no healthy place to linger at. A company of the 2nd Grenadiers, newly relieved, came up and also waited for the little train in the still moonlight night and drank hot tea while a spare engine was being coupled up. Every one thought (inevitable prelude to calamity!) that, after sixteen days in the trenches, his troubles were over. Then a gas-shell skimmed over the line which, at this point, had a cutting on one side and an embankment on the other. All hands fled to the embankment side and hugged it for precisely one hour while the air screamed to the curious whip-lash-like noise of gas-shells splintering, and filled with the fumes of them. The engine bolted down the line before it should be blown up, and when, on the stroke of ten, shelling ceased, Battalion Headquarters, Father Browne and the Doctor, Captain Woodhouse, and the Grenadiers' Company stumbled as best they could along the sleepers towards Arras. Every one missed every one else in the confusion, while the Irish orderlies raged through the crowd, like angry nurses, in search of their officers. But at last all hands were accounted for, blind, coughing, and, thanks to the nose-clips of the masks, mostly with sore noses. They got into Arras at midnight, and a good many of the Grenadiers had to be sent down for gas injuries.

The month closed with the Battalion nominally at Arras, and actually finding more than two-thirds of its strength for working-parties in the filthy front line – a favour which it had not received itself while there. Its casualty list for January was extraordinarily low, being only two men killed and twenty-six wounded, one officer, Captain Gordon, wounded and one, 2nd Lieutenant D. A. B. Moodie in hospital. During the month, 2nd Lieutenants A. S. Stokes and L. H. L. Carver joined, and 2nd Lieutenant A. W. G. Jamrack rejoined from the Reinforcement Battalion.

On the 1st February orders came that the line was to be held by all three Brigades of the Guards Division instead of two; for it must be remembered that each Brigade was short one battalion. The rearrangement drew more heavily on the working-parties in the forward area where a new, foul trench – Hyderabad Support – was under way. They supplied from two to four hundred men as need was, and lived in Arras prison in luxury – wire beds and palliasses for every man! – till the 6th February, when they relieved the 2nd Coldstream in the front line. The support-trenches here were the best they had found, being deep, duckboarded, well revetted and with plenty of dug-outs and an enviable system of cook-houses delivering hot meals in the actual trenches. They sent working-parties to the insatiable Engineers and the Brigade at large; for fresh trenches were being sketched out, if not built, against the impending German attack.

The front line from the 10th to the 13th February was remarkably quiet, but not easy. Their patrols found no enemy, nor any sign of them in No Man's Land; a little wiring of nights was possible; and there were no casualties. But the trench-strength of the Battalion was weak – 16 officers and 398 ranks, and every one had to work double-tides to keep the ways open.

They were relieved on St. Valentine's Day, two days after the 4th Guards Brigade, which took with them the 2nd Irish Guards, had been formed under Lord Ardee, and added to the Thirty-first Division.

Three days in Arras prison saw them back again in support just in time to get the full benefit of another day's thaw. It was a quiet tour. One man was killed by a trench-mortar, one badly wounded by a rifle-grenade, seven by shell-splinters outside a dug-out, and five men gassed. The enemy confined himself to long-range trench-mortars and an "increase in aerial activity." He was noticed to "object very strongly to our aircraft crossing his lines." Never was enemy more anxious not to draw attention to his moves. And, far behind our line at Arras and elsewhere, men dug and entrenched and sketched works of defence to meet the German rush, while the front trenches sat still and looked across deserts, apparently empty of life, till a head moved in the open. It was a season without parallel in our Armies' experience – this mere waiting for a certain blow to be dealt at a certain time. No written history records the psychology of those spring days. The Diary is concerned with the Battalion's own sorrow. Here is the story, as written: "During the month (February) the Household Battalion was disbanded and eighty men were allotted to the Battalion. This marks the beginning, and is the first official recognition of the fact that the Irish Guards cannot keep up the supply of Irish troops. A most regrettable epoch in the history of the Regiment." On the heels of this comes, comically enough, almost the sole personal expression of feeling in the entire Diary. They went, on the last day of February, into rest at Gordon Camp, christened after the 9th Gordons who made it. "It is without exception the most comfortable and best-laid-out camp I have ever been in. Everything that one could possibly wish for is here – even an officers' bath-room with porcelain bath and hot and cold water laid on." It was an all-too-short interval in cold and dirty work; for on the 2nd March the Scarpe trenches reclaimed them – Fampoux, Colt Reserve, Pepper and Pudding – in snow, sleet and unbroken monotony of working-parties.

On the 6th March the Diary notes that the 2nd Grenadiers, whom they relieved the next day, carried out a raid, successful in itself, and doubly so as drawing no retaliation on their own line. It resulted in two identifiable prisoners and a machine-gun. But battalions do not approve of their neighbours raiding when the enemy is "nervous."

THE MARCH PUSH

Their next front-line turn – 6th to 10th March – was utterly uneventful, and on the 12th they, being then in Stirling Camp, were ordered to "stand to" for the expected German offensive. It proved to be no more than a light shelling. So the still fine days, in line or in support, ran out till the dawn of the 21st March when the great shells suddenly descended on Arras, and rumours, worse than any shelling, followed their tracks. Says the Diary: "The German offensive has begun."

The evacuation of the town, during the next two days, was a nightmare of flying masonry, clouds of dust, the roar of falling brick-work, contradictory orders, and mobs of drifting civilians, their belongings pushed before or hauled after them, and no power to order them where to go. Arras, always in the front line, had been safe so long, it was inconceivable that there should be real danger now. Might they not camp out and return tomorrow? But the enemy were reported almost in sight, and ready to open on the town with their field-guns. They had broken through, men said, under cover of the heavy morning fog – broken through everywhere along the line of all our old gains from Lens to St. Quentin, and their whole strength was behind the blow. No one could understand it, though all men argued; and while the refugees fled forth, expostulating, blaming, but seldom weeping, that sunny day, eight hundred shells fell purposefully on the dishevelled town. By evening word came that our Somme line had not only broken but gone out – Infantry, Artillery and uncounted stores – between Chèrisy and Demicourt in the north. South of that, the old Cambrai Salient, which had not been hardly tried, was standing but would have to withdraw or be cut off, because, from Gouzeaucourt to La Fère, ten miles and more south of St. Quentin, the German tide had swept in from one to three miles deep, and was racing forward. It is not difficult to imagine what manner of reports the mere truth gave birth to, while the Battalion waited on in the Communal College where it was billeted, and was not encouraged to wander about the rocking, sliding streets.

By the evening of the 22nd March men began to understand it was no mere break-through but a collapse such as had never befallen British arms in the history of her people. Officers were sent out in the morning to reconnoitre the support-line of a third system of defence between Wancourt and Hénin-sur-Cojeul. But Hénin-sur-Cojeul was already under the hand of the enemy, who had gained three more miles in a few hours and, left and right, were widening the breach.

The morning of the 22nd March had been foggy again till noon and, under that cover, the Germans had again broken in on our surprised or withdrawing Divisions. Report said that whole Battalions and even Brigades had been cut off by the flood; their wireless working faithfully so long as it stood, and the sound of their small-arm fire continuing for a while after their last words had ceased. Late that evening orders came for the Battalion to move at midnight from Arras to Boisleux-St. Marc, some six miles due south of the town on a line, more or less, prepared against eventualities, and, with their Brigade, to give what help they could to the Divisions who might be falling back on that front. This was all that could be made out of the mass of contradictory orders that afflicted them, and the growing crop of rumours and alarms that upset men more than any countermanded orders.

The Battalion set to work on the 23rd March to dig a support-line in rear of what was called the Army Line which ran in front of Boisleux-St. Marc while the evacuation of Arras was being completed and "all details and drummers marched to the Reinforcement Battalion at Agnez-les Duisans," on the Scarpe well to the west of Arras. ("In those days we was throubled the way a man is disthressed in dhreams. All manner of things happening, ye'll understand, and him the only one able to do nothing. But I wish I'd been a musicaner.")

The Diary for the 24th March merely says, "remained in same positions," and refers to "repeated rumours." They sent their first-line transport back out of harm's way, and went on digging. Yet the 24th was a day no rumour could have painted much blacker than it was. From directly in front of the Guards Division at Boisleux, the line of the German gains in the past forty-eight hours dropped straight south to the Somme at Cléry, and thence skirted its western bank to Ham, where it broke across to the wide marshes of the Oise below La Fère. Two-thirds of the hard-bought ground of the Somme campaign, the scores of villages whose names smelt of blood, were lost, and the harvesting of the remainder was a matter barely of hours.

Next day saw Béhagnies, Grévillers, Irles of the wired bastions, Miraumont, Pys, Courcelette, Contalmaison, Thiepval and its myriad dead, and Pozières of the Australians – the very hearts of the deadliest of the first fightings – overrun; and the question rose in men's minds whether the drive would end, as was intended, in the splitting apart of the French and British Armies. For what was happening north of the Somme was play to the situation south of it. There the enemy's swarms of aeroplanes harried the Amiens hospitals, driving the civilians into the broadside of the country behind, where the moonlight nights betrayed them to fresh hosts in the air.

By the 26th March the tongue of the advancing tide had licked past Noyon and Roye and, next day, had encircled Montdidier. Meantime, our old Somme base on the Ancre, whence the great fights were fed and supplied from the hundred camps and dumps round Méaulte, and the railway-sidings between Albert and Amiens, had passed into the enemy's hands. To all human appearance, the whole of our bitter year's effort was abolished, as though it had never been. The enemy had prepared, brought together, and struck at the time that best suited himself, with seventy-three Divisions against thirty-seven British Divisions, and the outcome was appalling defeat of our arms.

It would thus seem that no amount of inspiring statesmanship at home, or anxious readjustment of Divisions at the front, will make troops where troops are not. Therefore the battalions and batteries in the full blast of the onset perished or were taken prisoners; and of the stores captured or destroyed, lest they should benefit the enemy, we may look to receive no account. Not the least depressing of the sights that adorned the landscape were the dumps lit by our own hands, flaring to heaven when, as turned out afterwards, there was really no need. Divisions were being raced up to reinforce the fluid front as fast as might be, but no one knew for certain when or where they would arrive, and Camp Commandants acted on their own judgements. The battalions in the line swayed to conflicting storms of orders.

"STANDING-TO"

On the 25th, being still at Boisleux-St. Marc, the 1st Irish Guards were detailed to relieve "several different units," but more specially the 1st Coldstream just east of Hamelincourt then practically in possession of the enemy. (One found out where the enemy were by seeing them come over the brows of unexpected slopes in small groups that thinned out and settled down to machine-gunning under cover of equally unexpected field-guns.) They spent the whole day being "hit and held" in this fashion, and, close on midnight, got definite instructions not to wait for any relief but to go off to the sugar-factory near Boyelles, which they did, and bestowed themselves in huts in the neighbourhood, and there were hotly shelled during the night. The German attack was well home on that sector now, and the German infantry might be looked for at any moment. They removed from those unhealthy huts to an old trench next morning, where their first set of orders was to relieve the 1st Scots Guards. (Order, provisional, definite and cancelled, all in two hours and a half!) Later came orders – equally definite, equally washed-out later – to relieve the 2nd Coldstream in another sector, and finally just before midnight they relieved the 1st Scots Guards after all. That Battalion had been in the Army Line between St. Léger and Hénin, but the enemy's advance had forced it back in the direction of Boisleux-St. Marc near the Arras – Albert railway-line. The Battalion found it a little before dawn, and lay out with all four companies in the front line, as did the other Battalions. By this time, though it would be not easy to trace their various arrivals in the confusion, the Guards Brigades had got into line between Boisleux-St. Marc and Ayette, on a front of roughly three and a half miles, while battalions of exhausted and withdrawing Divisions, hard pressed by the enemy, passed through them each with its burden of bad news. It was not an inspiriting sight, nor was the actual position of the Guards Brigades one to be envied. High ground commanded them throughout, and a number of huts and half-ruined buildings gave good cover to the gathering machine-guns. The German advance on that quarter resembled, as one imaginative soul put it, an encompassment of were-wolves. They slouched forward, while men rubbed tired eyes, in twos and threes, at no point offering any definite target either for small-arm or artillery, and yet, in some wizard fashion, always thickening and spreading, while our guns from the rear raged and tore uselessly at their almost invisible lines. Incidentally, too, our own gun-fire in some sectors, and notably behind the 4th Guards Brigade, did our men no service. But the most elaborate of preparations have an end, and must culminate in the charge home.

An intense barrage on the morning of the 27th March heralded the crsis, but luckily went wide of all the Battalion except No. 2 Company on the left. The attack followed, and down the trenched line from Ayette and Boisleux-St. Marc the Brigade answered with unbroken musketry and Lewis-guns. It was an almost satisfactory slaughter, dealt out by tired, but resolute, men with their backs to the wall. Except for occasional rushes of the enemy, cut down ere they reached the wire, there was nothing spectacular in that day's work. The Battalion shot and kept on shooting as it had been trained to do in the instruction-camps and on the comfortable ranges that seemed now so inconceivably far away. The enemy, having direct observation over the whole of our line, shot well and close. We suffered, but they suffered more. They ranged along the front from north to south as waves range down the face of a breakwater, but found nothing to carry away or even dislodge. Night closed in with a last rush at the wire on the Battalion's front that left a wreckage of German dead and wounded and two machine-guns, horribly hung up in the strands. Our losses in officers were 2nd Lieutenant Stokes severely wounded in the morning, and in the afternoon, Lieutenant Nash killed, and Captain Derek FitzGerald wounded and sent down. Lieut.-Colonel R. V. Pollok and Lieutenants Bence-Jones and Bagenal were also slightly wounded but remained at duty. When an officer dropped and could not get up again without help he was assumed to be unfit for work but not before.

("Ye'll understand, 'twas no question, those days, what ye could or could not do. Ye *did* it.")

And so ended the 27th of March with the German front from Lens to Albert held up, and destined, though men then scarce dared believe, not to advance to another effective surge. The French and British were perilously near forced asunder now and, the needs of the case compelling what might have been done long ago, General Foch, in the little city of Doullens, was, on the 26th March, given supreme command of all the hard-pressed hosts. The news went out at once into the front line where men received it as part and parcel of the immense situation. Nothing could have astonished them then, or, unless it directly concerned food or rest, have made them think.

The Battalion was placed where it was to endure, and was thankful that the 28th was a "fairly quiet day" but for heavy shelling on their right, and trench-mortars and shells on themselves. No. 2 Company, who had been unlucky with the big barrage the day before, suffered once again.

Next day (29th March), which was another "quiet" occasion, Lieutenant Zigomala was wounded and forty "of the most tired men" were relieved by an equal number from the Reinforcement Battalion, which relief became systematized, as it eased the strain a little to clear out visibly finished men day by day. All were worn down but "remained cheerful." Those who have full right to speak affirm that, in absolutely impossible situations, the Irish could be trusted to "play up" beyond even a Cockney battalion. The matter will always be in dispute, but none know better than the men who saw the Push through, how superbly the mud-caked, wire-drawn platoons bore themselves.

On the 30th March the attack rolled up again from the south where it had met no particular encouragement, and barraged the Battalion's sector with heavies for a couple of hours; causing forty-two casualties among the men and wounding Lieutenants Stacpoole and Bagenal. It then fell upon the 2nd Grenadiers and 1st Coldstream immediately to the Battalion's left and right, and was driven off with loss. There were other attacks, but with less venom in them, before the Hun could be induced to withdraw. Half the Battalion spent the night digging a line of posts in support which they occupied by dawn.

On the last of March "nothing of importance occurred." Everything, indeed, had occurred already. The old Somme Salient which, English fashion, had become an institution, was completely reversed on the ominous newspaper maps. The Germans stood a-tip-toe looking into Amiens, and practically the entire spare strength of the British Armies in France had been used and used up to bring them to that stand. The French were equally worn down. The American Armies were not yet in place, and what reinforcing Divisions were ready in England somewhat lacked training.

The Battalion, a straw among these waves, had in the month lost, besides officers, twenty-three other ranks killed and one hundred and seven wounded and one missing. It is even reported that there had been many days on which, owing to press of work, they had not shaved. ("That, ye'll understand, is being dirty, an' a crime. Believe me, now, there was times when we was all criminals, even Mr – , an' it disthressed him more than bloody war.")

The fierceness of the enemy's attack on the 28th March – ranging from Puisieux to north-east of Arras – had been, to an extent, his own undoing. For he had thrown his men in shoulder to shoulder in six lines at some spots, and our guns had caught them massed, forming up; But the check, severe as it was, did not choke off a final effort against the strained British and French cordon, on the 4th and 5th of April. The main weight of it, on the first day, fell south of the Somme, and on the second, north, from Dernancourt below Méaulte to Bucquoy which is on the same level as Gomiecourt. Except that the eastern side of Bucquoy was carried for a time, the northern attack was completely held, and so at last, after a heart-shattering fortnight, the Somme front came to rest. The Battalion, with its Headquarters under much too direct enemy observation near Boiry-St. Martin, reverted to its ancient routine of trench-work and reliefs under shell-fire.

The days included regular bursts of shelling, a large proportion of which was blue or yellow-cross gas, and when the Battalion lay in reserve they were kept awake by our energetic batteries on three sides of them.

Their St. Martin camp was a scientifically constructed death-trap. Most of it was under enemy observation and without ground-shelter. What shots ranged over our forward batteries, or short of our rear ones, found their camp. When our 15-inch guns retaliated, from a hundred and fifty yards behind them, the blast extinguished all candles. The Diary observes:

"The noise and the hostile retaliation made proper rest difficult." That was on the 4th April, when the attack south of the Somme was in full swing.

On the 5th April their huts in Brigade Reserve were shelled for half an hour, with six casualties, and when they went into the line on a new sector, held by scattered posts, nearly every one of their guides lost his miserable way in the dark. Headquarters here were pitched in an old German trench and then – for they were not even rain-proof – shifted to the edge of Boiry-St. Martin village. A cellar had to be dug out and supported, and the rain descended on the mud-pie that it was, and when Headquarters, and all their papers, had established themselves, the enemy gas-bombarded the village with perfect accuracy. The Commanding Officer, Lieut.-Colonel B. V. Pollok, the Assistant Adjutant Lieutenant J. N. Ward, and the M.O. Captain Woodhouse, had to be sent down suffering from yellow-cross gas after-effects.

Consider for a moment the woes of a Battalion Headquarters in the field. Late in January, Captain Gordon, the *pukka* Adjutant, riding to Arras for a bath, canters into a barrage of "heavies" and is wounded in the hand – a vital spot for Adjutants. This leaves only the C.O. and the Assistant Adjutant, Lieutenant J. N. Ward, to carry on, and whatever the state of the front, the authorities demand their regular supply of papers and forms. No sooner has the Assistant Adjutant got abreast of things, than all Battalion Headquarters are knocked out in an hour. Luckily, they were only away for three or four days. The enemy added a small and easily beaten off raid to the confusion he had made in Orderly room; Major Baggallay took over the command, and Captain Budd, adequate and untroubled as ever, who had held the ghostly F Post on the Scarpe, acted as Adjutant. Officers were beginning to wear out now. Three "of the most tired" were sent down and replaced by substitutes from the Reinforcement Battalion.

The following officers joined for duty on the 10th April: Lieutenant M. Buller, Lieutenant (Acting Captain) W. Joyce, Lieutenant Hon. B. A. A. Ogilvy, and 2nd Lieutenants T. B. Maughan, P. R. J. Barry, H. J. Lofting, G. C. MacLachlan and J. C. Haydon.

It was on the morning of the 9th April that the enemy opened his second great thrust on the Lys, and the three weeks' fighting that all but wiped out the Ypres Salient won him Messines, Kemmel, Armentières, Neuve Eglise, Bailleul, Merville, and carried him towards the Channel Ports, within five miles of Hazebrouck. That the stroke was expected made it none the less severe. Spring on that front had chosen to be unseasonably dry. The lowlands in the Lys valley, normally their own best defences, gave passage to men and guns when they should have been still impassable. Whatever else may have betrayed them, the Germans had no cause to complain of the weather throughout the war, or indeed of the foresight of their adversaries. They had to deal chiefly with Divisions that had been fought out in the Somme Push, reinforced with fillings from England and sent northward in a hurry. Sir Douglas Haig's despatches give the relative disparity thus:

> In the Lys Battle, prior to the 30th April, the enemy engaged against the British forces a total of 42 Divisions, of which 33 were fresh and 9 had fought previously on the Somme. Against these 42 German Divisions, 25 British Divisions were employed, of which 8 were fresh and 17 had taken a prominent part in the Somme battle.

Headquarters . . . shifted to the edge of Boiry-St.-Martin village. A cellar had to be dug out and supported, and the rain descended on the mud pie that it was, and when Headquarters . . . had established themselves, the enemy gas-bombarded the village with perfect accuracy.

Boiry-St.-Martin, April 1918.

These were worn out, and as the days of fighting continued many of them were so dead to the world that they laid them down and slept where they dropped by battalions. When orders came, it was a matter almost of routine that each senior, handing them on, should assault his junior into some sort of comprehension. Officers dared not trust themselves even to lean against walls for fear they should slide down dead asleep; and as a private of the Line put it in confession, "I don't know what the men would have done but for standing sentry. They got their sleep then." There is a story of a tattered Brigade, eight days, or it might have been ten, without closing an eyelid, which was flung back into the fight after assurance of relief, and, what was much worse, a few hours' rest. They returned, like sleep-walkers, and laid them down in some shallow hen-scratchings that passed for trench-work, where without emotion they resigned themselves to being blown out or up in detail. While they watched drowsily the descent and thickening of a fresh German shell-storm, preluding fresh infantry attacks, it occurred to them vaguely that there were high and increasing noises overhead – not at all like the deep whoop of "heavies." Then all the darkness behind the enemy lit with a low outlining ground-flare – the death-dance of innumerable 75's. Foch had sent up very many guns behind them, almost wheel to wheel, and when the French gunners at last shut off, the packed enemy trenches that were waiting to continue their march to the Channel, as soon as their own fire should have wiped up the few British bayonets before them, lay as still as the graves that they were. Then what remained of the Brigade that had seen this miracle was relieved by another Brigade, and stretched itself out to sleep behind it. Experts in miseries say that, for sheer strain, the Lys over went anything imagined in the War, and in this many who have suffered much are agreed.

The 4th Guards Brigade, which had been in billets near Villers-Brulin, after its heavy work on the Arras side, was despatched on the 10th April to the flat country round Vierhoek, and there – as will be told – spent itself in the desperate fighting round La Couronne and Vieux-Berquin that gave time to bar the enemy's way to Hazebrouck and – wiped out the 2nd Battalion.

The 1st Battalion, sufficiently occupied with its own front near Doiry, where the support-lines were targets by day and night, and the front-posts holes in the ground that seemed to shift at every relief, were told on the 12th April that a German attack was imminent, which report was repeated at intervals throughout the day. But their patrols found nothing moving in front of them, and their regular allowance of hostile mortar-bombs was not increased. The rumours from the Lys side were far more disturbing.

On the 13th April they were relieved by the 24th Lancashire Fusiliers, marched to Blaireville where they embussed for Saulty at the head of the little river that runs in stone channels through quiet Doullens, and there, "very cold, wet and muddy," found the best billets taken by Corps and Labour troops whom they knew not. The sentiments of men who have been digging and fighting without a break for ten weeks when confronted with warmly billeted Staffs and fat, back-area working-parties, need not be recorded.

At Saulty they rested from the 15th to the 23rd April under perpetual short notice: one hour from 8 a.m. till noon and three hours for the rest of the day and night. Thus "means of training were limited," and the weather varied from wet to snow-showers.

On the 24th of April the enemy captured Villers-Bretonneux, staring directly into Amiens, which ground, had they been allowed to hold uninterruptedly even for a day, might have been made too strong to reduce with the forces at our disposal then, and thus would have become the very edge of the wedge for splitting the French and English armies asunder. But that night, and literally at almost an hour's notice, a counter-attack by a Brigade of the Eighteenth Division, and the 13th and 15th Brigades of the Fourth and Fifth Australian Divisions, swept Villers-Bretonneux clear and established ourselves beyond possibility of eviction. Thus, the one last chance that might have swung the whole War passed out of the enemy's hands.

On that same day the 1st Irish Guards returned in lorries along the cramped and twisting roads by Bienvillers to Monchy, to relieve a battalion of the Royal Scots in the front line at Ayette, three miles south down the line from Boiry. Ayette village had been recaptured on the 3rd April by the Thirty-second Division, and had removed a thorn in the side of troops in that sector. Once again, their guides almost unanimously lost their way, and the multivious relief took half the night to accomplish.

It appeared as though the enemy had skinned his line here to feed his other enterprises in the north; for his outposts did nothing and, beyond shelling Monchy village from time to time, his guns were also idle.

So on the 29th April they arranged a Battalion raid on a German post (supposed to be held by night only) to occupy it if possible. But the enemy were in occupation and very ready. The little party returned with their officer, 2nd Lieutenant G. C. MacLachlan, and a Sergeant wounded. A few weeks later the Battalion worked out a most satisfactory little ten-minute return-raid without a single casualty, and so cleared their account.

April had been an inexpensive month for both men and officers. The Commanding Officer, the Assistant Adjutant, and the Medical Officer had, as we know, been slightly gassed at Headquarters, and 2nd Lieutenants C. L. Browne and MacLachlan wounded only. Three men had been killed and forty-one wounded. But no less than twenty-six were sent down sick – proof that the strain had told.

The enemy showed a certain amount of imagination unusual on that front. One of our forward posts, expecting the return of a patrol on the dawn on the 3rd May, saw a party of five approaching and challenged. "Irish Guards," was the reply, followed by a few bombs which did some damage. This peculiarly irritating trick had not been worked on the Battalion for some time, and they felt it – as their amused friends to left and right in the line took care that they should. Otherwise, the enemy devoted themselves to more and heavier gunnery, which, in a five-day tour, caused twenty casualties (wounded) and one killed. Brigade Reserve camps were outside Monchy-au-Bois, whence tired men were sent to the Details camp at Pommier (regularly bombed by aeroplane) and from Pommier were drawn occasional working-parties. One of these included the Battalion Drummers and Pipers, who enjoyed what might be called a "day out" in some old trenches.

On the 5th May Lieutenant Keenan arrived from the 2nd Battalion to take over the Adjutancy in place of Captain Gordon, who had been transferred to the 2nd Battalion as Second in Command, after almost three years' continuous service with the 1st Battalion.

On the 7th May they went up from Monchy, by the ever-hateful, ever-shelled Cojeul valley, to the Ayette subsector, relieving the 2nd Coldstream. Next day, the devil-directed luck of the front line, after a peaceful, fine night, caused the only trench-mortar sent over by the enemy that did not clean miss all our posts, to fall directly in No. 3 Post, right front Company (No. 4), instantly killing Captain Budd, M.C., commanding the Company, and with him 2nd Lieutenant E. C. G. Lord and seven men. Captain Budd's energy and coolness, proved on many occasions, were a particular loss to his comrades. He was a large silent man, on whom every one could, and did, lean heavily at all times. He knew no fear and was of the self-contained, intensely alive type, always in danger, but never by his friends connected with any thought of death. 2nd Lieutenant Lord ("Rosy" Lord) was a keen and promising young officer. Those were the only casualties of the tour. They were buried in the little Military Cemetery near Ayette.

Our guns had been working steadily from behind, but till this trench-mortar outburst, most of the enemy replies had been directed on Ayette itself or our support-lines.

The shelling throughout the month grew more and more earnest and our replies, roaring overhead, worried the dead-tired soldiery. The work was all at night – wiring and improving posts, and unlimited digging of communication-ways between them; for whether a trench-line held till Christmas, went up bodily next minute, or was battered down every hour, in the making there was but one standard of work that beseemed the Battalion; and though Divisional Commanders might, and as on the dreary Scarpe posts did, draw gratified Commanding Officers aside and tell them that for quantity and quality their trench-craft excelled that of other battalions, the Battalion itself was never quite contented with what it had accomplished.

Their next turn – May 16 to 21 – was fine and hot for a couple of mornings and regular barrages were put down on the support-line when they were standing-to. Four men were killed and thirteen, of whom two died later, were wounded.

They were heavily shelled in Brigade Reserve camp on the night of the 24th; four officers – Captain Bence-Jones, Lieutenants Riley and Buller, and 2nd Lieutenant Barry – wounded, one other rank killed and five wounded.

When they went up to relieve the 2nd Coldstream on the 25th May, they were caught in platoon-order at the corner of Adinfer Wood, a place of no good name to marching troops, and Lieutenant Williams was slightly wounded. Three-quarters of an hour's intense barrage was put down, on front and support lines, as soon as they were fairly in, causing several casualties.

The dawn of the 28th May began with another sharp barrage on the front line and the dinner-hour was a continuous barrage of 5·9's and 4·2's directed at Battalion Headquarters. They were missed, but a direct hit was made on an aid-post of the 2nd Grenadiers less than a hundred yards off on our left. As a distraction, orders came in from Brigade Headquarters the same morning that the Battalion would carry out a raid on one of the enemy's posts in front of the right Company. They were given their choice, it would seem, of two – one without artillery help and by day; the other with an artillery backing and by night. The Second in Command, Major R. Baggallay, elected for works of darkness – or as near as might be in spite of a disgustingly bright moon. Lieutenant C. S. O'Brien was detailed to command, with Sergeant Regan, a forceful man, as Sergeant. Only twenty-nine hands were required, and therefore sixty volunteered, moved to this, not by particular thirst for glory, of which the trenches soon cure men, as by human desire to escape monotony punctuated with shells. Extra rum-rations, too, attach to extra duties. As a raid it was a small affair, but as a work of art, historically worth recording in some detail. F Battery R.H.A. and 400th Battery R.F.A. supplied the lifting barrages which duly cut the post off from succour, while standing-barrages of 18-pounders, a barrage of 4·5 hows. and groups, firing concentrations at left and right enemy trenches, completed the boxed trap. In the few minutes the affair lasted, it is not extravagant to estimate that more stuff was expended than the whole of our front in 1914 was allowed to send over in two days.

The post had been reconnoitred earlier in the evening and was known not to be wired. All the raiders, with blackened faces and bayonets and stripped uniforms that betrayed nothing, were in position on the forming-up tape five minutes before zero. The moon forced them to crawl undignifiedly out in twos and threes, but they lined up with the precision of a football line, at one-yard intervals and, a minute before zero, wriggled to within seventy yards of their quarry. At zero the barrage came down bursting beautifully, just beyond the enemy post, and about two seconds ere it lifted the raiders charged in. No one had time to leave or even to make a show of resistance, and they were back with their five prisoners, all alive and quite identifiable, in ten minutes. The waiting stretcher-parties were not needed and – best of all – "retaliation was slight and entirely on Ayette" (One is not told what Ayette thought of it.) The motive of the raid was "to secure identity alive or dead." But when all was over without hurt, one single shell at morning "stand-to" (May 28) killed 2nd Lieutenant L. H. L. Carver in a front-line trench.

They held the raided post under close observation that day and the next (May 29), and discovered that it had been reoccupied by a machine-gun party. As they particularly did not wish it to put out wire or become offensive, they dosed it with constant bursts of their own machine-gun and were rewarded by hearing groans and cries, and our listening-patrol in No Man's Land saw a man being carried away.

On the 31st May the enemy set to, in earnest, to shell all reserve-lines and back-area for six hours; as well as the first-line transport in Adinfer Wood after dark, when wounded horses are not easy to handle. Their relief by the 2nd Grenadiers was badly delayed by heavy shelling all the way from the front line to Monchy, but instead of any number of casualties, which might reasonably have been expected, the Battalion got through unscathed.

The month's list was heavy enough as it stood. Five officers had been wounded and three killed in action; seventeen other ranks killed, and forty-eight wounded, and all this in the regular wear-and-tear front-line routine with nothing more to see than a stray German cap here and there. Twenty-two men were sent down sick, and the Diary begins to hint at the prevalence of the "Spanish fever," which was in a few months to sweep France and all the world.

June was a month of peace. It opened in reserve-trenches at the south-west end of Monchy-au-Bois, and when they next went up into line, a new route had been surveyed round the dreaded corner of Adinfer Wood which saved some shelling of reliefs.

On the 4th June the C.O., Lieutenant-Colonel Pollok, left the Battalion to take over command of Sixth Corps Army School, and Major R. R. C. Baggallay assumed command. Likewise three stray Germans were captured opposite one of our posts.

On the 5th, Major Gordon arrived from the 2nd Battalion for duty as Second in Command.

They were relieved by the 1st King's Regiment on the 6th June – a somewhat hectic performance, as the front-line track-ways were intricate, needing guides at almost every turn of them, and, for the run-up, one guide per platoon. After which, about one in the morning, it was discovered that the King's had come in without their Lewis-guns. Some Divisions were in the habit of leaving and taking over the Lewis-guns *in situ*; but the Guards Division always went in and out of the line with their very own weapons. One cannot delay a clear June dawn and, as the relieved Battalion had to get off in tightly packed and horribly conspicuous lorries, and as the last platoon could not reach those lorries till 3 a.m., it was touch-and-go whether daylight would not reveal them "like a Sunday School treat" to the German guns. But luck held. The last lorry was safe in Bavincourt Wood five miles behind Monchy before day had stripped the landscape, and the 1st King's were left to meditate on the wealth and variety of the Irish tongue, as delivered on empty stomachs, in whispers, down packed trenches.

The Battalion billeted at Bavincourt when the 2nd H.L.I. had got out of their quarters, and since, like the other camps, Bavincourt was regularly bombed, made earth walls round their Nissen huts, and slits near them to be used against 'planes or too extravagant shell-fire. Here they stayed till the end of the month, cleaning, refitting and training (in open warfare principally; and, this time, they were not to be disappointed) at Lewis-gunnery, bombing, and general physical smartening-up. When the Brigade Sports took place at Saulty, they won every event but three, and when the Corps Commander, the following week, inspected the different ways in the Divisional methods of carrying the eight Lewis-guns of each Company all on one limber, "the method employed by the Battalion was considered the best, and all units were ordered to copy." They had rigged a sort of false top on a rear-limber which accommodated all eight guns together.

A Divisional Horse-show was held on the 22nd, but there the Battalion did not get a single prize. They hammered on at their trainings and Brigade field-days – all with an eye to the coming open warfare, while the "Spanish fever," which was influenza of the post-war type, grew steadily worse among men and officers alike. When H.R.H. the Duke of Connaught visited Divisional Headquarters at Bavincourt Château on the 30th June, and the Battalion had to find not only the Guard of Honour but 160 men to line the avenue to the Château, there were seventy officers and men down with the pest, out of less than 900. Thirty-one men had been sent down sick; two had been killed in action presumably by overhead bombing, for the Diary does not mention any trench casualties, and twenty-three wounded.

The following officers joined during the month of June: Lieutenant C. A. J. Vernon, and 2nd Lieutenants E. B. Spafford, A. E. Hutchinson, H. R. Baldwin, G. F. Mathieson, J. A. M. Faraday, E. M. Harvey, M.C., and A. E. O'Connor, all on the 2nd June; Captain A. W. L. Paget on the 4th, and 2nd Lieutenant A. H. O'Farrell on the 10th June. Second Lieutenant C. S. O'Brien, who was in command of the model raid already mentioned, was awarded the Military Cross on the 9th of June.

After a sporting interlude on the 3rd July, when they met the 1st Munster Fusiliers at athletics and won everything except the hundred yards, they relieved the 15th H.L.I. in the intermediate line near Hendecourt. As a matter of fact, they were a sick people just then. All Battalion Headquarters except the Commanding Officer, and all the Officers of No. 2 Company, besides officers of other companies, were down with "Spanish fever" on going into the line. A third of the men were also sick at one time, and apparently the enemy too, for they hardly troubled to shell by day and let the night-reliefs go without attention. The only drawbacks were furious summer thunder-storms which, from time to time, flooded the trenches and woke up more fever. The front line held here by the Guards was badly knocked about and battered, and instructions ran that, in event of serious attack, it would not be contested.

There is no clear evidence of the state of the Battalion's collective mind at this time, but from home letters it might be gathered that the strain of the Push and its bewilderment had given place to the idea that great things were preparing. Battalions are very often told tales to this effect, but they suit themselves as to the amount that they swallow. No power on earth, for instance, could have persuaded the veterans of the Somme, after Cambrai, that there was "anything doing"; but as the summer of 1918 grew warmer in the wooded and orchard country behind the Amiens – Albert line, and our lines there held and were strengthened, and those who had been home or on the seas reported what they had heard and seen, hope, of a kind not raised before, grew in the talks of the men and the officers. ("Understand, I do *not* say there was anny of the old chat regardin' that the war would finish next Chuseday, the way we talked in '16. But, whatever they said acrost the water, *we* did not hould 'twould endure those two more extra years all them civilians was dishin' out to us. *What* did we think? That '19 would see the finish? 'Twud be hard to tell what we thought. Leave it this way: we was no more than waitin' on mercies to happen an' – 'twas mericles that transpired!")

They relieved their own Brigade Battalions with the punctilio proper to their common ritual, and for the benefit of over a hundred recruits. It was their ancient comrades under all sorts of terrors, the 2nd Coldstream, whose guides from Boiry-St. Martin one night lost their way in the maze of tracks and turns to the front line. But, as meekly set forth in the Diary, when it came the Battalion's turn to be relieved by the 2nd Grenadiers, "all tracks had been carefully picketed by this Battalion to assist Grenadier Companies coming in and ours going out." The occasions when the guides of the 1st Irish Guards lost their way must be looked for in the reports of others.

"Little shelling and no casualties" were the order of the fine days till, on the 29th July, taking over from the 2nd Coldstream, they found six platoons of the 3rd Battalion, 320th Regiment, U.S.A., which had come into line the night before and were attached for instruction. These were young, keen, desperately anxious to learn, and not at all disposed to keep their heads down.

Next day the enemy opened on them, and "were rather offensive in their shelling." The front platoon of the Americans, attached to the Battalion's front Company, caught it worst, but no casualties were reported. Then things quieted down, and a patrol of Special Battalion Scouts, a new organization of old, trusty No Man's Landers, under Lieutenant Vernon as Intelligence Officer, went out on reconnaissance, across the Cojeul valley, and wandered generally among ancient trench-lines in bright moonlight. They found a German party working on fresh earth, but no signs of enemy patrols on the move in the valley. This was as well. No one wished to see that dead ground occupied, until by our own people at the proper time.

July's bill of casualties was the lowest of all. No officer and but one man had been killed, and two wounded. This last was when the enemy shelled Doiry to celebrate the arrival of the American platoons. Seventeen men were sent down sick. Fifty other ranks were transferred to the 1st from the 2nd Battalion, now acting as a feeder to its elder brother.

On the 1st of August the Battalion was still in the peaceful front line watching the six American platoons being relieved by other six platoons from the 2nd Battalion of the 320th Regiment. It was observed, not without some envy – "They did not know enough to save 'emselves throuble, an' they would not ha' done it if they had. They was too full of this same dam' new ould war." Even at this immense distance of time, one can almost hear the veterans commenting on the zeal and excitement that filled the stale lines where, to those young eyes from across the water, everything was as shining-new as death.

On the 3rd August the Battalion made a reconnaissance of a post with the idea of raiding it, which was a complete though bloodless failure. Some of our back guns chose the exact moment when the raiders were setting out (on the sure information of a scouting-party, who had just come in) to wipe up the unconscious little garrison and their machine-gun, and woke the night with heavy shell dropped *in* our own wire and in front of our objective. Naturally nothing could be done, and the affair was called off till the next evening (4th August), when a "crawling-party," under Lieutenant Vernon, of a corporal and six men went out along the same route that the scouts had taken the night before. They were expected and welcomed with enthusiasm. A sentry gave the alarm, a little party ran out to cut them off, the machine-gun (a heavy one), which had not betrayed itself before, promptly opened fire, but wide of our prone men, and a German, as promptly, hove bombs in the wrong direction. All this, says the report, happened as soon as some one inside the post gave "short decisive orders." Then Véry lights flared without stint, and, being some way from home, with much unlocated wire between, the raiders got away swiftly, and safely. The tracks of the scouts through the long grass the night before had put the enemy on the alert. But if our guns had only held their tongues on that occasion, our coup might have been brought off. Instead of which, the enemy woke up and shelled a front company for a quarter of an hour with 60-pounders before he could be induced to go to bed.

THE BEGINNINGS OF THE END

But all this was as light, casual, and unrelated as the throwing of the ball from hand to hand that fills time before an innings; and, by the latter part of July, men began half unconsciously to speculate when our innings would begin. In the North, the enemy, crowded into the Lys salient, which they had been at such pains to hack out over the bodies of the 2nd Battalion, were enjoying some of the pleasures our men had tasted round Ypres for so many years. Our gathering guns, cross-ploughing them where they lay, took fresh toll of each new German Division arriving to make good the wastage. In the South, outside Amiens, the Australians, an impenitent and unimpressionable breed, had, on the 4th of July, with the help of four Companies of the Thirty-third American Division, and sixty tanks, gone a-raiding round the neighbourhood of Hamel and Vaire Wood, with results that surprised everybody except themselves. They did not greatly respect the enemy, and handled him rudely. Meantime, Amiens, raked over by aeroplanes almost every hour, was being wrecked and strangled; and all the Labour Corps, which, from the soldier's point of view, could have been better used in saving poor privates cruel fatigues, were working day and night at railway diversions and doublings that, by some route or another, should bring the urgent supplies of both French and British armies to their destinations. Men argued, therefore, that the first job to be taken in hand would be the deliverance of Amiens. There was talk, too, that all French Divisions in Flanders were withdrawn and concentrated behind Amiens city. This might be taken for a sign that the Lys salient was reckoned reasonably secure, and as confirming the belief that upon the Lys, also, we had abundance of artillery. On the other hand (these are but a few of the rumours of the time), away in the unknown south-east of France, where few British troops had penetrated in the memory of present fighting men, some five or six Divisions, making the Ninth British Corps, had been sent for a "rest" after the March Push, and had been badly mauled by a sudden surprise-attack on the Aisne where, together with the Fifth French Army, they had been driven back towards the Marne, which all the world thought was a river and a battle long since disposed of. The enemy there were sitting practically outside the Forest of Villers-Cotterêts, a name also belonging to ancient history. Much-enduring men, whom Fate till now had spared, recounted how the 4th (Guards) Brigade, as it was then, had first "caught it" there, among the beech-trees very nearly four years back. Moreover, there was fresh trouble between Montdidier and Noyon, where the enemy were again throwing themselves at the French. Then, too, Foch, who was in charge of all, but who, so far, had made no sign, had borrowed four more of our Divisions – the whole of the Twenty-second Corps this time – and they were off on some French front, Heaven and Headquarters alone knew where. Likewise one composite "scrum" of French, American, English and Italian troops was holding, it might be hoped, a German capital attack near Rheims. The old war-line that in the remote days of winter would have called itself the Somme Front, discussed and digested these news and many more. There was nothing doing on their beat to write home about, even were they allowed to do so. The question was whether they would be called on to repair to the Lys and free Hazebrouck, which was undoubtedly still in a dangerous position, or stand still and await what might befall at Amiens. There was no limit to speculation and argument any more than there had been when the Somme Front went in March, and the more they argued the more confused men grew over the confidential information that was supplied them. ("Them Gen'rals, and their Staffs, must ha' done quite a little lyin' – even for them. They had *us* believin' their word! I've heard since even Jerry believed 'em.')

That would appear to have been the trouble with the enemy. It was evident to the most hardened pessimist that a French counter-attack launched out of the Villers-Cotterêts forests, to begin with (and in several other places at, apparently, the same time), was *not* the flash-in-the-pan that some people foretold. For the second time the enemy was withdrawing from the Marne, and, under pressure, continuing his withdrawal. His great attack near Rheims, too, seemed to have stuck. On the Lys, from time to time, sites of villages with well-remembered names were occasionally returning to their lawful trustees. Hopeful students of the war hinted that, with fresh troops in vast numbers, more guns, and a share of luck, 1918 might see the foundations laid for a really effective finish in 1919. A report had come up from the South that the French down Amiens way had made an experimental attack, or rather a big raid, on the enemy, and had found him there curiously "soft" and willing to shift.

The air thickened with lies as the men, who moved about the earth by night or under cover, increased, and our aircraft were told off to circle low and noisily

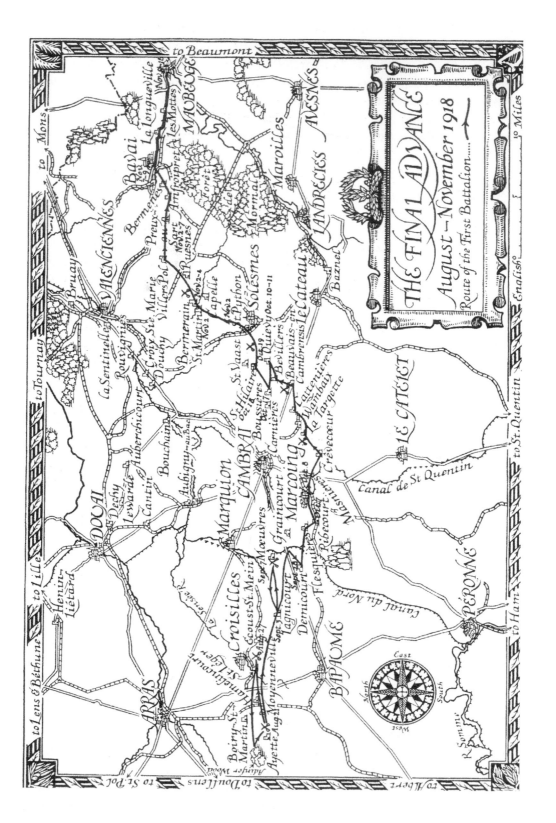

at certain points and drown the churn of many tanks trailing up into their appointed areas. All the Canadian Divisions, men said, were moving off to recapture Kemmel Hill. All our forces round Amiens were digging themselves in, said others, preparatory to a wait-and-see campaign that would surely last till Christmas. For proof, it was notorious that our guns in that sector were doing nothing (As a matter of fact they were registering on the sly.) Everybody round Amiens, a third party insisted, would be sent off in a day or two to help the French in Champagne. The weaknesses of human nature in possession of "exclusive information" played into the hands of the very few who knew; and young Staff Officers of innocent appearance infernally bamboozled their betters.

So it happened, on the 4th August, on a misty dawn, that the Fourth Army (Rawlinson's) with four hundred tanks, backed by two thousand guns, and covered by aeroplanes to a number not yet conceived in war, declared itself as in being round Amiens at the very nose of the great German salient. In twenty-four hours that attack had bitten in five miles on an eleven-mile front, had taken twelve thousand prisoners and some three hundred guns, and was well set to continue. At the same time the French, striking up from the South, had cleared their front up to the Amiens – Roye road from Pierrepont, through Plessier to Fresnoy, and had taken over three thousand prisoners and many guns. Caught thus on two fronts, the enemy fell back, abandoning stores and burning dumps, which latter sight it cheered our men to watch. But the work and the honour of the day, as of the Fourth Army's campaign from this point on, rested with the Canadian and Australian Divisions who made up the larger part of it. The Australians Sir Archibald Montgomery describes in his monumental *Story of the Fourth Army* as "always inquisitive and seldom idle." The Canadians had exactly the same failings, and between the two Dominions the enemy suffered.

By the 12th August he had been forced back on to the edge of the used, desolate, and eaten-up country where he had established himself in 1916 – a jungle of old wire, wrecked buildings, charred woods and wildernesses of trench. It was ideal ground for machine-gun defence; with good protection against tanks and cavalry. There he went to earth, and there, after a little feeling along his line, was he left while the screw was applied elsewhere. Our front at that time ran from Bray-sur-Somme due south to Andechy, where we joined the French almost within machine-gun range of Roye.

North of Bray, to the western edge of the town of Albert, the left wing of the Fourth Army had the enemy held, worried and expectant. Now was the Third Army's turn to drive in the wedge, from north of Albert up the line to Arras where the right of the First Army would assist. What Headquarters knew of the enemy's morale on that sector was highly satisfactory. Moreover, he was withdrawing out of his Lys salient as his Divisions were sucked down south to make up wastage there. But our men still expected that they would tramp their weary way back across every yard of their battle-fields and burial-grounds of the past two years, finishing up, if luck held, somewhere round the Hindenburg Line by Christmas. That the wave, once launched, would carry to the Rhine was beyond the wildest dreams.

The Battalion, after their little raid already mentioned, had spent from the 5th to the 9th August in reserve-trenches at Ransart, doing musketry and route-marching. They returned to the support-trenches at Hendecourt les-Ransart, relieving the 2nd Coldstream, and stayed there till the 16th August, when they relieved the same Battalion in the front line opposite Boiry-St. Martin.

They had to patrol the No Man's Land in front of them a good deal at night (because it would, later, be their forming-up area), but suffered nothing worse than the usual shelling and trench-mortaring, and their share in the work of the opening day, August 21, was small and simple. "At 5 a.m. the 2nd Guards Brigade on our right attacked Moyenneville with their objective just east of the railway. The 1st Coldstream was next on our right." There was a thick fog when the barrage opened, as well as a smoke barrage. The tanks forming up made noise enough to wake a landful of Germans, but apparently drew no fire till they were well away, lunging and trampling over the enemy machine-gun-posts that had annoyed our folk for so long. The only serious work for the Battalion was to secure a small trench, cover the north side of the railway with their fire, and establish a post at the railway crossing "as soon as a tank had passed over." The trench had been occupied early in the night after a small bombing-brawl with the enemy. The tank detailed to pass by that way in the morning was warned of the occupation and told not to fire into it as it came along, and all was well. There was an idea that a couple of companies assisted by eight tanks should capture Hamelincourt, a mile east of Moyenneville, which latter had been taken, before the fog lifted, by the 2nd Guards Brigade. But this was cancelled after much waste of time, and the Battalion lay still under a shelling of mustard-gas, and pleasantly watched prisoners being sent back.

The enemy's front was giving before the attack of eight Divisions, but not without sudden and awkward resistances, due to the cut-up and trenched state of the ground, that hid too many machine-guns for comfort; and the gas-nuisance grew steadily worse.

The Battalion lay where they were the next day (August 22), but sent out a patrol under 2nd Lieutenant Faraday to work up a trench near Hamel Switch, to the north of Hamelincourt. After capturing four Germans it came under machine-gun fire from Hamelincourt. A platoon was sent to support it, but was withdrawn, as the Hamelincourt attack had been postponed till the next day. Then the patrol had to retire across abominable shallow trenches, clogged with wire and lavishly machine-gunned. The Germans tried to cut them off. They withdrew, fighting. Their Lewis-gun was knocked out and five men wounded. While these were being helped back, the Lieutenant and two men, Sergeant Dolan and Private Tait, covered the retreat among the wire. Next, Faraday was wounded badly in the foot, and the sergeant and private carried him in turn, he being six feet long and not narrow, while the rest of the party threw bombs at the Germans, and tried to close with them. Eventually they all reached home safe. Dolan's one comment on the affair was: "Tis heavy going out yonder." Lieutenant Faraday was awarded the M.C. and Dolan the D.C.M. Later on, in 1919, Dolan also received the Médaille Militaire for gallantry on many occasions.

Seen against the gigantic background of the opening campaign, it was a microscopical affair – a struggle of ants round a single grain – but it moved men strongly while they watched.

For the reason that always leads a Battalion to be hardest worked on the edge of battle, they were taken out of the line on the 23rd, cautiously, under gas and common shell, and marched back seven miles in five hours to Berles-au-Bois behind Monchy-au-Bois in order to be marched back again next day to Boiry-St. Martin, where they spent the day in the Cojeul Valley, and afterwards (August 25) moved up into support in the Hamel Switch between Hamelincourt and St. Leger. Hamelincourt had been taken on the 23rd by the 2nd Brigade, and as the night came down wet, the "men made what shelters they could from corrugated iron and wood lying about." The trenches hereabouts had every disadvantage that could be desired. Some were part of the Army Line and had been dug a foot or two deep with the spade as lines to be developed in case of need. Presumably, it was nobody's business to complete them, so when the trouble arrived, these gutters, being officially trenches, were duly filled by the troops, and as duly shelled by the enemy.

For example, when the Battalion moved forward on the 26th their trenches were but waist-deep, which, to men who had spent most of the day in the dry bed of the Cojeul river, under gas and common shell, was no great treat.

Since the 21st August the Guards Division had been well employed. Its 2nd Brigade, with the Second Division on its right, had captured the Ablainzevelle – Moyenneville spur; and the Second Division had taken Courcelles. By the night of the 23rd, when the 3rd Guards Brigade relieved the 2nd, and the Second Division had captured Ervillers on the Arras-Bapaume road, the Guards Division, with their 1st Brigade in support, was within half a mile of St. Léger, and in touch with the Fifty-sixth Division on their left, which was trying to work round the head of the Hindenburg Line and turn in from the north. At this point resistance stiffened. The hilly ground, cut and cross-cut with old trenches and the beginnings of new ones, lent itself to the stopping game of well-placed machine-guns equally from round Croisilles, where the Fifty-sixth Division was engaged; from about St. Léger Wood, where the 3rd Guards Brigade, supported by tanks, was renewing its acquaintance with the German anti-tank-rifle; and from Mory, where the Sixty-second Division was delayed by the Division on its right being held up. An enemy balloon or two hung on the horizon and some inquisitive, low-fighting aeroplanes hinted at coming trouble. The line expected as much, but they did not seem so well informed farther back.

THE AFFAIR OF ST. LEGER

On the 26th August orders arrived that the 1st Guards Brigade would now take up the running from the 3rd, and advance eastward from St. Léger towards Ecoust till opposition was met. There were, of course, refinements on this idea, but that was the gist of it. The 2nd Grenadiers and the 2nd Coldstream would attack, with the Battalion in support. The men were in their trenches by tea-time on the 26th, No. 1 Company in Jewel Trench just east of the entrance to the little Sensée river valley, and the others disposed along the line of Mory Switch, an old trench now only a foot deep. Battalion Headquarters lay in an abandoned German stores dug-out. Final orders did not arrive till after midnight on the 26th, and there was much to arrange and link up between then and seven o'clock, barrage time. The Grenadiers were on the right and the Coldstream on the left of the Battalion, the latter following a quarter of a mile behind, with Nos. 1 and 3 Companies to feed the Grenadiers and Nos. 4 and 2 for the Coldstream. As the front was so wide, they split the difference and kept as close as might be to the dividing line between the two leading Battalions, which ran by Mory Switch and Hally Avenue. The hot day broke with a gorgeous sunrise over a desolate landscape that reeked in all its hollows of gas and cordite. A moment or two after our barrage (field-guns only) opened, the enemy put down a heavy reply, and into the smoke and dust of it the Companies, in artillery formation, walked up the road without hesitation or one man losing his place. No. 1 Company leading on the right disappeared at once after they had passed their jumping-off point at Mory Switch. Almost the first shells caught the leading platoon, when Lieutenant J. N. Ward was killed and Lieutenant P. S. MacMahon wounded. As soon as they were clear of the barrage, they came under full blast of machine-gun fire and saw the Grenadiers presently lie down enfiladed on both flanks. Four of our machine-guns tried to work forward and clear out the hindrances, but the fire was too strong. Both Battalions were finally held up, and the Grenadiers were practically cut to pieces, with their reserve companies, as these strove to reinforce the thinned line. After what seemed an immense time (two hours or so) Captain Thompson, seeing that, as far as that sector was concerned, the thing was hung up, ordered his men to dig in in support, and they spent till nightfall "recovering casualties" – their own, those of the Battalions ahead, and of the Guards Machine-Guns.

No. 3 Company, which followed No. 1, suffered just as heavily from the barrage. Very soon their commander, Captain Joyce, was wounded and Lieutenant H. R. Baldwin killed. Second Lieutenant Heaton, who took over, was gassed in the course of the afternoon, and C.S.M. O'Hara then commanded. There was nothing for them to do either save dig in, like No. 1, behind the Grenadiers, and a little to the right of them.

No. 4 Company, under Captain Hegarty, following the Coldstream, got the worst barrage of all as soon as they were clear of their trenches, and found the Coldstream held up, front and flank, within fifty yards of the sunken road whence they had started. No. 15 platoon of the Irish Guards was almost wiped out, and the remains of it joined with No. 13 to make a defensive flank, while No. 14 crawled or wriggled forward to reinforce the Coldstream, and No. 16 lay in reserve in a sunk road. Sunk roads were the only shelter for such as did not wish to become early casualties.

There was a thick fog when the barrage opened, as well as a smoke barrage. The tanks forming up made noise enough to wake a landful of Germans, but apparently drew no fire till they were well away.

Barrage at dawn, 21st August 1918.

No. 2 Company (Captain A. Paget) following No. 4 had been held back for a few minutes by the C.O. (Major R. Baggallay) on the fringe of the barrage, to be slipped through when it seemed to lighten. They also launched out into a world that was all flank or support, of Battalions which could be neither seen nor found, who were themselves outflanked by machine-guns in a landscape that was one stumbling-block of shallow trenches which suddenly faded out. They crossed the St. Léger – Vraucourt road and bore east, after clearing the St. Léger wood, till they reached the St. Léger reserve trench, and held it from the Longatte road to where it joined the Banks Reserve. Says one record: "At this time, Captain Paget was in ignorance of the success or location of the attacking Battalions, and both of his flanks exposed as far as he knew." The enemy machine-guns were hammering home that knowledge, and one of the platoons had lost touch altogether, and was out in the deadly open. So in the trench they lay till an officer of the Coldstream came over and told Paget the "general situation," which, unofficially, ran: "This show is held up." He borrowed a section from No. 5 platoon to help to build up a flank to guard the east side of St. Leger and vanished among the increasing shell-holes.

Well on in the morning a message arrived from Captain Hegarty, No. 4 Company, that he and his men were on the St. Léger – Vraucourt road and held up like the rest. Captain Paget went over, in the usual way, by a series of bolts from shell-hole to shell-hole, trying to clear up an only-too-clear situation. On the way he found a lost platoon, sent it to dig in on the left of No. 2 Company, and also saw the C.O. 2nd Coldstream and explained his own dispositions. They were not made too soon, for in a short time there was an attack on No. 2 Company which came within sixty yards before it was broken up by our small-arm fire. The Germans were followed up as they returned across the Ecoust – Mory ridge by long-range shooting in which, for the sake of economy, captured enemy rifles and ammunition were used.

By this time the whole front was split up into small or large scattered posts in trenches or under cover, each held down by machine-guns which punished every movement. Two Companies (2 and 4) were near the St. Leger Trees, a clump of nine trees on the St. Léger – Ecoust road, mixed up with the Coldstream posts. The other two were dug in behind the Grenadiers on the right. Battalion Headquarters circulated spasmodically and by rushes when it saw its chance, from one point to the other of the most unwholesome ground. Even at the time, some of its shell-hole conferences struck the members as comic; but history does not record the things that were said by dripping officers between mouthfuls of dirt and gas.

Every battle has its special characteristic. St. Leger was one of heat, sunshine, sweat; the flavour of at least two gases tasted through respirators or in the raw; the wail of machine-gun bullets sweeping the crests of sunken roads; the sudden vision of wounded in still-smoking shell-holes or laid in the sides of a scarp; sharp whiffs of new-spilt blood, and here and there a face upon which the sun stared without making any change. So the hours wore on, under a sense of space, heat and light; Death always just over the edge of that space and impudently busy in that light.

About what would have been tea-time in the real world, Captain Paget, a man of unhurried and careful speech and imperturbable soul, reported to the C.O., whom he found by the St. Leger Trees, that there were "Huns on his right – same trench as himself." It was an awkward situation that needed mending before dusk, and it was made worse by the posts of the Coldstream and some Guards Machine-Guns' posts, as well as those of our No. 4 Company, being mixed up within close range of No. 2. The C.O. decided that if a barrage could be brought to bear on the trench and its rather crowded neighbourhood, No. 2 might attack it. A young Gunner, Fowler by name cast up at that juncture and said it might be managed if the Battalion withdrew their posts round the area. He had a telephone, still uncut, to his guns and would observe their registration himself. The posts, including those of the Guards Machine-Guns, were withdrawn, and Fowler was as near as might be killed by one of his own registering shots. He got his 18-pounders to his liking at last, and ten minutes' brisk barrage descended on the trench. When it stopped, and before our men could move, up went a white flag amid yells of "Kamerad," and the Huns came out, hands aloft, to be met by our men, who, forgetting that exposed troops, friend and foe alike, would certainly be gunned by the nearest enemy-post, had to be shooed and shouted back to cover by their officers. The prisoners, ninety of them, were herded into a wood, where they cast their helmets on the ground, laughed, and shook hands with each other, to the immense amusement of our people. The capture had turned a very blank day into something of a success, and the Irish were grateful to the "bag." This at least explains the politeness of the orderly who chaperoned rather than conducted the Hun officer to the rear, with many a "This way, sir. Mind out, now, sir, you don't slip down the bank." They put a platoon into the captured trench and lay down to a night of bursts of heavy shelling. But the enemy, whether because of direct pressure or because they had done their delaying work, asked for no more and drew back in the dark.

When morning of the 28th broke "few signs of enemy movement were observed." Men say that there is no mistaking the "feel of the front" under this joyous aspect. The sense of constriction departs as swiftly as a headache, and with it, often, the taste that was in the mouth. One by one, as the lovely day went on, the patrols from the Companies made their investigations and reports, till at last the whole line re-formed and, in touch on either flank, felt forward under light shelling from withdrawing guns. An aeroplane dropped some bombs on the Battalion as it drew near to the St. Leger Trees, which wounded two men and two Gunner officers, one of whom – not Fowler, the boy who arranged for the barrage – died in Father Browne's arms. On the road at that point, where the wounded and dying of the fight had been laid, only dried pools of blood and some stained cotton-wads remained darkening in the sun. Such officers as the gas had affected in that way went about their routine-work vomiting disgustedly at intervals.

Battalion Headquarters, which had nominally spent the previous day in a waist-deep trench, set up office at the St. Léger Trees, and the advance of the Guards Division continued for a mile or so. Then, on a consolidated line, with machine-guns chattering to the eastward, it waited to be relieved. As prelude to their watch on the Rhine, the affair was not auspicious. The Grenadiers, on whom the brunt of the fight fell, were badly knocked out, and of their sixteen officers but four were on their feet. The Coldstream were so weakened that they borrowed our No. 4 Company to carry on with, and the Irish thought themselves lucky to have lost no more than two officers (Lieutenant J. N. Ward and Lieutenant H. R. Baldwin) dead, and six wounded or gassed, in addition to a hundred and seventy other ranks killed or wounded. The wounded officers were Captain W. Joyce; Lieutenants P. S. MacMahon and C. A. J. Vernon, who was incapacitated for a while by tear-gas in the middle of action and led away blinded and very wrath; also 2nd Lieutenants H. Connolly, G. T. Heaton, and A. E. Hutchinson.

The Division was relieved on the night of the 28th: the Battalion itself, as far as regarded No. 1 Company, by the 1st Gordons, from the Third Division, Nos. 2 and 4 Companies by another battalion, and No. 3 Company under the orders of the 2nd Grenadiers. They marched back to their positions of the night before the battle "very glad that it was all behind us," and their shelters of bits of wood and rough iron seemed like rest in a fair land.

On the 29th August, a hot day, they lay in old trenches over the Moyenneville spur in front of Adinfer Wood facing Douchy and Ayette, where "three weeks ago no man could have lived." They talked together of the far-off times when they held that line daily expecting the enemy advance; and the officers lay out luxuriously in the wood in the evening after Mess, while the men made themselves "little homes in it."

Next day they rested, for the men were very tired, and on the last of the month the whole Battalion was washed in the Divisional Baths that had established themselves at Adinfer. But the enemy had not forgotten them, and on the 1st of September their shelters and tents in the delightful wood were bombed. Six men were injured, five being buried in a trench, and of these two were suffocated before they could be dug out.

TOWARDS THE CANAL DU NORD

And that was all the rest allowed to the Battalion. On the 2nd September the Canadian Corps of the First Army broke that outlying spur of the Hindenburg System known as the Drocourt–Quéant Switch, with its wires, trenches and posts; and the Fifty-seventh and Fifty-second Divisions, after hard work, equally smashed the triangle of fortifications north-west of Quéant where the Switch joined the System. The gain shook the whole of the Hindenburg Line south of Quéant and, after five days' clean-up behind the line, the Guards Division were ordered to go in again at the very breast of Hindenburg's works. No one knew what the enemy's idea might be, but there was strong presumption that, if he did not hold his defence at that point, he might crack. ("But, ye'll understand, for all that, we did *not* believe Jerry would crack past mendin'.")

The Battalion spent the night of the 2nd September, then, in shelters in Hamel Switch Trench on their way back from Adinfer Wood to the battle. The front had now shifted to very much the one that we held in April 1917, ere the days of Cambrai and Bourlon Wood. The 1st Guards Brigade were in Divisional Reserve at Lagnicourt, three miles south-west of Ecoust-St. Mein, where the Battalion had to cross their still fresh battle-field of less than a week back, as an appetizer to their hot dinners. They occupied a waist-deep, old trench, a little west of Lagnicourt, and noticed that there was no shelling, though the roads were full of our traffic, "a good deal of it in full view of Bourlon Wood." Going over "used" ground for the third time, and noting one's many dead comrades, does not make for high spirits even though one's own Divisional General has written one's own Brigadier, "All Battalions of the 1st Guards Brigade discharged their duty splendidly at St. Léger."

Lagnicourt was shelled a little by a high-velocity gun between the 4th and the 6th of September, and seventeen bombs were dropped on the Battalion, wounding two men.

By all reason there should have been a bitter fight on that ground, and full preparation for it was made. But the enemy, after St. Léger saw fit to withdraw himself suddenly and unexpectedly out of all that area. For one bewildering dawn and day "the bottom fell out of the front," as far as the Guards Division was concerned. It is a curious story, even though it does not directly concern the Battalion. Here is one detail of it:

On the 3rd September the 2nd Brigade toiled in from Monchy, in full war-kit, and, tired with the long day's heat, formed up west of Lagnicourt before dawn, detailed to win, if they could, a thousand yards or so of chewed-up ground. They "went over the top" under a creeping barrage, one gun of which persistently fired short, and – found nothing whatever in front of them save a prodigious number of dead horses, some few corpses and an intolerable buzzing of flies! As they topped the ridge above Lagnicourt, they saw against the first light of the sun, dump after German dump blazing palely towards the east. That was all. They wandered, wondering, into a vast, grassy, habitationless plain that stretched away towards the Bapaume – Cambrai road. Not a machine-gun broke the stupefying stillness from any fold of it. Yet it was the very place for such surprises. Aeroplanes swooped low, looked them well over, and skimmed off. No distant guns opened. The advance became a route-march, a Sunday walk-out, edged with tense suspicion. They saw a German cooker wrecked on the grass, and, beside it, the bodies of two clean good-looking boys, pathetically laid out as for burial. The thing was a booby-trap arranged to move our people's pity. Some pitied, and were blown to bits by the concealed mine. No one made any comment. They were tired with carrying their kit in the sun among the maddening flies. The thousand yards stretched into miles. Twice or thrice they halted and began to dig in for fear of attack. But nothing overtook them and they installed themselves, about dusk, in some old British trenches outside Boursies, four miles and more, as the crow flies, from Lagnicourt! At midnight, up came their rations, and the punctual home-letters, across that enchanted desert which had spared them. They were told that their Brigade Artillery was in place behind the next rise, ready to deliver barrages on demand, and in due course the whole of our line on that sector flowed forward.

The Battalion relieved the 1st Scots Guards in the front line near Moeuvres on the 7th – a quiet relief followed by severe gassing. Here they passed two days in the delicate and difficult business of feeling all about them among the mass of old trenches, to locate enemy's posts and to watch what points of vantage might offer. The wreckage of the houses round Moeuvres, into which the trenches ran, lent itself excellently to enemy activity; and men played blind-man's buff round bits of broken walls wherever they explored. Their left was in the air; their right under the care of Providence; and their supports were far off. No. 3 Company (Captain G. L. Bambridge, M.C.), while trying to close a gap between the two front Companies (3 and 1) by peaceful penetration with a bombing-party, found enemy in the trench, drove him up it as far as they could, built a barricade and were then heavily counter-raided by a couple of officers and twenty men whom they ejected after, as the Company justly owned, "a good attempt." The enemy "attempted" again about midnight on the 8th, when he was bombed off, and again on the afternoon of the 9th in an outlying trench, mixed up with smashed cellars and broken floors, where he captured two unarmed stretcher-bearers and three men who had not been in the line before. Though it does new hands no harm to realize that front-line trenches are not Warley Barracks (and stretcher-bearers, like order-lies, are prey to all the world), still the matter could not be passed over. Our trench-mortars attended vigorously to the enemy posts whence the raid had been launched, and in the afternoon sent a strong patrol to make the outraged trench secure. Later on, a platoon of No. 1 Company got into touch with the battalion (8th King's) on their left, and took part in a small "bicker," as it was described, but with no casualties.

They were relieved the same night, though they did not expect it, by the 1/5th Battalion Loyal North Lancs who had not made sure of their route beforehand, and so, in wet darkness, lost their way, failed to meet the guides at the rendezvous, and were heavily shelled. The relief dragged on till well towards dawn, when the Battalions straggled off into some drenching trenches without any sort of accommodation. ("The whole thing the most appalling mess and agony I have ever experienced.") The worst was when a stray light went up and showed the relieved Battalion under pouring rain "following my leader" in a complete circle like caterpillars, in the hopeful belief that they were moving to their destination. They next took the place of the 3rd Guards Brigade in reserve-trenches near Edinburgh Support, where they stayed till the 14th September and were not even once shelled. Salvage and cleaning up was their fatigue – a dreadful job at any time, for the ground was filled with ancient offal as well as new – lost French of '14 mingled grotesquely with the raw produce of yesterday's bombing-raid. Yet men's feelings blunt so by use that they will scavenge yard by yard over the very clay of the pit into which they themselves may at any instant be stamped, nor turn a hair at shapes made, last year, in their likeness. The Battalion was complimented by Major-General on the extent and neatness of its dump. No mere campaigning interferes with the Army's passion for elaborate economies. A little before this, the entire British Expeditionary Force was exhorted to collect and turn in all solder from bully-beef tins and the like. Naturally, the thing became a game with betting on results between corps; but when a dark, elderly, brooding private of the Irish spent three hours stalking a Coldstream cooker with intent to convey and melt it down, every one felt it had gone far enough.

On the 15th September they relieved the 1st Scots Guards in the old trenches west of Lagnicourt. There they managed to put in a little box-respirator drill which at the best is a dry fatigue, but, be it noted with gratitude, "beer was obtained for the men and sent up from transport-lines."

The whole area reeked of the various gases which the enemy were distributing with heavies. They hung in the hollows and were sucked up by the day's heat, and no time or place was safe from them. Gas-discipline had to be insisted on strongly, for even veterans grow careless of a foe they cannot see, and the new hands are like croupy babies.

On the 17th September they the 2nd Scots Guards in support, and No. 2 Company took over from a Company of the Welsh Guards. Their trenches were in what had been the British front line of the old time – Fish Avenue, Sprat Post, Shark Support, Rat and Rabbit Avenue, and so forth.

There was desultory shelling on the morning of the 18th, and heavier work in the afternoon, causing six casualties, and slightly wounding Captain Vernon, Intelligence Officer. Then the silence of preparation for battle falls on the record. It was nothing to the Battalion that on the 18th September the enemy "apparently attacked south of the Divisional front along the Bapaume – Cambrai road." The dead must bury their dead on the Somme. They had their own dispositions to arrange and rearrange, as men, for one cause or other, fell out and no unit could afford to take chances, with the Hindenburg Line ahead of them. ("An' we knowin' we was told off to cross that dirty ditch in front of 'em all.") Their world, as with every other Division, was limited to the Reserves behind them, who should come up to make good their casualties; their trench-mortar batteries alongside them; and their own selves, about to be used in what promised to be one of the bloodiest shows of the war.

Those who were for the front line enjoyed a week to work and think things over. Those who were set aside for the second course were bombed by night and – went mushroom-picking in back-areas between parades, or played riotous cricket-matches with petrol-tins for wickets!

Their Divisional Commander, Major-General Feilding, had left on September 11 to succeed Sir Francis Lloyd in command of the London District, and General T. G. Matheson, C.B., had been appointed to the command of the Guards Division. The Battalion was full strength, officers and men, for there had been little during the past month to pull it down.

THE CROSSING OF THE CANAL DU NORD

Operations against the Hindenburg Line were to open on the 27th September with the attack of fourteen Divisions of the First and Third Armies on a twelve-mile front from opposite Gouzeaucourt in the south to opposite Sauchy-Lestrée, sister to Sauchy-Cauchy – under the marshes of the Sensée river in the north. It would be heralded by two days' solid bombardment along the entire fronts of the First, Third and Fourth Armies, so that the enemy might be left guessing which was to hit first. When the First and Third Armies were well home, the Fourth would attend to the German position in the south, and heave the whole thing backward.

The share of the Guards Division in the northern attack was to cross the Canal du Nord at Lock Seven, north of Havrincourt, on a front of a mile; then work through the complicated tangle of the Hindenburg support-line directly east along the ridge from Flesquières village to Premy Chapel which stands at the junction of the roads from Noyelles, Marcoing and Graincourt, and to consolidate on the line of the Marcoing – Graincourt road. Meantime, the Third Division on their right would take the village of Flesquières; the Fifty-second Division would take the Hindenburg Line that lay west of the Canal in the bend of it, and would then let the Sixty-third through who would swing down from the north and attend to Graincourt and Anneux villages. The total advance set for the Guards Division was three miles, but, if the operations were fully successful, they were to push on to the outskirts of Noyelles; the Third Division to Marcoing; while the Fifty-seventh, coming through the Sixty-third, would take Cantaing and Fontaine-Notre-Dame. In the Guards Division itself, the 2nd Brigade was to move off first, and ferret its way through a knot of heavily wired trenches that lay between them and the Canal, take the Hindenburg support-trenches, and then form a defensive flank to the left of the next advance till the Fifty-second and Sixty-third Divisions should have secured Graincourt. The 1st Brigade would pass through them and capture the trenches across the Canal to the north and north-east of Flesquières. If resistance were not too strong, that Brigade was to go on to the spur running from Flesquières to Cantaing, and help the Sixty-third turn the Graincourt line. The 3rd Brigade, passing through the 1st, would carry on and take the high ground round Premy Chapel.

Enough rain fell the day before to grease the ground uncomfortably, and when at 3.30 a.m. the Irish Guards moved off from their reserve trenches west of Lagnicourt to their assembly positions along the Demicourt – Graincourt road to Bullen Trench, the jumping-off place, it was pouring wet. They were not shelled on the way up, but the usual night-work was afoot in the back-areas, and though our guns, as often the case on the eve of an outbreak, held their breath, the enemy's artillery threatened in the distance, and the lights and "flaming onions" marked their expectant front. Just before the Battalion reached the ruins of Demicourt, there was an explosion behind them, and they saw, outlined against the flare of a blazing dump, Lagnicourt way, a fat and foolish observation-balloon rocking and ducking at the end of its tether, with the air of a naughty baby caught in the act of doing something it shouldn't. Since the thing was visible over half a Department, they called it names, but it made excuse for a little talk that broke the tension. Tea and rum were served out at the first halt – a ritual with its usual grim jests – and when they reached the road in front of Demicourt, they perceived the balloon had done its dirty work too well. The enemy, like ourselves, changes his field-lights on occasion, but, on all occasions, two red lights above and one below mean trouble. "Up go the bloody pawnbrokers!" said a man who knew what to expect, and, as soon as the ominous glares rose, the German trench-mortars opened on the Battalion entering the communication-way that led to Bullen Trench. Our barrage came down at Zero (5.20) more terrifically, men said, than ever they had experienced, and was answered by redoubled defensive barrages. After that, speech was cut off. Some fifty yards ahead of Bullen Trench – which, by the way, was only three feet deep – lay the 1st Scots Guards, the first wave of the attack. On, in front of, and in the space between them and the Irish, fell the rain of the trench-mortars; from the rear, the Guards Machine-Guns tortured all there was of unoccupied air with their infernal clamours. The Scots Guards went over among the shell-spouts and jerking wires at the first glimmer of dawn, the Irish following in a rush. The leading Companies were No. 3 (Lieutenant H. A. A. Collett) on the left, and No. 4 (2nd Lieutenant C. S. O'Brien) on the right. The 1st Guards Trench Mortar Battery (2nd Lieutenant O. R. Baldwin, Irish Guards) was attached experimentally to No. 3 Company in the first wave instead of, as usual, in support. No. 2 Company (Captain C. W. W. Bence-Jones) supported No. 3, and No. 1 (Lieutenant the Hon. B. A. A. Ogilvy) No. 4. They stayed for a moment in the trench, a deep, wide one of the Hindenburg pattern, which the Scots Guards had left. It was no healthy spot, for the shells were localised here and the dirt flung up all along it in waves. Men scrambled out over the sliding, flying edges of it, saw a bank heave up in the half-light, and knew that, somewhere behind that, was the Canal. By this time one of the two Stokes guns of the Mortar Battery and half the gunners had been wiped out, and the casualties in the line were heavy; but they had no time to count. Then earth opened beneath their feet, and showed a wide, deep, dry, newly made canal with a smashed iron bridge lying across the bed of it, and an unfinished lock to the right looking like some immense engine of war ready to do hurt in inconceivable fashions. Directly below them, on the pale, horribly hard, concrete trough, was a collection of agitated pin-heads, the steel hats of the Scots Guards rearing ladders against the far side of the gulf. Mixed with them were the dead, insolently uninterested, while the wounded, breaking aside, bound themselves up with the tense, silent preoccupation which unhurt men, going forward, find so hard to bear. Mobs of bewildered Germans had crawled out of their shelters in the Canal flanks and were trying to surrender to any one who looked likely to attend to them. They saluted British officers as they raced past, and, between salutes, returned their arms stiffly to the safe "Kamerad" position. This added the last touch of insanity to the picture. ("We'd ha' laughed if we had had the time, ye'll understand.")

. . . Then earth opened beneath their feet and showed a wide, deep, dry, newly-made canal with a smashed iron bridge lying across the bed of it, and an unfinished lock to the right of it looking like some immense engine of war ready to do hurt in inconceivable fashions.

The Canal du Nord, 28th September 1918.

None recalls precisely how they reached the bottom of the Canal, but there were a few moments of blessed shelter ere they scrambled out and re-formed on the far side. The shelling here was bad enough, but nothing to what they had survived. A veil of greasy smoke, patched with flame that did not glare, stood up behind them, and through the pall of it, in little knots, stumbled their supports, blinded, choking, gasping. In the direction of the attack, across a long stretch of broken rising ground, were more shells, but less thickly spaced, and craters of stinking earth and coloured chalks where our barrage had ripped out nests of machine-guns. Far off, to the left, creaming with yellow smoke in the morning light, rose the sullen head of Bourlon Wood to which the Canadians were faithfully paying the debt contracted by the 2nd Battalion of the Irish Guards in the old days after Cambrai.

At the crest of the ascent lay Saunders Keep, which marked the point where the Scots Guards would lie up and the Irish come through. Already the casualties had been severe. Captain Bence-Jones and 2nd Lieutenant Mathieson of No. 2 Company were wounded at the Keep itself, and 2nd Lieutenant A. R. Boyle of No. 1 earlier in the rush. The Companies panted up, gapped and strung out. From the Keep the land sloped down to Stafford Alley, the Battalion's first objective, just before which Lieutenant Barry Close was killed. That day marked his coming of age. Beyond the Alley the ground rose again, and here the Irish were first checked by some machine-gun fire that had escaped our barrages. Second Lieutenant O'Brien, No. 3 Company, was hit at this point while getting his men forward. He had earned his Military Cross in May, and he died well. The next senior officer, 2nd Lieutenant E. H. R. Burke, was away to the left in the thick of the smoke with a platoon that, like the rest, was fighting for its life; so 2nd Lieutenant O'Farrell led on. He was hit not far from Stafford Alley, and while his wound was being bandaged by Sergeant Regan, hit again by a bullet that, passing through the Sergeant's cap and a finger, entered O'Farrell's heart. The officer commanding the remnants of the Mortar Battery took on the Company, and his one gun. Meantime; Collett and a few of No. 3 Company had reached Silver Street, a trench running forward from Stafford Alley, and he and Lieutenant Brady were bombing down it under heavy small-arm fire from the enemy's left flank which had not been driven in and was giving untold trouble. No. 2 Company, with two out of three of its officers down, was working towards the same line as the fragment of No. 3; though opinion was divided on that confused field whether it would not be better for them to lie down and form a defensive flank against that pestilent left fire. Eventually, but events succeeded each other like the bullets, Collett and his men reached their last objective – a trench running out of Silver Street towards Flesquières. Here he, Brady and Baldwin drew breath and tried to get at the situation. No. 4 Company lay to the right of No. 3, and when 2nd Lieutenant E. H. R. Burke, with what was left of his platoon before mentioned, came up, he resumed charge of it without a word and went on. No. 1 Company (Lieutenant the Hon. B. A. A. Ogilvy) had, like the rest, been compelled to lead its own life. Its objective was the beet-sugar factory in front of Flesquières ahead of and a little to the right of the Battalion's final objective, and it was met throughout with rifle, bomb and flanking fire. Lieutenant Ogilvy was wounded at a critical point in the game with the enemy well into the trench, or trenches. (The whole ground seemed to the men who were clearing it one inexhaustible Hun-warren.) As he dropped, Lieutenant R. L. Dagger and Sergeant Conaboy, picking up what men they could, bombed the enemy out, back and away, and settled down to dig in and wait; always under flank-fire. The Sergeant was killed "in his zeal to finish the job completely" – no mean epitaph for a thorough man. By eleven o'clock that morning all the Companies had reached their objectives, and, though sorely harassed, began to feel that the worst for them might be over. There were, however, two German "whizz-bangs" that lived in Orival Wood still untaken on the Battalion's left, and these, served with disgusting speed and accuracy, swept Silver Street mercilessly. The situation was not improved when one of the Sergeants quoted the ever-famous saying of Sergeant-Major Toher with reference to one of our own barrages: "And even the wurrums themselves are getting up and crying for mercy." The guns were near enough to watch quite comfortably, and while the men watched and winced, they saw the "success" signal of the Canadians – three whites   rise high in the air in front of Bourlon Wood. Then No. 1 Company. reported they were getting more than their share of machine-gun fire, and the 1st Guards Brigade Trench Mortar Battery, reduced to one mortar, one officer, one sergeant, four men, and ten shells, bestowed the whole of its ammunition in the direction indicated, abandoned its mortar and merged itself into the ranks of No. 3 Company. It had been amply proved that where trench-mortars accompany a first wave of attack, if men are hit while carrying two Stokes shells apiece (forty pounds of explosives), they become dangerous mobile mines.

Enemy aeroplanes now swooped down with machine-gun fire; there seemed no way of getting our artillery to attend to them and they pecked like vultures undisturbed. Then Battalion Headquarters came up in the midst of the firing from the left, established themselves in a dug-out and were at once vigorously shelled, together with the neighbouring aid-post and some German prisoners there, waiting to carry down wounded. The aid-post was in charge of a young American doctor, Rhys Davis by name, who had been attached to the Battalion for some time. This was his first day of war and he was mortally wounded before the noon of it.

The trench filled as the day went on, with details dropping in by devious and hurried roads to meet the continual stream of prisoners being handed down to Brigade Headquarters. One youth, who could not have been seventeen, flung himself into the arms of an officer and cried, "Kamerad, Herr Offizier! Ich bin sehr jung! Kamerad!" To whom the embarrassed Islander, brutally: "Get on with you. *I* wouldn't touch you for the world!" And they laughed all along the trench-face as they dodged the whizz-bangs out of Orival Wood, and compared themselves to the "wurrums begging for mercy."

About noon, after many adventures, the 2nd Grenadiers arrived to carry on the advance, and Silver Street became a congested metropolis. The 2nd Grenadiers were hung up there for a while because, though the Third Division on the right had taken Flesquières, the Sixty-third on the left had not got Graincourt village, which was enfilading the landscape damnably. Orival Wood, too, was untaken, and the 1st Grenadiers, under Lord Gort, were out unsupported half a mile ahead on the right front somewhere near Premy Chapel. Meantime, a battalion of the Second Division, which was to come through the Guards Division and continue the advance, flooded up Silver Street, zealously unreeling its telephone wires; Machine-Gun Guards were there, looking for positions; the 2nd Grenadiers were standing ready; the Welsh Guards were also there with intent to support the Grenadiers; walking wounded were coming down, and severe cases were being carried over the top by German prisoners who made no secret of an acute desire to live and jumped in among the rest without leave asked. The men compared the crush to a sugar-queue at home. To cap everything, some wandering tanks which had belonged to the Division on the right had strayed over to the left. No German battery can resist tanks, however disabled; so they drew fire, and when they were knocked out (our people did not know this at first, being unused to working with them), made life insupportable with petrol-fumes for a hundred yards round.

About half-past four in the afternoon a Guards Battalion – they thought it was the 1st Coldstream – came up on their left, and under cover of what looked like a smoke-barrage, cleared Orival Wood and silenced the two guns there. The Irish, from their dress-circle in Silver Street, blessed them long and loud, and while they applauded, Lieut.-Colonel Lord Gort, commanding the 1st Grenadiers, came down the trench wounded on his way to a dressing-station. He had been badly hit once before he thought fit to leave duty, and was suffering from loss of blood. The Irish had always a great regard for him, and that day they owed him more than they knew at the time, for it was the advance of the 1st Grenadiers under his leading, almost up to Premy Chapel, which had unkeyed the German resistance in Graincourt, and led the enemy to believe their line of retreat out of the village was threatened. The Second Division as it came through found the enemy shifting and followed them up towards Noyelles. So the day closed, and, though men did not realize, marked the end of organized trench-warfare for the Guards Division.

The Battalion, with two officers dead and five wounded out of fifteen killed: Lieutenant B. S. Close, and 2nd Lieutenant A. H. O'Farrell; wounded: Captain the Hon. B. A. A. Ogilvy, Captain C. W. W. Bence-Jones, and 2nd Lieutenants A. R. Boyle, G. F. Mathieson; and C. S. O'Brien, M.C., died of wounds), and one hundred and eighty casualties in the ranks, stayed on the ground for the night. It tried to make itself as comfortable as cold and shallow trenches allowed, but by orders of some "higher authority," who supposed that it had been relieved, no water or rations were sent up; and, next morning, they had to march six thousand yards on empty stomachs to their trench-shelters and bivouacs in front of Demicourt. As the last Company arrived a cold rain fell, but they were all in reasonably high spirits. It had been a winning action, in spite of trench-work, and men really felt that they had the running in their own hands at last.

Back-area rumours and official notifications were good too. The Nineteenth and Second Corps of the Second Army, together with the Belgian Army, had attacked on the 28th September, from Dixmude to far south of the Ypres – Zonnebeke road; had retaken all the heights to the east of Ypres, and were in a fair way to clear out every German gain there of the past four years. A German withdrawal was beginning from Lens to Armentières, and to the south of the Third Army the Fourth came in on the 29th (while the Battalion was "resting and shaving" in its trench-shelters by Demicourt) on a front of twelve miles, and from Gricourt to Vendhuille broke and poured across the Hindenburg Line, then to the St. Quentin Canal. At the same time, lest there should be one furlong of the uneasy front neglected, the Fifth and Sixth Corps of the Third Army attacked over the old Gouzeaucourt ground between Vendhuille and Marcoing. This, too, without counting the blows that the French and the Americans were dealing in their own spheres on the Meuse and in the Argonne; each stroke coldly preparing the next.

The Germans had, during September, lost a quarter of a million of prisoners, several thousand guns, and immense quantities of irreplaceable stores. Their main line of resistance was broken and over-run throughout; and their troops in the field were feeling the demoralization of constant withdrawals, as well as shortage from abandoned supplies. Our people had known the same depression in the March Push, when night-skies, lit with burning dumps, gave the impression that all the world was going up in universal surrender.

TOWARDS MAUBEUGE

But work was still to do. Between Cambrai, which at the end of October was under, though not actually in, our hands, and Maubeuge, lay thirty-five miles of France, all open save for such hastily made defences as the enemy had been able to throw up after the collapse of the Hindenburg systems. There, then, the screw was turned, and on the 8th October the Third and Fourth Armies attacked on a front of seventeen miles from Sequehart, north of Cambrai, where the Cambrai – Douai road crosses the Sensée, southward to our junction with the French First Army a few miles above St. Quentin. Twenty British Divisions, two Cavalry Divisions, and one American Division were involved. The Battalion faced the changed military situation, by announcing that Companies were "at the disposal of their Commanders for open warfare training." After which they were instantly sent forward from their Demicourt trenches, to help make roads between Havrincourt and Flesquières!

On the 3rd October they had orders to move, which were at once cancelled – sure sign that the Higher Command had something on its mind. This was proved two days later when the same orders arrived again, and were again washed out. Meantime, their reorganization after the Flesquières fight had been completed; reinforcements were up, and the following officers had joined for duty; Lieutenants H. E. Van der Noot and G. F. Van der Noot, and 2nd Lieutenants A. L. W. Koch de Gooreynd, the Hon. C. A. Barnewall, G. M. Tylden-Wright, V. J. S. French and R. E. Taylor.

. . . No German battery can resist tanks, however disabled; so they drew fire, and when they were knocked out (our people did not know this at first, being unused to working with them), made life insupportable with petrol-fumes for a hundred yards round.

Near Flesquières towards the end of September 1918.

On the 4th October the Commanding Officer went on leave, and Major A. F. L. Gordon, M.C., took command of the Battalion. Once more it was warned that it would move next day, which warning this time came true, and was heralded by the usual conference at Brigade Headquarters, on the 7th October, when the plans for next day's battle in the sector of the line were revealed. The Second Division, on the left, and the Third; right of the Guards Division, were to attack on the whole of the front of the Sixth Corps at dawn of the 8th October. The Guards Division was to be ready to go through these two Divisions on the afternoon of that day, or to take over the line on the night of it, and continue the attack at dawn on the 9th. The 1st Guards Brigade would pass through the Third Division, and the 2nd Brigade through the Second Division. As far as the 1st Brigade's attack was concerned, the 2nd Coldstream would take the right, the 2nd Grenadiers the left of the line, with the 1st Irish Guards in reserve. It was all beautifully clear. So the Battalion left Demicourt, recrossed the Canal du Nord at Lock 7, and were "accommodated" in dug-outs and shelters in the Hindenburg Line, near Ribecourt.

On the 9th October the Battalion moved to Masnières, four miles or so south of Cambrai. Here, while crossing the St. Quentin Canal, No. 3 Company had three killed and three wounded by a long-range gun which was shelling all down the line of it. They halted in the open for the rest of the day. A curious experience followed. The idea was to attack in the general direction of Cattenières, across the line of the Cambrai – Caudry railway, which, with its embankment and cuttings, was expected to give trouble. The New Zealand Division was then on the right of the Guards Division; but no one seemed to be sure, the night before the battle, whether the Third Division was out on their front or not. ("Everything, ye'll understand, was all loosed up in those days. Jerry did not know his mind, and for that reason we could not know ours. The bottom was out of the War, ye'll understand, but we did not see it.") However, it was arranged that all troops would be withdrawn from doubtful areas before Zero (5.10 a.m.), and that the 2nd Coldstream and the 2nd Grenadiers would advance to the attack under a creeping barrage with due precautions which included a plentiful bombardment and machine-gunning of the railway-embankment.

The Battalion, in reserve, as has been said, moved from Masnières to its assembly-area, among old German trenches near the village of Seranvillers, in artillery formation at 2.40 a.m., and had its breakfast at 5 a.m., while the other two battalions of the Brigade advanced in waves, preceded by strong patrols and backed by the guns. There was no shelling while they assembled, and practically none in reply to our barrage; nor did the leading battalions meet opposition till after they had cleared out the village of Seranvillers, and were held up by screened machine-guns in a wood surrounding a sugar-factory north of Cattenières. The Battalion followed on in due course, reached the railway-embankment, set up Headquarters in a road-tunnel under it (there was no firing), and received telephonic orders that at 5 a.m. on the 10th October they would pass through the other two battalions and continue the advance, which, henceforth was to be "by bounds" and without limit or barrage. Then they lay up in the railway-embankment and dozed.

They assembled next morning (the 10th) in the dark, and, reinforced by seven Corps Cyclists and a battery of field-guns, went forth into France at large, after a retiring enemy. Nothing happened for a couple of miles, when they reached the outskirts of Beauvais-en-Cambrensis, on the Cambrai – Le Cateau road, where a single sniper from one of the houses shot and killed 2nd Lieutenant V. J. S. French, No. 4 Company. A mile farther on, up the Beauvais – Quievy road, they found the village of Bevillers heavily shelled by the enemy from a distance, so skirted round it, and sent in two small mopping-up parties. Here No. 4 Company again came up against machine-gun and sniper fire, but no casualties followed. Their patrols reported the next bound all clear, and they pushed on, under heavy but harmless shelling, in the direction of Quievy. At eight o'clock their patrols waked up a breadth of machine-gun nests along the whole of the front and that of the battalions to their left and right. They went to ground accordingly, and when the enemy artillery was added to the small-arm fire, the men dug slits for themselves and escaped trouble. For some time past the German shell-stuff had been growing less and less effective, both in accuracy and bursting power, which knowledge cheered our troops. In the afternoon, as there were signs of the resistance weakening, our patrols put forth once more, and by five o'clock the Battalion had reached the third bound on the full battalion front. Then, in the dusk, came word from the New Zealand Division on their right, that the Division on *their* right again, had got forward, and that the New Zealanders were pushing on to high ground south of Quievy. With the message came one from No. 4 Company, reporting that their patrols were out ahead, and in touch with the New Zealanders on their right. There is no record that the news was received with enthusiasm, since it meant "bounding on" in the dark to the fourth bound, which they accomplished not before 10.30 that night, tired officers hunting up tired companies by hand and shoving them into their positions. These were on high ground north-east of Quievy, with the Battalion's right on a farm, called Fontaine-au-Tertre, which signifies "the fountain on the little hill," a mile beyond the village. The 1st Scots Guards were on their left holding the village of St. Hilaire-les-Cambrai. Then, punctual as ever, rations came up; Battalion Headquarters established itself in a real roofed house in the out- skirts of Quievy, and No. 1 Company in reserve was billeted in the village.

Next morning (11th October) when the 3rd Guards Brigade came through them and attacked over the naked grass and stubble fields towards St. Python and Solesmes, the Battalion was withdrawn and sent to very good billets in Quievy. "The men having both upstairs and cellar room. All billets very dirty," says the Diary, "owing to the previous occupants (Hun) apparently having taken delight in scattering all the civilian clothes, food, furniture, etc., all over the place." Every one was tired out; they had hardly slept for three nights; but all "were in the best of spirits." Brigade Headquarters had found what was described as "a magnificent house" with "most comfortable" bed in "a large room." Those who used it were lyric in their letters home.

The total casualties for the 10th and 11th October were amazingly few. Second Lieutenant V. J. S. French was the only casualty among the officers, and, of other ranks, but three were killed and nine wounded.

The Officers who took part in the operations were these:

No. 1 Company

Lieut. H. E. Van der Noot
2nd Lieut. J. C. Haydon

2nd Lieut. R. E. Taylor.

No. 2 Company

Lieut. E. M. Harvey, M.C.
2nd Lieut. G. T. Todd

2nd Lieut. A. L. W. Koch de Gooreynd.

No. 3 Company

Lieut. F. S. L. Smith, M.C.
Lieut. G. E. F. Van der Noot

2nd Lieut. J. J. B. Brady.

No. 4 Company

Capt. D. J. Hegarty
2nd Lieut. Hon. C. A. Barnewall

2nd Lieut. V. J. S. French (killed).

Battalion Headquarters

Major A. F. Gordon, M.C.
Capt. J. B. Keenan

Capt. G. L. St. C. Bambridge, M. C.

They lay at Quievy for the next week, employed in cleaning up dirty billets, while the 8th and 2nd Brigades of the Division were cleaning out the enemy rear-guards in front of them from the west bank of the Selle river, and roads and railways were stretching out behind our Armies to bring redoubled supply of material. One of the extra fatigues of those days was to get the civil population out of the villages that the enemy were abandoning. This had to be done by night, for there is small chivalry in the German composition. Quievy was shelled at intervals, and no parades larger than of a platoon were, therefore, allowed. The weather, too, stopped a scheme of field-operations in the back-area between Quievy and Bevillers; and a washed and cleanly clothed Battalion were grateful to their Saints for both reliefs.

On the 17th October the Sixty-first Division took over the Guards area, and that afternoon the Battalion left Quievy by cross-country tracks for Boussières, and moved into position for what turned out to be all but the last stroke of the long game.

The enemy on that front were by now across the steeply banked Selle river, but the large, straggling village of Solesmes, of which St. Python is practically a suburb, was still held by them and would have to be cleaned out house-to-house. Moreover, it was known to be full of French civils, and getting them away in safety would not make the situation less difficult.

ST. PYTHON

It was given out at Brigade conference on the 17th that the Sixty-first Division would take place on the right of the Guards Division and the Nineteenth on its left in the forthcoming attack, and that the Sixty-first would attend to Solesmes, while the Guards Division pushed on north-east between St. Python and Haussy on a mile-wide front through the village of Escarmain to Capelle, a distance of some three and a half miles. The 1st and 3rd Brigades would lead, the 2nd in reserve, and the passage of the Selle would be effected in the dark by such bridges as the Sappers could put up.

The Battalion moved nearer their assembly-areas to St. Hilaire-les-Cambrai, on the night of the 18th after Company Commanders had thoroughly explained to their men what was in store; and on the 19th those Commanders, with the Intelligence Officer, Captain Vernon, went up to high ground overlooking the battlefield. It was a closer and more crumpled land than they had dealt with hitherto, its steep-sided valleys cut by a multitude of little streams running from nor'-west to south-east, with the interminable ruled line of the Bavai road edging the great Forest of Mormal which lay north of Landrecies. The wheel was swinging full circle, and men who had taken part in that age-ago retreat from Mons, amused themselves by trying to pick out familiar details in the landscape they had been hunted across, four years before. But it was misty and the weather, faithful ally of the Germans to the last, was breaking again. Just as the Battalion moved off from St. Hilaire to their area on the railway line from Valenciennes to Le Cateau, rain began and continued till six next morning, making every condition for attack as vile as it could. They dug them shallow trenches in case of shell-fire, and sent down parties to reconnoitre the bridges over the Selle. Four bridges were "available," i.e. existed in some shape, on or near the Battalion front, but no one had a good word to say for any of them.

There is a tale concerning the rivers here, which may be given (without guarantee) substantially as told: "Rivers round Maubeuge? 'Twas *all* rivers – the Aunelle and the Rhonelle and the Pronelle, an' more, too; an' our Intelligence Officer desirin' to know the last word concernin' each one of 'em before we paddled it. Michael an' me was for that duty. Michael was a runner, afraid o' nothing, but no small liar, and him as fed as myself with reporting on these same dam' rivers; and Jerry expendin' the last of his small-arm stuff round and round the country I forget which river 'twas we were scouting, but he was ahead of me, the way he always was. Presently he comes capering back, 'Home, please, Sergeant,' says he. 'That hill's stinking with Jerries beyond.' 'But the river?' says I. 'Ah, come home,' says Michael, 'an' I'll learn ye the road to be a V.C.!' So home we went to the Intelligence Officer, and 'twas then I should have spoke the truth. But Michael was before me. I had no more than my mouth opened when he makes his report, which was my business, me being Sergeant (did I tell ye?), to put in. But Michael was before me. He comes out with the width of the river, and its depth, and the nature of its bottom and the scenery, and all and all, the way you'd ha' sworn he'd been a trout in it. When we was out of hearing, I told him he was a liar in respect to his river. 'River,' says he; 'are ye after calling *that* a river? 'Tis no bigger than a Dickiebush ditch,' he says. 'And anyway,' says he, 'the Battalion'll rowl across it in the dark, the way it always does. Ye can not get wetter than wet, even in the Micks!' Then his conscience smote him, an' when his Company went down to this river in the dark, Michael comes capering alongside whishpering between his hands: 'Boys!' says he, 'can ye swim, boys? I hope ye can all swim for, Saints be my witness, I never wint near the river. For aught I know it may be an arrum of the sea. Ah, lads, *thry* an' learn to swim!' he says. Then some one chases him off before the officer comes along; an' we wint over Michael's river the way he said we would. Ye can not get wetter than wet – even in the Micks."

It was a quiet night, except for occasional bursts of machine-gun fire, but there was no shelling of the assembly-area as the 2nd Grenadiers formed up on their right, with the 2nd Coldstream in reserve. Nos. 1 and 2 Companies (Captain A. W. L. Paget, and Lieutenant E. M. Harvey, M.C.) moved off first, No. 3 in support (Captain Bambridge), and No. 4 (2nd Lieutenant O. R. Baldwin) in reserve. The barrage opened with a percentage of demoralising flame-shells. There was very little artillery retaliation, and beyond getting rather wetter than the rain had already made them, the Battalion did not suffer, except from small-arm fire out of the dark. The first objective, a section of the Solesmes – Valenciennes road gained in an hour, with but eight casualties, mainly from our own "shorts" in the barrage, and several prisoners and machine-guns captured. The prisoners showed no wish to fight.

The Companies had kept direction wonderfully well in the dark, and reached the second and last objective under increased machine-gun fire, but still without much artillery. The 3rd Guards Brigade on their left had been hung up once or twice, which kept No. 2 Company, the left leading Company, and Nos. 3 and 4 (in support) busy at odd times forming defensive flanks against sniping. By half-past five, however, they were all in place, and set to dig in opposite the village of Vertain. Then dull day broke and with light came punishment. The enemy, in plain sight, opened on them with everything that they had in the neighbourhood, from 7 a.m. to 10 p.m. of the 20th. The two front Companies were cut off as long as one could see, and a good deal of the stuff was delivered over open sights. It was extremely difficult to get the wounded away, owing to the continuous sniping. But, through Providence, or the defect of enemy ammunition, or the depth of the slits the men had dug, casualties were very few. Battalion Headquarters and the ground where No. 4 Company lay up, were most thoroughly drenched, though an officer of No. 3 Company, whose experience was large, described his men's share as "about the worst and most accurate shelling I have been through." They were, in most places, only a hundred yards away from a dug-in enemy bent on blessing them with every round left over in the retreat. During the night, which was calmer, our Artillery dealt with those mixed batteries and groups so well that, although no man could show a finger above his shelter in some of the Company areas, the shelling next day was moderate. The forward

"Rivers round Maubeuge? 'Twas all rivers – Aunelle and the Rhonelle and the Bonelle, an' more, too; an' our Intelligence Officer desirin' to know the last word concernin' each one of 'em before we paddled it . . ."

First Battalion advance guard in front of Maubeuge, 9th November 1918.

posts were still unapproachable, but they sent out patrols from Nos. 1 and 2 Companies to "report on the River Harpies," the next stream to the Selle, and to keep it under observation. This was an enterprise no commander would have dreamed of undertaking even three months ago. The enemy sniping went on. The 2nd Coldstream, who had been moved up to protect the right flank of the 2nd Grenadiers (the Sixty-first Division, being delayed some time over the clearing up and evacuation of Solesmes, was not yet abreast of them), were withdrawn to billets at St. Hilaire in the course of the afternoon; but word came that neither the Grenadiers nor the Irish need look to be relieved. It rained, too, and was freezing cold at night. Another expert in three years of miseries writes: "One of the worst places I have ever been in. Heavy rain all day and night. . . . More shelling if we were seen moving about. Heavy rain all day. . . . Soaked through and shivering with cold." The Diary more temperately: "The men were never dry from the time they left their billets in St. Hilaire on the evening of the 20th, and there was no shelter whatever for any of the Companies." So they relieved them during the night of the 21st, front Companies 1 and 2 returning to the accommodation vacated by their supports, 3 and 4.

Battalion relief came when the 24th Battalion Royal Fusiliers (Second Division) took over from them and the Grenadiers and got into position for their attack the next morning. An early and obtrusive moon made it difficult to fetch away the front-posts, and though the leading Company reached the Selle on its way back at a little after five, the full relief was not completed till half-past nine, when they had to get across-country to the main road and pick up the lorries that took them to "very good billets" at Carnières. Their own Details had seen to that; and they arrived somewhere in the early morning "beat and foot-sore," but without a single casualty in relieving. Their losses for the whole affair up to the time of their relief were one officer (Captain and Adjutant J. B. Keenan) wounded in the face by a piece of shell, the sole casualty at Battalion Headquarters; ten other ranks killed; forty-two wounded, of whom two afterwards died, and two missing – fifty-five in all.

The Companies were officered as follows:

No. 1 Company	No. 2 Company
Capt. A. W. L. Paget, M.C.	Lieut. E. Harvey, M.C.
No. 3 Company	No. 4 Company
Capt. G. L. St. C. Bambridge	2nd Lieut. O. R. Baldwin

Battalion Headquarters

Major A. F. Gordon, M.C.	Capt. J. B. Keenan	Capt. C. A. J. Vernon

Cleaning up began the next day where fine weather in "most delightful billets" was cheered by the news that the Second Division's attack on Vertain had been a great success. In those days they looked no farther than their neighbours on either side.

Every battle, as had been pointed out, leaves its own impression. St. Python opened with a wild but exciting chase in the wet and dark, which, at first, seemed to lead straight into Germany. It ended, as it were, in the sudden rising of a curtain of grey, dank light that struck all the actors dumb and immobile for an enormously long and hungry stretch of time, during which they mostly stared at what they could see of the sky above them, while the air filled with dirt and clods, and single shots pecked and snarled round every stone of each man's limited sky-line; the whole ending in a blur of running water under star-light (that was when they recrossed the Selle river) and confused memories of freezing together in lumps in lorries, followed by a dazed day of "shell-madness," when all ears and eyes were intolerably over-burdened with echoes and pictures, and men preferred to be left alone. But they were washed and cleaned and reclothed with all speed, and handed over to their Company Officers for the drill that chases off bad dreams. The Regimental Sergeant-Major got at them, too, after their hair was cut, and the massed Brigade Drums played in the village square of Carnières, and, ere the end of the month, Inter-Company Football was in full swing.

A draft of ninety-one other ranks joined for duty on the 22nd October. Lieutenant-Colonel Baggallay, M.C., came back from leave and, in the absence of the Brigadier, assumed command of the Brigade, and Captain D. W. Gunston joined.

THE BREAK-UP

On the last day of October they moved from Carnières to St. Hilaire and took over the 3rd Grenadiers' billets in the factory there, all of which, house for house, officers and men, was precisely as before the attack on the 20th, ten days ago. But those ten days had borne the British Armies on that front beyond Valenciennes in the North to within gun-shot of Le Quesnoy in the centre, and to the Sambre Canal, thirty miles away, in the South. Elsewhere, Lille had been evacuated, the lower half of Western Flanders cleared, from the Dutch frontier to Tournai, while almost every hour brought up from one or other of the French and American Armies, on the Meuse and the Argonne, fresh tallies of abandoned stores and guns, and of prisoners gathered in rather than captured. Behind this welter, much as the glare of a mine reveals the façade of a falling town-hall, came word of the collapse of Bulgaria, Turkey and Austria. The whole of the herd of the Hun Tribes were on the move, uneasy and afraid. It remained so to shatter the mass of their retiring forces in France, that they should be in no case to continue any semblance of further war without complete destruction. Were they permitted to slink off unbroken, they might yet make stand behind some shorter line, or manufacture a semblance of a "face" before their own people that would later entail fresh waste and weariness on the world.[1]

---

[1] This, be it remembered, gives roughly the idea at the close of 1918.

The weather and the destruction they had left in their wake was, as on the Somme, aiding them now at every turn, in spite of all our roadmen and Engineers could do. Our airmen took toll of them and their beasts as they retreated along the congested ways; but this was the hour when the delays, divided counsels and specially the strikes of past years had to be paid for, and the giant bombing-planes that should have taught fear and decency far inside the German frontiers were not ready.

A straight drive from the west on to the German lateral communications promised the quickest return. It was laid in the hands of the First, Third and Fifth Armies to send that attack home, and with the French and American pressure from the south, break up the machine past repair.

Men, to-day, say and believe that they knew it would be the last battle of the War, but, at the time, opinions varied; and the expectations of the rank and file were modest. The thing had gone on so long that it seemed the order of life; and, though the enemy everywhere fell back, yet he had done so once before, and over very much the same semi-liquid muck as we were floundering in that autumn's end. "The better the news, the worse the chance of a knock," argued the veterans, while the young hands sent out with high assurance, at draft-parades, that the War was on its last legs, discovered how the machine-gun-fenced rear of retirements was no route-march. ("There was them that came from Warley shouting, ye'll understand; and there was them that came saying nothing at all, and liking it no more than that; but I do not remember any one of us looked to be out of it inside six months. No – not even when we was dancing into Maubeuge. We thought Jerry wanted to get his wind.")

On the 4th November, one week before the end, twenty-six British Divisions moved forward on a thirty-mile front from Oisy to north of Valenciennes, the whole strength of all their Artillery behind them.

The Guards' position had been slightly shifted. Instead of working south of Le Quesnoy, the Division was put in a little north of the town, on the banks of the river Rhônelle, between the Sixty-second Division on their right and the Forty-second on their left. The Battalion had marched from St. Hilaire, in the usual small fine rain, on the 2nd November to billets in Bermerain and bivouacs near-by. It meant a ten-mile tramp of the pre-duckboard era, in the midst of mired horse and lorry-transport, over country where the enemy had smashed every bridge and culvert, blocked all roads and pulling-out places with mine-craters, and sown houses, old trenches and dug-outs with fanciful death-traps. The land was small-featured and full of little hills, so heavily hedged and orcharded that speculative battalions could be lost in it in twenty minutes. There were coveys, too, of French civils, rescued and evacuated out of the villages around, wandering against the stream of east-bound traffic. These forlorn little groups, all persuaded that the War was over and that they could return to their houses to-morrow, had to be shifted and chaperoned somehow through the chaos; but the patience and goodwill of our people was unending.

The wet day closed with a conference at Brigade Headquarters, but the enemy had thrown out our plan for action on that sector by thoughtlessly retiring on both flanks of the Division, as well as a little on the front of it, and final orders were not fixed till after midnight on the 3rd November.

The 1st and 2nd Guards Brigades were to attack, the 3rd in reserve. Of the 1st Brigade, the 2nd Coldstream would take the line as far as the first objective; the 2nd Grenadiers would then come through and carry on to the next line, the Irish Guards in support. The Brigade's assembly-area was across the Rhônelle river, east of the long and straggling village of Villers-Pol, on the Jenlain – Le Quesnoy road. Zero was fixed for 7.20. The Battalion marched from Bermerain, and met its first enemy shell as it was going under the Valenciennes railway-embankment. What remained of the roads were badly congested with troops, and one gets the idea that the Staff-work was casual. To begin with, the Battalion found the 3rd Grenadiers and the 1st Scots Guards between themselves and the 2nd Grenadiers, which was not calculated to soothe any C.O. desirous of keeping his appointment. Apparently they got through the Scots Guards; but when they reached the Rhônelle, its bridge being, of course, destroyed, and the R.E. working like beavers to mend it, they had to unship their Lewis-guns from the limbers, tell the limbers to come on when the bridge was usable, and pass the guns over by hand. While thus engaged the Scots Guards caught them up, went through them triumphantly, made exactly the same discovery that the Irish had done, and while they in turn were wrestling with their limbers, the Irish, who had completed their unshipping, went through them once more, and crossed the Rhônelle on the heels of the last man of the 3rd Grenadiers – "one at a time, being assisted up the bank by German prisoners." By the mercy of the Saints, who must have been kept busy all night, the shelling on the bridge and its approaches ceased while that amazing procession got over. They were shelled as they re-formed on the top of the steep, opposite bank, but "by marvellous good-luck no casualties"; got into Artillery formation; were shelled again, and this time hit, and long-range machine-gun fire met them over the next crest of ground. It was all ideal machine-gun landscape. The 2nd Grenadiers, whom they were supporting, had been held up by low fire from the village of Wagnies-le-Petit on their left, a little short of the first objective, which was the road running from Wagnies, south to Frasnoy. The Battalion dug in behind them where it was, and after an hour or so the enemy opened fire with one solitary, mad trench-mortar. Not more than a dozen rounds were sent over, and these, very probably, because the weapon happened to lie under their hands, and was used before being abandoned. And luck had it that this chance demonstration should kill Lieutenant A. L. Bain ("Andy" Bain), who had joined for duty not a week ago. He was the last officer killed in the Battalion, and one of the best. Lieutenant F. S. L. Smith, M.C., was also wounded. They stayed in their scratch-holes till late in the afternoon, as the troops of the Forty-second Division on their left were held up too, but the 2nd Guards Brigade on their right gradually worked forward. Some of their Divisional field-guns came up and shelled Wagnies-le-Petit into silence, and at half-past four orders arrived for the Battalion to go through the 2nd Grenadiers and continue at large into the dusk that was closing on the blind, hedge-screened country. There was no particular opposition beyond stray shells, but the boggy banked Aunelle had to be crossed on stretchers, through thick undergrowth, in a steep valley. Everything after that seemed to be orchards, high hedges, and sunk and raised roads, varied with soft bits of cultivation, or hopelessly muddled-up cul-de-sacs of farm-tracks. The Companies played blind-man's buff among these obstacles in the pitch-dark, as they hunted alternately for each other and the troops on their flanks. There was "very heavy shelling" on the three most advanced Companies as well as on Brigade Headquarters throughout the night. The men dug in where they were; and casualties, all told, came to about twenty. Very early on the 5th November the 3rd Guards Brigade passed through them and continued the advance. Preux-au-Sart, the village behind them, had been taken by the 2nd Brigade the evening and the night before, so the Battalion "came out of its slits" and went back to billet in its relieved and rejoicing streets, where "the inhabitants on coming out of their cellars in the morning were delighted to find British troops again, and showed the greatest cordiality." If rumour be true, they also showed them how easily their Hun conquerors had been misled and hoodwinked in the matter of good vintages buried and set aside against this very day. "The men were very comfortable."

The fact that Austria was reported out of the War did not make the next day any less pleasant, even though it rained, and "all the windows in the Battalion Headquarters were broken by one shell." Battalion Headquarters had come through worse than broken glass in its time, but was now beginning to grow fastidious.

On the afternoon of the 7th November the Battalion marched to Bavai over muddy roads in drizzle. Even then, men have said, there was no general belief in the end of Armageddon. They looked for a lull, perhaps; very possibly some sort of conference and waste of time which would give the enemy breath for fresh enterprise. A few, however, insist that the careful destruction of the roads and railway-bridges and the indifference of the prisoners as they poured in warned them of the real state of affairs. ("It looked as if the Jerries had done all the harm they could think of, and were chucking it – like boys caught robbing an orchard. There wasn't an atom of dignity or decency about any of 'em. Just dirt and exhausted Jerrydom.") What the Battalion felt most was having to make detours round broken bridges, and to dig ramps in mine-craters on the roads to get their Lewis-guns across. They jettisoned their second-line transport at a convenient Château outside Bavai on this account; found that there were no arrangements for billeting in the town, so made their own, and, while Bavai was being shelled, got into houses and again were "very comfortable." The 2nd Brigade were in the front line on the railway, and next day the 1st Brigade were to lead and capture Maubeuge, seven miles down a road which cut across the line of their earlier stages in the retreat from Mons, and three miles, as a shell ranges, from the village of Malplaquet.

They began their last day, half an hour after midnight, marching "as a battalion" out of Bavai with their Lewis-gun limbers. Twice they were slightly shelled; once at least they had to unpack and negotiate more mine-craters at cross-roads. It was a populous world through which they tramped, and all silently but tensely awake – a world made up of a straight, hard road humped above the level of the fields in places, rather like the Menin road when it was young, but with untouched tiled houses alongside. Here and there one heard the chatter of a machine-gun, as detached and irrelevant as the laugh of an idiot. It would cease, and a single field-gun would open as on some private quarrel. Then silence, and a suspicion, born out of the darkness, that the road was mined. Next, orders to the Companies to spread themselves in different directions in the dark, to line ditches and the like for fear of attack. Then an overtaking, at wrecked cross-roads, of some of the 2nd Brigade, who reported patrols of the 3rd Grenadiers had pushed on into Maubeuge without opposition, and that the rest of that Battalion was gone on. Just before dawn, No. 4 Company of the Irish, marching on a road parallel to the highway, ran into a company of Germans retiring. The Diary says: "A short sharp fight ensued in which five of the enemy were wounded and twelve captured, the rest getting off in the dark." But there is a legend (it may have grown with the years) that the two bodies found themselves suddenly almost side by side on converging tracks, and that the Irish, no word given, threw back to the instincts of Fontenoy – faced about, front-rank kneeling, rear-rank standing, and in this posture destroyed all that company. It was a thing that might well have come about darkling in a land scattered with odds and ends of drifting, crazed humanity. No. 2 Company solemnly reported the capture of two whole prisoners just after they had crossed the railway in the suburbs of Maubeuge, which they passed through on the morning of the 9th, and by noon were duly established and posted, Company by Company, well to the east of it. No. 2 Company lay in the village of Assevant, with pickets on the broken bridge over the river there, an observation-line by day and all proper supports; No. 4 Company in posts on the road and down to the river, and Nos. 1 and 3 in reserve; Yeomanry and Corps Cyclists out in front as though the War were eternal.

AFTER THE ARMISTICE

And, thus dispersed, after a little shelling of Assevant during the night, the Irish Guards received word that "an Armistice was declared at 11a.m. this morning, November 11."

Men took the news according to their natures. Indurated pessimists, after proving that it was a lie, said it would be but an interlude. Others retired into themselves as though they had been shot, or went stiffly off about the meticulous execution of some trumpery detail of kit-cleaning. Some turned round and fell asleep then and there; and a few lost all holds for a while. It was the appalling new silence of things that soothed and unsettled them in turn. They did not realize till all sounds of their trade ceased, and the stillness stung in their ears as soda-water stings on the palate, how entirely these had been part of their strained bodies and souls. ("It felt like falling through into nothing, ye'll understand. Listening for what wasn't there, and tryin' not to shout when you remembered for why.") Men coming up from Details Camp, across old "unwholesome" areas, heard nothing but the roar of the lorries on which they had stolen their lift, and rejoiced with a childish mixture of fear as they topped every unscreened rise that was now mere scenery such as tourists would use later. To raise the head, without thought of precaution against what might be in front or on either flank, into free, still air was the first pleasure of that great release. To lie down that night in a big barn beside unscreened braziers, with one's smiling companions who talked till sleep overtook them, and, when the last happy babbler had dropped off, to hear the long-forgotten sound of a horse's feet trotting evenly on a hard road under a full moon, crowned all that had gone before. Each man had but one thought in those miraculous first hours:" – even I myself, here – have come through the War!" To scorn the shelter of sunken roads, hedges, walls or lines of trees, and to extend in unmartial crowds across the whole width of a *pavé*, were exercises in freedom that he arrived at later. 'We cannot realize it at all." . . . "So mad with joy we don't feel yet what it all means." The home letters were all in this strain.

The Battalion was relieved on the 12th November by the 2nd Grenadiers and billeted in the Faubourg de Mons. All Maubeuge was hysterical with its emotions of release, and well provided with wines which, here as elsewhere, had somehow missed the German nose. The city lived in her streets, and kissed everybody in khaki, that none should complain. But the Battalion was not in walking-out order, and so had to be inspected rigorously. Morning-drill outside billets next day was in the nature of a public demonstration – to the scandal of the grave Sergeants.

On the 14th a great thanksgiving-service was held in the Cathedral for all the world, the Battalion providing the Guard of Honour at the Altar, and lining the Place d'Armes at the presentation of a flag by the Mayor of Maubeuge to the Major-General. The massed drums of the Division played in the square in the afternoon, an event to be remembered as long as the Battalion Dinner of the evening. They were all route-marched next morning for an hour and a half to steady them, and on the 16th, after dinner, set off in freezing weather for the first stage of their journey to Cologne. It ran via Bettignies and then to Villers-Sire-Nicole, a matter of five and a half miles.

On the 17th they crossed the Belgian frontier at Givet and reached Binche through a countryside already crowded with returning English, French, Italian and Belgian prisoners. One Diary notes them like migrating birds, "all hopping along the road, going due west." Binche mobbed the Drums as one man and woman when they played in the town at Retreat, but it was worse at Charleroi on the 19th, where they could hardly force their way through the welcoming crowds. The place was lit from end to end, and the whole populace shouted for joy at deliverance.

Now that they had returned as a body to civilization, it was needful they should be dressed, and they were paraded for an important inspection of great-coats, and, above all, gloves. That last, and the fact that belts, when walking out, were worn over the greatcoats, were sure signs that war was done, and His Majesty's Foot Guards had come into their own. But they found time at Charleroi, among more pleasant duties, to arrest three German soldiers disguised as civilians.

On the 23rd they left for Sart-St.-Laurent, whose Mayor, beneath a vast Belgian flag, met and escorted them into the town. The country changed as they moved on, from flat coal-districts to untouched hills and woods. On the 24th they picked up a dump of eighty-four guns of all calibres, handed over according to the terms of the Armistice; passed through a tract of heavily wired country, which was "evidently intended for the Meuse Line that the Germans were to have fallen back on"; and a little later crossed (being the first of the Division to do so) the steeply banked, swiftly running Meuse by a pontoon bridge. Next their road climbed into Nanine, one of the loveliest villages, they thought, they had ever seen. But their hearts were soft in those days, and all that world of peace seemed good. They dared not halt at Sorinne-la-Longue the next day, as the place was infected with influenza ("Spanish fever"), so pushed on to Lesves, and on the 26th November to Sorée, where was another wayside dump of thirty or forty Hun guns. It is noteworthy that the sight of the discarded tools of their trade frankly bored them. Where a Hun, under like circumstances, would have re-triumphed and called on his servile Gods these Islanders (of whom almost a half were now English) were afflicted with a curious restlessness and strong desire to get done with the work in hand. All their world was under the same reaction. They had to wait at Sorée for three days, as supplies were coming up badly. Indeed, on the 28th November, the Diary notes bitterly that "for the first time in the War the supplies failed to arrive. The Quartermaster managed to improvise breakfasts for the Battalion." It was not all the fault of bad roads or the dispersion of the troops. The instant the strain was taken off, there was a perceptible slackening everywhere, most marked in the back-areas, on the clerical and forwarding sides. Every one wanted to get home at once, and worked with but half a mind: which, also, is human nature.

They were on the road again by December 5 with the rest of their Brigade, and reached Mean in the afternoon over muddy roads. By the 6th they were at Villers-St.-Gertrude hill-marching through beautiful scenery, which did not amuse them, because, owing to the state of communications, supplies were delayed again. So, on the 8th December at Lierneux, fifteen miles from Villers-St.-Gertrude, another halt was called for another three days, while Company Officers, homesick as their men, drilled them in the winter dirt. On the 11th they crossed the German frontier line at Recht, and the drums played the Battalion over to the Regimental March. ("But, ye'll understand, we was *all* wet the most of that time and fighting with the mud an' our boots. 'Twas Jerry's own weather the minute we set foot in his country, and we none of us felt like conquerors.

We was just dhrippin' Micks.") At Vielsalm, almost the last village outside Germany, they picked up a draft of sixty men to share with them the horrors of peace ahead, and a supply-system gone to bits behind them.

Their road wound through small and inconspicuous hamlets among wooded hills, by stretches of six or seven hours' marching a day. The people they had to deal with seemed meek and visibly oppressed with the fear of rough treatment. That removed from their minds, they stepped aside and looked wonderingly at the incomprehensible enemy that tramped through their streets, leaving neither ruin nor rape behind. By the 18th December the advance had reached Lovenich, and, after two days' rest there, they entered Cologne on the 23rd December with an absence of display that might or might not have been understood by the natives. They had covered more than two hundred miles over bad roads in bad boots that could not be repaired nor thrown away, and but one man had fallen out. The drums played "Brian Boru" when they entered the Hohenzollern Ring; their Major-General beheld that last march, and they were duly photographed in the wet; while the world that saw such photographs in the weekly illustrated papers was honestly convinced that the Great War and all war was at an end for evermore.

Then really serious trouble overtook them, which was, in some sort, a forecast of the days to come. Their billets at Nippes, in the suburbs of Cologne, were excellent and clean, though, of course, in need of the usual "improvements" which every Battalion of the Brigade is bound to make; but on Christmas Day, owing to transport difficulties, the men's Christmas Dinner did not arrive! This thing had never happened in the whole history of the War! Pressure of work in the front line had delayed that dinner, as on the Somme; enemy attentions had caused it to be eaten in haste, a sort of Passover, as in the dread Salient, but complete breakdown was unheard of. The Battalion, rightly, held it mortal sin, and spoke their minds about the transport which was fighting mud and distance across the hills as loyally as ever. It was the back-areas that had been caught unprepared by the peace. But, on Christmas Night (superb and unscrupulous Staff-work went to secure it), a faithful lorry ploughed in from Paris with what was wanted, and on Boxing Day the full and complete Christmas dinner was served, and for the fifth and last time their Commanding Officer performed the sacred ritual of "going round the dinners."

They sat them down, twenty-two officers and six hundred and twenty-eight other ranks, and none will know till Judgment Day how many ghosts were also present. For the first time since August '14 the monthly returns showed no officer or man killed, wounded or missing. The two Battalions had lost in all two thousand three hundred and forty-nine dead, including one hundred and fifteen officers. Their total of wounded was five thousand seven hundred and thirty-nine. Of both these the 1st Battalion, by virtue of thirteen months longer in the field, could reckon more than a generous half.

They were too near and too deeply steeped in the War that year's end to realize their losses. Their early dead, as men talked over the past in Cologne, seemed to belong to immensely remote ages. Even those of that very spring, of whom friends could still say, "If So-and-so had only lived to see this!" stood as

271

far removed as the shadowy great ones of the pre-bomb, pre-duckboard twilight; and, in some inexpressible fashion, they themselves appeared to themselves the only living people in an uncaring world. Yet Cologne was alive with soldiery; roads were roaring full, as communications were restored; men stood guard over visible gun and ammunition dumps. The Battalion joined in marches to the bridge-heads, attended football matches, saw hosts of new faces belonging to new troops of all breeds; and watched about them, in the wet, grey weather, the muddy-faced Hun-folk, methodically as usual, trying to find out just how far it was expedient to go with the heralds of the alleged new order.

"But ye'll understand, when everything was said and done, there was nothing real to it at all, except when we got to talking and passing round the names of them we wished was with us. We was lonely in those days. The half of us was Church of England by then, too. But we were lonely, ye'll understand, as units. And our billets, mind ye, magnificent, with walls and lockers and doors and all. The same for the Officers! And there was Mr. – that I'd known well any time these last two winters, freezing and swearing alongéside of me in any shell-hole we could find, and glad to be out of the wind – and now, him cursin' in his quarters because he had not the Jerry-talk for the German for: 'Turn off that dam' steam-heat!' And that's war *all*so.

"But ye might tell that we was lonely, most of all. Before God, we Micks was lonely!"

COMMANDING OFFICERS
1ST BATTALION

From August 12, 1914

Rank	Name	From	To
B.E.F.			
Lt.-Col.	Hon. G. H. Morris	12.8.14	1.9.14
Major	H. H. Stepney	2.9.14	17.9.14
Lt.-Col.	Lord Ardee, C.B., C.B.E.	18.9.14	3.11.14
Lt.-Col. (temp)	Hon. J. F. Trefusis, D.S.O.	4.11.14	15.8.15
Lt.-Col. (temp)	G. H. C. Madden	16.8.15	1.11.15
Lt.-Col. (temp)	R. C. A. McCalmont, D.S.O.	2.11.15	2.3.17
Lt.-Col. (actg)	H. R. Alexander, D.S.O., M.C.	3.3.17	23.5.17
Lt.-Col. (actg)	C. E. Rocke, D.S.O.	24.5.17	11.7.17
Lt.-Col. (actg)	R. V. Pollok, C.B.E., D.S.O.	12.7.17	19.6.18
Lt.-Col. (actg)	R. R. C. Baggallay, D.S.O., M.C.	20.6.18	To return to England

APPENDIX A

OFFICERS: KILLED IN ACTION OR DIED OF WOUNDS
WOUNDED IN ACTION
MISSING
REWARDS

KILLED IN ACTION OR DIED OF WOUNDS
Lieut.-Colonel C. FitzClarence, V.C.
(Temp. Brigadier-General),
In Command of 1st Guards Brigade, 12.11.14.
Lieut.-Colonel G. C. Nugent, M.V.O. (Temp. Brigadier-General),
In Command of 5th London Infantry Brigade, 31.5.15
Lieut.-Col. The Hon. J. F. Hepburn-Stuart-Forbes-Trefusis, D.S.O.
(Temp. Brigadier-General),
In Command of the 20th Brigade after Commanding 1st Battalion, 24.10.15.
Lieut.-Colonel The Hon. G. H. Morris, 1.9.14

MAJORS
T. M. D. Bailie, 15.9.16
The Lord Desmond FitzGerald, MC., 3.3.16
The Earl of Rosse, 15.6.18
H. F. Crichton, 1.9.14
H. A. Herbert-Stepney, 6.11.14
G. H. C. Madden (Temp. Lieut.-Col.), 12.11.15
G. E. S. Young, 31.3.17

CAPTAINS
H. H. Berners, 14.9.14
The Lord Arthur Hay, 14.9.14
The Hon. A. E. Mulholland, 1.11.14
E. G. Mylne, 12.6.15
The Hon. P. J. H. Ogilvy, M.C., 9.10.17
E. C. Stafford-King-Harman, 6.11.14
C. A. Tisdall, 1.9.14
V. C. J. Blake, 28.1.16

M. V. Gore-Langton, M.C., 10.10.15
E. J. F. Gough, 30.12.14
J. N. Guthrie, 13.5.15
The Lord John Hamilton, 6.11.14
L. R. Hargreaves, MC., 25.9.16

LIEUTENANTS

A. L. Bain, 4.11.18
R. St. J. Blacker-Douglass, M.C., 1.2.15
E. Budd, M.C. (Acting Captain) 8.8.18
S. E. F. Christy, 12.7.16
L. S. Coke, 31.10.14
H. J. B. Eyre, 15.7.17
J. K. M. Greer, MC., 3.10.16
R. H. W. Heard, MC., died 3.3.19
K. R. Mathieson, 1.11.14
J. H. Nash, 27.8.18
F. L. Pusch, D.S.O., 27.6.16
H. Shears, 4.7.17
T. K. Walker, 24.4.16
L. C. Whitefoord, 15.9.16
H. R. Baldwin, 29.8.18
G. Brooke, 7.10.14
T. Butler-Stoney, 1.10.17
B. S. Close, 27.9. 18
N. F. Durant, 30.11.17
V. W. D. Fox, 18.5.15
The Lord Guernsey, 14.9.14
W. E. Hope, 6.11.14
G. M. Maitland, 1.11.14
T. Musgrave, 6.2.15
C. Pease, 18.9.16
R. J. P. Rodakowski, 9.10.17
C. R. Tisdall, E. MC., 15.9.16
J. N. Ward, 29.8.18

2ND LIEUTENANTS

T. Allen, 25.2.15
N. Butler, 15.9.16
H. A. Connofly, 27.8.18
V. J. S. French, 10.10.18
F. H. N. Lee, 4.7.16
E. C. G. Lord, 8.5.18
C. S. O'Brien, M.C., 27.9.18
T. S. V. Stoney, 9.10.17
N. L. Woodroffe, 6.11.14
G. P. Boyd, 3.9.17
T. A. Carey, 5.12.17
L. H. L. Carver, 26.5.18
H. V. Fanshawe, 11.10.17
H. S. Keating, 20.1.15
L. C. L. Lee, 1.2.15

H. Marion-Crawford, 16.4.15
J. M. Stewart, 1.4.15

OFFICERS ATTACHED TO 1ST BATTALION
Capt. Rev. J. Gwynne, 11.10.15
Lieut. C. de B. G. Persse (7th Dragoon Guards), 18.5.15
Capt. H. J. S. Shields, R.A.M.C., 26.10.14
2nd Lieutenant Davis (U.S.A. Medical Service), 27.9.18

IRISH GUARDS OFFICERS WITH OTHER REGIMENTS
Lieut. J. N. Marshall, V.C., MC. (Acting Lieut.-Colonel attached Lancs. Fusiliers), 4.11.18
2nd Lieut. C. H. Eilcart (Guards Machine-Gun Regiment), 27.9.18
2nd Lieut. E. H. Fallows (att. Guards Machine-Gun Regiment), 25.3.18
2nd Lieut. A. G. Hunt (Guards Machine-Gun Regiment), 4.11.18
2nd Lieut. N. King (att. Guards Machine-Gun Regiment), 26.5.18
Lieut. C. H. Lord Settrington (died of wounds received in action with the Russian Relief Force), 24.8.19
Lieut. J. C. Zigomala, M.B.E. (killed whilst serving with the Russian Relief Force), 25.8.19

WOUNDED IN ACTION

Major Lord D. FitzGerald, M.C. (twice w.)	1.9.14; Oct. 1915
R. St. J. Blacker-Douglass, MC.	1.9.14
Capt. Hon. H. W. Gough, M.C.	14.9.14
Capt. J. N. Guthrie (twice w.)	14.9.14; (v. slightly) 16.4.15
Lieut. Col. E. B. Greer, MC.	28.10.14
Capt. W. C. N. Reynolds.	31.10.14
Major R. H. Ferguson (twice w.)	31.10.14; 23.6.17
Lieut.-Col. Hon. H. Alexander, L. of H. (twice w.) D.S.O., M.C.	1.11.14; Oct. 1917
Capt. M. V. Gore-Langton, M.C.	1.11.14
Capt. Lord Kingston	1.11.14
Lieut.-Col. Hon. T. Vesey (twice w.)	31.10.14; 27.9.15
Col. Lord Ardee, C.B.	7.11.14; gassed 4.4.18
Major R. S. Webber	12.11.14
Capt. C. R. Harding	12.11.14
Capt. P. H. Antrobus, M.C.	13.11.14; gassed July 1917
Capt. G. P. Gough	25.12.14
Capt. F. H. Witts, MC. (three times w.)	25.12.14; Oct. 1917; 25.5.18
J. T. Robyns (accidentally)	17.1.15
Major P. S. Long-Innes, M.C. (twice w.).	1.2.15; 15.9.16
Capt. A. H. Blom	1.2.15; 5.5. 25.9.16
Capt. F. F. Graham	2.2.15
Capt. Hon. H. A. V. St. G. Harmsworth (twice w.)	11.2.15; 2.8.15
Capt. T. E. G. Nugent (accidentally) (twice w.)	24.3.15; 3.3.16
Capt. C. Pease (twice w.)	16.5.15; 15.9.16
Capt. R. B. H. Kemp	17.5.15
Capt. E. G. Mylne	17.5.15
Capt. S. G. Tallents	17.5.15
Lieut. Col. P. L. Reid	18.5.15
Capt. H. T. A. H. Boyse	18.5.15
Major W. E. Earl of Rosse	18.5.15
Capt. R. S. G. Paget (twice w.)	18.5.15; 18.7.17
Major G. E. S. Young (twice w.)	18.5.15; 16.3.17
E. W. Campbell	18.5.15

Capt. J. R. Ralli	18 5.15
Capt. Hon. W. S. P. Alexander, D.S.O.	18.5.15
J. K. M. Greer, MC. (twice w.)	18.5.15; 15.9.16
Capt. A. W. L. Paget (twice w.)	19.5.15; 27.7.17
Capt. Sir G. H. Burke, Bt	19.5.15
L. S. Straker	17.6.15
K. W. Hogg	31.7.15
Brig.-Gen. R. J. Cooper, C.B., C.V.O. (M.E.F.)	16.8.15
W. B. Stevens	27.9.15
R. H. S. Grayson (twice w.)	27.9.15; Oct. 1917
R. H. W. Heard	7.10.15; gassed 26.4.18
J. Grayling-Major	8.10.15
Lieut.-Col. G. H. C. Madden	11.10.15
Capt. F. P. H. Synge, M.C. (twice w.)	21.10.15; July 1916
T. F. Tallents, MC. (twice w.)	21.10.15; Oct. 1917
Capt. G. N. Hubbard	16.11.15
S. E. F. Christy	20.12.15
Capt. R. J. P. Rodakowski (twice w.)	25.3.16; 25.9.16
F. H. N. Lee	18.6.16
Temp. Major J. N. Marshall, V.C., MC., attached Lancs. Fus. (twice w.)	19.6.16; June 1917
Lieut.-Col. R. V. Pollok, D.S.O. (twice w.)	25.7.16; 28.3.18; gassed 11.4. 18
Capt. D. C. Parsons	13.9.16
J. C. Zigomala (twice w.)	13.9.16; 30.3.18
Capt. A. C. W. Innes, MC.	15.9.16
Count J. E. de Salis (twice w.)	15.9.16 July 1917
H. C. Holmes	15.9.16
T. Butler-Stoney	15.9.16
D. J. Hegarty	16.9.16
J. N. Ward (twice w.)	15.9.16; 9.4.18
Capt. R. Rankin	15.9.16
Major C. E. A. Rocke, D.S.O	15.9.16
G. V. Williams, M.C. (twice w.)	25.9.16; 13.10.18
T. C. Gibson (twice w.)	25.9.16; 13.9.17
Capt. P. B. Woodhouse, MC., R.A.M.C.(attached) (twice w.)	25.9.16; Oct. 1917
Rev. F. M. Browne, MC. (attached) (twice w.)	25.9.16; Oct. 1917
Capt. L. R. Hargreaves, MC.	25.9.16
C. E. R. Hanbury	Jan. 1917
J. Orr	2.2.17
D. S. Browne (twice w.)	25.2.17; 9.10.17
W. C. Mumford, MC.	15.3.17
N. B. Bagenal (three times w.)	13.7.17; Oct. 1917; 30.3.18
H. J. Lofting	18.7.17
Capt. J. B. Keenan (twice w.)	21.7.17; 21.10.18
H. H. Maxwell (twice w.)	26.7.17; 10.10.17
R. L. Dagger	29.7.17
N. M. Buller (twice w.)	31.7.17; 24.5.18
E. H. Dowler (twice w.)	31.7.17; Oct. 1917
Capt. H. F. d'A. S. Law, MC.	1.8.17
H. E. Van der Noot	3.8.17
Major R. R. C. Baggallay, M.C.	14.8.17
Capt. T. F. MacMahon, M.C.	11.9.17
B. S.Close	Oct. 1917
T. Corry, D.C.M.	Oct. 1917

E. M. Harvey, M.C.	Oct. 1917
Capt. R. B. S. Reford, M.C.	Oct. 1917
Capt. Hon. H. V. Harmsworth, M.C.	27.11.17
P. M. Riley (twice w.)	30.11.17; 24.5.18
G. K. Thompson, M.C.	30.11.17
G. E. Van der Noot	30.11.17
Capt. W. Joyce (twice w.)	30.11.17; 29.8.18
A. F. L. Gordon, M.C.	19.1.18
Capt. the Hon. H. B. O'Brien	26.3.18
D. J. B. Fitzgerald	27.3.18
F. G. de Stacpoole	2.4.18
A. S. Stokes	2.4.18
Lieut.F. S. L. Smith, M.C. (twice w.)	12.4.18; 4.11.18
C. L. Browne	13.4.18
Capt. G. L. Bambridge	14.4.18
C. A. J. Nicholson	25.4.18
G. C. MacLachlan	29.4.18
T. B Maughan	2.5.18
Capt. C. W. W. Bence-Jones (twice w.)	24.5.18; 27.9.18
P. R. J. Barry	24.5.18
D. R. Williams	25.5.18
Lieut. J. A. M. Faraday	22.8.18
Lieut. P. S. MacMahon	29.8.18
G. T. Heaton	29.8.18
H. Connolly	29.8.18
A. E. Hutchinson	29.8.18
Lieut. C. A. J. Vernon	18.9.18; gassed 29.8.18
Lieut. G. F. Mathieson	27.9.18
A. R. Boyle	27.9.18
Capt. the Hon. B. A. A. Ogilvy	27.9.18

MISSING

Capt. Viscount Castlerosse (wounded and since found)	1.9.14
Hon. A. Herbert (wounded and since found)	1.9.14
Lord R. Innes-Ker (wounded and since found)	1.9.14
G. M. Maitland	1.11.14
Capt. Lord A.J. Hamilton	6.11.14

REWARDS
VICTORIA CROSS

Acting Lieut. Colonel J. N. Marshall	13.2.19

C.B.E.

Brig.-General R. Le N. Lord Ardee (Base Comdt.)	3.6.19
Major R. V. Pollok (Comdt. Sch. of Instr.)	3.6.19

D.S.O.

Major H. R. L. G. Alexander	1.1.16
Captain W. S. P. Alexander	20.8.17
Major R. R. C. Baggallay	1.1.19
Major Hon. A. C. S. Chichester (Staff)	3.6.18
Captain A. F. L. Gordon	12.12.19
Colonel R. C. A. McCalmont	1.1.17
Major R. V. Pollok	28.12.17

Lieut. F. L. Pusch (19th Bn. London Regiment)	Sept. 1915
Lieut.-Colonel C. E. A. S. Rocke	28.12.17
Major (Temp. Brig.-Gen.) Hon. J. F. Hepburn	16.2.15
Captain F. H. Witts (Staff)	2.6.19

O.B.E

Major Hon. A. C. S. Chichester (Staff)	3.6.19
Captain T. C. Gibson	–
Major C. R. Harding	3.6.19
Major St. J. R. Pigott	–
Lieut.-Colonel P. L. Reid	4.6.18
Captain W. C. N. Reynolds	3.6.19
Captain S. G. Tallents	3.2.20
Captain R. G. C. Yerburgh	3.6.19

M.B.E.

Captain J. S. N. FitzGerald (Staff)	–
Captain and Qr. H. Hickie	12.12.19

MILITARY CROSS

Major H. R. L. G. Alexander	1.1.16
Captain P. H. Antrobus	28.12.17
Major R. R. C. Baggallay(Staff)	1.1.17
Captain G. L.St. C. Bambridge	13.9.18
Lieut. P. R. J. Barry	10.11.18
Lieut. R. St. J. Blacker-Douglass	10.3.15
Captain H. Bracken (att.20th K.L. Regt.)	–
Lieut. P. B. Brown	1917
Lieut. D. S. Browne	10.12.19
Rev. F. S.du Moulin Browne (att. 1st Ba. I.G.)	11.1.19
Lieut. E. Budd	7.4.17
Lieut. H. A. A. Collett	10.11.18
Lieut. J. A. M. Faraday	15.10.18
Lieut. W. D. Faulkner	1.1.19
Major Lord D. Fitzgerald	22.6.15
Captain J. S. N. Fitzgerald	–
2nd Lieut. R. Gamble	1.1.17
Captain A. F. L. Gordon	1.1.17
Captain M.V. Gore-Langton	6.9.15
Major H. W. Gough	1.1.15
Lieut.-Colonel E. B.Greer	22.6.15
Lieut. J. K. M. Greer	Sept.1916
Captain D. W. Gunston	28.10.17
Lieut. C. E. Hammond	3.1.18
Captain L. R. Hargreaves	14.11.16
Captain H. A. V. St. G. Harmsworth	1.1.18
Lieut. E. M. Harvey	5.11.17
Lieut. D. J. Hegarty	10.1.19
Captain and Qr. H. Hickie	3.6.18
Lieut. A. E. Hutchinson	15.10.18
Captain A. C. W. Innes	10.3.15
Captain H. F. d'A. S. Law	5.6.17
Lieut. M. B. Levy	30.10.17
Major P. 5. Long-l	14.11.16
Lieut. (Acting Lieut.-Col.) J. N. Marshall	7.11.18
Captain T. F. MacMahon	14.11.16
Lieut. D. A. B. Moodie	3.1.18

Captain W. C. Mumford	14.11.15
Captain T. E. G. Nugent	30.9.18
2nd Lieut. C. S. O'Brien	30.9.18
Captain Hon.H. B. O'Brien (Staff)	26.7.18
Captain Hon. P. J. H. Ogilvy	14.11.16
Lieut. Hon. B. A. A. Ogilvy	10.11.18
Captain A. W. L. Paget	15.10.18
Lieut. R. B. S. Reford	23.4.18
Lieut. F. S. L. Smith	26.7.18
Captain G. K. Thompson	15.3.16
Lieut. C. R. Tisdall	1916
Captain C. A. J. Vernon	10.11.18
Lieut.G. V. Williams	2.10.16
Captain F. H. Witts	1.1.17
Captain Randal Woodhouse, R.A.M.C. (att.lst Bn. 1G.)	31.5.16

CROIX DE GUERRE

Major Hon. C. A. S. Chichester (Staff)	16.5.19
Major R. V. Pollok	28.12.17
Lieut.-Colonel T. E Vesey	17.8.18
Captain R. G. C. Yerburgh (Staff)	21.8.19

APPENDIX B

W.O.s, N.C.O.s AND MEN KILLED IN ACTION
OR DIED OF WOUNDS OR DISEASE

Abbey, John, 3913, L.-Cpl., *k. in a. 8.8.15*

Adams, Henry, 8555, Pte., *k. in a. 2.8.17*

Ahern, Patrick, 5888, Pte., *k. in a. 17.9.16*

Ahern, William, 6045, Pte., *k. in a. 18.6.16*

Allen, Charles, 1535, Pte., *k. in a. 18.11.14*

Allgood, Henry, 5600, L.-Cpl., *d. 16.2.15*

Allingham, Edward V., 11433, Pte., *k. in a. 27.8.18*

Anstis, Robert, 6390, Pte., *d. of w. 27.9.16*

Antrobus, Fred, 8399, Pte., *d. of w. 5.11.18*

Appleby, Francis, 8571, Pte., *k. in a. 14.1.18*

Arlow, Samuel J., 7905, Pte., *d. of w. 30.11.15*

Armstrong, Thomas, 1200, Pte., *k. in a. 6.11.14*

Aspell, Michael, 9116, Pte., *k. in a. 17.9.16*

Atherton, Leonard, 12180, Pte., *k. in a. 27.3.18*

Bailey, Abraham, 1627, Sgt., *k. in a. 6.11.14*

Bailey, Herbert C., 11865, Pte., *k. in a. 30.11.17*

Baines, James, 12235, Pte., *k. in a. 12.4.18*

Bannon, John, 8333, Pte., *k. in a. 9.10.17*

Barry, William, 2413, Pte., *k. in a. 1.11.14*

Barter, Joseph, 5962, L.-Cpl., *k. in a. 25.1.16*

Bass, Joseph, 6401, Pte., *k. in a. 2.12.15*

Bates, Oliver, 4686, Pte., *k. in a. 18.5.15*

Beardmore, George E., 12345, Pte., *d. of w. 26.7.19*

Beazley, Christopher, 11551, Pte., *k. in a. 11.9.17*

Beggen, John, 10962, Pte., *k. in a. 9.10.17*

Beirne, John, 1596, L.-Cpl., *d. 2.11.14*

Bell, John A., 3568, Pte., *k. in a. 1.9.14*

Bell, John, 12343, Pte., *k. in a. 27.8.18*

Bell, Patrick, 5195, Pte., *k. in a. 5.12.17*

Bell, Robert, 2872, L.-Cpl., *k. in a. 1.2.15*

Benbow, Edwin J., 2783, Pte., *k. in a. 18.5.15*

Bigger, Robert J., 12090, Pte., *k. in a. 30.11.17*

Biggins, Richard, 2375, Pte., *k. in a. 14.9.14*

Birmingham, Patrick, 3802, Pte., *k. in a. 6.11.14*

Birney, John, 2942, Pte., *k. in a. 6.11.14*

Black, George, 4301, Pte., *k. in a. 6.11.14*

Black, Peter, 3168, Pte., *d. of w. 16.11.16*

Blakely, John F., 7673, Pte., *k. in a. 27.11.17*

Blood, Michael, 2925, Pte., *d. of w. 6.9.14*

Boland, Henry, 9528, Pte., *k. in a. 9.10.17*

Boland, John, 9775, Pte., *k. in a. 9.10.17*

Boland, Patrick J., 3358, Pte., *k. in a. 15.9.14*

Boland, William, 5779, Pte., *k. in a. 10.10.15*

Bolger, William, 4412, Pte., *k. in a. 6.11.14*

Boner, James, 10453, Pte., *k. in a. 9.10.17*

Boothman, George T., 12246, Pte., *k. in a. 27.8.18*

Bourke, William, 9965, L.-Cpl., *d. of w. 8.9.18*

Bourne, George H., 12621, Pte., *k. in a. 20.10.18*

Bowyer, Edward A., 11838, Pte., *k. in a. 27.8.18*

Boyce, Patrick C., 8206, Pte., *d. of w. 1.7.18*

Boylan, Michael, 8274, Pte., *k. in a. 15.9.16*

Boyle, Francis, 5282, L.-Cpl., *k. in a. 11.9.16*

Bracken, Samuel, 4596, Pte., *k. in a. 22.10.14*

Brady, Edward, 12315, Pte., *d. 15.3.19*

Brady, James, 10070, Pte., *k. in a. 31.7.17*

Brady, Joseph, 12573, Pte., *d. of w. 28.3.18*

Bray, Edward, 4956, Pte., *k. in a.1.2.15*
Brazill, John, 11051, Pte., *d. of w. 1.12.17*
Breen, James, 5387, Pte., *k. in a. 18.5.15*
Brennan, Christopher, 4961, Pte., *d. of w.*
   1.2.15
Brennan, Edward, 9793, Pte., *k. in a. 9.10.17*
Brennan, George P., 3536, L.-Sgt., *k. in a.*
   9.11.14
Brennan, John, 7476, L.-Sgt., *d. of w. 27.4.18*
Brennan, John, 8441, Pte., *k. in a. 9.1 0.17*
Brennan, Michael, 4048, Pte., *k. in a. 6.11.14*
Brennan, Nicholas, 8836, L.-Cpl., *k. in a.*
   3.8.17
Brennock, William, 3258, Pte., *k. in a. 6.11.14*
Breslin, Andrew, 3103, Pte., *k. in a. 1.11.14*
Brett, John, 9408, Pte., *k. in a. 10.10.17*
Brewster, John C., 5008, Pte., *k. in a. 11.7.15*
Brien, Charles, 3790, L.-Sgt., *d. of w. 10.5.17*
Brien, Cornelius, 6336, Pte., *k. in a. 17.9.16*
Brien, James, 9435 Pte., *d. ofw. 26.9.16*
Brine, Michael, 3975, L.-Cpl., D.C.M., *d. of*
   w. 5.5.15
Britt, Rody, 2663 L.-Cpl., *k. in a. 1.11.14*
Broderick, John, 11156, Pte., *d. of w. 29.12.16*
Brogan, Edward, 5999, Pte., *d. of w. 12.1.16*
Brogan, Philip, 2761, Pte., *k. in a. 1.11.14*
Brosnahan, Timothy, 5963,I *d. of w. 1.1.16*
Brown, Albert E., 9262, Pte., *k. in. 25.9.16*
Brown, John,2913, Pte., *k. ma. 14.9.14*
Brown, John, 3582, Pte., *k. in a. 1.11.14*
Brown, John, 9566, Pte., *k. in a. 17.9.16*
Brown, Samuel W., 5370, Pte., *d. 6.8.15*
Browne, David, 4558, Pte., *d. of w. 5.11.14*
Browne, Michael, 1655, Pte., *k. in a. 1.11.14*
Browne, William, 4533, Pte., *k. in a. 8.8.15*
Bruce, William J., 4446, Pte., *k. in a. 29.6.17*
Bruton, Charles, 7859, Pte., *d. of w. 22.9.16*
Buckley, Patrick, 10249, Pte., *k. in a. 10.10.17*
Buggy, William, 11333, Pte., *d. 18.2.17*
Burgess, Francis C., 4838, Pte., *d. of w.*
   18.9.16
Burke, Edmund, 4406, Pte., *k. in a. 18.5.15*
Burke, James, 1228, Pte., *k. in a. 18.5.15*
Burke, Joseph, 10878, Pte., *k. in a. 30.11.17*
Burke, John, 11052, Pte., *d. of w. 16.12.17*
Burke, Michael, 5244, Pte., *d. of w. 1.8.15*
Burke, Michael, 9437, Pte., *d. of w. 5.10.16*
Burke, Richard B., 9002, Pte., *d. of w. 29.3.18*
Burne, Maurice, 4237, Pte., *k. in a. 4.8.15*
Burns, Patrick, 4189, Pte., *k. in a. 4.9.14*
Butler, William, 558, Pte., *k. in a. 1.11.14*
Byrne, Edward, 3049, Pte., *k. in a. 2.11.14*
Byrne, George, 4108, Pte., *k. in a. 8.11.14*
Byrne, James, 4867, L.-Sgt., *k. in a. 15.9.16*

Byrne, John, 1462, Pte., *d. of w. 30.10.14*
Byrne, John, 3849, Pte., *k. in a. 2.11.14*
Byrne, John, 4836, Pte., *d. of w. 19.9.16*
Byrne, Leo J. P., 12051, L.-Cpl., *k. in a.*
   27.8.18
Byrne, Malachy, 7691, Pte., *d. of w. 11.4.18*
Byrne, Michael J., 12273, Pte., *k. in a. 27.9.18*
Byrne, Patrick. 9921, Pte., *d. of w. 15.10.17*
Byrne, Terence, 6376, L.-Cpl., *k. in a.*
   30.11.17
Byrne, Thomas, 7851, Pte., *k. in a. 9.10.17*
Byrne, Thomas, 9758, L.-Cpl., *k. in a.*
   10.10.17
Byrne, William, 2894, Pte., *k. in a. 1.12 14*
Byrne, William, 3564, Pte., *k. in a. 26.10.14*
Byrnes, Denis, 4195, Pte., *k. in a. 6.11.14*
Caffrey, John J., 11306, Pte., *k. in a. 23.2.17*
Cahill, Patrick, 4340, Pte., *d. of w. 30.12.14*
Cahill, Patrick, 7714, Pte., *d. of w. 23.10.15*
Callaghan Patrick. 5474. Pte., *k. in a. 18.5.15*
Campbell, James, 4121, Pte., *k. in a. 11.3.15*
Campbell, Michael, 4371, Pte., *d. of w.*
   27.5.15
Campbell, Patrick, 516, Pte., *k. in a. 1.11.14*
Campbell, Thomas, 5619, Pte., *k. in a.*
   22.10.15
Canavan, Michael, 5872, L.-Cpl., *k. in a.*
   8.8.15
Carberry, Thomas, 2742, Pte., *k. in a. 1.11.14*
Carey, Daniel, 9440, Pte., *k. in a. 15.9.16*
Carey, Edward, 3490, L.-Cpl., *k. in a. 18.5.15*
Carey, Michael, 3262, L.-Sgt., *k. in a. 14.2.15*
Carey, Thomas, 5563, Pte., *d. of w. 24.3.15*
Carlisle, Herbert, 4106, Pte., *k. in a. 14.9.14*
Carr, John, 3332, Pte., *k. in a. 6.11.14*
Carr, Patrick, 3848, Pte., *k. in a. 6.11.14*
Carroll, James, 3483, L.-Cpl., *d. 15.12.16*
Carroll, John, 3868, Pte., *k. in a. 6.11.14*
Carroll, John, 4716, Pte., *k. in a. 18.5.15*
Carroll, Thomas, 4449, Pte., *k. in a. 1.11.14*
Carson, Thomas, 4418, Pte., *d. of w. 17.5.15*
Carton, Hugh, 3132, Sgt., MM., *k. in a.*
   15.9.16
Carton, Joseph, 2987, Pte., *k. in a. 1.11.14*
Casey, William, 1765, Pte., *k. in a. 1.11.14*
Cassidy, Thomas, 3452, Pte., *d. of w. 9.11.14*
Caulfield, Patrick, 5321, Pte., *d. of w. 1.4.18*
Caves, Thomas R., 2068, Pte., *k. in a. 6.11.14*
Cawley, Michael, 6659, Pte., *k. in a. 8.5.18*
Clancy, William, 4882, Pte., *k. in a. 3.8.17*
Clarke, Cornelius, 4581, Pte., *k. in a. 4.9.14*
Clarke, Joseph, 4260, Pte., *d. of w. 4.3.17*
Clarke, John, 9550, Pte., *d. of w. 6.12.17*
Clarke, Patrick, 1813, L.-Cpl., *k. in a. 1.12.17*

Clarke, Patrick, 5267, Pte., *d. of w. 19.5.15*

Clarke, Richard, 2297, Pte., *k. in a. 4.9.17*

Cleeve, John, 1453, Pte., *k. in a. 1.11.14*

Cleland, Richard, 740, Pte., *k. in a. 1.11.14*

Clenaghan, William, 5286, Pte., *k. in a. 29.1.16*

Clerkin, Owen, 9441, Pte., *k. in a. 15.9.16*

Coalpoise, Frank, 4586, Pte., *d. of w. 17.11.14*

Coffey, John. 4582. Pte., *k. in a. 8.5.18*

Coffey, Maurice, 3844, Pte., *k. in a. 15.9.16*

Coghlan, Charles, 8039, Pte., *k. in a. 27.9.18*

Coghlan, Michael, 3663, Sgt., *k. in a. 17.9.16*

Coldwell, Christopher J., 6278, Pte., *k. in a. 12.10.15*

Colfer, Patrick, 7762, L.-Sgt., *d. of w. 22.4.17*

Collins, Michael, 5979, Pte., *d. of w. 31.5.15*

Comerford, John, 2802, Pte., *k. in a. 26.10.14*

Conaboy, John, 6439, L.-Sgt., *k. in a. 27.9.18*

Conboy, Bernard, 3732, Pte., *k. in a. 6.11.14*

Concannon, Patrick, 4646, Pte., *d. of w 14.5.15*

Condell, John H., 9563, Ptc., *k. in a. 26.9.16*

Condon, David, 10076, Pte., *k. in a. 15.3.17*

Condon, John, 5222, Pte., *d. of w. 13.9.17*

Conlon, John, 7912, Pte., *k. in a. 9.9.17*

Conlon, Patrick W., 5673, Pte., *k. in a. 15.9.16*

Connell, Michael, 6621, Pte., *k. in a. 25.10.15*

Connell, Thomas, 1938, Pte., *d. of w. 4.8.15*

Connolly, Alexander, 5991, Pte., *d. of w. 3.11.16*

Connolly, John, 2003, L.-Sgt., *d. of w. 28,12,14*

Connolly, John, 4861, Pte., *k. in a. 6.2.15*

Connolly, Patrick J., 1397, Pte., *k. in a. 6.11.14*

Connolly, Patrick, 10040, Pte., *k. in a. 9.10.17*

Connor, John, 4778, Pte., *k. in a. 8.5.18*

Connor, Patrick, 706, L.-Sgt., *k. in a. 23.10.14*

Connor, Thomas, 4977, Pte., *k. in a. 12.9.16*

Conron, Patrick, 12259, Pte., *k. in a. 30.3.18*

Conroy, John, 9238, Pte., *d. of w. 26.9.16*

Considine, Thomas, 11569, Pte., *k. in a. 9.10.17*

Convay, Edward, 1395, Pte., *k. in a. 10.1.15*

Conway, Edward J., 4881, Pte., *d. of w. 25.4.16*

Conway, George, 1688, Pte., *k. in a. 27.12.14*

Conway, Hugh, 7554, Pte., *k. in a. 14.11.16*

Conway, Thomas, 10660, Pte., *k. in a. 14.11.16*

Cook, Robert J., 11094, L.-Sgt., *k. in a. 20.10.18*

Cooney, Frank, 5549, Pte., *k. in a. 9.10.19*

Cooper, William V., 10161, L.-Cpl., D.C.M., *k. in a. 9.10.17*

Copeland, James, 11679, Pte., *d. of w. 29.9.18*

Corcoran, William, 4523, L.-Cpl., *k. in a. 1.9.14*

Cornally, Joseph, 2696, Pte., *k. in a. 1.2.15*

Cornally, Patrick, 10729, Pte., *k. in a. 12.9.17*

Corrigan, Patrick, 5367, Pte., *k. in a. 26.5.18*

Cosgrave, Denis, 4920, Pte., *k. in a. 15.9.16*

Cosgrave, Hugh, 10570, Pte., *k. in a. 30.3.18*

Cox, James J., 1972, Pte., *d. of w. 28.10.14*

Coyle, Michael, 9402, Pte., *d. of w. 28.9.16*

Coyle, Peter, 4570, L.-Cpl., *d. of w. 25.11.14*

Crawley, Martin, 5177, Pte., *k. in a. 15.9.16*

Croft, Victor, 8600, Pte., *k. in a. 26.7.17*

Crompton, Leonard, 12655, L..Cpl., *k. in a.* (formerly 3842, Household Battalion) *4.11.18*

Crone, David, 5366, Pte., *k. in a.12.7.16*

Cronin, Robert, 6602, Pte., *k. in a. 27.9.18*

Croskerry, Patrick, 11575, Pte., *d. of w. 7.12.17*

Crosson, William, 3720, Ptc., *d. of w. 2.11.14*

Crowe, Michael, 7753, Pte., *k. in a. 12.10.15*

Cruikshank, Stafford, 5110, Pte., *d. of w. 22.2.15*

Cullen, Edward, 9481, Pte., *k. in a. 9.10.17*

Cullen, John, 4322, Pte., *k. in a. 1.11.14*

Cullen, Maurice, 6901, Pte., *k. in a. 9.9.18*

Cullen, Michael, 2193, Pte., *k. in a. 18.5.15*

Cullen, Nicholas, 4700, Ptc., *k. in a. 18.5.15*

Cullen, Patrick, 4321, Pte., *k. in a. 6.9.14*

Cullen, William B., 11293, Pte., *k. in a. 9.10.17*

Culleton, Martin, 1458, Pte., *k. in a. 6.11.14*

Cummins, Michael, 6321, Pte., *k. in a. 11.10.15*

Cunningham, Hugh, 10097, Pte., *k. in a. 1 6.10.17*

Cunningham, James F., 2114, L.-Cpl., *d. of w. 20.11.14*

Cunningham, John, 1398, Pte., *k. in a. 6.11.14*

Cunningham, John, 1651, Pte., *k. in a. 3.11.14*

Cunningham, Patrick, 10995, Pte., *k. in a. 30.3.18*

Cunningham, William, 6280, Pte., *k. in a. 12.9.16*

Curnan, Thomas, 10384, L.-Cpl., *d. of w 24.2.17*

Curry, Michael, 2508, Pte., *k. in a. 6.11.14*

Curtin, Martin, 11392, Pte., *d. of w. 7.9.18*

Curtis, Patrick, 3351, Pte., *k. in a. 5.11.14*

Custy, Edward, 5203, Pte., *k. in a. 19.5.15*

Dagg, Michael, 4338, Pte., *k. in a. 17.10.14*
Dalton, John, 11953, Pte., *k. in a. 27.3.18*
Dalton, Peter, 4564, Pte., *d. of w. 15.11.14*
Daly, Edward, 4298, Pte., *k. in a. 25.10.14*
Daly, James, 4701, Pte., *k. in a. 10.10.17*
Daly, Jeremiah, 9304, Pte., *k. in a. 28.6.16*
Daly, John C., 392, L.-Cpl., *k. in a. 26.10.14*
Daly, John E., 6463, L.-Sgt., *k. in a. 25.9.16*
Daly, John, 9022, Pte., *k. in a. 17.9.16*
Daly, Joseph, 11687, Pte., *d. of w. 6.6.18*
Daly, Michael, 1926, Pte., *k. in a. 1.11.14*
Daly, Michael, 4471, Pte., *k. in a. 1.11.14*
Daly, Patrick, 1301, Pte., *k. in a. 18.5.15*
Daly, Richard, 4916, Pte., *k. in a. 15.9.16*
Darcy, Patrick, 4672, Pte., *d. of w. 4.2.15*
Daughton, Richard, 1478, Pte., *k. in a. 31.10.14*
Day, Patrick, 3923, Pte., *k. in a. 1.11.14*
Deacey, John, 10709, Pte., *k. in a. 30.3.18*
Dean, Cecil P. W., 3329, L.-Sgt., *k. in a. 18.5.15*
Deignan, Michael F., 4644, Pte., *d. of w. 6.5.15*
Delaney, James, 9443, Pte., *d. of w. 1.4.18*
Delaney, Michael, 10623, L.-Cpl., *k. in a. 22.5.18*
Delaney, Patrick, 6281, L.-Cpl., *k. in a. 26.7.17*
Delplanque, Charles, 1807, Pte., *k. in a. 21.10.14*
Dempsey, Simon, 6282, L.-Cpl., *k. in a. 9.6.15*
Dennehy, James, 9537, Pte., *k. in a. 3.9.17*
Devaney, Bernard, 3798, Pte., *k. in a. 27.9.18*
Dever, Patrick, 6979, Pte., *d. of w. 14.10.16*
Devereux, Michael, 3927, Pte., *k. in a. 1.11.14*
Devine, Andrew, 4019, Pte., *k. in a. 1.11.14*
Devins, Owen, 2981, Pte., *k. in a. 15.9.16*
Digan, Edward, 10102, Pte., *d. of w. 6.1.19*
Dillon, Robert L., 6389, L.-Cpl., *d. of w. 30.9.16*
Dixon, John, 12170, Pte., *d. of w. 17.4.18*
Docherty, James, 1645, Pte., *k. in a. 17.11.14*
Dolan, Edward, 2199, Pte., *k. in a. 26.10.14*
Dolan, John, 2581, Pte., *k. in a. 1.11.14*
Dolan, Patrick, 1180, Pte., *d. of w. 6.11.14*
Donagher, Michael, 4543, Pte., *k. in a. 1.11.14*
Donaldson, Patrick, 4737, Pte., *k. in a. 1.2.15*
Donelan, Michael, 543, Pte.,*d. 20.1.15*
Donnelly, Thomas, 5298, Pte., *k. in a. 17.9.16*
Donoghue, John, 8746, Pte., *k. in a. 9.10.17*
Donoghue, Michael, 12213, Pte., *k. in a. 10.10.18*
Donoghue, Patrick, 8193, Pte., *k. in a. 3.8.17*

Donohoe, Joseph, 1659, Pte., *k. in a. 15.5.15*
Donohoe, Patrick, 3056, Sgt., MM, *k. in a .30.3.18*
Donovan, Cornelius, 10459, Pte., *d. of w. 9.4.18*
Donovan, David, 7042, Pte., *d. of w. 21.7.16*
Donovan, Michael, 982, Pte., *k. in a. 27.10.14*
Doonan, John, 6101, Pte., *k. in a. 28.3.18*
Dooney, Edward, 8046, L.-Cpl., MM., *k. in a. 30.3.18*
Doran, John, 4729, Pte., *d. of w. 1.2.16*
Doran, Patrick, 11026, Pte., *d. of w. 1.12.17*
Doran, Roger, 8643, Pte., *k. in a. 15.9.16*
Dore, John, 3307, Pte., *d. of w. 13.2.16*
Dorgan, Peter, 7841, Pte., *d. of w. 1.9.18*
Dougan, James, 1844, Pte., *k. in a. 15.9.16*
Dowd, James, 5101, Pte., *k. in a. 8.1 0.15*
Dowler, John, 10524, Pte., *d. of w. 9.10.17*
Dowler, Michael, 7128, Pte., *k. in a. 10.12.16*
Dowling, Bernard, 1978, L.-Cpl., *k. in a. 18.5.15*
Dowling, Edward, 2648, Pte., *k. in a. 6.11.14*
Doyle, Denis, 4003, Pte., *k. in a. 1.11.14*
Doyle, Edward, 4077, Pte., *k. in a. 18.2.15*
Doyle, James, 9918, Pte., *k. in a. 9.10.17*
Doyle, Michael, 2269, Pte., *k. in a. 6.11.14*
Doyle, Michael, 2875, Pte., *k. in a. 18.5.15*
Doyle, Thomas, 3973, L.-Cpl., *d. of w. 15.10.16*
Doyle, William, 4932, L.-Cpl., *d. of w. 1.12.15*
Drumm, Frank, 2667, Pte., *d. of w. 10.11.14*
Duane, Stephen C., 2191, L.-Sgt., *k. in a. 6.11.14*
Ducey, Martin, 5834, Pte., *k. in a. 18.5.15*
Duff, Edward, 3015, Pte., *k. in a. 6.11.14*
Duffy, Martin, 7806, Pte., *k. in a. 28.5.18*
Duffy, Owen, 10263, Pte., *k. in a. 27.9.18*
Duggan, Joseph, 5505, Pte., *k. in a. 26.3.16*
Duggan, Patrick, 5893, Pte., *k. in a. 25.9.16*
Duncan, William, 11239, Pte., *k. in a. 1.8.17*
Dunleavy, James, 5038, Pte., *k. in a. 18.2.15*
Dunleavy, Michael, 3850, Pte., *k. in a. 1.9.14*
Dunne, John T., 2272, Pte., *k. in a 1.11.14*
Dunne, Joseph, 778!, Pte., *d. of w. 30.11.15*
Dunne, Patrick, 34 Pte., *k. in a. 1.2.15*
Dunne, Patrick, 4132, L.-Sgt., *k. in a. 6.11.14*
Dunne, William P., 1O53; *k. in a. 18.5.15*
Dunne, William, 4390, Pte., *k. in a. 1.11.14*
Dunwoody, Robert A., 2805, Pte., *k. in a. 6.11.14*
Earl, Daniel, 4228, L.-Cpl., *k. in a. 15.9.16*
Echlin, Richard, 4431, Pte., *k. in a. 1.11.14*
Edens, Thomas, 2611,Pte., *k. in a. 1.11.14*
Edgar, Thomas, 3537, Pte., *k. in a. 1.11.14*

Egan, James, 4161, L.-Cpl., *k. in a* . *22.2.15*
Egan, Michael, 3829, Pte., *k. in a. 1.11.14*
Egan, Michael, 4255, Pte., *k. in a. 1.11.14*
Elliott, James, 5623, L.-Cpl., *d. of w. 27.3.16*
Ellis, James, 6814, L.-Sgt., *d. of w* . *8.9.18*
Ellis, William S., 6131, Pte., *d. of w. 20.9.16*
Emerson, Thomas, 11473, Pte., *k. in a.*
10.10.17
Emery, George J. E., 12762, Pte., *d. of w.*
1.10.18
Emmett, John P., 3856, Pte., *k. in a. 6.11.14*
English, Theobald F., 5618, Pte., *k. in a.*
30.11.1 7
Enright, John, 6158, Pte., *k. in a. 12.9.16*
Eogan, John F., 3038, L.-Cpl., *k. in a. 6.9.14*
Fagan, John, 2992, Pte., *k. in a. 6.11.14*
Fallon, William, 2400, Pte., *k. in a. 8.5.18*
Farrell, Edward, 3999, Pte., *k. in a. 6.11.14*
Farrell, Luke C., 4915, Pte., *k. in a. 1.2.15*
Farrelly, Patrick, 6160, Pte., *k. in a. 15.9.16*
Farry, Patrick, 4504, Pte., *k. in a. 6.11.4*
Faulkener, Thomas, 1885, Pte., *k. in a.*
18.5.15
Feeley, Peter, 10428, Pte., *k. in a. 26.7.17*
Fennessy, William, 4694, Pte., *k. in a. 27.6.16*
Fenning, Thomas, 3143, Pte., *k. in a .6.11.14*
Ferguson, Andrew, 327, Sgt., *k. in a. 1.11.14*
Ferris, Charles, 2416, L.-Cpl., *k. in a.*
25.10.14
Ferris, Joseph, 10045, Pte., *d. of w. 2.12.17*
Fingleton, Thomas, 3408, Pte., *k. in a.*
29.12.14
Finn, Patrick, 10174, Pte., *k. in a. 9.10.17*
Finn, Timothy M., 12690, Pte., *k. in a. 27.8.18*
Finnegan, John, 12030, Pte., *d. of w. 1.12.17*
Finnegan, Tobias, 5808, Pte., *k. in a. 18.5.15*
Fisher, John, 4198, Pte., *k. in a. 15.9.16*
Fitzgibbon, Michael, 10921, Pte., *d. of w.*
1.7.18
Fitzgibbon, Patrick, 6419, Pte., *k. in a.*
15.9.16
Fitzmaurice, John, 9951, Pte., *k. in a. 30.3.18*
Flanagan, James J., 3560, Pte., *k. in a. 15.9.16*
Flanagan, James, 5664, Pte., *k. in a. 9.10.17*
Flanagan, James, 12002, Pte., *k. in a. 25.9.18*
Flanagan, Patrick, 3407, Pte., *k. in a. 1.11.14*
Fleming, David, 7814, L.-Cpl., *d. of w.*
11.9.17
Fleming, William, 1370, Sgt., *d. of w. 4.11.14*
Flynn, Christopher, 10103, Pte., *k. in a.*
28.7.17
Flynn, Denis, 4913, Pte., *k. in a. 27.6.18*
Flynn, Edward, 3425, Pte., *k. in a. 1.11.14*
Flynn, John, 1235, Pte., *k. in a. 6.11.14*

Flynn, Michael, 3572, Pte., *k. in a. 18.5.15*
Flynn, Patrick, 11233, Pte., *d. of w. 4.9.17*
Flynn, Thomas, 4179, Pte., *k. in a. 14.9.14*
Foley, Michael, 3545, Pte., *d. ofw* . *6.7.15*
Foley, Patrick, 7123, Pte., *k. in a. 9.10.17*
Foran, John, 9605, Pte., *k. in a. 30.3.18*
Forbes, Timothy, 8963, Pte., *k. in a. 15.11.16*
Ford, William, 354, Pte., *d. of w. 25.2.15*
Ford, William W. M. C. W., 12736, Pte., *k. in*
a. 27.9.18
Forde, William, 7733, Pte., *k. in a. 9.10.17*
Forrestal, David, 3517, Pte., *k. in a. 1.11.14*
Foster, John, 11507, Pte., *d. of w. 27.2.18*
Fovargue, John, 12508, Pte., *d. of w. 30.10.18*
Fox, Patrick, 5861, Pte., *k. in a. 15.9.16*
Foynes, Timothy, 4158, Pte., *k. in a. 6.11.14*
Frankish, Alfred, 12866, Pte., *d. 7.7.18*
Franklin, John, 5490, L.-Cpl., *k. in a. 25.9.16*
Freeman, Joseph, 794, Pte., *k. in a. 13.9.17*
French, William, 8741, Pte., *d. of w. 8.2.16*
Frize, John, 5513, Pte., *k. in a. 17.4.15*
Fry, William, 1245, Pte., *d. of w. 15.11.14*
Fulton, William, 380, Pte., *k. in a. 1.11.14*
Gaffney, Joseph, 4067, Pte., *d. of w. 2.7.15*
Gallacher, Daniel, 5591, Pte., *d. of w. 9.8.15*
Gallacher, John, 5066, Pte., *k. in a. 18.5.15*
Gallagher, James, 5739, Pte., *d. of w.19.5.15*
Gallagher, James, 9595, Pte., *k. in a. 1.12.17*
Gallagher, James, 11770, Pte., *k. in a.*
30.11.17
Gallagher, John, 2769, Pte., *k. in a. 27.3.18*
Gallagher, Martin, 1581, Pte., *k. in a.*
26.10.14
Gallagher, Michael, 4394, Pte., *d. 21.2.19*
Gallagher, Patrick, 5317, Pte., *k. in a. 4.8.15*
Gallagher, Teague, 6504, L.-Cpl., *k. in a.*
9.10.17
Gallagher, Thomas, 2860, Pte., *k. in a.*
14.9.14
Gallagher, William, 2631, Pte., *k. in a. 1.11.14*
Galvin, Richard, 4542, Pte., *k. in a. 18.5.15*
Galway, Thomas, 9953,Pte., *k. in a. 15.3.17*
Gardiner, Thomas, 3812, Pte., *k. in a. 12.7.16*
Gardiner, Walter J., 6139, L.-Cpl., *k. in a.*
27.9.18
Garvey, David, 917, Pte., *k. in a. 1.11.14*
Gaye, James, 3141, Pte., *k. in a. 6.11.14*
Geaney, William, 1823, Pte., *k. in a. 6.11.14*
Geary, Patrick, 3760, Pte., *k. in a. 22.10.15*
Geelan, John, 4452, Pte., *k. in a. 1.11.14*
Geraghty, James, 5012, Pte., *d. of w. 4.12.17*
Geraghty, Patrick, 5140, Pte., *k. in a. 22.5.18*
Gerrard, Samuel, 3522, Pte., *k. in a. 8.9.14*
Gibson, Patrick, 4465, Pte., *k. in a. 15.9.16*

Gibson, William, 4635, Pte., *k. in a. 15.9.16*
Gibson, William, 10013, Pte., *k. in a. 9.10.17*
Gilhooly, Patrick, 5860, Pte., *k. in a. 18.5.15*
Gill, Frank, 3148, L.-Sgt., *k. in a. 9.10.17*
Gilligan, Michael, 6393, L.-Cpl., *k. in a.*
  15.9.16
Gilmartin, John, 11032, Pte., *d. of w. 19.3.17*
Gleeson, John, 7679, Pte., *d. of w. 17.9.16*
Glenn, William D., 2599, Pte., *k. in a. 1.2.15*
Glynn, Michael, 3162, Pte., D.C.M., *k. in a.*
  6.11.14
Gonnelly, Patrick, 6285, Pte., *k. in a. 17.9.16*
Gough, Michael, 11431, Pte., *k. in a. 27.9.18*
Gough, William, 8459, Pte., *k. in a. 26.9.16*
Grace, Simon, 7918, Pte., *k. in a. 27.11.15*
Grace, Thomas, 1856, Pte., *d. of w. 19.5.15*
Grady, Richard, 3972, C.Q.M.S., M.M., *d. of*
  w. 16.9.16
Graham, John, 2057, L.-Sgt., *k. in a. 1.9.14*
Graham, John, 7902, Pte., *k. in a. 10.10.15*
Graham, Robert, 7018, Pte., *d. of w. 31.5.16*
Graham, William, 4531, Pte., *k. in a. 6.11.14*
Graham, William, 5389, Sgt., *k. in a. 22.4.15*
Graves, John, 5698, Pte., *k. in a. 15.9.16*
Gray, John, 1812, Pte., *k. in a. 18.5.15*
Gray, Owen, 10345, Pte., *k. in a. 25.9.16*
Greene, Daniel, 11287, Pte., *k. in a. 15.3.17*
Greene, William F. S., 3762, Pte., *k. in a.*
  5.11.14
Greenlee, James, 2328, Pte., *k. in a. 26.7.17*
Greer, John, 1821, Pte., *k. in a. 14.9.14*
Grey, Edward, 4283, Pte., *k. in a. 12.9.14*
Griffin, Francis, 4351, Pte., *d. of w. 6.9.14*
Griffin, James, 4629, Pte., *k. in a. 19.3.15*
Griffin, Patrick, 10031, Pte., *d. of w. 8.10.18*
Griffith, George, 4457, Pte., *k. in a. 1.11.14*
Grogan, James, 1946, Pte., *k. in a. 1.9.14*
Grogan, John M., 9444, Pte., *k. in a. 15.9.16*
Guckien, Peter, 8393, Pte., *d. of w. 4.10.16*
Guina, Edward, 4000, Pte. *k. in a. 6.11.14*
Guinan, John, 5685, L.-Cpl., *k. in a. 30.11.17*
Gwilt, Jesse, 11827, Pte., *d. of w. 20.10.18*
Haggerty, Jeremiah, 5344, L.-Sgt., *k. in a.*
  18.5.15
Hall, Thomas, 7633, Pte., *k. in a. 6.10.15*
Halligan, Michael, 4897, Pte., *d. of w. 20.5.15*
Halton, Mathew, 1850, Pte., *d. of w. 6.8.16*
Hamill, James, 5033, Pte., *k. in a. 1.2.15*
Hamilton, Frederick C., 509, Pte., *k. in a.*
  1.9.14
Hamilton, James, 3886, Pte., *k. in a. 1.11.14*
Hamilton, John, 5594, Pte., *k. in a. 10.5.15*
Hamilton, William, 1673, Pte., *k. in a. 6.11.14*
Hamilton, William, 2673, Pte., *k. in a. 17.5.15*

Hannan, James M., 4495, Pte., *k. in a. 14.9.14*
Hannan, Martin, 8244, Pte., *k. in a. 28.3.18*
Hannaway, Patrick J., 9571, Pte., *k. in a*
  30.3.18
Hannigan, Denis, 11395, Pte., *k. in a. 3.9.17*
Hanningan, Thomas G., 2969, Sgt., *k. in a.*
  4.9.14
Hannon, Martin, 11471, Pte., *d. of w. 1.5.18*
Hanrahan, Matthew, 4664, Pte., *d. of w.*
  19.5.15
Hanton, John C., 5141, Pte., *d. of w. 17.6.16*
Haran, James, 4655, L.-Sgt., *k. in a. 1.2.15*
Hardiman, John, 12146, Pte., *d. of w. 6.6.18*
Harding, George, 2720, Sgt., *d. of w. 6.7.17*
Hare, Frederick, 9716, Pte., *d. of w. 12.10.16*
Harkin, James, 5947, Pte., *d. of w. 7.8.15*
Harney, Denis, 3712, Pte., *k. in a. 6.11.14*
Harpur, Walter, 4539, Pte., *k. in a. 6.2.15*
Harrington, Ernest, 4407, Pte., *k. in a.*
  6.11.14
Harrington, Michael, 8872, Pte., *d. of w.*
  26.7.17
Harris, James, 4185, Sgt., *k. in a. 18.5.15*
Harris, John, 3784, Pte., *k.. in a. 4.9.14*
Harris, William, 6597, Pte., *k. in a. 8.8.15*
Harrison, Robert, 2249, Pte., *d. of w. 19.5.15*
Hart, Thomas, 5677, Pte., *k. in a. 25.4.15*
Hart, William, 79, Pte., *k. in a. 16.9.14*
Harte, George, 11320, Pte., *d. of w. 11.10.17*
Harte, James, 8339, Pte., *k. in a. 9.4.18*
Haughney, Patrick, 11559, Pte., *d. of w.*
  10.10.1 7
Hawkes, James W., 9298, Pte., *k. in a 27.9.18*
Hay, Joseph A., 9670, Pte., *d. of w. 21.3.18*
Hayden, Harold, 12706, Pte., *k. in a. 27.8.18*
Hayden, William, 4479, Pte., *k. in a. 13.4.15*
Hayes, James, 5332, Pte., *d. of w. 7.7.17*
Hayes, John E., 6309, Pte., *k. in a. 17.9.16*
Hayes, Patrick, 4505, Pte., *d. of w. 25.7.17*
Healy, John J., 4852, Pte., *k. in a. 18.5.15*
Healy, Joseph, 3317, L.-Cpl., *d. of w. 18.5.15*
Healy, Michael, 5550, Pte., *k. in a. 15.9.16*
Heaney, Edward, 2438, Sgt., *k. in a. 30.11.17*
Heary, Thomas, 4676, Pte., *k. in a. 10.1 .15*
Heatherington, Nathaniel, 2070, Pte., *k. in*
  a. 6.11.14
Heenan, Martin, 12055, Pte., *k. in a. 1.12.17*
Heffernan, Patrick, 11743, Pte., *k. in a.*
  9.10.17
Heffernan, Robert, 9682, Pte., *k. in a. 27.9.18*
Heggarty, Patrick, 4576, Pte., *k. in a. 6.2.15*
Hennessy, James, 5054, Pte., *d. of w. 8.8.15*
Heslin, Patrick, 2440, Pte., *d. of w. 13.7.18*
Heydon, Patrick J., 2206, Pte., *k. in a. 4.9.14*

Hickey, James, 10764, Pte., *d. of w.* 30.3.18

Hickey, Michael P., 4099, Pte., *d. of w.* 20.11.14

Hickmann, Alfred, 12341, Pte., *k. in a.* 26.5.18

Higgins, John, 6947, Pte., *k. in a.* 27.9.15

Higginson, Richard, 2533, Pte., *k. in a.* 18.5.15

Higgiston, James, 5584, Pte., *k. in a.*17.9.l

Hinds, Patrick J., 4506, Pte., *k. in a.* 1.11.14

Hoare, Joseph, 3544, Pte., *k. in a.* 5.12.17

Hoarey, Edward, 4745, Pte., *k. in a.* 18.5.15

Hoban, Michael, 11882, Pte., *d. of w.* 1.12.17

Hoey, James, 5045, Pte., *k. in a.* 25.4.16

Hogan, James, 8447, Pte., *k. in a.* 9.10.17

Hogan, Joseph W., 2192, Pte., *d. of w.* 8.11.14

Hogan, Michael, 11090, Pte., *k. in a.* 4.9.17

Hogan, Patrick, 10589, Pte., *d. of w.* 10.10.17

Holloran, Thomas, 4960, Pte., *k. in a.* 25.1 0.15

Holloway, Reginald, 3246, L.-Cpl., *k. in a.* 6.11.11

Holloway, Thomas, 5544, Pte., *k. in a.* 18.5.15

Holmes, William B., 5848, Pte., *k. in a.* 18.5.15

Holmes, William J., 5816, L.-Cpl., *k. in a.* 31.12.1 5

Holton, John, 8848, Pte., *d.* 5.11.16

Hood, James, 9352, Pte., *k. in a.* 12.11.16

Horrigan, Garrett, 11131, Pte., *k. in a.* 27.8.18

Howie, Walter, 4434, Pte., *k. in a.* 3.11.14

Hughes, Bernard, 4376, Pte., *d. of w.* 29.4.15

Hughes, Peter, 11590, Pte., *k. in a.* 8.5.18

Humphreys, Thomas T., 3311, Pte., *d. of w.* 8.11.14

Hunt, John, 5825, Pte., *k. in a.* 18.5.15

Hunt, Patrick, 9486, Pte., *k. in a.* 26.7.17

Hunter, Hugh, 3116, Pte., *k. in a.* 25.10.14

Hunter, James, 4272, Pte., *k. in a.* 3.11.14

Hyland, John, 9619, Pte., *d. of w.* 24.9.16

Igoe, Herbert, 9873, Pte., *k. in a.* 9.1 0.17

Ireland, Henry, 4803, Pte., *k. in a.* 18.5.15

Irwin, George, 1623, Sgt., *d. of w.* 11.9.14

Izzard, Seymour A., 4557, Pte., *k. in a.* 27.8.18

Jackson, Thomas, 3862, L.-Cpl., *k. in a.* 15.3.17

Jackson, William, 8738, Pte., *k. in a.* 19.6.18

Jackson, William, 9448, Pte., *k. in a.* 25.4.16

Jacob, Peter, 305, Pte., *k. in a.* 4.9.14

Jameson, William J.;3 L.-Cpl., *k. in a.* 6.11.14

Jervois, Eugene W., 4210, 1 *d. of w.* 7.11.14

Johnston, James, 3985, Sgt., *d. of w.* 1.12.17

Johnston, Joseph, 8416, Pte., *d. of w.* 25.9.16

Johnston, Stephen, 5871, Pte., *k. in a.* 18.5.15

Johnstone, Howard, 5348, Pte., *k. in a.* 17.9.16

Jones, William, 7121, Pte., *k. in a.* 16.3.17

Jordan, Nicholas, 7299, Pte., *d. of w.* 1.2.16

Joyce, Stephen, 6636, L.-Cpl., *k. in a.* 30.9.15

Kane, Alexander, 10475, Pte., *k. in a.* 6.7.17

Kane, Peter, 2819, L.-Cpl., *d. of w.* 9.4.16

Kavanagh, Francis, 8361, Pte., *k. in a.* 24.1.18

Kavanagh, James, 4050, Pte., *k. in a.* 3.11.14

Kavanagh, James, 5546, Pte., *k. in a.* 9.10.17

Kavanagh, Patrick, 3509, Pte., *k. in a.* 6.11.14

Kavanagh. Patrick. 10329, L.-Cpl., *d. of w.* 3.5.18

Kavanagh, Thomas, 7325, Pte., *k. in a.* 26.2.17

Kavanagh, William, 1258, Pte., *k. in a.* 1.11.14

Kavanagh, William P., 4058, L.-Sgt., *k. in a.* 1.11.14

Keane, William, 2545, Pte., *k. in a.*1.11.14

Kearney, James, 9875, Pte., *k. in a.* 15.3.17

Kearney, Patrick, 4957, Sgt., MM., *k. in a.* 30.11.1 7

Keating, Andrew, 5251, Pte., *k. in a.* 15.9.16

Keating, Joseph, 6505, L.-Cpl., *k. in a.* 5.12.17

Keating, Thomas, 1424, Pte., *k. in a.* 4.9.14

Keaveny, John, 12514, L.-Cpl., *k. in a.* 8.5.18

Keegan, Frederick, 4904, Pte., *k. in a.* 19.3.15

Keegan, Matthew, 3751, L.-Cpl., *k. in a.* 6.11.14

Keith, Robert, 5393, Pte., *k. in a.* 10.1 0.17

Kelleher, Daniel, 6288, L.-Cpl., *k. in a.* 16.9.16

Kelly, Edward, 11364, Pte., *k. in a.* 29.7.17

Kelly, Francis, 2777, Pte., *k. in a.* 6.11.14

Kelly, James, 1888, Pte., *k. in a.* 14.9.14

Kelly, James, 2075, Pte., *d. of w.* 21.5.18

Kelly, James, 5346, L.-Cpl., *k. in a.* 18.5.15

Kelly, James, 5410, L.-Cpl., *d. of w.* 18.12.16

Kelly, James, 6255, Pte., *d.* 24.6.16

Kelly, James, 12809, Pte., *k. in a.* 20.10.18

Kelly, John, 1697, Pte., *d. of w.* 6.11.14

Kelly, John, 8779, Pte., *k. in a.* 13.12.16

Kelly, John, 11460, Pte., *k. in a.* 2.8.17

Kelly, John J., 4876, Pte., *d. of w.* 25.2.15

Kelly, Michael, 3800, Pte., *d. of w.* 14.1 15

Kelly, Michael, 1936, L.-Cpl., *k. in a.* 6.11 14

Kelly, Patrick, 11832, Pte., *k. in a.* 27.9.18

Kelly, Thomas, 1889, Pte., *d. of w.* 9.11 14

Kelly, William, 2903, Pte., *k. in a.* 22.9.14

Kelly, William, 7306, Pte., *k. in a.* 15.9.16

Kelly, William, 11446, Pte., *k. in a. 3.8.17*
Keneally, Charles, 1130, Pte., *k. in a. 30.12.14*
Kenneally, John, 9495, Pte., *d. of w. 26.9.16*
Kennedy, Charles, 7382, Pte., *k. in a. 28.6.16*
Kennedy, Percy, 3982, Pte., *k. in a. 2.11.14*
Kennedy, Patrick, 5349, Pte., *k. in a. 18.5.15*
Kennedy, Robert T., 2610, Pte., *k. in a. 17.10.14*
Kennedy, Thomas E., 10168, Pte., *k. in a. 9.10.1 7*
Kennelly, Michael, 6640, Sgt., *k. in a. 3.9.17*
Kenny, Francis, 12735, Pte., *k. in a. 2.8.18*
Kenny, Michael, 4608, Pte., *d. of w. 29.6.16*
Kenny, Patrick, 8568, Pte., *k. in a. 26.9.16*
Kenny, Thomas, 3306,Pte., *k. in a. 1.11.14*
Kent, Patrick J., 9232, Pte., *d. of w. 24.9.16*
Keogh, James, 10818, Pte., *k. in a. 26.2.18*
Keogh, Thomas, 1621, Pte., *k. in a. 18.5.15*
Kerr, Patrick, 8305, Pte., *k. in a. 9.10.17*
Kerrigan, Thomas, 4197, Pte., *d. of w. 10.9.14*
Kiely, Patrick, 10970, L.-Cpl., *d. of w. 4.9.17*
Kiely, William, 3541, L.-Cpl., *k. in a. 6.11.14*
Kiernan, Thomas, 11482, Pte., *d. of w. 31.3.18*
Kilbane, Michael, 6291, L.-Cpl., *k. in a. 15.9.16*
Kilbride, Edward, 4520, Pte., *k. in a. 29.10.14*
Kilduff, Patrick, 4088, Pte., *k. in a. 9.1.15*
Kilpatrick, James, 12535, L.-Cpl., *k. in a. 8.10.18*
Kinder, Arthur, 6132, Pte., *k. in a. 26.9.16*
King, James, 12075, Pte., *k. in a.1.12.17*
Kinsella, James F. J., 2350, Pte., *k. in a. 1.9.14*
Kinsella, James, 2469, Pte., *k. in a. 15.3.17*
Kinsella, Lawrence, 3129, Pte., *k. in a. 1.11.14*
Kinsella, Matthew, 1848, Pte., *k. in a. 30.3.18*
Kinsella, Patrick, 8114, Pte., *d. of w. 30.9.16*
Kirk, Edmund, 2511, Sgt., *d. of w. 18.11.14*
Kirk, John, 108, Sgt.-Major, M.C., *d. of w. 2.4.16*
Kirk, Thomas, 6361, Pte., *k. in a. 23.7.16*
Lacey, Maurice, 8498, Pte., *d. of w. 11.9.17*
Lacey, William, 10770, Pte., *k. in a. 27.9.18*
Lafferty, Bernard, 9454, Pte., *k. in a. 9.10.17*
Lafferty, George, 5392, Pte., *k. in a. 18.5.15*
Laffey, Bernard, 4304, Pte., *k. in a. 4.9.14*
Lally, Peter, 3281, Pte., *k. in a. 18.5.15*
Lambert, Thomas, 12096, Pte., *k. in a. 1.12.17*
Lamont, William, 11191, Pte., *k. in a. 15.3.17*
Lane, Sydney, 3526, Pte., *d. of w. 30.5.15*
Lane, Timothy J., 4872, Sgt., *k. in a. 7.12.15*
Lanegan, William, 3900, Pte., *d. of w. 18.9.16*
Lang, Francis W., 11297, Pte., *k. in a. 27.8.18*

Langford, Francis D., 7234, Pte., *d. 13.2.17*
Langley, John, 11843, Pte., *k. in a. 9.10.17*
Langrill, Henry, 3345, L.-Cpl., *k. in a. 3.11.14*
Larkin, James, 9969, Pte., *k. in a. 27.9.18*
Larkin, Thomas, 9340, Pte., *k. in a. 15.3.17*
Lavin, James, 7069, Pte., *k. in a. 14.11.16*
Lawless, George, 5451, Pte., *k. in a. 15.9.16*
Lawless, Michael, 4112, Pte., *k. in a. 15.9.16*
Lawlor, Michael, 6934, Pte., *d. of w. 28.8.18*
Lawlor, Patrick J., 11932, Pte., *d. of w. 27.9.18*
Lawson, Thomas, 8563, Pte., *k. in a. 25.9.16*
Lawton, Michael, 2207, Pte., *k. in a. 26. 7.17*
Lawton, Peter F., 3957, Pte., *k. in a. 18.5.15*
Leahy, John, 2699, Pte., *d. of w. 15.9.14*
Leahy, William, 4155, Pte., *k. in a. 6.11.14*
Leak, Ernest W., 8673, Pte., *d. of w. 19.4.16*
Lee, Patrick J., 4254, L.-Cpl., *d. of w. 28.9.18*
Leggett, Ernest 5094, Pte., *k. in a. 17.5.15*
Lehane, Michael, 9293, Pte., *d. of w. 30.3.18*
Lennon, James, 4859, Pte., *k. in a. 26.7.17*
Lennon, William H., 8169, Pte., *k. in a. 9.9.17*
Lennox, George, 9157, Pte., *k. in a. 26.5.18*
Lernan, Ronald, 5467, Pte., *k. in a. 27.8.18*
Levey, John F., 4270, Pte., *k. in a. 3.11.14*
Lewis, Michael, 10028, Pte., M.M., *k. in a. 14.7.1 7*
Leydon, Frank, 9765, Pte., *k. in a. 17.9.16*
Liddane, Thomas J., 9456, Pte., *k. in a. 15.3.17*
Liston, John, 1194, Pte., *k. in a. 8.3.15*
Lockhart, William H., 4062, Pte., *k. in a. 16.11.14*
Logan, Robert, 2466, Pte., *k. in a. 9.10.17*
Loghan, Malachy, 4760, Pte., *d. of w. 10.1.15*
Logue, Thomas, 10285, Pte., *k. in a. 9.10.17*
Lonergan, Daniel, 11603, Pte., *k. in a. 27 8.18*
Lonergan, Edward, 4853, Pte., *k. in a. 1.4.15*
Lonergan, Jeremiah, 4774, Pte., *k. in a. 10.1.15*
Long, Patrick, 9799, Pte., *d. of w. 1.11.18*
Long, William, 7861, Pte., *k. in a. 17.9.16*
Longmore, Wilson, 2700, L.-Sgt., *k. in a. 19.3.15*
Loobey, Edward, 6191, Pte., *k. in a. 26.9.16*
Looney, James, 10138, Pte., *k. in a. 2.6.18*
Loughlin, William, 3650, Pte., *k. in a. 1.11.14*
Loughren, Leslie J., 3192, L.-Sgt., *d. 13.5.15*
Lowndes, Thomas, 9714, Pte., *d. of w. 24.9.16*
Love, Thomas A., 6209, L.-Cpl., *k. in a. 8.10.15*
Loye, Patrick J., 5928, Pte., *d. of w. 24.4.16*
Lucey, Timothy, 8268, Pte., *k. in a. 17.9.16*
Lucitt, Edward, 2225, Pte *d. of w. 14.9.14*

Lucitt, John, 3947, L.-Cpl., *k. in a. 6.11.14*
Luttrell, Ernest, 4515, Pte., *k. in a. 6.11.14*
Lydon, James, 4821, Pte., *k. in a. 15.9.16*
Lydon, John, 12331, Pte., *k. in a. 27.8.18*
Lynam, John, 10986, Pte., *k. in a. 3.8.17*
Lynch, Edward, 10953, Pte., *k. in a. 15.11.16*
Lynch, John, 3304, Pte., *k. in a. 6.11.14*
Lynch, Patrick, 4458, Pte., *k. in a. 6.11.14*
Lyons, Peter, 4602, Pte., *k. in a. 25.9.16*
Macken, John, 5558, Pte., *k. in a. 18.5.15*
Macken, Patrick F., 6163, L.-Cpl., *d. of w. 11.10.1 7*
Madden, Thomas, 6731, Pte., *k. in a. 27.9.18*
Magee, William J., 3139, Pte., *k. in a. 4.9.14*
Maher, Denis, 870, Pte., *k. in a. 1.11.14*
Maher, James, 865, Pte., *k. in a. 18.5.15*
Maher, James, 4475, Pte., *k. in a. 2.11.14*
Maher, Lawrence, 3971, Pte., *d. of w. 18.5.15*
Mahon, John, 10707, Pte., *k. in a. 4.11.18*
Mahoney, James, 4786, Pte., *d. of w. 21.5.15*
Mahoney, John M., 5455, Pte., *d. of w. 19.3.15*
Mahoney, John, 11092, Pte., *k. in a. 9.10.17*
Mahoney, Timothy, 5883, Pte., *k. in a. 18.5.15*
Malone, Edward, 10080, Pte., *d. of w. 27.12.16*
Mann, Joseph, 2763, Pte., *d. of w. 19.5.15*
Mansfield, Joseph, 2845, Pte., D.C.M.., *k. in a. 27.9.18*
Marley, John, 10763, Pte., *k. in a. 2.8.17*
Marnell, Walter, 6414, Pte., *d. of w. 1.7.16*
Martin, Christopher 11782, Pte., *k. in a. 27.8.18*
Martin, Michael, 6314, Pte., *k. in a. 15.9.16*
Martin, William, 2632, Pte., *d. 26.9.14*
Mason, James, 4489, Pte., *k. in a. 6.11.14*
Massey, John J., 4202, Pte., *d. of w. 10.11.14*
Masterson, Andrew, 4306, Pte., *k. in a. 6.11.14*
Masterson, Michael, 5597, Pte., *k. in a. 23.10.15*
Matthews, Edmund C., 12865, Cpl., MM., *k. in a. 27.8.18*
Matthews, Edward, 9627, L.-Cpl., *d. of w. 13.9.17*
Matthews, Henry, 6392, Pte., *k. in a. 30.11.17*
Mathews, Roger, 4160, L.-Sgt., *k. in a. 22.9.15*
Meagher, John, 3243, Pte., *k. in a. 4.9.14*
Meehan, Hugh, 3251, Pte., *k. in a. 1.11.14*
Meehan, Lawrence, 5021, L.-Cpl., *k. in a. 18.5.15*
Meehan, Peter, 2841, Pte., *d. of w. 17.11.14*

Merrick, William, 10111, L.-Cpl., *k. in a. 30.11.1 7*
Mescal, Mark S., 11452, L.-Cpl., *k. in a. 1.12.17*
Mills, Alexander, 1994, Pte., *k. in a. 1.11.14*
Mills, John, 11398, Pte., *k. in a. 9.10.17*
Minihane, William, 8816, Pte., *k. in a. 2.8.17*
Mitchell, Michael, 6297 Pte., *k. in a. 15.9.16*
Mitchell, Reginald E., 12439, Pte., *k. in a. 20.10.18*
Moffatt, Thomas, 5185, Pte., *k. in a. 11.9.16*
Molloy, Arthur B., 3525, Pte., *k. in a. 1.11.14*
Molloy, Denis, 1604, Pte., *k. in a. 6.11.14*
Molloy, Robert, 1545, Pte., *k. in a. 1.9.14*
Montague, John, 5465, Pte., *k. in a. 25.4.16*
Montgomery, Irvine, 10344, Pte., *k. in a. 25.9.16*
Moody, William T., 12921, Pte., *k. in a. 27.9.18*
Mooney, John, 7391, Pte., *k. in a. 15.9.16*
Mooney, Peter, 4129, Pte., *k. in a. 6.9.14*
Moore, William, 4015, Pte., *d. of w. 24.11.14*
Moore, William, 9701, Pte., *k. in a. 24.9.16*
Moran, John, 3498, Pte., *k. in a. 6.11.14*
Moran, Michael, 1934, Pte., *k. in a. 18.5.15*
Moran, Michael, 3632, C.S.M., D.C.M.., *d. of w. 20.9.16*
Moran, Patrick, 1991, Pte., *k. in a. 1.11.14*
Moran, Patrick, 11560, Pte., *k. in a. 9.10.17*
Morgan, John, 1276, Pte., *k. in a. 23.10.14*
Morgan, John, 3622, Pte., *k. in a. 1.11.14*
Morgan, Thomas H., 11096, Pte., *k. in a. 16.10.17*
Morley, John, 9581, Pte., *k. in a. 9.10.17*
Moroney, Martin, 11600, Pte., *k. in a. 10.10.17*
Morris, John M., 12716, Pte., *d.of w. 28.8.18*
Morrissey, James, 10438, Pte., *d. 2.6.18*
Mulgrew, James, 5245, Pte., *d. 23.6.15*
Mullaney, James, 4788, Pte., *k. in a. 15.9.16*
Mullen, Charles, 9420, Pte., *k. in a. 25.9.16*
Mullholland, William P., 2280, Pte., *k. in a. 6.11.14*
Mulqueen, Jack, 8565, Pte., *k. in a. 15.9.16*
Mulvihill, William, 11916, Pte., *d. of w. 3.12.17*
Munns, Arthur, 552, C.S.M. D.C.M.., *k. in a. 17.11.14*
Murphy, Andrew, 11440, Pte., *k. in a. 9.10.17*
Murphy, Bernard 10105, Pte., *k. in a. 30.8.17*
Murphy, Daniel, 12287, Pte., *k. in a. 27.8.18*
Murphy, James, 5199, L.-Cpl., *k. in a. 6.3.15*
Murphy, James, 5666, Pte., *k. in a. 18.5.15*
Murphy, Jeramiah, 8957, Pte., *d. of w. 21.10.16*

Murphy, John, 4364, Pte., *k. in a. 1.11.14*
Murphy, John, 5233, Pte., *k. in a. 18.5.15*
Murphy, John T., 6036, Pte., *k. in a. 23.11.15*
Murphy, Joseph, 9940, Pte., *d. of w. 4.8.17*
Murphy, Joseph P., 6430, L.-Sgt., *k. in a. 30.3.18*
Murphy, Michael, 6133, Pte *k. in a. 28.6.16*
Murphy, Michael, 8466, Pte., *k. in a. 25.9.16*
Murphy, Michael J., 10166, Pte *d. of w. 8.3.18*
Murphy, Michael J., 12005, Pte *k. in a.
1.12.17*
Murphy, Michael, 12428, Pte., *k. in a. 27.9.18*
Murphy, Myles, 5402, Pte., *k. in a. 23.10.18*
Murphy, Patrick, 4410, Pte., *k. in a. 6.11.14*
Murphy, Richard, 11334, Pte., *d. of w. 27.9.18*
Murphy, Thomas, 6364, Pte., *k. in a. 16.11.16*
Murphy, William, 5142, Pte., *k. in a. 18.5.15*
Murphy, William, 10337, Pte., *k. in a. 9.9.17*
Murray, James, 2924, Pte., *k. in a. 29.10.14*
Murray, Patrick, 7887, Pte., *k. in a. 27.8.18*
Murrin, Patrick, 2247, Pte., *k. in a. 5.4.15*
Murtagh, Patrick, 4356, Pte., *d. 23.4.16*
Murtagh, William, 3291, Pte., *k. in a. 17.2.15*
Murtagh, William, 4411, Pte., *k. in a.
30.11.17*
McAdoo, Samuel, 9462, Pte., *d. 21.9.16*
McAviney, James, 3694, Pte., *k. in a. 1.11.14*
McAviney, Thomas, 5586, Pte., *k. in a.
15.9.16*
McCall, James, 5662, Pte., *k. in a. 18.5.15*
McCann, Bernard, 5051, Pte., *d. of w. 31.3.15*
McCarroll, Francis, 4598,Pte., *k. in a. 25.5.18*
McCarte, Charles, 10526, Pte., *d. of w. 9.4.18*
McCarthy, Charles, 3775, Pte., *k. in a. 18.5.15*
McCarthy, Charles E. M., 2728, Sgt., *d. of w.
15.11.14*
McCarthy, Daniel, 10918, Pte., *d. of w.
14.12.16*
McCarthy, Daniel T., 12089, L.-Cpl., *d. of w.
22.9.18*
MacCarthy, Harry, 4370, Pte., *k. in a.
26.10.14*
McCarthy, James, 4640, Pte., *k. in a. 10.10.17*
McCarthy, James, 11432, Pte., *k. in a. 26.7.17*
McCarthy, Joseph, 4675, Pte., *k. in a. 25.4.16*
McCarthy, Michael, 4670, Pte., *k. in a.
18.5.15*
McClinton, Samuel, 4381, Pte., *d. of w.
18.11.14*
McClory, John, 5155, Pte., *k. in a. 6.2.15*
McCloskey, James J., 6167, Pte., *k. in a.
28.8.18*
McCluskey, Joseph, 1959, Pte., *k. in a.
6.11.14*
McCluskey, Thomas, 4031, Pte., *k. in a. 6.11.14*

McColgan, Robert, 2437, Pte., *k. in a.
26.10.14*
McConaty, Patrick, 3173, Pte., *k. in a.
26.10.14*
McConnell, Charles, 3428, Pte., *k. in a.
1.11.14*
McConnell, Philip, 507, L.-Cpl., *k. in a.
29.10.14*
McConnell, Walter, 6343, L.-Cpl., M.M., *d. of
w. 19.9.18*
McConniff, Terence, 11972, Pte., *k. in a.
5.12.17*
McConnon, Matthew J., 5162, Pte., *k. in a.
16.3.15*
McCormac, Thomas, 8125, Pte., *k. in a.
30.11.17*
McCormack, Joseph, 4094, Pte., *d. of w.
1.11.14*
McCormack, Robert, 10692, Pte., *k. in a.
3.11.18*
McCrory, Thomas, 5927, Pte., *d. of w. 4.2.16*
McCue, Patrick, 10991, Pte., *k. in a. 9.10.17*
McDermott, Robert, 4429, L.-Cpl., *k. in a.
6.11.14*
McDevitt, Patrick, 10018, Pte., *d. of w.
25.9.16*
McDonagh, James, 10706, L.-Cpl., *k. in a.
30.3.18*
McDonagh, Thomas, 3156, Pte., *d. of w.
8.9.14*
McDonald, Bartholomew, 4093, L.-Cpl., *k.
in a. 4.9.14*
McDonnell, John, 3458, Pte., *k. in a. 31.10.14*
McDonnell, Loftus J., 11245, Pte., *k. in a.
30.11.17*
McDonough, John, 3310, Pte., *d. of w.
28.10.14*
McDonough, Patrick, 10975, Pte., *d. of w.
4.7.17*
McDonough, Richard, 3432, Sgt., *d. 13.5.18*
McDonough, Stephen, 7343, L.-Cpl., *k. in a.
11.9.16*
McErlean, James, 10017, Pte., *k. in a. 27.3.18*
McEvoy, Joseph, 9082, Pte., *d. of w. 17.7.16*
McEvoy, Thomas, 3930, L.-Sgt., MM., *d. of
w. 3.12.17*
McFadden, George, 4834, Pte., *d. of w. 3.6.15*
McGann, Thomas, 3356, Pte., *k. in a. 6.11.14*
McGarrigal, John J., 5672, Pte., *h. in a.
12.7.17*
McGee, James, 11612, Pte., *d. of w. 10.9.17*
McGill, William J., 5246, Pte., *d. of w. 19.5.15*
McGinn, James, 2487, Pte., *k. in a. 6.11.14*
McGonigal, Charles, 4738, Pte., *k. in a. 14.2.15*

McGourty, John, 9377, Pte., *k. in a. 3.6.18*

McGrane, William, 5450, Pte., *k. in a. 16.3.15*

McGrath, Denis, 9560, Pte., *k. in a. 11.9.16*

McGrath, John, 4594, Sgt., *d. of w. 3.10.15*

McGrath, John, 8688, Pte., *k. in a. 17.9.16*

McGrattan, John, 10482, Pte., *d. 6.1.17*

McGuckion, Thomas, 2422, Pte., *k. in a.*
6.11.14

McGuinness, John, 3099, Pte., *k. in a. 29.3.18*

McGuinness, Joseph, 10575, Pte., *d. of w.*
30.11.1 7

McGuinness, Stephen, 12919, Pte., *k. in a.*
27.9.18

McGuinness, William, 6136, Pte., *d. of w.*
23.11.15

McGuinness, William, 11039, Pte., *d. of w.*
9.9.17

McGuire, Hugh, 5891, Pte., *k. in a. 1.12.17*

McGuirk, Thomas, 3294, Pte., *d. 30.7.17*

McGurk, Charles, 2873, Pte., *k. in a. 4.9.14*

McHugh, Martin, 5902, Pte., *d. of w. 6.4.18*

McHugh, Richard, 4804, Pte., *k. in a. 15.9.16*

McInerney, 4078, Pte., *k. in a. 15.4.16*

McIntee, Arthur, 2187, L.-Cpl., *k. in a.*
6.11.14

McIntosh, John, 5289, Pte., *k. in a. 27.9.15*

McIntyre, Alexander, 326, Sgt., *d. of w. 5.8.17*

McKenna, John, 9978, Pte., *k. in a. 9.10.17*

McKenna, Patrick, 3661, Pte., *k. in a. 6.2.15*

McKenna, Peter, 10334, L.-Cpl., *d. 22.1.17*

McKenna, Richard, 1121, Pte., *k. in a. 1.11.14*

McKeon, James, 2459, Pte., *k. in a. 6.11.14*

McKeon, Michael, J., 10440, Pte., *k. in a.*
20.10.18

McKeown, Peter, 9098, Pte., *k. in a. 15.9.16*

McKittrick, Peter, 3874, Pte., *k. in a. 18.5.15*

McLean, Henry, 2396, Pte., *k. in a. 10.9.17*

McLester, James, 1533, Pte., *k. in a. 22.6.15*

McLaughlin, Bernard, 4045, L.-Sgt., *k. in a.*
2.11.14

McLaughlin, John, 3331, Pte., *k. in a. 3.11.14*

McLoughlin, Patrick, 12951, Pte., *k. in a.*
27.9.18

McLoughlin, William, 1473, Pte., *d. of w.*
20.9.16

McMahon, Daniel, 3936, Pte., *k. in a. 1.11.14*

McMahon, Martin, 11283, Pte., *k. in a.*
10.10.17

McManus, Hugh M., 14, Pte., *k. in a. 18.5.15*

McManus, Robert, 12183, Pte., *k. in a.*
27.8.18

McManus, Eugene, 4850, L.-Sgt., *k. in a.*
17.9.16

McMillan, Robert, 2327, Pte., *k. in a. 1.11.14*

McMonagle, Francis, 3093, Pte., *k. in a.*
1.9.14

McNally, William J., 10967, Pte., *k. in a.*
25.9.16

McParland, John J., 5865, Pte., *k. in a.*
25.9.16

McRoberts, James, 3009, Pte., *k. in a. 14.1.15*

McSharry, John, 6086, Pte., *k. in a. . 23.11.15*

McVeigh, William, 3024, Pte., *k. in a.*
29.10.14

McWilliams, Donald, 11840, Pte., *d. of w.*
28.3.18

McWilliams, John, 9642, Pte., *k. in a. 25.9.16*

Nancollas, George, 2816, Sgt., *d. of w.*
12.9.17

Neely, James G., 8785, Pte., *k. in a. 27.9.16*

Neill, James, 4771, Pte., *k. in a. 6.2.15*

Neill, Michael, 4802, Pte., *k. in a. 1.2.15*

Nichols, Richard, 1822, Pte., *k. in a. 26.10.14*

Nicholas, Thomas H., 3880, Pte., *k. in a.*
1.11.14

Nicholson, John, 7276, Pte., *d. of w. 6.9.17*

Nixon, Edward, 3086, L.-Cpl., *k. in a. 1.11.14*

Noble, John, 3326, Pte., *k. in a. 10.10.17*

Nolan, James, 4696, Sgt., *d. of w. 8.10.16*

Nolan, John, 3649, Pte., *d. of w. 9.11.14*

Nolan, Laurence, 3497, L.-Sgt., *d. of w.*
19.9.16

Nolan, Patrick, 4862, Pte., *k. in a. 18.5.15*

Nolan, Patrick, 5196, Pte., *k. in a. 26.3.18*

Nolan, Thomas, 8934, Pte., *k. in a. 9.10.17*

Noonan, Joseph, 3017, Pte., *k. in a. 17.6.15*

Noonan, Matthew, 5395, Pte., *k. in a. 18.5.15*

Norris, Thomas, 3647, Pte., *k. in a. 6.11.14*

Norris, Thomas, 9562, Pte., *k. in a. 15.9.16*

Nowlan, William, 2430, Pte., *k. in a. 1.9.18*

Nugent, Thomas H., 3524, Pte., *k. in a.*
1.11.14

Nyhan, Thomas, 8158, Pte., *d. of w. 26.9.16*

O'Boyle, William, 10491, Pte., *d. of w. 2.11.17*

O'Brien, Daniel, 8808, Pte., *k. in a. 8.11.17*

O'Brien, Denis, 7468, Pte., *k. in a. 5.4.18*

O'Brien, Edmond, 8362, Pte., *k. in a. 17.9.16*

O'Brien, Henry, 4637, Sgt., *k. in a. 28.6.16*

O'Brien, James, 4699, Pte., *k. in a. 8.1.15*

O'Brien, James, 11755, Pte., *d. of w. 2.4.18*

O'Brien, John, 2290, Pte., *k. in a. 1.11.14*

O'Brien, John, 4016, Pte., *k. in a. 1.11.14*

O'Brien, John, 8871, Pte., *d. of w. 16.9.16*

O'Brien, Thomas, 11502, Pte., *d. of w. 7.5.18*

O'Connell, Patrick J., 2434, L.-Sgt., *k. in a.*
1.11.14

O'Connell, Peter, 9412, Pte., *k. in a. 20.10.18*

O'Connor, Francis, 1930, Pte., *k. in a. 6.11.14*

O'Connor, Jeremiah, 5198, L.-Sgt., *k. in a.*
31.7.18

O'Connor, John, 7604, Pte., *k. in a. 16.11.16*

O'Connor, John, 9092, Pte., *k. in a. 9.7.17*

O'Connor, Michael, 4839, Pte., *k. in a.*
15.9.16

O'Connor, Michael, 5735, Pte., *d. of w.*
8.10.15

O'Connor, Stephen, 11106, Pte., *k. in a.*
22.5.18

O'Connor, Thomas, 5347, Pte., *k. in a.*
28.6.17

O'Connor, Thomas, 5593, Pte., *k. in a.*
9.10.15

O'Doherty, Denis, 7427, Pte., *k. in a. 27.8.18*

O'Donnell, John, 1319, L.-Cpl., *d. of w.*
16.3.15

O'Donnell, Joseph, 2320, Pte., *d. of w. 20.5.15*

O'Donnell, John, 3838, L.-Sgt., *k. in a.*
15.9.16

O'Donnell, Michael, 5854, Pte., k. in a.
17.9.16

O'Donnell, William, 9891, *d. 28.4.19*

O'Driscoll, Jeremiah, 9849, Pte., *k. in a.*
20.10.18

O'Dwyer, Denis, 9156, Pte., *k. in a. 17.9.16*

O'Flaherty, Arthur, 6261, Pte., *k. in a. 26.3.16*

O'Flynn, Cornelius, 5894, Pte., *k. in a.*
14.9.17

O'Grady, Timothy, 10864, Pte., *k. in a.*
9.10.17

O'Halloran, Bernard, 12194, Pte., *d. of w.*
26.5.18

O'Halloran, John, 1736, L.-Cpl., *d. 7.4.15*

O'Hara, James, 1763, Pte., *k. in a. 8.10.15*

O'Hare, Patrick, 9398, Pte., *k. in a. 12.7.16*

O'Keeffe, Michael, 3687, Sgt., *d. of w. 26.7.17*

O'Keeffe, Michael, 5827, Pte., *k. in a.*
23.10.15

O'Keeffe, Patrick, 3757, Pte., *d. 3.12.17*

O'Leary, Cornelius, 7575, Pte., *k. in a. 7.7.17*

O'Leary, Daniel S., 10144, Pte., *k. in a.*
25.9.16

O'Leary, Henry, 5607, L.-Cpl., *k. in a. 15.9.16*

O'Loughlin, James, 3123, Sgt., *d. of w. 6.9.14*

O'Loughlin, Patrick, 4762, Pte., *k. in a.*
29.12.14

O'Mahoney, Jeremiah, 4070, Pte., *d. 1.7.15*

O'Malley, Patrick, 9174, L.-Sgt., *k. in a.*
5.12.17

O'Neil, Patrick, 7952, Pte., *d. of w. 26.6.16*

O'Neill, Bernard, 4966, Pte., *k. in a. 31.3.18*

O'Neill, James, 1191, L.-Sgt., *k. in a. 6.11.14*

O'Neill, James, 7898, Pte., *k. in a. 9.10.17*

O'Neill, James, 12192, Pte., *k. in a. 10.10.18*

O'Neill, Michael, 2960, Pte., *k. in a. 6.11.14*

O'Neill, Thomas, 9761, Pte., *k. in a. 10.12.16*

O'Reilly, Christopher, 6366, L.-Cpl., *d. of w.*
28.3.18

O'Reilly, Peter, 3828, Pte., *k. in a. 6.9.14*

O'Reilly, Thomas, 7854, L.-Cpl., *d. of w.*
28.8.18

Ormsby, John, 2050, Pte., *k. in a. 1.11.14*

O'Rourke, James, 2820, Pte., *k. in a. 6.11.14*

O'Rourke, Michael, 7507, Pte., *k. in a.*
17.9.16

O'Rorke, Thomas, 10877, Pte., *k. in a. 9.10.17*

Osborne, Harry, 12519, Pte., *k. in a. 27.9.18*

O'Shaughnessy, Michael, 3308, Pte., *k. in a.*
5.10.14

O'Shea, Charles, 4440, Pte., *k. in a. 4.9.14*

O'Shea, Daniel, 7656, Pte., *k. in a. 2.4.16*

O'Shea, John, 11921, Pte., *k. in a. 1.4.18*

O'Sullivan, Bartholomew, 3646, Pte., *d. of w.*
22.5.15

O'Sullivan, Daniel, 10513, Pte., *k. in a.*
9.10.17

O'Sullivan, David, 12125, Pte., *d. of w.*
31.10.18

O'Sullivan, John, 4669, Pte., *d. of w. 27.5.19*

O'Sullivan, Michael, 3709, L.-Cpl., *k. in a.*
18.5.15

O'Toole, John J., 1761, Sgt., *k. in a. 4.11.14*

Owen, John, 9626, L.-Cpl., *k. in a. 25.9.16*

Owens, William, 4847, Pta., *d. of w. 3.1.15*

Parish, Albert, 1118, Pte., *d. of w. 23.5.15*

Parisotti, Joseph, 12322, Pte., *d. of w. 2.4.18*

Parr, Francis, 4229, Pte., *d. of w. 6.11.14*

Paton, Henry, 3773, L.-Cpl., *k. in a. 1.11.14*

Payne, Henry, 999, Drill-SgL, *k. in a 10.10.17*

Payne, Robert, 151, Sgt., *k. in a. 6.11.14*

Peakin, Thomas, 5972, Pte., *k. in a. 16.5.15*

Pearson, Thomas, 12740, Pte., *d. of w. 29.8.18*

Perry, Frank, 5048, Pte., *k in a. 30.3.18*

Phair, Edward, 10490, Pte., *d. of w. 10.10.17*

Phelan, Francis A., 11945, Pte., *k. in a.*
1.12.17

Phelan, James, 4764, Pte., *k. in a. 6.2.15*

Phelan, Thomas, 1514, Pte., *k. in a. 19.5.15*

Phibbs, Thomas, 3843, Pte., *k. in a. 6.11.14*

Philips, John H., 12798, Pte., *k. in a. 21.9.18*

Pitman, Percy, 2972, Drummer., *k. in a.*
4.12.14

Plenderleith, David, 4978, Pte., *k. in a. 9.1.15*

Porter, George D., 4051, L.-Cpl., *k. in a.*
1.11.14

Power, John, 10035, Pte., *d. of w. 27.9.16*

Power, Martin, 10362, Pte., *k. in a. 10.10.17*

Power, Michael, 2260, Pte., *k. in a. 17.2.15*
Power, Michael, 10188, Pte., *d. of w . 7.5.18*
Power, William, 6043, Pte., *d. of w. 17.6.16*
Prendergast, Bartholomew, 8617, *Pte., k. in a. 31.7.17*
Proudfoot, Richard, 4296, Pte., *k. in a. 15.3.17*
Purcell, Stephen, 7526, Pte., *d. of w. 29.3.18*
Quigley, Samuel, 3631, L.-Cpl., *k. in a. 15.9.16*
Quinn, Charles, 11277, Pte., *k. in a. 1.9.18*
Quinn, John, 5408, Pte., *k. in a. 23.10.15*
Quinn, Joseph 2885, Pte., *k. in a. 1.11.14*
Quinn, Michael, 1810, Pte., *d. 24.2.19*
Quinlan, Patrick J., 4687, L.-Cpl., *k. in a. 8.10.15*
Quirke, John, 10464, Pte., *k. in a. 15.3.17*
Rafferty, Daniel, 4799, Pte., *k. in a. 5.2.15*
Rafter, John, 3185, L.-Cpl., *k. in a. 9.11.14*
Raftery, Guy, 3763, Pte., *d. of w. 22.5.15*
Ralph, Michael, 3777, Pte., *k. in a. 25.10.14*
Rankin, Thomas, 805, Pte., *k. in a. 1.11.14*
Reardon, Edward, 2403, Pte., *k. in a. 1.11.14*
Reardon, James S., 6033, Pte., *k. in a. 30.4.15*
Redden, Patrick, 4860, Pte., *k. in a. 11.9.16*
Redmond, James, 6445, L.-Cpl., *k. in a. 16.3.17*
Regan, John, 11808, Pte., *k. in a. 20.1.18*
Reid, Albert, 5802, Pte., *k. in a. 29.1.16*
Reid, Joseph, 436, Pte., *d. 20.2.15*
Reilly, Francis, 3642, L.-Sgt., *k. in a. 17.9.16*
Reilly, James, 1068, Pte., *k. in a. 8.10.15*
Reilly, James, 5740, Pte., *d. of w. 9.10.17*
Reilly, John, 3754, Pte., *k. in a. 31.7.17*
Reilly, John, 4086, Pte., *k. in a. 1.11.14*
Reilly, John, 11007, Pte., *d. of w. 9.10.17*
Reilly, William, 2635, Sgt., *k. in a. 4.8.17*
Reynolds, John J., 2042, L.-Cpl., *d. of w. 12.9.14*
Reynolds, John, 4976, L.-Cpl., *k. in a. 15.9.16*
Richardson, Ernest, 551, C.S.M., *k. in a. 1.9.14*
Riordan, Jerom, 3728, Pte., *d. of w. 1.11.14*
Riordan, Maurice, 2618, Sgt., D.C.M. and bar, *k. in a. 15.9.16*
Riordan, Timothy, 6058, Pte., *k. in a. 17.9.16*
Ritchie, David, 5551, Pte., *k. in a. 18.5.15*
Roane, John, 5159, L.-Cpl., *k. in a. 30.11.17*
Roberts, Jonathan, 8695, L.-Cpl., *k. in a. 15.9.16*
Roberts, Patrick, 4398, Pte., *k. in a. 1.11.14*
Robinson, James, 1236, Pte., *k. in a. 6.11.14*
Roe, Joseph, 10534, Pte., *d. of w. 24.8.16*
Rogers, James, 5133, Pte., *k. in a. 18.5.15*

Rogers, John, 1448, Pte., *k. in a. 6.11.14*
Rogers, Patrick, 3048, *k. in a. 14.9.14*
Rogers, Thomas, 9424, Pte., *k. in a. 15.9.16*
Ronan, Daniel, 3799, Pte., *d. 19.2.19*
Rooker, Charles W. H., 9090, L.-Sgt., *d. of w. 28.8.18*
Rooney, Francis, 1521, Pte., *k. in a. 6.11.14*
Rooney, Thomas, 1703, *d. 14.11.14*
Rose, James, 2880, L.-Sgt., *k. in a. 27.7.16*
Rowlands, John, 2189, Pte., *k. in a. 6.11.14*
Roy, John, 5989, Pte., *k. in a. 18.5.15*
Ruane, Garrett, 3561, Pte., *k. in a. 18.5.15*
Ruffley, John, 7910, Pte., *k. in a. 15.9.16*
Russell, Gilbert W., 5449, L.-Cpl., *d. of w. 21.3.17*
Russell, Peter, 8677, Pte., *k. in a. 17.9.16*
Russell, Thomas, 3944, Pte., *k. in a. 1.11.14*
Ryall, Charles, 2105, Pte., *k. in a. 13.9.17*
Ryan, Edward, 3738, Pte., *k. in a. 6.11.14*
Ryan, Francis, 5590, Pte., *k. in a. 8.8.15*
Ryan, James, 12129, Pte., *k. in a. 26.11.17*
Ryan, John, 2698, Pte., *k. in a. 16.9.14*
Ryan, John, 3216, Pte., *k. in a. 1.9.14*
Ryan, John, 5382, Pte., *d. 6.8.15*
Ryan, Joseph, 5543, Pte., *d. of w. 16.4.15*
Ryan, Patrick, 3385, Pte., *k. in a. 1.11.14*
Ryan, Thomas, 3441, Pte., *k. in a. 4.9.14*
Ryan, William, 2594, Pte., *k. in a. 18.5.15*
Ryan, William, 5807, Pte., *k. in a. 18.5.15*
Ryan, William, 10592, Pte., *k. in a. 9.10.17*
Sales, John, 2261, Sgt., *k. in a. 18.5.15*
Salter, Peter, 3882, Pte., *k. in a. 1.11.14*
Sammons, Henry H., 12674, Pte., *k. in a. 27.8.18*
Sangster, William, 5005, Pte., *k. in a. 15.7.15*
Sargent, Robert, 5264, Pte., *k. in a. 25.9.16*
Saunders, John, 11944, Pte., *k. in a. 27.9.18*
Scally, Joseph, 3608, Sgt., *k. in a. 9.10.17*
Scally, Joseph, 5044, Pte., *k. in a. 30.11.17*
Scanlon, James, 10981, Pte., *k. in a. 26.7.17*
Scott, William, 10004, Pte., *k. in a. 25.9.16*
Scully, Michael, 4480, Pte., *k. in a. 1.11.14*
Sedge, Percy G., 12709, Pte., *k. in a. 20.10.18*
Sexton, Cornelius, 8512, Pte., *d. of w. 23.7.16*
Shanahan, William, 642, Pte., *k. in a. 1.11.14*
Sharp, John T. B., 12524, Pte., *d. of w. 29.5.18*
Shaw, William J., 10272, Pte., *k. in a. 9.10.17*
Shea, John, 4309, Pte., *d. of w. 16.5.15*
Sheehan, Michael, 12088, Pte., *d. of w. 28.3.18*
Sheehy, John, 11491, Pte., *d. of w. 1.8.17*
Sheppard, Robert, 1262, L.-Cpl., *k. in a. 18.5.15*
Sheridan, Nicholas J., 5090, Pte., *d. of w. 13.4.15*

Sheridan, Patrick, 7977, Pte., *k. in a. 11.9.16*
Sheridan, William, 5949, Pte., *k. in a. 18.5.15*
Sherlock, Mathew, 6042, Pte., *k. in a. 3.8.15*
Sherwood, William R., 3752, Pte., *k. in a.
5.11.14*
Sherry, Matthew, 5365, Pte., *d. 17.6.18*
Shields, Henry, 11615, Pte., *k. in a. 27.5.18*
Shields, Terence, 4517, Pte., *k. in a. 1.11.14*
Shotton, John, 12756, L.-Cpl., *k. in a.
20.10.18*
Simpson, Edward, 2025, Pte., *k. in a. 1.11.14*
Simpson, Robert, 2607, Pte., *k. in a. 8.9.14*
Singleton, Isaiah, 3400, L.-Cpl., *k. in a.
1.11.14*
Sloane, John, 1176, Pte., *k. in a. 4.9.14*
Slowey, Patrick, 1299, Pte., *d. of w. 22.4.15*
Smith, Benjamin J., 12603, Pte., *k. in a.
27.9.18*
Smith, John, 2213, Pte., *k. in a. 1.11.14*
Smith, Richard, 8837, L.-Cpl., *k. in a. 17.9.16*
Smyth, Gerald C., 4568, Pte., *k. in a. 27.10.14*
Smyth, John, 4231, Pte., *k. in a. 6.11.14*
Smyth, Patrick, 10655, Pte., *k. in a. 1.12.17*
Smyth, Samuel, 10068, Pte., *k. in a. 24.9.16*
Smythe, Albert, 4480, Pte., *k. in a. 1.11.14*
Snow, Joseph, 2778, L.-Sgt., *k. in a. 26.9.16*
Spillane, John, 6055, L.-Cpl., *k. in a. 31.7.17*
Sprowle, Robert, 3387, Pte., *d. of w. 2.11.14*
Spragg, William, 4951, Pte., *k. in a. 26.3.18*
Stanton, John, 11166, Pte., *k. in a. 9.10.17*
Starr, Denis, 3951, Pte., *k. in a. 1.11.14*
Stedman, William, 3782, Pte., *d. 12.4.15*
Steepe, William, 4438, Pte., *k. in a. 1.2.15*
Stiven, James, 11066, Pte., *k. in a. 15.7.17*
Stokes, John, 1778, Pte., *d. of w. 19.5.15*
Stokes, John, 1873, Pte., *k. in a. 1.9.14*
Streatfield, Walter T., 12909, Pte., M.M., *k. in
a. 21.10.18*
Strickland, John F., 4988, L.-Cpl., *k. in a.
1.2.15*
Stuart, Eugene, 6092, Pte., *d. of w. 10.12.15*
Stuart, John, 3044, Pte., *k. in a. 1.11.14*
Styles, Albert, 5995, Pte., MM., *k. in a.
20.10.18*
Sullivan, Cornelius, 4812, Pte., *d. of w.
22.5.15*
Sullivan, Edward J., 4921, Pte., *k. in a.
12.3.15*
Sullivan, John, 3749, Pte., *d. of w. 28.7.15*
Sullivan, John, 8646, Pte., *d. of w. 8.10.18*
Sullivan, Michael, 11906, Pte., *d. of w.
5.12.17*
Sullivan, Philip, 1903, L.-Cpl., *k. in a. 1.11.14*
Sullivan, William, 4783, L.-Sgt., *k. in a. 25.9.16*

Sutton, John, 1365, Pte., *k. in a. 6.11.14*
Swanton, Charles, 4098, Pte., *d. of w. 17.4.16*
Sweeney, Edward, 9471, Pte., *d. of w. 16.3.17*
Sweeney, John, 5013, Pte., *k. in a. 12.10.15*
Sweeney, John, 8120, Pte., M.M., *k. in a.
9.10.17*
Sweeney, Patrick, 6437, Pte., *k. in a. 26.9.16*
Sycamore, Ernest, 12525, Cpl., *d. of w.
18.5.18*
Synnott, James, 4677, Pte., *k. in a. 23.3.15*
Taaffe, John, 371, Pte., *d. of w. 6.11.14*
Taaffe, William, 5617, Pte., *k. in a. 9.10.17*
Taggart, Edward, 12451, Pte., *k. in a. 19.8.18*
Taylor, Daniel, 5994, Pte., *d. of w. 3.8.15*
Teanby, Harry, 1046, Pte., *k. in a. 4.9.14*
Tether, Arthur R. C., 12734, Pte., *k. in a.
10.10.18*
Thompson, James, 9551, Pte., *k. in a. 23.2.17*
Thorneycroft, John F., 12340, Pte., *d. of w.
22.5.18*
Thynne, Patrick, 3179, L.-Cpl., *k. in a.
17.5.15*
Tighe, Patrick, 5470, Pte., *k. in a. 17.9.16*
Timoney, James, 6556, Pte., *k. in a. 3.9.17*
Tobin, Francis, 12003, Pte., *k. in a. 1.12.17*
Tobin, Patrick, 1743, Pte., *k. in a. 14.9.14*
Togher, James, 6171, Pte., *k. in a. 15.9.16*
Toomey, William, 5769, Pte., *k. in a. 18.5.15*
Topping, John, 4164, Sgt., *k. in a. 5.2.15*
Townsend, Patrick, 4530, Pte., *k. in a. 14.9.14*
Tracey, William, 5148, Pte., *k. in a. 25.2.15*
Travers, William, 5521, L.-Sgt., *k. in a. 15.3.17*
Troy, James J., 3889, Pte., *d. of w. 15.12.17*
Tuohy, Michael, 11319, Pte., *k. in a. 30.4.18*
Tuohey, William, 4566, Pte., *k. in a. 1.9.14*
Tyrrell, Patrick, 9927, L.-Sgt., M.M., *d. of w.
28.9.18*
Underhill, Ernest J., 12685, Pte., *k. in a.
27.8.18*
Underwood, Harry, 12758, Pte., *d. of w.
22.10.18*
Vancroft, Evan, 2335, Pte., *k. in a. 3.11.14*
Walker, Alfred, 5958, Pte., *d. of w. 28.5.15*
Walker, Patrick, 6080, Pte., *d. of w. 28.9.15*
Walker, Thomas, 12569, Pte., *k. in a. 26.3.18*
Wallace, James F., 1575, L.-Cpl., *k. in a.
25.10.14*
Wallace, James, 1605, Pte., *k. in a. 4.9.14*
Wallace, Mark, 10425, Pte., *d. of w. 31.3.18*
Wallace, Patrick J., 8455, Pte., *k. in a. 11.9.16*
Walpole, George H., 12272, Pte., *d. of w.
20.10.18*
Walsh, Daniel, 3030, Pte., *k. in a. 1.11.14*
Walsh, Edward, 3409, Pte., *k. in a. 18.11.14*

Walsh, James, 4562, Pte., *k. in a. 26.10.14*
Walsh, Martin, 4572, Pte., *k. in a. 1.11.14*
Walsh, Nicholas, 10775, Pte., *k. in a. 2.8.17*
Walsh, Patrick, 10061, Pte., *d. of w. 24.9.16*
Walsh, Patrick J., 10900, Pte., *k. in a. 26.7.17*
Walsh, Richard, 4250, Pte., *d. of w. 18.12.14*
Walsh, Thomas, 7738, Pte., *k. in a. 13.7.17*
Walsh, William, 5901, Pte., *k. in a. 15.9.16*
Walsh, William, 9636, Pte., *d. of w. 14.12.16*
Walshe, Thomas, 9259, Pte., *d. of w. 10.10.17*
Warde, William, 2032, Pte., *k. in a. 18.5.15*
Warner, William, 5653, Sgt., *d. of w. 1.12.17*
Webb, Leonard, 3890, Pte., *d. of w. 11.9.14*
Wellspring, Owen, 5099, Sgt., *k. in a. 2.8.17*
Whelan, Edward, 12309, Pte., *k. in a. 8.5.18*
Whelan, John P., 5095, Pte., *d. of w. 17.9.16*
Whelan, Martin, 3323, Pte., *d. of w. 20.1.15*
Whelan, Richard, 6094, Pte., *k. in a. 28.6.16*
Whelan, Thomas, 5679, L.-Sgt., *d. of w.
1.12.17*
White, John, 2695, L.-Cpl., MM., *k. in a.
10.10.17*
White, William, 8192, Pte., *k. in a. 15.9.16*
Whitty, John, 10942, Pte., *k. in a. 9.10.17*
Williams, John, 5464, Pte., *k. in a. 6.10.15*

Wilmott, William, 5524, Pte., *k. in a. 26.3.16*
Willoughby, Charles, 1729, Pte., *k. in a.
18.5.15*
Willoughby, Charles, 9266, Pte., *k. in a.
17.6.16*
Woods, Joseph H., 10221, Pte., *k. in a.
23.2.17*
Woods, Robert, 5990, Pte., *k. in a. 17.9.16.*
Woodcock, Ernest E., 12571, Pte., *d. of w.
30.3.18*
Woodroffe, Robert, 3268, L.-Cpl., *k. in a.
1.11.14*
Woulfe, Michael, 2486, Pte., *k. in a. 1.11.14*
Wright, William, 988, Drummer, *k. in a.
1.11.14*
Wylie, Charles, 4188, Sgt., *k. in a. 10.12.16*
Wynne, Christopher, 10850, Pte., *k. in a.
30.3.18*
Wynne, John, 9611, Pte., *k. in a.,12.9.17*
Yates, Edward H., 11315, Pte.;, *d. of w.
15.4.17*
Young, Algernon A. L., 5116, L. Cpl., *d. of w.
22.2.15*
Younge, Anthony, 4182, Pte., D.C.M., *k. in
a. 20.6.16*

APPENDIX C

W.O.s, N.C.O.s, AND MEN
FIRST AND SECOND BATTALIONS
REWARDS

VICTORIA CROSS
7708 L.-Sgt. Moyney, J.
3556 L.-Cpl. O'Leary, M.
8387 L.-Cpl. Woodcock, T.

MILITARY CROSS
3578 C.S.M. Kennedy, M
108 SM. Kirk, J.

DISTINGUISHED CONDUCT MEDAL

No.	Rank	Name
7218	Sgt.	Anstey, C. E.
5722	Pte.	Barry, H.
12501	Sgt.	Bishop, T.
5841	Pte.	Boyd, J.
10133	L.-Sgt.	Bray, H.
3975	Pte.	Brine, M.
3221	Sgt.	Burling, D
7321	L.-Sgt.	Butler, T.
918	SM.	Cahill, T.
525	Pte.	Cannon, J.
10161	Pte.	Cooper, W.
2384	C.S.M.	Corry, T.
3507	Sgt.	Curtin, J.
4455	Sgt.	Daly, P.
2195	L.-Cpl.	Deacons, J.
2853	L.-Cpl.	Delaney, W.
4039	Pte.	Dempsey, B.
4116	L.-Sgt.	Dignan, J.

6193	Sgt.	Dolan, P.
2372	Sgt.	Feighery, W.
9210	Pte.	Finnegan, J.
11712	L.-Cpl.	Flanagan, M.
1226	Sgt.	Foley, J.
7570	L.-Sgt.	Frawley, J.
12124	Pte.	Gallagher, M.
2793	Pte.	Geon, R.
3303	Sgt.	Glynn, J.
2535	C.S.M.	Harradine, C.
4613	Pte.	Hennigan, P.
4906	Pte.	Henry, J.
1155	Sgt.	Hiscock, H.
55	C.S.M.	Holmes, W.
2807	Sgt.	Keown, F.
10210	L.-Cpl.	Lecky, W.
5973	Pte.	Lynch, M.
2845	Pte.	Mansfield, J.
8149	Pte.	McCarthy, T.
2385	Sgt.	McClelland, T.
3726	Sgt.	McGoldrick, P.
8384	Sgt.	McGuinness, J.
5741	Pte.	McKendry, W.
7830	Pte.	McKinney, P.
4432	L.-Sgt.	McMullen, T.
2112	C.S.M.	McVeigh, H.
3567	Pte.	Meagher, W.
3235	Sgt.	Milligan, J.
7683	L.-Sgt.	Mohide, P.
4015	Pte.	Moore, W.
3632	C.S.M.	Moran, M.
1664	Sgt.	Moran, C.
9500	Pte.	Morrison, P.
552	C.S.M.	Munns, A.
3655	C.S.M.	Murphy, G.
3006	Sgt.	Murphy, F.
8828	Sgt.	Murray, T.
6484	Sgt.	Nolan, P.
5743	Pte.	O'Brien, D.
2760	Pte.	O'Connor, J.
4389	Sgt.	O'Hare, E.
4612	Sgt.	Pearce, W.
10757	Pte.	Priesty, J.
6311	L.-Cpl.	Quinn, P.
6301	Pte.	Regan, J.
2506	Sgt.	Reilly, T.
2618	Sgt.	Riordan, M.
5446	Pte.	Roche, J.
5279	Pte.	Rochford, J.
3072	Pte.	Russell, W. G.
8255	L.-Cpl.	Smith, R.
2623	Sgt.	Spicer, W.
2303	Sgt.	Usher, W.
2767	Sgt.	Voyles, D.

5910	Sgt.	Wain, F.
1033	C.S.M.	Walsh, J.
8050	Sgt.	Walsh, W.
3987	Sgt.	Wilkinson, J.
4182	Pte.	Younge, A.

BAR TO DISTINGUISHED CONDUCT MEDAL

No.	Rank	Name
4432	L.-Sgt.	McMullen, T.
2760	Pte.	O'Connor, J.
4389	Sgt.	O'Hare, E.
6301	Pte.	Regan, J
2618	Sgt.	Riordan, M.
2303	Sgt.	Usher, W.

MILITARY MEDAL

No.	Rank	Name
7218	Sgt.	Anstey, C. E.
6157	Pte.	Armstrong, W.
8922	Pte.	Arthor, S.
9093	L.-Sgt.	Baker, C.
4512	Sgt.	Balfe, J.
5132	Sgt.	Barrett, J.
6351	Pte.	Barry, P.
11794	L.-Cpl.	Bishop, M.
6276	L.-Sgt.	Black, P.
6402	L.-Cpl.	Bonham, J.
6273	L.-Cpl.	Boyle, F.
10732	Pte.	Boyle, P.
7967	Pte.	Boyton, R.
4751	Pte.	Brabston, M.
6332	Sgt.	Brennan, J.
6202	L.-Cpl	Brien, P.
6271	L.-Sgt	Browne, M.
5115	Pte.	Bruton, P.
9632	Pte.	Buckley, S.
8106	Pte.	Byrne, J.
1730	Sgt.	Byrne, J. G.
6186	Pte.	Byrnes, P.
6457	Sgt.	Cahill, T.
9309	Pte.	Callaghan, P.
1985	Cpl.	Campbell, D.
4435	Pte.	Carberry, M.
4009	Pte.	Carroll, J.
3483	Pte.	Carroll, J.
3132	Sgt.	Carton, H.
7043	Pte.	Caulfield, W.
3659	Pte.	Cawley, J.

1579	Pte.	Cleary, J.
8395	L.-Cpl.	Coard, J.
6196	Sgt.	Cole, M.
11099	L.-Sgt.	Collins, M.
12234	Pte.	Collins, R.
6277	L.-Sgt.	Comesky, J.
3515	Sgt.	Connor, G.
9014	L.-Cpl.	Conroy, M.
7109	Pte.	Corliss, J.
6044	L.-Cpl.	Cousins, A.
6583	Pte.	Courtney, J.
3146	Pte.	Coyne, F.
6509	L.-Cpl.	Cronin, J.
9349	Pte.	Cunnane, J.
11321	Pte.	Curley, M.
3507	Sgt.	Curtin, J.
4529	L.-Cpl.	Daly, J.
6523	Pte.	Daly, J.
1999	Sgt.	Denn, A.
7958	Pte.	Devine, J.
5752	Pte.	Docherty, G.
11271	L.-Cpl.	Doherty, C. M.
9376	L.-Cpl.	Dollar, W.
2922	Sgt.	Donnelly, J.
3056	Sgt.	Donohoe, P.
2786	Pte.	Doolan, J.
2867	Sgt.	Doolan, P.
8046	L.-Cpl.	Dooney, E.
7750	Pte.	Driscoll, T.
3003	L.-Cpl.	Duff, J.
4488	Pte.	Dunne, D.
4658	Cpl.	Dunne, J.
4944	Pte.	Durkin, J.
11858	L.-Sgt.	English, S.
10521	Pte.	Erwin, R.
8773	Pte.	Evans, T.
9794	Pte.	Farley, P.
6698	Sgt.	Farrell, F.
4166	Sgt.	Fawcett, J.
2372	Sgt.	Feighery, W.
4993	L.-Cpl.	Fitzgerald, M.
6768	L.-Sgt.	Flaherty, J.
11712	L.-Cpl.	Flanagan, M.
5797	Sgt.	Flynn, J.
6266	Pte.	Fox, A.
10358	Pte.	Furlong, M.
8743	L.-Cpl.	Galbraith, J.
11985	Pte.	Gardiner, H.
10436	Pte.	Gault, J.
7954	Pte.	Glacken, C.
6970	Pte.	Gorbey, R.
8229	Pte.	Gowan, F.
3972	C.Q.M.S.	Grady, R.
3847	Sgt.	Grean

2858	L.-Cpl.	Green, A.
7032	Pte.	Greene, L.
7695	Sgt.	Griffin, J.
3477	Cpl.	Gunning, M.
12958	Sgt.	Hamill, R.
6632	Cpl.	Hanlon, W.
5004	Pte.	Hannan, J.
10449	L.-Cpl.	Hannan, L.
6135	L.-Sgt.	Harris, T.
7739	Pte.	Hawthorne, J.
8572	L.-Cpl.	Heaney, J.
7493	L.	Higgins, M.
6471	Sgt.	Hillock, E.
4068	Sgt.	Hodgson, W.
4632	Pte.	Horan, J.
7475	Pte.	Horton, A.
10848	L.-Cpl.	Hunt, J.
10059	Pte.	Hurley, M.
11681	Pte.	Hynes, J.
11501	L.-Sgt.	Jenkins, D.
8517	L.-Cpl.	Jenkins, J.
11956	Pte.	Johnson, S.
1767	Sgt.	Joyce, P.
10039	Pte.	Kane, H.
4957	L.-Sgt.	Kearney, P.
10595	L.-Cpl.	Keenan, E.
8228	Pte.	Keenan, P.
7871	Pte.	Kelleher, D.
11034	L.-Cpl.	Kelly, E.
2746	Sgt.	Keniry, T.
8702	Pte.	Kennedy, M.
11008	L.-Cpl.	Kennedy, W.
112	Sgt.	Kenny, M.
5939	Pte.	Kenny, M.
8465	Sgt.	Kenny, T.
2807	Sgt.	Keown, F.
5319	Pte.	Kilkenny, A.
7628	Sgt.	King, H.
3346	Pte.	Langrill, J.
12233	Pte.	Larkin, J.
6474	Pte.	Lavelle, J.
10028	Pte.	Lewis, M.
3686	Sgt.	Looney, D.
3272	L.-Sgt.	Looran, J.
3734	Pte.	Lowe, D.
5764	Pte.	Luby, T.
3948	Pte.	Lydon, J.
7075	Pte.	Madden, P.
6648	Pte.	Maguire, J.
9458	Pte.	Maguire, T.
12681	L.-Cpl.	Manning, J.
6078	Pte.	Martin, J.
2494	Sgt.	Mason, T.
6939	L. Cpl.	Matear, H.

12856	Pte.	Matthews, E.
10443	Pte.	McAteer, J.
5237	Sgt.	McCabe, J.
7866	Pte.	McCaffrey, S.
5096	Sgt.	McCarthy, G.
9754	Pte.	McCarthy, P.
6258	C.S.M.	McCarthy, R.
8662	L.-Sgt.	McConnell, R.
6343	L.-Cpl.	McConnell, W.
3224	Cpl.	McCullagh, E.
1910	Sgt.	McCusker, F.
4386	Sgt.	McDonald, J.
7937	Cpl.	McDonnell, M.
6643	Pte.	McElroy, J.
6448	Sgt.	McFarlane, R.
5532	Pte.	McGinnis, C.
5728	Pte.	McGowan, T.
7053	Pte.	McGurrin, W.
10171	L.-Cpl.	McHale, S.
7777	L.-Sgt.	McKiernan, M.
9230	Pte.	McKinney, I.
8078	Pte.	McNulty, J.
5806	Pte.	McNulty, P.
6021	Pte.	McQuillan, T.
6782	L.-Sgt.	Mehegan, D.
10020	B'dsman	Mills, F.
7586	L.-Sgt.	Moran, J.
12747	Pte.	Morgan, E.
7763	Pte.	Moore, P.
1964	Pte.	Morrison, J.
10354	L.-Sgt.	Morrissey, M.
11659	Pte.	Murphy, J.
6211	Sgt.	Murphy, M.
6892	Sgt.	Murphy, M.
4140	Pte.	Murphy, T.
8720	Pte.	Naylor, H.
10823	Pte.	Neagle, T.
6484	Sgt.	Nolan, P.
4029	Pte.	Nolan, P.
11888	Pte.	Nott, P.
7520	Pte.	Nulty, S.
2727	Pte.	O'Brien, M.
10437	Pte.	O'Brien, M.
6229	Pte.	O'Brien, W.
3261	L.-Sgt.	O'Byrne, J.
2289	Pte.	O'Connor, J.
4256	Sgt.	O'Connor, M.
10251	L.-Cpl.	O'Dea, T.
11897	Pte.	O'Farrell, J.
11425	Pte.	O'Flaherty, J.
8810	Pte.	O'Flynn, W.
7167	Sgt.	O'Hagan, J.
6184	Sgt.	O'Neill, J.
8122	Pte.	O'Neill, J.

5786	Sgt.	O'Reilly, J.
3969	Sgt.	O'Shea, C.
7541	Pte.	O'Sullivan, T.
9565	Pte.	Patton, T.
5508	Sgt.	Pennington, J.
3096	Sgt.	Pogue, A.
10550	Pte.	Power, G.
2596	L.-Cpl.	Purdy, McD.
9882	Pte.	Quinn, J.
3836	Cpl.	Redmond. J.
7295	L.-Cpl.	Redmond, T.
3122	Sgt.	Reid, L.
2506	Sgt.	Reilly, T.
10826	Pte.	Richerby, G.
5279	Pte.	Rochford, J.
776	Pte.	Roche, P.
7400	Cpl.	Rolls, E.
3638	Pte.	Rowe, M.
8552	Pte.	Ruth, J.
4817	Pte.	Ryan, D.
9188	L.-Cpl.	Ryan, M.
9783	Pte.	Savage, H.
12523	Sgt.	Savin, J.
8096	Sgt.	Scully, J.
7327	Pte.	Shanahan, W.
6653	Pte.	Shannon, T.
8932	Pte.	Sharkey, P.
4548	L.-Cpl.	Sheehan, P.
6860	Pte.	Sheil, P.
6701	Pte.	Slattery, P.
2640	L.-Sgt.	Smith, J.
8112	Pte.	Somers, L.
12400	Pte.	Southern, N.
5995	Pte.	Styles, A.
7223	Sgt.	Sussex, H.
9084	Pte.	Sweeney, D.
8120	Pte.	Sweeney, J.
5837	Pte.	Taylor, G.
2955	Sgt.	Taylor, R.
1725	C.S.M.	Toher, D.
12339	Pte.	Tomlyn, F.
7381	Pte.	Troy, W.
10180	Pte.	Tuffy, P.
2208	L.-Sgt	Tynan, P.
9927	L.-Cpl.	Tyrrell, P.
4133	L.-Cpl.	Vanston, J.
6508	Pte.	Waidron, P.
11765	Pte.	Walsh, E.
2759	Sgt.	Weedon, W.
12691	Sgt.	Westbrook, A.
3494	Pte.	Whearty, J.
2695	Pte.	White, J.

BAR TO MILITARY MEDAL

No.	Rank	Name
11794	L.-Cpl.	Bishop, M.
7967	Pte.	Boyton, R.
1999	Sgt.	Denn, A.
2786	Pte.	Doolan, J.
4993	L.-Cpl.	Fitzgerald, M.
12958	Sgt.	Hamill, R.
10354	L.-Sgt.	Morrissey, M.
6484	Sgt.	Nolan, P.
5279	Pte.	Rochford, J.

FOREIGN DECORATIONS

CROIX DE GUERRE

No.	Rank	Name
918	SM.	Cahill, T.
4107	C.S.M.	Farrell, J.
6467	Pte.	Gallagher, J.
6448	Sgt.	Macfarlane, R.
3006	Sgt.	Murphy, F.
4884	Pte.	O'Brien, D.
3987	Sgt.	Wilkinson, J.

MÉDAILLE MILITAIRE

No.	Rank	Name
6193	Sgt.	Dolan, P.
7708	L.-Sgt.	Moyney, J.
1800	C.S.M.	Proctor, J.
1073	C.S.M.	Rodgers, J.

MÉDAILLE D'HONNEUR
4751 Pte. Brabston, M.
ITALIAN BRONZE MEDAL
3235 Sgt. Milligan, J.
RUSSIAN DECORATIONS

3556 L.-Cpl. O'Leary, M.	Cross of the Order of St. George, 3rd Class
2303 Sgt. Usher, W.	Medal of the Order of St. George, 2nd Class

MERITORIOUS SERVICE MEDAL

No.	Rank	Name
4874	O.R. Sgt.	Ashton, A.
2900	C.Q.M.S;	Curtis, P.
10374	Sgt.	Donovan, P.
4215	Sgt.	Halpin, G.
4707	Sgt.	Hogan, P.
6631	Pte.	Hurley, J.
1175	Sgt.	King, W.
1134	Q.M.S.	Mathews, P.
3374	Q.M.S.	McCarthy, T.
1699	Cpl.	McFadden, J.
121	S.C.	McKenna, J.
7525	Pte.	Millett, L.
6892	Sgt.	Murphy, M.
2098	Sgt.	O'Brien, J.
216	O.R.Q.M.S.	O'Gorman, R.
4972	S.M.	Dr. Price, G.
1158	Sgt.	Smith, G.
2087	O.R.Q.M.S.	Smythe, J.
1549	Q.M.S.	Thompson, W.
2103	Sgt.	Walsh, J.

INDEX